A Vigilant Society

A Vigilant Society

Jewish Thought and the State in Medieval Spain

Javier Roiz

Translated by
Selma L. Margaretten

SUNY PRESS

Published by State University of New York Press, Albany

Printed in the United States of America

For information, contact State University of New York Press, Albany, NY
www.sunypress.edu

Production by Ryan Morris
Marketing by Michael Campochiaro

Library of Congress Cataloging-in-Publication Data

Roiz, Javier.
[Sociedad vigilante y mundo judío en la concepción del estado. English]
A vigilant society : Jewish thought and the state in medieval Spain / Javier Roiz ; translated by Selma L. Margaretten.
p. cm.
Includes bibliographical references (p.) and index.
ISBN 978-1-4384-4563-2 (hc : alk. paper)—978-1-4384-4562-5 (pb : alk. paper)
1. Judaism and politics—History. 2. Political science—History. I. Title.

BM645.P64R6513 2013
296.3'82—dc23
2012012853

10 9 8 7 6 5 4 3 2 1

To my teacher Harry Eckstein

Contents

Preface

This book is envisioned as a chance to enter into a dialogue with the reader, as the author also seeks to learn and contrast ideas. Like all books of an interdisciplinary nature or ones that touch on different fields, there may be errors or imprecision. Moreover, I wish to advance that I have not attempted a historical investigation or a reconstruction of a period, but simply a reflection on our own time.

Leaving aside the Aristotelian principle of identity as dealt with in this work, we see that it is possible to consider a long period of time without having to hold to a strict order of centuries or a precise linking of arguments.

Likewise, the internal world of the individual is a central matter of study in the book, even as the principle of identity does not operate in it, *in foro interno*. All this gives us a freedom that is perhaps one of the greatest conquests that political science will bring to the twenty-first century. By thinking in this way, we can appreciate profound realities that would otherwise be hidden from us. Values and deeds will be revealed that can now be understood in a different light. One example of this is the vigilant society that I study in this book.

I found that, to a large extent, the so-called vigilant society had its origins in the thirteenth century in Western Europe and produced a new vision of the public sphere and the individual that are still in effect today. As witnesses to this, we find major institutions that in time came to be the most successful franchises in European history, such as the State and the colleges of liberal arts, that is, the universities. The Atlantic projection of Western Europe would be carried out by means of the vehicle of its languages that, in turn, became intercontinental languages.

At the present time political theory finds itself in a globalized society where life is presented, on the one hand, full of doubts, while on the other, facing an extraordinarily broad horizon.

The State is at its peak, and, at the same time, it is in the process of being revised. Its global extension confirms its formidable success as a mechanism of public engineering, a device that articulates our society throughout the planet. Of course there are also criticisms of its dysfunctions. Some countries think that more State is needed to organize authority, safeguard the security of its citizens, and stimulate progress. Sometimes we speak of "development" as if societies were waiting for someone to unwrap them in order to reveal their values. In other cases the question is whether or not the State is even capable of defending its borders. Finally, there are places where the State clearly goes too far and shuts the door on any outside interference, maintaining law and order by tyrannical procedures or dragging its people into disastrous civil wars. And in spite of all this, invading nations still continue to exist.

Thus the State is again becoming an object of primary interest for political theory. Some might argue that it has never stopped being so. Now, however, the novelty lies in that the State is not what it was at the beginning of the twentieth century when a young Eric Voegelin presented his science of the Staatslehre in Vienna, or when the experts in political science taught—and some continue to teach—that the State is the supreme institution that will provide the key to the politics of a country.

However, much of this renewed interest in the State has to do with the cessation of harassment—after 1989—by the romantic ideologies that attempted to explain the State as a superstructure loaded with falsehood and an entity that melts in the air. Now that this *vindiciae contra tyrannos* has been overcome, there has been a continual interest in examining not only the mechanisms of the State and its functioning, but also its appearance as a supreme institution and the way in which it arose.

In this book I have attempted to propose a certain genealogy of the State and study some aspects of its political foundation. But I have not done so with historical techniques, a task for which I do not feel competent. Nor have I used a historicist approach, a deformation that is very common in twentieth-century political theory and with which I disagree.[1] By returning to the origins of the State, the idea is to understand the reasons behind certain hidden elements in its architecture and to listen to the sounds of the society from which it came. This is how, in the course of my research, I came upon a new Western world that arose in the thirteenth century and that, starting from its medieval traditions, was beginning to give evidence of the profound changes that would convert it into a new reality: a *vigilant society*.

In order to understand this new society that I believe is still in effect today, I have studied a segment of the Jewish population of the Diaspora. This group of people lived embedded in and, in some cases, were subjected to conditions of extreme subordination within other communities, while exhibiting an extremely high level of literacy and a great sensitivity to their political surroundings. We have to take into account that this Jewish population was spread out over a wide area of Europe and North Africa and that it had no political autonomy, no army, and no borders. It lived under political regimes that were set up and ruled by others.

This situation of dependence on and, at the same time, immersion of the Jewish communities in Christian or Muslim territory, exposed them to the dissemination of those cultures which they themselves were a part of as subjects. Not only did they speak the language of the land, but they were also born in that land, a land in which their Jewish ancestors had settled long before the advent of those conquerors who now ruled over them and saw them as strangers in their realm. [2]

Now then, what was so special about these Jewish groups was the fact that they could communicate between themselves, having access to other members of their religion from the most remote parts of those lands. This would produce what I refer to in this book as a cultural cross-pollination that encouraged and accelerated the exchange of ideas and experiences in the face of the new events that were occurring in Western Europe. In 1100 a professor of logic at the University of Paris could not communicate with the sages of Córdoba or Sicily, but the rabbis of the Rhine could travel to Toledo and Barcelona where they met up with fellow Jews with whom they shared a common identity, and could converse with each other in Hebrew or Aramaic.

My point of departure, therefore, is this unique and privileged horizontal position that favored communication between the Jewish communities of Western Europe. It encouraged an intellectual and scientific encounter that, understood from a present-day vantage point, would anticipate by several years phenomena that would occur a century later in the Christian sphere that was already established as a monolithic force in Western Europe.

My interest in these European Jewish communities is an imperative, to which I have willingly submitted myself. It arose from the need to understand in its very origin the evolution of that new vision of the public sphere and the political culture that came into being in Western Europe in the twelfth century and would be consolidated in the thirteenth century. This is why it is necessary to study the ways and means of living that gave rise to this vigilant society.

In cases where political theory attempts to delve deeply into highly specialized sectors of knowledge, some scholars might be bothered by, and even suspicious of, such a daring approach. Therefore I apologize at the outset to any expert who might detect an incorrect detail due to my insufficient knowledge. It should also be noted, however, that heated debates and disagreements abound in the very heart of these specialties. In my work I have tried to understand the moment when certain standards of living and a new public vision were born and when a new appreciation of the role of the public sphere took place, factors that have been decisive ever since.

This book, then, is a work of political theory that has occasionally come up against a scarcity of means and knowledge about the matter. We should recall that Leo Strauss was the first to put Moses Maimonides on the map of worldwide political theory in his 1963 essay, "How to Begin to Study *The Guide of the Perplexed*." Until then, the Cordoban sage was unknown to this field and contrary to that of the young Thomas Aquinas, who was so indebted to the *Guide of the Perplexed*, Maimonides' work did not appear in the manuals of the history of political science, except for an occasional anecdotal reference. If it were not for Strauss's audacity and talent, we would never have thought of this book as an important step in the history of political ideas. The well-deserved incorporation of this masterpiece into European theoretical tradition, in fact leads us in the present book to suggest that this tradition is intertwined with the rhetorical humanism of southern Europe. The reader will soon find that my book falls within a theoretical line that at present is considered of some importance in contemporary political theory: the reopening of the case for rhetoric. This line of thinking criticizes the executive face of politics and recovers the tradition of the authentic and genuine rhetoric. It assumes a liberation from the assumptions currently in force in twentieth-century political science that are centered on the vigilant characteristics of the State. The new political theory defends the importance of the democratic government of the life of each person. This is something similar to what, from another perspective, Sheldon S. Wolin called the democratization of the citizen's self.[3]

In regard to my sources, I have searched extensively for those works available on this subject. There is, however, the eternal problem of transcriptions, which the scholars in this field have complained about. I have tried to resolve the problem as best I could, looking, whenever possible, for homogeneity and consensus. In general, I have respected the original transcription of the authors, especially in regard to translated fragments.

The very idea of Sepharad itself has been questioned, in spite of the fact that the term has been used for over a thousand years. Although the *Real Academia de la Lengua Española* clearly identifies Sepharad with Spain,[4] not everyone has accepted this definition of Sepharad. H. J. Zimmels points out that "The problem of the relations between the Ashkenazim and the Sephardim has always been of interest to Jewish circles, and is nowadays more than ever of paramount importance."[5] Zimmels is referring to "those (Jews) of Spain," a Spain understood in the broadest sense and generally referring to the "Golden Age" from the tenth to the fourteenth centuries. At that time this notion of Sepharad also included regions in the south of present-day France such as the domains of Montpellier and Provence.[6]

Another aspect that sometimes clouds the idea of Sepharad is the religious confrontation that always lies below the surface. Baer tells us that "the contest between Judaism and Christianity, which the Middle Ages inherited from ancient times, took on here [in the Iberian Peninsula] more poignant form than anywhere else."[7]

Today there is frequent disagreement about the way some people interpret the idea of *lo español* (what is Spanish, or Spanishness), and this contaminates the topic. Because of their nationalistic tendencies, a certain intellectual sector refuses to recognize that the Jews of Catalonia are called Sephardim. They also reject as aberrant Baer's idea that in the thirteenth century, when all the Hispanic Jews, with the exception of Granada, had undergone the historical process "which transferred the Jews of Spain from the political jurisdiction of the Moslems to that of the Christians [it can be said that] . . . the basic problems confronting all of Spanish Jewry were intrinsically the same."[8] Some people would even have difficulty accepting Jonathan Ray's more flexible proposal that the study of Sephardic Jewry should be carried out within the context of "the history of medieval Iberia."[9] Moreover, what should we say about the heated quarrels between historians on the origins of Spain and the significance of the Reconquest?

Nowadays, on an international level there are those who use the word "Sephardic" to refer to an orientalized or Eastern, non-European Jewry. For this line of thought, the true European part of Judaism is the Ashkenasic one, while the Sephardic tradition is relegated to a virtually meaningless and almost residual minority: a culture of an exotic and premodern nature. Finally, there are many who do not think we can make a proper comparison between the Sephardic and the Ashkenazic Jews because they do not consider Sephardic identity to be sufficiently defined or clarified as such.

I would ask all these factions to be patient and allow this book to carry out its small task of recovery, an effort that is not intended to demean anyone or combat any other perspective.

I hope that the reader will merely see in this book an attempt to reopen the doors to lost historical values and a theoretical-political line of profound democratic worth that was gradually relegated to the background of Western European thought. It is a call for help from other scholars and an attempt to facilitate their work so that they will easily improve our own in the near future. It is a matter of recovering a few *lost objects*, in a sense well understood by Melanie Klein (1882–1925), Franz Kafka (1883–1924), and Walter Benjamin (1892–1940). The absence of these values takes on a special interest in view of the confusion being generated by the major changes taking place in the twenty-first century. These important transformations are occurring now in the splendid vigilant society that, in our opinion, was created in earlier times with not a few convulsions and renunciations.

Acknowledgments

I wish to express my gratitude to Rosa María Ramos, librarian of the Biblioteca de la Universidad Complutense for her invaluable help, efficiency, and kindness. I am also indebted to Antoni Jordà, of the Universitat Rovira i Virgili, and Selma Margaretten of Boston University for their advice and encouragement, as well as my collaborators Laura Adrián, Daniel Blanch, Juan Dorado, Jorge Loza, and Marta Martínez for their help in the preparation of the manuscript.

1

Knowledge and Power

> Modern man is the historical prolongation of medieval man who still survives within him. Our life is the second power of the superimposed medieval life.[1]
>
> —José Gaos

The need to live perpetually under the protection of a foreign entity has always been a characteristic of the Jewish people in the Diaspora. The life of its communities has always depended on the laws of those regimes and their territorial protection. As a consequence, the Jewish quarters have always had to rely on the law of the land and its authorities in order to survive. Lacking weapons, an army, and sovereignty, the tradition of Jewish public life intensely reveals the influences of their hosts.

However, their presence within empires and kingdoms of widely differing conditions had impregnated them with public substances that they frequently transferred to their sister communities.[2] We are dealing here with *aljamas*[3] or *calls* (communities) or, in some cases, mere Jewish neighborhoods embedded in very different cultures. This, then, was how the task of political cross-pollination began that had far-reaching consequences for the construction of Europe.

It was not unusual for those rabbis who emigrated to other lands to bring with them their customs and to sometimes show their lack of understanding toward local practices, resulting in friction with Jews in their adopted countries. This is the reason Rabbi Simon ben Zemah Duran (1361–1444)[4] gave for revoking a decision by another Spanish rabbi in Algeria: "The rabbi's inhibition is due to the fact that in Christian countries whence we hail no such custom exists, and consequently, it was difficult for the rabbi to regard as permissible a matter for which he had found no precedent."[5]

It was in the midst of this Diaspora that the life of Moses Maimonides, or Rambam (1138–1204),[6] an important thinker for southern Europe, transpired. As a prominent member of the Sephardic minority, he represents medieval thought at its highest point.[7] Nevertheless, as a teacher, Rambam had many adversaries within Judaism who considered his ideas to be extremely rationalistic. Others felt that he was a danger to the integrity of the Jewish faith and a threat to the preservation of its people.

In spite of all this, Maimonides attempted to synthesize a rich tradition of thought, while at the same time he tried to make it comprehensible to those who were living in a very different time, one of major transformations.

He did this from the standpoint of a man who was assaulted on all sides to convert. Because of the situation of the Jewish community, always in the minority, ill-adapted to, and in the midst of two great empires, Moses had the task of sustaining his identity in the face of great demands and pressure for him to convert. In this respect, it was a world not very far from our own time.

His personal life is an example of the situation in which his own coreligionists found themselves in general: always on the brink of leaving, looking for safer lands, or fleeing from persecution, and always tempted to renounce their convictions for a more profitable faith. Maimonides represented a minority that was forced to live under difficult conditions, both civil and political, and under which the easiest choice would have been to convert. Sometimes it was simply the only outlet to use in order to save one's life.

Moreover, there is an additional aspect to his work. Judaism is also vulnerable to the plague of false messiahs who appear from time to time to put an end to the long wait of its people. They bring with them the hope of redemption for Israel's woes and the promise of independence. This would be the omnipotent attainment of what, in another context, the romantics of the nineteenth and twentieth centuries would call *the final solution*.

But the essence of Judaism lies precisely in the renunciation of omnipotence, in other words, of the magical solutions to life's hardships. Therefore, in order to keep the faith alive and preserve the Jewish people, it is necessary to avoid falling into the trap of those false messiahs. Centuries before the birth of Maimonides many of those so-called messiahs had caused problems for the communities and their rabbis. Some were hotheads, others demented, and others simply opportunists. But in every one of these cases, there was always a sizeable number of Jews who were tempted to believe that freedom had come at last, that finally a political and religious leader had appeared who would deliver them from so much humiliation and so many postponements.

When these false hopes were shown to be hoaxes, the consequence was discouragement. Many young people became disoriented when faced with three disparate attractions: the country in which they had grown up and that they saw as their home, those leaders who frequently seduced them into believing in miraculous solutions, and the strict interpreters of Judaic law who, in the face of such dangers for their identity, locked themselves up tighter in their ritual orthodoxy.

Maimonides arose out of the shadows as a key figure in science, an eminent scholar and rabbi, and a famous physician. The purpose of his work was to furnish his coreligionists with a guide to cope with so much confusion. His study of the texts of the Torah and the Talmud will serve him to give an account of a tradition of thought (*halakhah*)[8] and its significance for the twelfth century. His education in al-Andalus (Córdoba and Lucena) and his knowledge, by way of his Andalusian teachers of the Greek and Judaic traditions, will prepare him for a new understanding of the city, public life, and religion. Such notables as Rabbi Isaac Alfasi, the first compiler of *halakhah* in Sepharad,[9] Rabbi Joseph Levita ibn Míguez, principal of the Academy of Lucena; Joseph ibn Zadik; and his own father, Rabbi Maimon, a judge from Córdoba, influenced his early education, in addition to the lessons of Rabbi Solomon ibn Gabirol's Platonism, Rabbi Abraham ibn Daud's Aristotelianism, and the mathematics and astronomy of Rabbi Abraham bar Hiyya of Barcelona.[10]

The European Chessboard

Greek influence can easily be seen in the Sephardic tradition. Rambam probably received it by way of Mediterranean cultural and commercial centers. The Greek schools did not die out with the Cynics, Skeptics, or Epicureans, as young Western students were traditionally taught, but rather continued their activity until the fifth century CE. Their work spread from Athens to Alexandria, one of the most brilliant cities in this tradition,[11] as well as Constantinople, the capital of Greek-speaking Europe. Thus, a figure such as Themistius, the great fourth-century teacher of Greek philosophy, was, for Maimonides, well known and esteemed, something that was unthinkable in Latin-speaking Europe. The rupture of the tradition of the Greek schools which, in the West, was the consequence of the confrontation between the two Europes—Greek and Latin—had no effect on the North African Jewish tradition. Jewish science, by way of its active community in Alexandria, cultivated that knowledge and passed it along to future generations. It is enough to recall the extremely important figure of Philo of Alexandria (25BCE?–50CE) to understand the scope of this transmission. In like manner, the wealth of the Muslim culture and economy would take up all this knowledge and transmit it to medieval Andalusia.

Today the complete vision of those two Europes enables us to see what was hidden in the past, such as the Crusades against Byzantium or the importance of Venice as a hinge of luxury between both worlds. The commercial, fluvial, maritime, and overland routes were the fundamental arteries for the growth of European culture.

Jewish understanding of the reality of Europe enables us to understand that constant struggle between Greek and Latin Europe, in which the latter was ultimately more predatory and efficient in its expansion than the Orthodox model. This animosity between the two Europes explains why Greek culture had to find other, more circuitous ways of making inroads into the West. To a certain extent the rise of Christian scholasticism would attempt to reply to the "Greco-Arabic tidal wave"[12] that was perceived as a veritable menace. The great transfusion of Greek to Latin, already anticipated in the fourteenth century, occurred in 1453 with the fall of Constantinople to the Turks. European Greece was definitively left behind in the fifteenth century. It was time for the Renaissance to begin.

During the medieval period prior to the eleventh century, the culture inherited from the Greek schools found its way through the Mediterranean by slipping in between Christianity and Islam, the two empires of the period. The Jewish minority played an essential role in the preservation and development of European culture by serving as the transmitter of this knowledge. It performed an important function in the cross-pollination of the urban cultures of the West. Jerusalem was the symbol of this Mediterranean contribution, which, together with the Greek world, made up the foundations of our civilization. Later on, Leo Strauss would theorize about this in the twentieth century.

Curiously, Maimonides' biography moves inversely to this expansion. It goes from western Andalusia to the Middle East and the birthplace of Mediterranean civilization. Obviously it is an approximation to Jerusalem, the source of knowledge of his people. This movement is not unusual, especially within Sephardic culture. Nahmanides (1194–1270),[13] himself, another great figure in thirteenth-century Jewish thought, would end up at the age of seventy-three as a refugee in Akko and Jerusalem after his exile from Catalonia in 1267.

It is important to analyze the essential differences between the public life as practiced by Jewish tradition and that of the Christian world, or so-called Christianity, in which Westerners do not usually include the Greek world. From a Western point of view, Orthodox culture is considered to be archaic and too hieratic.

We have seldom paid tribute to a world like Byzantium, obviously more learned and more developed commercially and culturally. We are indebted to it for introducing the fork, so we do not have to eat with our hands,[14] the habit of daily bathing, and the code of Justinian (483–565),[15] the great regulator of maritime life in the world that Byzantium contributed to the civilized world. From it would also come the tradition of noteworthy schools of philosophy that, in spite of the fact that they were no longer interesting to the West, would continue to be taught to generations of important thinkers and politicians. However, it is shocking that Western political engineering does not study the Byzantine Empire more thoroughly, if only as an example of efficiency and endurance.[16]

The rise of a tradition that extended from Alexandria, Aleppo, Tunis, Crete, Venice, Naples, Palermo, Siracusa, and Fez to Córdoba, speaks of an invaluable commercial, religious, and maritime world. This was how a great accumulation of philosophical, astronomical, mathematical, medical, botanical, and historical knowledge passed from Constantinople to Western Europe.[17]

Greek culture has come down to us in part from the Jewish circles that lived in these cities, Islamic or Christian, and continued to maintain its science and knowledge in spite of always being in danger of persecution or expulsion.

This was a minority that never had an independent political organization or an army of its own, and it always had to rely on the legal capacity and security provided by its countries of adoption. These human groups were also confronted with another danger—that of assimilation—a perennial fear of the people of Israel, established within monarchies that were very bellicose and often dogmatic. Forced to live as a minority in situations of harrowing civil clashes between Christians or headlong confrontations of mutual conquest between two religions of enormous transcendence, their mere survival was extremely difficult.

Education in Sephardic Culture

Maimonides was born in Córdoba in 1138 into a Jewish community that lived under a regime governed by changing versions of Islam, which gradually became more rigid. At the same time, his city was very close to the border with the Christian world, which was equally belligerent. This Christian society was more backward economically and endowed with fewer comforts, and religious orthodoxy was about to impose itself on its inhabitants.

After the Almohad persecution of 1148, he had to emigrate with his family to other cities in Hispaniae. Although it is known that many Jewish families went to Saragossa, there is no record of where his family ended up. They may have gone to Almería, a prosperous city at that time. Around 1159 the family crossed over to Fez, where they resided until 1165.[18] From there, again because of religious persecution, Maimonides went to the Holy Land and finally to Egypt, where it is known that he settled down and worked for many years as a physician at the court of Saladin (Salah al-Din). He died in Fustat, a district of Cairo, in 1204.

Maimonides was always concerned that young people might become converted or *assimilated* for convenience, either because of ignorance or the need to become integrated in society. When Maimonides was thirteen he began a pilgrimage between the interstices of the two great powers, a situation that must have put him in a rather uncomfortable position. Those were influential years filled with unforgettable experiences.

The Sephardic or Hispanic world represented a substantial part of medieval Judaism. Specifically, the period between 900 and 1200 is considered to be the "Golden Age of Spanish Jewry."[19] It was this tradition that preserved elements relevant for political theory.

The first element is their view of education as an individual matter. In this sense, it does not seem probable that Maimonides intended for his works to merely regularize and systematize the knowledge of the Jewish religion. It is true that his *Mishneh Torah* made him an excellent codifier of *ḥalakhah*,[20] that tradition of discourse and law that gives political and moral substance to the people of Israel and is the artifice of the recovery and protection of the identity of Judaism. His work, however, is not merely a compilation, but it is also a profound and learned review of its opportune meaning for the times in which he lived.

His knowledge of philosophy includes those Greek texts that he received from his teachers in Córdoba. But he also takes up the wisdom of Hebrew tradition regarding the public life of the *kehillah* or *cahal*, the *aljama*, or Jewish quarter.[21]

The world in which he was educated consisted, on the one hand, of Muslim scholars who had studied the Platonic and Aristotelian tradition and, on the other, of his Jewish teachers at Lucena who were undoubtedly familiar with these sources. Lucena had an important Jewish community, and its intellectual activity was of the highest level. It was also the seat of the famous school founded by Rabbi Isaac Alfasi.

We should point out that if in his medical knowledge there are echoes of the Mediterranean culture of several religions, the same is true of his philosophical knowledge. This is not the case with the Roman tradition, which in any case may have reached him by way of his contacts with the Ashkenazic schools and those Christian centers in Toledo, Catalonia, and Provence.

While it is true that his works were widely read and discussed,[22] it is also true that some of his books were sometimes rejected and even burned[23] in those places where he had strong adversaries. Rambam undoubtedly had fierce enemies within the Sephardic community. His most important contender must have been Jonah Gerondi,[24] a cousin of Nahmanides, who devoted his writings to attacks on the *Guide of the Perplexed* (*Moreh Nevukim*) and was instrumental in convincing several Christian communities to burn this book. But when later on the attack extended to other important Jewish books such as the Talmud itself, Jonah Gerondi recanted and adopted a position of repentance and respect for the teacher from Córdoba that lasted for many years. In a letter to Rabbi Hillel of Verona,[25] a devotee of Maimonides, he expressed his contrition for his earlier views.

Nahmanides himself, an admirer of the Cordoban and a follower of his teachings, had expressed his confusion over the proposals put forth in the *Guide*: "We were therefore surprised by Maimonides, who detracts from the miraculous, and accentuates naturalism."[26]

In 1232, at the height of the tension, Nahmanides exhorts the rabbis of Castile and Aragon to unite in support of the cause of Solomon ben Abraham of Montpellier. This venerable and prestigious Talmud scholar had already raised his voice several years earlier against Maimonides' work, specifically his code, the *Mishneh Torah*: "I became exercised to protect Israel and its sanctities . . . when I saw that belief in bodily resurrection was being lost in this land among many of his dispersed peoples . . . even before the book which perplexes the guides (*Guide of the Perplexed*) had reached here, part of the nation had rebellious ideas about faith in the Creator."[27]

The translation of the *Guide of the Perplexed* from Arabic to Hebrew had far-reaching and prolonged repercussions. It provoked a crisis—whose echoes can still be heard even today!—in Jewish communities under Christian domination by opening the doors to the knowledge of Aristotle and Averroes (1126–1198).[28] As a consequence, a very controversial Averroist current appeared among those Jews. It sparked a fierce polemic between the supporters of philosophy and others who were adherents of rabbinical tradition.[29] A third element in discord—the kabbalah—arose in the thirteenth century. In this sense, Gerona was an important center in the gestation of the kabbalah.[30]

Why did Maimonides present such a menace to Jewish tradition? Why was he so dangerous for the Jewish citizens of Western Europe?

Rambam wrote his *Guide* in Arabic perhaps because he feared that his work would not be properly understood. He wrote it in Arabic with Hebrew characters (*aljamiado*) and instructed his copyists to transcribe it only in those letters.[31]

It should be emphasized that Maimonides was more debated and attacked for his work in Christian Europe than in Muslim lands.[32] One of the reasons might be the different relationship between Judaism and Islam in contrast to the relationship Judaism has always had with Christianity. Contrary to the Christians, Muslims never held that the Jews had tortured and killed their founder.[33] Mohammad died of natural causes; therefore, there was no reason for "propheticide."[34] It is enough to read any reference by Maimonides to Jesus of Nazareth to understand the depth of this animosity and the difficult solution to this clash between them:

> Jesus the Nazarene, may his bones be ground to dust. He was a Jew because his mother was a Jewess although his father was a Gentile. For in accordance with the principle of our law, a child born of a Jewess although his father was a Gentile, or of a Jewess and a slave, is legitimate (Yevamot 45a). Jesus is only figuratively termed an illegitimate child. He impelled people to believe that he was a prophet sent by God to clarify perplexities in the Torah, and that he was the Messiah that was predicted by each and every seer. He interpreted the Torah and its precepts in such a fashion as to lead to their total annulment, to the abolition of all its commandments and to the violation of its prohibitions. The sages, of blessed memory, having become aware of his plans before his reputation spread among our people, meted out fitting punishment to him.[35]

The Jewish rejection of the Christian world (the successors of Edom or Esau) is especially virulent, since the origin of the exile of the Jewish people is attributed to it. In the words of Bahya ben Asher, a preacher, exegete, and judge of Saragossa at the end of the thirteenth and beginning of the fourteenth centuries: "It is well known that, although we live dispersed and oppressed in their lands [both Islamic and Christian], the origin of our exile lies with Edom, *those who eat the flesh of the pig*, for he expelled us and destroyed our Temple."[36]

On the contrary, the welcome given to the Sephardim from Spain after the 1391 crisis is proof of the swift integration of the Jews into the Muslim kingdoms of North Africa. Rabbi Simon Duran speaks of the case of Algeria in his *responsa*.[37] The Sephardic emigrants arrived in a country that was "backward, underdeveloped, uncivilized,"[38] people of good feelings "that prompted its rulers to throw open the doors to the fugitives, and to afford them therein a secure asylum."[39] The same could also be said of the welcome given to the 1492 exiles in the Turkish Empire.

Maimonides' work is a contribution of the West to European culture, given that the culture of Córdoba represents the development in Arabic, Hebrew, and romance of a very advanced civilization in the sciences, philosophy, poetry, and urban culture within the territory of Hispania. It was a world in which the Jewish communities had felt themselves well integrated for centuries—Jewish settlements date from the beginning of the Christian era—and in which they collaborated actively. In reality, the level of Sephardic cultural and theological development both in Arabic and the romance languages was considered, for centuries, superior to Ashkenazic Judaism. The beliefs of the Sephardim and Ashkenazim were the same with regard to the principles of Judaism, given that both groups considered the Talmud to be their highest authority. There were, however, many differences in relation to their customs and views of everyday life: "Sephardim follow the rulings of Rabbi Joseph Caro, a Spanish Jew . . . whereas Ashkenazim adhere to the particular traditions outlined in the same work by Rabbi Moses Isserles, a Polish Jew. In general, Rabbi Caro's perspective represents a more liberal and permissive tendency than the one approved by Ashkenazi authorities such as Isserles."[40]

Jews and Christians

Historians have taught us that Sephardic culture was widespread in the Iberian Peninsula and that it continued without many problems until the conversion of the Visigoths to Christianity: "The Jewish settlement on the Iberian Peninsula was a very ancient one and in its early stages had prospered. Even after the Visigoths had established their rule over the land, the condition of the Jewish communities remained favorable for a long time. They earned their livelihood with dignity, and they fulfilled the laws of the Torah and observed its commandments without hindrance."[41]

This situation changed with the coming of the Visigoths throughout the fifth century thanks to an agreement with the Roman province of Tarraco that would alter the situation. The Visigoths were Arian Christians who became unified with the Catholicism predominant in the Hispano-Roman world at the Councils of Toledo that culminated in 589. The situation was different from then on. Their king Reccared[42] even converted to Catholicism to encourage the alliances and bring the population together. Then the panorama changed with the entrance on stage of the Christian synods that began to promote a very restrictive legislation for the Jews.

The policy of obligatory baptism gave rise to the *anusim* (coherced)[43] or crypto-Jews who practiced their religion in secret, something that the new Spanish Inquisition would plainly label as "Judaizing" in the sixteenth century. In this climate the arrival of Islam in the Golden Age was a relief from this situation. However, by entering into the political sphere of Islam, the Spanish synagogues were able to establish contact with Babylonian Jewry and, thus, gradually assume "leadership of the majority of the world Jewish community."[44]

Sephardism evolved in the midst of the Muslim and Christian cultures. It flourished in Arabic as well as the romance languages, particularly in Castilian.[45] But in the Christian world, Jewish culture may have had a component of guilt that was lacking in its relationship with Arabic culture. This feeling of sorrowful guilt is expressed eloquently by Sem Tob ben Yishaq Ardutiel, also known as Don Santo de Carrión:[46] "Many a sword of good and fine steel comes from a torn sheath, and it is from the worm that fine silk is made . . . For being born on the thornbush, the rose is certainly not worth less, nor is good wine if taken from the lesser branch of the vine. Nor is a hawk worth less, if born in a poor nest; nor are good proverbs [of less value] if spoken by a Jew."[47]

In contrast, it is obvious that the *aljamas* in the south were living a period of great splendor, "one of the longest and most glorious chapters in Jewish history."[48] But when the Christian Reconquest became stronger as it pushed south—in 1212 the Almohads suffered a decisive defeat at Las Navas de Tolosa and Seville fell in 1248—the Jewish community living in the Muslim world would have great difficulty in transplanting itself to Christian territory. As Jonathan Ray points out: "The delicate flower of Andalusi Jewish culture could not be easily transplanted in the soil of Christian Spain. In contrast to the cosmopolitan cities and glittering courts of the Andalusi princes, the Christian castles of the north seemed crude and uninviting, and provided little to assuage the Jew's bitterness over the fall of their illustrious communities."[49]

The Jewish lamentation for the Sepharad of the south—in this case, that of the refined poet Abraham ibn Ezra—is different from the shameful laments of their coreligionists in the Christian territories.

I weep like the ostrich[50] for Lucena.
Her remnant dwelt innocent and secure,
Unchanged for a thousand years;
Then came her day and her people were exiled and she a widow . . .

I will shave my head and cry bitterly over the exiles from Seville,
Over her noble men that were slain and their sons enslaved,
Over refined daughters converted to the foreign faith.

Alas, the city of Córdoba is forsaken, her ruin as vast as the sea!
Her sages and learned men perished from hunger and thirst.
Not a single Jew was left in Jaén or Almería;
Mallorca and Malaga struggle to survive.

The Jews who remain are a beaten and bleeding wound.
For this I mourn and learn a dirge and wail with bitter lamentation;
I shout in my distress: They have vanished like water.[51]

In any case, the Christian kings favored the arrival of Jewish refugees, given that they helped these rulers in the repopulation of the newly conquered territories. The charters granted to some cities specify royal protection for the Jews who had been harassed first, by the intolerance of the Almoravids and later on, by the Almohads. This is the case of Ramón Berenguer IV in the Charter of Tortosa (1145):[52] "If more Jews come to settle, I shall give them homes to occupy and settle . . . I grant you those good laws and all customs and usages which the Jews of Barcelona enjoy."[53]

The situation changed definitively in 1391. This was "the beginning of the end of the Jewish communities in Spain." That year was marked by numerous popular uprisings against the Jews, many of whom died in the revolts. Among them was the only son of the chief rabbi of Saragossa, Hasdai ben Judah Crescas. The battle was not so much about exterminating the Jews but rather about forcing them to convert. During this same period there was an institutional schism within Christianity with two popes claiming the throne of St. Peter in 1378. The Jewish community saw itself in serious danger of dispersion or assimilation, a situation that prompted some Jewish teachers to feel as if they were in "an obligatory war" against Christianity and write theological refutations in reply.[54] This is the case of Hasdai Crescas and his *Refutation of the Christian Dogmas.*[55]

Theory and Prophecy: Inherence and Contingence

For a student familiar with Aristotle's works it is obvious that *dialectic* and *rhetoric* are twins, inseparable parts of politics.[56] Moreover, the rhetorical heart of life incorporates both the inherent and the contingent. The teachings of the rhetoricians counted on not only the syllogism but also the *enthymeme.* It was obvious, therefore, that the dialectical process implicated both the teacher and the pupil. The idea of *isegoria,* so well understood in the Mediterranean, and the democratic rhetoric of Isocrates, Cicero, and Quintilian implied precisely that idea: that one cannot teach a subject or what one would consider to be truth without taking into account the feelings and participation of one's students. In this way, instead of the truth, the most believable or credible is established. In the Talmudic tradition of the Mediterranean, this is the very essence of daily life in the *aljama.* Even when revealed truth exists, its everyday interpretation for the life of the quarter is based on constant study and consensus. Justice is not so much an abstract expression as the honest and constant practice of good judgment.

Maimonides does not specifically pretend to conceal his work, but rather, he does not want to give something to someone who cannot share it, either because that person is not prepared or because of excess. For him, learning is not a dialectic process. It is a matter that will come to the fore centuries later, that is, if it was ever out of sight. To begin with, the dialect practiced in the Greek *poleis* had nothing to do with what the Central Europeans—and by the Ashkenazim by contact—understood as such. It arose in nineteenth-century romanticism. But neither Hegelian dialecticism, nor the Marxist variety, the School of Frankfurt, nor "the dialectic of fists and pistols" of the fascist ideologues had anything to do with what the Greek citizens understood as the dialectic that was the inseparable twin sister of rhetoric.

Of course, for the devotees of that romantic dialectic, decisively molded by the Calvinists, a certain rhetoric still exists. But for these people—and for the journalists who echo such a rhetoric—it is a matter of *ars fallendi,* of speaking for the sake of speaking or manipulating facts with words. The rhetoric is lacking in and devoid of *inventio*. Drama has been expelled from the university by Petrus Ramus (Pierre de la Ramée, 1515–1572), and the entire space is taken over by a new dialectic, all-conquering and ubiquitous. Only a few were able to correct this serious error of perception, and among the most sublime examples of this are Shakespeare's *Hamlet*, Bach's *Inventions*,[57] and the works of Giambattista Vico. The absolute domination of the Ashkenazic version in these matters established a vision that made Maimonides' political theory almost incomprehensible. In this line there are some who assimilate Maimonides and his understanding of the monarchy with John Locke.[58] It is curious to see that critics accused the teacher from Córdoba of being mysterious and slightly esoteric, while he was really being wisely prudent.

It must be recognized that Leo Strauss, with his extraordinary intuition, is one of the few who, even when he participated in this intellectual mess, with the ins and outs typical of his style, penetrated intelligently into Rambam's thought without destroying it, and even made some magnificent contributions. Initially he was responsible for having brought Maimonides to the foreground of political theory and of having rescued him in this field from unjustified oblivion.

Isadore Twersky, a great Maimonides scholar, attempts to justify him in a modern way. On the one hand, he recognizes that "discrepancy" that he has been accused of sometimes in his writings between the principles and the application of norms. On the other hand, he excuses Rambam by using German romantic explanations to exculpate him. Thus, he explains (in his literary style) "There is an unpredictable and spontaneous factor of creativity, both conscious and unconscious . . . *das unbewusste Schaffen* from which creativity stems or sometimes erupts."[59]

Strauss was more to the point when he perceived a particular enchantment in Maimonides' *Guide*. He saw that, aside from its extraordinarily well-thought-out structure, the work encourages the reader to become immersed in the pleasure of reading to the point where he will not put it down. Undoubtedly Strauss would also have found the same pleasure in *Don Quixote*, a work that exercises a similar enchantment on its reader.

Fortunately contemporary theory does understand the meaning of rhetoric as it was understood by the Sephardic teachers, more refined and cultured than the Germanicized and Latinized Ashkenazim, and has reopened the case for its study. Now we have begun to address the problem of teaching political science with the complexity that the subject demands, instead of relying on the omnipotence of the dialectic teacher who sometimes plans his class as if his pupils were merely complements to his teaching.

The very fact that the *Guide of the Perplexed* is designed *to teach one on one* is something that makes us think even more about the work. This procedure would culminate in the nonidentification of knowledge with power. As Maimonides reflects, God (omnipotence) knows his being as it is for, in him, knowledge, power, and being are fused into one: "For our knowledge and ourselves are separate."[60] Thus the insistence of Maimonides on teaching being directed to wakefulness as well as lethargy and that learning takes place especially through dreams at night. He insists on this from the point of view of a physician who spent hours attending to his patients in practice, and with great fervor, he reclaims the importance of the body and the practical. This should make us think: "While it is a duty to study by day and by night, most of one's knowledge is acquired at night . . . [W]hosoever occupies himself with the study of the Torah by night—a mark of spiritual grace distinguishes him by day . . . A house wherein the words of the Torah are not heard at night will be consumed by fire . . . 'A fire not blown by man shall consume him'" (Job 20:26).[61]

Dream and prophecy are inextricably intertwined. As Rambam explains, "no prophecy and no prophetic revelations come in any other way except *in a dream* or *in a vision* and through the agency of an angel."[62]

These prophecies come in a state of extreme agitation and terror. They appear as a vision and afterwards, as Daniel, himself[63]—the exile from Judah—tells us, the prophet was exhausted, weak, and fell into a deep sleep with his face to the ground:[64] "In a state such as this the senses too cease to function, and the overflow in question comes to the rational faculty and overflows from it to the imaginative faculty so that the latter becomes perfect and performs its function."[65] Thanks to this vision, in which "deep and secret things" hidden in the dark are revealed to Daniel, the prophet can interpret the king's "dreams and the visions of [his] head" so that he may "know the thoughts of [his] heart."[66]

On the other hand, there are "fantasms of the imagination" that present themselves during our sleep and go beyond the simple psychic representation of external objects by the senses and can exist in the imagination "after the object of which it is the form is no longer manifest to the senses."[67]

In view of the way Maimonides sees the life of the mind and the importance he gives to wakefulness and lethargy, we can draw the conclusion that the only thinker of Ashkenazic origin who links up with Maimonides is, astonishingly, Sigmund Freud.[68] His genius coincides with the teacher from Córdoba, not only in his fundamental view of the world, which is evident, but also in the importance he gives to lethargy and to the opening up of the individual's being to a complexity that is inexhaustible in the executive power of a person, the "red memory,"[69] and the will that sometimes becomes atrophied and empties out the rest of the *self* or *oneself*. Freud's demand that dreams be taken into account as material for knowledge and as an essential cognitive source, the dismantling of the executive power of the individual, and the recovery of the *infantes*, in the rhetorical meaning of the word, were all concepts familiar to the Sephardic tradition and understood as well by the rhetoricians of Mediterranean humanism.

The learning process cannot be one-sided, nor is it the outcome of a critical dialectic confrontation (*disputatio*) of clashing swords. Freud culminated his brilliant finding with a discovery that Leo Strauss was also aware of: the principle of identity does not function inside the human brain, in its inner world. Maimonides, too, was aware of this, and therein lies his splendor. Time and space do not exist in dreams, in the enchanted world of the *Guide of the Perplexed*,[70] or in the enchantment of *Don Quixote*, the greatest and most healing book in this tradition of political theory. Perhaps this is a well-known perception in Jewish tradition. For this reason, in a dream it is possible to be in two places at once, and things can appear for which no words can be found in the dictionary. In view of this complexity, the Sephardic teachers knew they could not rely on programmed knowledge, directed by a know-it-all decisive executive, to draw up guidelines and protocols for the sake of functionality and order.

For this same reason, in the *medina* (city), which, for the republicans of the classical world, would always be written man *in extenso*, not all its problems could be solved with such a decisive reliance on the executive, whether it was the Gentile power of the crown or the laws of the land that the *aljamas* found in the states where they settled.[71]

The Law of the Kingdom Is the Law

According to medieval documents, the *aljama* was the legal institution that brought the Jews together in the great medieval cities under Muslim domination. In smaller cities, however, the minorities were insufficient to make up a legal organism that could serve a variety of functions. In other places they had different names. Thus, in Catalonia they were known as *calls* (perhaps from the Hebrew *cahal*) and in other territories of the kingdoms of Aragon and Castile they were called *juderías* (Jewish quarters).

The Aragonese *aljamas* were made up of both the Jewish inhabitants and their institutions. In general they enjoyed a considerable degree of autonomy.[72] They occupied their own sections of town that could even be separate from the rest of the inhabitants. The Moriscos (converted Muslims) also lived in separate sections of the cities in Christian territories, and in keeping with the policies of repopulation, the Christians themselves were grouped in parishes around their churches.

In practice, the Jewish communities or quarters were made up of autonomous corporations with their own norms in religious, legal, administrative, and economic matters similar to those of medieval cities, whose institutions they often imitated: "According to privileges granted by the Aragonese monarchs, the *aljamas* arbitrated within their jurisdictions disputes for insults and civil suits, levied fines and excommunicated the guilty, and had the authority to expel them from the community and the city. Some *aljamas* could also impose the death penalty or sanction informers (*mosrim* or *malsvinim*) in their midst who denounced their members to the Christian authorities, thus putting in serious danger the existence of entire communities."[73]

In contrast to the Moriscos, the Jewish inhabitants did not have the status of "conquered on the battlefield," which was to their advantage. Their communities usually accepted royal authority and with it the obligation to be loyal subjects and pay their taxes. In the special case of Aragon, James I frequently offered the Jewish communities in conquered territories the same favorable status as the Jews of Barcelona.

The Jewish communities varied in size and were governed by an executive council of secretaries or deputies who attended to the daily needs of the population. Moreover, an assembly of all the adult men of the quarter could be convened to ratify a statute or an especially important decision.[74] If the volume of work required it, there were more officials in charge of economic, religious, legal, or administrative matters of lesser importance. The religious leaders were a rabbi-judge (*dayyan*) and in some cases, assistant rabbis with special functions for specific cases.[75] The inhabitants of the neighborhood were normally grouped around their synagogue, although sometimes the increase in population obliged them to spread out to another part of the city. Within the quarter there were usually a butcher shop, oven, market, tavern, hospice, and ritual bath, and outside the quarter, a cemetery.[76] And naturally, they had their own judges: "The *mucaddemim* also exercized penal jurisdiction; they were responsible, in the name of the *aljama*, for the religious and moral conduct of each of its members, and especially vigilant in persecuting informers. In addition to the *mucaddemim*, the Aragonese and Valencian *aljamas* also had a *bet-din*, a court composed of two or three judges who had the authority to act in lesser trials and conduct interrogations by order of the *mucaddemim*, and impose fines. These special judges were called *berorim*."[77]

As the Christian conquest advanced, royal laws began to take precedence in the Jewish quarters over the laws of Israel, that is, the Torah and the Talmud. This is what Ashkenazic philosophy brought to Barcelona and Castile in the extraordinary figures of Solomon ibn Adret (1235–1310) and Asher ben Yehiel (1250–1327) in Toledo. Little by little good judgment became blurred as the central focus of public life. In the *aljamas* of Sepharad, however, public life was understood as an everyday reality in which, thanks to good judgment, contingencies were taken into account in order to resolve daily problems. Thus, offenses, tensions, conflicts, fears and malaise, superstitions and unfounded terrors were worked out through a close-knit web of good judgment, which had been preserved through a long tradition of discourse (*halakhah*) and legal rulings. *Halakhah* is based on the laws of Israel, but it is the result of the consensus between different interpretations and applications. Decisions were always made with its support by taking into account the contingency of emotions, specific interests, and public conditions at that particular moment.

But that was not the line that would win out. Throughout the thirteenth and fourteenth centuries Ashkenazic public philosophy gradually became more firmly rooted in the peninsula, perhaps because of its ability to respond to more immediate political interests. The fact is that, with it, the way was laid for a Jewish society that would become much more assimilated into Christian society.

The Disputation of Barcelona held in July 1263 marked a turning point in this history. It was a public event that came to signify "the setting for the new situation of Judaism in the heart of Christianity."[78]

In this confrontation there appeared the new spirit of the orders born to preach as a form of conquest of souls and territories. Raimundo de Penyafort (1175–1275), who became a Dominican friar in 1221 and was chosen general of the Order of Preachers in 1237, was present at the Disputation. He had been the pope's confessor since 1230, an influential post from which he resigned in 1240 to return to Aragon and devote his life to preaching in the heart of the communities of infidels, mainly the Jews. Penyafort stands in contrast to that other great figure of Christian apologetics, Raimundo Lulio or Llull (1232–1316), who was also a preacher, of aristocratic origin, and a Franciscan terciary. He tended to look for the coincidences between Christianity and other beliefs in order to open the doors to those who wished to be assimilated. To a certain extent, Llull tried to be an advocate for the infidels. Both Penyafort and Llull were preachers and missionaries on the Catalan frontier, and they are examples of the two opposing methods of Christian apologetics in the thirteenth century. Both of these great figures had access to and influence on the king of Aragon.[79]

The relationship between Christians and Jews never recovered from the blow dealt by the Disputation of Barcelona, an event that motivated the expulsion of Nahmanides, by then an old man. Until then, the Jew had been a useful *servus regis* to society and, as such, well regarded by the Crown. But after the royal decrees of September 1263 and the papal bull of Clement IV from Viterbo, Jewish residents began to undergo constant surveillance and humiliation. As a consequence of the Disputation they were forced to open their homes to the Jewish apostate Paulo Christiani—personally assigned by the pope—and his Dominican companions. Jews everywhere, no matter what their status, were to comply "with humility, reverence, and without slander or subterfuge." They were to show the visitors all the books in their possession so that they could expurgate and cleanse their collections. The cost of these visits was to be paid for by the Jews themselves, although the expense could be deducted from the tribute they owed to the king.[80]

This process of militarization of consciences started off very forcefully, culminating in the sixteenth century in the deformation of and subsequent emptying out of rhetoric. Thus, rhetorical *inventio* passed over into the realm of dialectic in a pedagogical transformation carried out by the Calvinist Ramus. All this would have a lasting effect on the public life of Europe.

A Vigilant Society

At the end of the thirteen century Jewish philosophy would go far beyond Maimonides' expression in his Code that "the person who spies on his neighbor breaks a prohibition."[81] From this time on, its philosophy would become assimilated to the vision that was more in tune with a Christian world that was advancing, unstoppable and definitively in Western Europe. In this sense, Maimonides represents an important obstacle in the progress of the *vigilant society*. This vision, however, with due respect for the gigantic stature of Maimonides, is truly incomprehensible. From Christian Catalonia the king does not look upon Maimonides as someone nearby, and in one royal decree, he is mentioned as Moses "the Egyptian" or "Maimonides of Cairo." In other words, he is an outsider.[82]

Curiously enough, the apostate Paolo Christiani refers to him with praise during the Disputation. Although Rambam is admired as a teacher within the Jewish communities of the kingdom of Aragon, he is regarded with suspicion because his position is uncomfortable for those who are in favor of a greater adaptation to the Christian view of the public. Submission to Christian laws required many changes within the Jewish communities such as the rejection of polygamy, the acceptance of the death penalty, the recognition of Christian notaries, and a new understanding of public life. Even in the fourteenth century this is apparent in Ibn Adret, who accepts allegiance to the prince or the homeland in a way that Maimonides would never have accepted. The elimination of the public philosophy of the southern teachers, headed by the great Maimonides, signifies not only progress in the modernization of Judaism, in the interpretation of some present-day scholars. That idea is anachronistic here. What happens is that a transmutation of public life is building up that leans toward the executive, with the consequent deterioration of good judgment. Democratic aspects will slowly fall, only to survive, as will also happen later on to rhetoric, in a few sublime European literary creations such as *Hamlet* and *Don Quixote*.

In this way we arrive at the *barbarism*[83] of some present-day critics who interpret Rambam from a dialectical mentality borrowed from nineteenth-century Christian romanticism. It is an error made even by eminent Jewish scholars educated in German academic romanticism or American Calvinist positivism who do not know how to interpret this wise contribution to European culture that is exceptional for the West.

Some will understand him through his Aristotelianism,[84] influenced by Averroes, which supposedly led Rambam toward that badly matched duality of philosophy and theology; others will explain him as an avant-garde dialectical universalistic theologian, who is unbearable in times of scepticism like our own. Some have unashamedly dared to label the teacher from Córdoba as the author of a political model that "appears to violate the most basic human rights, as is true of all theocratic models."[85]

On the other hand, Leo Strauss would be an admirable example of that Ashkenazic interpretation of Maimonides that lacked a rhetorical or Mediterranean humanistic education. Nevertheless, thanks to his extraordinary intuition and interpretive brilliance, Strauss was capable of learning a great deal from the Cordoban. At times he adopts an excessively prosecutorial tone in speaking of the person he considers to be his teacher. But at least he allows himself to approach with genuine interest such an exceptional work as the *Guide of the Perplexed* and to read it from the point of view of its "*enchantment*" and without confusing the rhetorical enchantment with romantic intoxication. Unfortunately this is not the case with certain followers of Strauss, who try to imitate an almost inimitable teacher and fall into the arrogant simplification of things.

Maimonides understood that the law of the land is the law of the Jews, but he understood it in the Talmudic sense that the Jews should be loyal and constructive to the power that gives them asylum. This does not mean, however, that they must identify patriotically with those new entities that emerge such as the Prince, the Gentile king, or a homeland to which one must surrender enthusiastically, even at the cost of going against the law of Israel, which is divine law.

On the other hand, he knows that if man is very keen on learning, he also frequently looks for the easiest road. He often wants to find the immediate solution to problems without taking into account the effort which it entails: "For man has in his nature a desire to seek the ends; and he often finds preliminaries tedious and refuses to engage in them."[86]

Another danger lies in the teaching of improper material, not because it contains hidden dangers, but because the teacher's attitude might hide a high degree of omnipotence. One should not use illustrations or arguments where it is not possible to do so. Not everyone can teach everything, nor even learn everything. More than an elitist mistrust, we find a serious concern for the truth.

Two ideas are intertwined in this vision: (1) a horizontal understanding of existence, in which the flow of life is like a melody in which time lets us enjoy the melodic richness of public life, and (2) the transcendence of a harmonic reading of society in which several voices are superimposed simultaneously. Harmony implies the timeless understanding of public life in which several voices and meanings not only live together in a single instant, but they change shape, activate and reactivate, and glorify each other. In other words, the sum of various voices and sounds exalts a new musicality between them, creating, in turn, a reality encouraged by that harmony.

This view of the public sector allows for a complexity of thought that could hardly be expressed from the viewpoint of the agora, the corporeal setting of life, with its constant movement in time and space.

With the comprehension of life *ex-auditu*, there arises the possibility of contact not only with sounds and words but also with silence. "One should always cultivate the habit of silence . . . 'A fence to wisdom is silence.'"[87] Just as in a musical score the notation marks the silences (rests) with its exact measurement, in this tradition, silence appears as the root of public agreement.

Curiously, this concept already existed in Greek and Roman rhetorical tradition,[88] but it was gradually replaced in Latin Europe by a life of presences. After this, the logos was understood as a world of signs and public appearance as the visual perception of reality. This reality was composed of men in action, occupied with their things and interests (*inter homines esse*).

Maimonides concedes a great deal of importance to withdrawing from worldly things. But this does not mean that he recommends isolation or reclusion in caves or mountains like the early Jewish *therapeutae*. He believes that man should avoid the many distractions that the crowd and daily life offer him. In order to advance along the road, he should remain alone for a time in order to meditate, think calmly about his situation, and receive tranquil and undisturbed the data and reflections of a world that is sometimes tenuous. This is not an antipolitical solitude.[89] The *Katima*, as later on, with Baroque *solitude*, refers to this. *Katima* means reclusion as well as seal. It is something that the privileged few need in order to travel through the celestial kingdoms. "O solitude, my sweetest choice! / Places devoted to the night, / Remote from tumult and from noise."[90]

Sometimes our teacher uses ambiguous concepts, which clashes with his devotion to clarifying the terms and passages of the sacred texts in order to avoid confusion. Maimonides does not seek to play with the reader because that would imply that he was addressing the voluntarist reader, the one who is identified with the executive power of the very government of his life, that is, with his memory and will. On the contrary, Maimonides addresses the identity of the reader as a whole. For this reason he knows that, while he has to clarify the meanings for him to avoid confusion, he also has to feed that part of the reader that is not his vigilant executive side.

The *Katima* alludes to the need to close out matters only when they have been lived and thought about wisely; and for this, a lethargic tranquility is needed, in other words, reverie, rest, enchantment. The seal, *sigillum cerae*, is the requirement that guarantees the necessary reclusion into the internal world of persons and kingdoms in which unique realities are hidden. Maimonides frequently refers to the idea of interior space: the sultan's palace, the sealed-off interior of things, the inner part of the body. The road to progress in perfection or in wisdom goes from outside to inside. There are seven spheres of virtue, and each of them communicates with an interior that is not enclosed but is open to the most precious spaces. For Maimonides, to enter into certain realms is not to become a recluse, but, on the contrary, to proceed toward a reality that becomes wider and ever changing.

Ezekiel, the villager, sees the sultan riding his horse in the desert and then goes back to tell his people about his clothes, his troops, his cortège, and his wanderings. Likewise, Maimonides feels obligated to explain the paraphrases of the sacred texts and the visions of the prophets that are sometimes incomprehensible at a first hearing or reading. These texts were often read aloud or recited like a musical score. There are obscure parables that are not always identified as such, and for this reason it is necessary to explain them. The wise man is like an interpreter of music.

Total devotion to God demands absolute concentration, the absence of distractions that prevent us from acquiring wisdom. This is why one has to protect oneself from the crowd and not shut oneself up needlessly. The wise person must know how to protect himself from the multitude. He should know the true nature of the crowds in order to save himself and not be carried away by distractions. The isolation that Maimonides proposes is an external and partial solitude that enables one to think. It is not like retreating to the wilderness or the monastery. It is a condition for the perfection of life, as well as it is the care for the health of the body. It is not an antisocial or antipolitical separation, but a solitude that enables one to take charge of the government of oneself.

The body is important. If a person undergoes hunger, cold, heat, or pain, he cannot think calmly. The protection of the body is a requisite to attain wisdom and perfection in life. Humans should retreat in the face of the multitudes. They should not think of the crowd except to protect themselves from the harm that it can cause. This claustrophilia of thought and work is interesting as it recalls the *call jueu*, the Jewish quarter of Gerona with its houses without windows.

To Accept Payment for Teaching

Another important point in the life and works of Maimonides is his refusal to take payment for his teaching. The mere fact of warning us about the inequality between knowledge and power implies protecting us from the temptation of assuming the opposite, that is, that power is automatically knowledge: "The notion of knowledge is in us other than the notion of power, and the latter other than the notion of will."[91]

Maimonides makes this distinction in reference to the attributes of Yahveh and his omnipotence, in whom that identification is absolute. With it, he makes it quite clear that in the human sphere such identification is not real, unless we are caught up in the delirium of human omnipotence, religious sectarianism, or madness itself.

This equating of essences between *knowledge* and *power*, widely accepted by thinkers, citizens, and modern politicians—and put into words by Francis Bacon (1521–1626)—takes for granted the idea that power can exalt unwise men and improper knowledge in the temples. Its influence in molding the reality of life makes what a few people want to be valued as wisdom as long as it is proposed by them. Maimonides' teaching tries to protect us from this situation. Just because they are powerful does not mean that the way is wide open to them to fame, admiration, and what is more substantial, to the capacity to consecrate that which is wise and that which is wisdom.

Another great warning is that, in view of these fears, we should not take payment for our teaching. In reality, charging for lessons is, in this case, a fraudulent initiative because it is a question of establishing an external action agreed upon between two executive powers—the will and memory of two people, pupil and teacher—who decide on payment in the name of the complete reality of both participants in the transaction. The scholar who serves as arbitrator in religious matters and the teacher who studies the problems of life should be free of all ties. Thus Maimonides warns his pupil that it is more respectable to earn one's living with a trade than to receive remuneration for teaching.[92]

The reason for this is that payment interferes with the entrance into lethargy that is sought after and is necessary to begin the productive relationship between teacher and pupil. In reality, it would ruin the possibility of *isegoria* in the Greek sense of the word. For someone to enter into lethargy, aside from a vigilant acceptance, a long period of effort, work, and cooperation is required; and after that, the contingency may happen. There is an element of chance and improvisation in all this that will decide whether or not that deep and transrational bonding will take place. This connection goes beyond the executive power of the participants because it implies complete thought, that is, on the one hand, a vigilant intellectual effort and, on the other, whatever passes through the hidden cables of the lethargic relationship. We should take into account that the executive element of the government of a person includes red memory and will.[93]

Maimonides realizes that this relationship between teacher and pupil is very complex. Its influence is sometimes massive, occasionally disproportionate, and at other times, filled with obstacles. In this slow process of apprenticeship and life, payment is hardly recommended.[94] It makes no sense because how can this process be evaluated with a fair judgment, and who can do it? Moreover, how can a strict and executive ingredient such as payment be woven into such a complex living experience that is not merely executive? In sum, if we consider how important the exercise of good judgment under the protection of the law is for Rambam, how is it possible to introduce payment into this procedure?

When transactions move back and forth between various levels of life and consciousness and in different spheres of the identity of two people, how can payment be made and to whom? And with what, how much, and by whom?

The introduction of this factor of payment alters the essence of the therapeutic content of teaching between two persons. It affects the relationship of the two powers of government in question, and consequently it is harmful to the very purpose of teaching. Whenever the government of the whole self of the individual is involved, no payment can be made except when the proper sensibility is lacking, for this is an indication that the teacher-pupil relationship has not been properly understood.

It is interesting to see how one of his greatest pupils, Sigmund Freud, differs from Maimonides on this point. This is striking because psychoanalysis is surprisingly close to the depth and objective of this tradition of teaching and government.

To a certain extent Freud seems incredibly close to the Sephardic teacher,[95] although I have not found any evidence that he was actually familiar with his work. Nevertheless, he did not follow Maimonides' advice because he did receive payment for psychoanalytic therapy. It is true, of course, that in modern psychotherapy it is customary to accept payment for consultation in accordance with the going market price. This idea is hard to accept, however, in dealing with a science such as psychoanalysis, which distanced itself from the sterility of positivism and attempted to correct the overemphasis on the scientific theories of the time. Even though it was difficult to abandon his blind faith in the science of that period, Freud actually renounced his medical career and distanced himself from the atheistic and enlightened obsession of his youth. These early ideas helped him to become assimilated into the Viennese world by adopting an attitude that was, in reality, more anti-Christian than atheist, as was true of many other young people in his position. This was a very subtle way to become assimilated for an extraordinarily intelligent young Jew from a poor immigrant family in Vienna. This was why it was so important for him to reject all the Jewish rituals and even music,[96] which indicates an inclination toward the visual Catholic type of learning as opposed to auditory learning.

It is odd that Freud rejected the profession of medicine, which he had hardly begun to practice, in order to devote himself to the more psychological and philosophical-political part of his work. Maimonides did practice medicine throughout his life, partly to obtain the economic benefits, so he could continue his didactic pursuits. Freud embarked on a long journey from his rigorously scientific training to the moment when he devoted his life to what would become his masterpiece, *The Interpretation of Dreams*. This was a not a very positivistic subject and one that was held to be extravagant by his psychiatrist colleagues. With it, the young Freud left behind forever his intent to become assimilated into the Germanic culture of the Austro-

Hungarian Empire and become converted into a true Joseph, son of Jacob, which was actually the name of his father.

Nevertheless, on the matter of accepting payment for knowledge and helping his patients overcome the misgovernment of their lives, Freud did not completely resolve his own inner struggle. He was not helped by the circumstances. We should realize, however, that he, himself, never did see the connections in life that, for Moses Maimonides, prevent a person from receiving payment in this world of learning and the governance of our lives. Perhaps Freud did see them but was unable to find an alternative.

Reason and Revelation

It is hard to understand why Maimonides insists that divine law, as expressed through the Torah, is more moderate and fair than the human laws of the *nomos*, which are of an artificial nature. In our time, in which we are so proud of the achievements of reason, it is hard to admit that a people or an individual could give his or herself over to a divine law. If a person is an atheist, the question is meaningless on principle. But, even if this is not the case, to accept the deliberation and clemency of divine law is tantamount to accepting a miracle.

A believer can be confident that his divine law, that which was entrusted to him, contains more wisdom than the law of the human *nomos*. But, in view of so many divine laws as expressed in the different religious confessions, it is difficult to admit that each believer has the right to think that way. Even under the umbrella of pluralism, Maimonides' position is uncomfortable for present-day scholars. It is a question of accepting the fact that there can be various conflicting divine laws. Naturally this leads to confrontation between religious idealism and multiculturalism, ecclesiastic dogmatism, and democratic freedom.

It is necessary to clarify this point. Maimonides was the rabbi of a people that was always in the minority. The Jews were a small part of cities that lived immersed in their own closed faith of the majority. The religious truth of the regime is alien to them. It, too, is a revealed, divine truth, on which public life—the way in which laws are made and obeyed—is based. How did Maimonides view this? What was his point in defending divine law so forcefully?

We are accustomed to thinking about political theory in terms of inherent categories. Maimonides' *dicta* can be interpreted rationally as if they were abstract affirmations that fit general laws of knowledge. But he is probably not in that situation. He usually speaks with contingency in mind. The Jewish minority discovered its God—a *locus* of omnipotent power—and has a tradition of life based on its covenant, face to face, with the Almighty.[97] This is expressed in the Torah, and it is in the Torah where the Jewish people should seek not only wisdom, but the *good judgment* that emanates from daily life and arises from a fundamental alliance. This is a mutual agreement in which, on the one hand, Israel rejects the omnipotence and accepts both the existence of Yahveh as well as his impositions; and on the other hand, Yahveh assures the protection of what would be his chosen people. Obviously being the chosen people is not the result of an impulsive act by either of the two parties but is the fruit of that free mutual recognition, because "Jacob chose God and God therefore chose Jacob, while the other nations chose idolatry."[98]

Not remembering this truth of the Jewish people is equivalent to distorting everything. For this reason, Rambam defends the Torah as an essential tool for a Jew, given that it includes, summarizes, and protects very profound truths. These certainties have not merely been guarded in the coffer of secrets, but they have evolved in the centuries-old life of Israel, and in the accumulation of its interpretations of the Law by many wise men.

It is possible to leave all of this behind, and it can be done abruptly But this would mean rejecting the fabric that it has woven, not like a library of the people or a central finance bank of knowledge, but as something that was slow in the making, like something unfolding within the inner part of its citizenry. It is the result of its public life and has been defining itself in daily judgments, in which much of the intelligence of the city has been produced.

To dismantle all of this would be to extirpate a knowledge that arose from the Torah and was continued on in the prophetic beliefs. For Israel, Yahveh is the absolute *locus* of omnipotence, and that is tantamount to recognizing the limitations of human beings, born to die, and having to live with the limitations of body and mind.

To annul this would mean renouncing the most transcendental wisdom of the Jewish people and the risk of losing their identity and the dissolution of their very existence. If they did so there would be no rational progress or the overcoming of prejudices by other religions. Nor would it mean that they had overcome those antiscientific deficiencies implied in religious faith, even though that is precisely what the rationalist philosophers believe. They believe that religion ends up tying rational knowledge to a faith, a revelation that can only be accepted blindly and it is not necessary to justify in the long run. This is a mystification of rationalism that needs to be clarified. In this sense we can understand Nahmanides' indignation over the Christian comprehension of faith. For the Christians faith shows itself by means of a belief in something that is not understood or not known. Nahmanides, on the contrary, states categorically that one can only believe in what one knows for sure: "No one can believe in something they cannot understand."[99]

Sephardic tradition does not accept the fact that knowledge in public questions is based on the logos or on the extraction of knowledge with appropriate methods. Knowledge is not the product of human minds working on the unknown in life. Maimonides sees that man is full of possibilities for thinking, feeling, sleeping, and acting. He sees man's richness in every age in life. And he doesn't understand that knowledge is merely the task of adults disposed to think just because they are loaded up with ideas. The baby, the child, the ignorant, the disabled, the wise man, and the simple citizen are all involved in the business of living and working on the government of their lives. However, not everyone has the same tools to work with. Each person has to face up to that government that is sometimes in the hands of others, as in the case of children, slaves, the disabled, and the oppressed.

In order to take charge of the government of our self, we need laws that deal with problems inherent in our lives. But we also need wise and often very simple rules that can release us from the contingencies of life, to overcome the pain of existence and care for the weaknesses of our bodies. To begin with, if our body hurts, we cannot think properly. Therefore, it should be attended to before we attempt to think on a higher plane. Human suffering erodes our thought and life itself. Rambam knows very well what he is saying. Something similar happened to him with the death of his brother, which plunged him into despair for over a year and caused him to become almost incapable of working. How can we get out of something like this? What kind of wisdom can help us put up with this confusion and bewilderment? This misgovernment of life requires inherent knowledge, clear and accurate diagnoses, legal opinions, and advice. But all that must be lived on a day-to-day basis in order to improve our health and enable our abilities to work in our favor.

To live in public life requires much more than inherence. In accord with some rhetoricians, Maimonides does not fall into the fiction of identifying scientific knowledge with the magic wand of scientifistic omnipotence of Christian theology and the exaggerated omnipotence also preserved by extremist sects and miracle workers in their time.

Living requires careful knowledge, quiet and honest study, and virtuous actions, but the entire matter of public living also demands good judgment on a daily basis that cannot be attained if it is not based on the Torah.[100] For the Jewish people, "The Torah speaks according to the language of man."[101]

For Maimonides, by closing the door to this wisdom and proclaiming the logical neutrality of scientific wisdom, we attempt to establish the predominance of the intellect over life. This fanaticism of reason is just as erroneous as the fanaticism of the ideologues of religion or *mutakallimun.*

The dogmatic process is the same in both of them. The iconic figure of the *mutakallim* is that of the sage who knows the revealed law and tries to explain or cultivate it with refinement according to the truth in its highest degree of purity. The ideologue, no matter whether he is a dogmatic ideologue of religion or an atheist with an overemphasis on science, neither the atheist nor the *mutakallim* take into account the fact that contingency demands its place and attention in everyday life as an essential part of public life. We are dealing here with the problem of *the governance of our lives.* For Rambam, this should be the first topic of study for political science.[102]

By resurrecting this idea, Maimonides revolutionized political theory. Political science must study the life of public realm, that is, the business of who rules and who obeys and how to dismantle corruption, whether it is *in foro interno*, in the city, or in the nation of nations.[103]

The government of oneself deals with the patterns of behavior and customs, whether good or bad. We must work with them in order to govern ourselves. This is what the philosophers call vices and virtues. The government of one man by another is carried out through the law. Cities have always made rules and guidelines to regulate human associations. These standards are what the Greek philosophers called the *nomoi.* Maimonides reminds us that "the philosophers have many books that have been translated into Arabic," although "perhaps those that have not been translated are even more numerous."[104] But he adds another definitive clarification[105] clearly addressed to mark the distance between the teachings of the Greek masters and the true Jewish wisdom: "But in these times we do not need all these laws and *nomoi*, for divine laws govern human conduct."[106]

While this understanding of public life does not view the Torah as if it were a kind of second nature, it does hold that the Torah is innate within man because of his political nature.

This is why Maimonides' work deals with the search for the best government. He considers that it is possible to say that one government is better than another according to the qualities of each type of government. His inquiry into the best government indicates his knowledge of the Greek teachers Plato, Aristotle, and Themistius.[107] For Leo Strauss, Maimonides' rigorous analysis of Jewish philosophy makes him a natural model for teaching a person to think.[108]

Moreover, Jewish tradition holds that the politics of the here and now is very important. In other words, it deals with everyday political activity, which is evident and expressed in the *responsa*.[109] For this reason, the idea of civil politics expressed in Jewish *halakhah* should be understood very carefully. Occasionally it refers to the nobility of the soul, the spiritual welfare of its citizens, and the search for what is true and correct. But at the same time it speaks to us of a second intention: the welfare of the body. In this sense, politics consists largely in making possible the physical welfare of its citizens, in giving satisfaction to its most contingent values and needs. Its primary concerns are food, health, shelter, security, fear, anxiety, and physical and mental pain in relation to others.

The soul represents the inherent in life, that part of the human being that remains fixed with the passing of time and concrete actions. The body changes, hurts, complains, ages, deteriorates, or is ennobled on a daily basis. It is pure temporality and limitation and reflects our affects and most immediate emotions. The former represents the philosophical search for truth, and the latter, the politics of man. Which of the two is more important for Maimonides?

Undoubtedly the second is the most relevant, the one for which every effort has been made to show it in its particular details. The fact is that truth, the first aim, can only be attained after achieving the second, the welfare of the body.[110] It is equally clear that politics takes precedence, for it is primary in the search for human perfection. The Torah and the sages who interpret it clearly refer to the commandment to "preserve perpetually . . . the achievement of a *world in which everything is well and everything is long* . . . His dictum [in the Law of Moses] *That He might preserve us alive, as it is at this day* refers to the first and corporeal preservation, which lasts for a certain duration and which can only be well ordered through political association, as we have explained."[111]

Given the circumstances of human nature and man's need to be governed, Maimonides admits that sometimes some governments can be less worthy, no matter how legitimate they may be. Rambam sees two essential ingredients in the politics of a kingdom: power and law. Power without law is blind; law without power is empty. Power has the ability to oblige people to obey the rules and inspires fear in order to dissuade citizens from breaking the law. The law represents adequate order in society.

An essential question is how to balance both ingredients. The law has its limits and its scope; power has its intensity and its regulation. The search for the middle way between two extremes is an important point for the Cordoban teacher: "The right way is the mean in each group of dispositions common to humanity; namely, that disposition which is equally distant from the two extremes in its class, not being nearer to the one than the other."[112]

This is an Aristotelian moral tactic that he combines with the search for Solomonic wisdom. By joining the two, he hopes to avoid those fanatic phobias he suffered from as a member of a fragile minority in the hands of Gentile or Muslim power.

Seen from another angle, apprenticeship should not be extravagant, lurching from side to side and passing from one extreme to the other, as was usual in those conversions that Rambam hated so much. On the contrary, progress in knowledge is slow because it is not only a matter of voluntary or memorized intellectual perception but also of going beyond powerful human limitations. "A sudden transition from one opposite to another is impossible. And therefore man, according to his nature, is not capable of abandoning all to which he was accustomed."[113]

To begin with, "the Law does not pay attention to the isolated. The Law was not given with a view to things that are rare."[114] The law takes into account things "that occur in the majority of cases and pays no attention to what happens rarely."[115] It seeks the reasoned order of public life. It deals with that which is inherent in the life of the city, and as such, it cannot stop to consider the contingencies of rare or isolated cases.

Law is a divine matter. Sometimes it may go against the interests of a particular individual, but we should understand that not everything that is derived from it is actualized in every individual.[116] Laws do not have to depend on time and place, but must deal with the most common aspects and more general cases in the life of a city or a kingdom. In the genesis of the law, contingencies are not to be considered.

The laws that articulate a government are made for general cases and the most common needs. It follows that by adhering to those standards, the government acquires legitimacy with them and with the rules that emanate from them. Usually they have a broad and more universal scope, but sometimes they do not because the matters they regulate are not of a universal nature. In this case, the law has to adapt to practical usage even if the solution is knowingly incorrect or imperfect. Maimonides is not worried about it because he understands that this imperfection is not due to the law itself but rather to the very matter that the law wishes to regulate. The law takes charge of the imperfection of the actions in a realistic way.

The law must be universal and must affect everyone alike, even those who are not normally included in its sphere of influence. This is the servitude of the law, a part of its imperfection. But it has to be this way because, if it were adjusted to fit particular cases, it would be corrupt from the very beginning, and the entire kingdom would be corrupted. Like any system of rules, the law aspires to or tries to serve society as a whole, the entire life of the kingdom. We shall see to what extent law and politics are intertwined in public life.

Does the law try to imitate nature? It is, in fact, obligated to do so, given the fact that if it were applied to all individuals strictly and precisely, it could harm them. Although the law is given with broad intentions, it is not always applied to everyone with the same intensity, and in daily life it does not affect everyone equally. The fact is that individuals frequently escape from the law or do not live completely under its influence. In this way the law, de facto, is tempered, which is not always a bad thing. Universal law can sometimes be harmful for the life of individuals and for their daily life. In order for the law to be fair, not only must it have a reasonable content that is best for society, but it should also be *applied by persons who are moved by noble ends.*

The harm that men do to one another comes from ignorance, from being deprived of knowledge: "Through cognition of the truth, enmity and hatred are removed and the inflicting of harm by people on one another is abolished."[117] Knowledge has the capacity to transform, but not in the Socratic sense. Maimonides believes that the best government is one that would create the conditions for prosperity and justice and cultivate knowledge. Of course we should not forget that, for him, this includes the knowledge of the Torah, which separates him from Greek teaching. Both enable humans to devote themselves to the knowledge of and devotion to God. Knowledge is the result, not the cause, of this prosperity and peace. In these conditions a spirit of wisdom and intuition will flourish.

The Messianic Era

No one knows exactly what the arrival of the Messianic era will be like. It can happen at any time, but it is not possible to predict how it will occur. One thing is certain, however: the Diaspora will end. The Jewish people live in exile in alien lands. The arrival of the Messiah will bring political sovereignty and freedom. The Messianic era will become a reality in this world. Life will continue along its normal course "except that independent sovereignty will be restored to Israel. The ancient sages already said: 'The only difference between the present and the Messianic era is that political oppression will be ceased.'"[118] The main difference between Messianic Israel and the non-Messianic faction is the arrival of complete political life free from outside oppression.

In the Messianic kingdom the Torah is the law, and the king is triumphal. If he is assassinated or does not fulfil his aim, then he is not the

Messiah. When the Messiah does come, the good king will be known by his submission to the law. The king will be guided by virtue and piety. There is a constant tension in Judaism between preserving the integrity of divine law and the political regime. The government of the people will always be in conflict with divine law, valid for any context in the Jewish community. For a religious people, two authorities are interwoven: the Sanhedrin and the king. Both make laws and sanction conduct.

Religion is a political matter for Maimonides. It emanates from divine law, which, in turn, gives us man's condition. This does not mean that religion has the authority of a state to establish itself, but it can generate political actions and can have a great influence on the political process. It is neither a theocratic vision nor the subordination of politics to religion. Maimonides always gives priority to the worldly, to the body, from which the rest of the government of the city should emanate.

The king's right to govern entails his capacity to legislate and oblige his subjects to comply with the law. The king can sentence a citizen to death, particularly if he has rebelled against his majesty, which is tantamount to endangering Israel itself. The death penalty is not mentioned in the Torah, but the king can apply it in extreme cases. The king's authority is independent of the Torah. It is a spontaneous activity that is not ordained by law.

The Sanhedrin makes the laws, while the king, in principle, remains outside the legislative process. The king is in charge of inspiring fear and respect and instilling compliance in his subjects.[119] He must keep order, for if there is no order, there is no rule of law. A powerful monarch is essential for the rule of law in the city.

The ruler has a series of extralegal powers, including the power to impose penal punishments. Nevertheless, he cannot interfere with the rules of the Sanhedrin and its legislative activity. The king can declare war, but the Sanhedrin has to approve it in the majority of cases, except if it is a religious war.

Here we can see the religious gap that allows the Sanhedrin to withdraw and leave the way open for the king to declare war and lead his people into it. In any case, it is the task of the king to convince the people to go to war and to keep up the spirit of its citizens. Moreover, one of the king's most important obligations is to fight against corruption.[120]

The king's position is hereditary. Maimonides concedes that the Sanhedrin can intervene only in the nomination of the first in line of the dynasty. Here he reinforces the figure of the king against the influence of the Sanhedrin that is chosen by the people.

Nevertheless, the law must always be sanctioned with the approval of the people, and a law can never be implemented without the will of the people. An edict can never be proclaimed or a law sanctioned without the assurance that the people can comply with it. Moreover, if the public reacts against it, the law should be rescinded. In sum, Maimonides believes that the law should be made by those who are qualified to do so, but always by popular consent. The law cannot be imposed on the people by cohersion.[121]

In order to disqualify a candidate for office, what counts is not his professional incompetence but his moral incapacity and lack of religious piety. This is interesting because it involves what is known in contemporary political theory as *internal public spaces*. Once the way is open for religious or moral criteria, the importance of the internal forum (*foro interno*) of persons is recognized, although the way is also open for the interference of the rabbis in the politics of the moment.

The king must be named with honors and must be someone who belongs to the tribe. He cannot be an outsider. He must inspire fear and respect in the inhabitants in order for them to respect the law. But the king has no access to the personal wealth of his people. That shows that the king is not above the law, assuming that the power of the king is essential to maintaining the external rule of the law. The king should have an innate capacity for this function and be disposed to accept that responsibility. The law confers a high honor on him that should be respected, but at the same time, the law demands that he too should be respectful and obliging, "merciful with the high and the low . . . poor and rich, and always concerned with their welfare and honor"[122] He must sustain all the weight of the workload that falls on him and hear the complaints and objections of the people, for the Bible considers him to be their good shepherd.

For their part, the judges are in charge of managing the contingencies in the application of laws, taking into account the changes that occur in everyday practice. As Menachem Lorberbaum points out, "Judicial activity is geared to contingency."[123]

Maimonides and Aristotle

Maimonides is often seen as an Aristotelian. The fact is that he was familiar with and admired Aristotle. He had also studied enthusiastically the interpretations of the Muslim sages, among them, Averroes. But some scholars mistakenly exaggerate his Aristotelianism. They do this probably because they do not take into account the idea of *isegoria* and the essential rhetorical component of public life that Aristotle not only theorized but also lived like any citizen of Athens. For Aristotle, as for the Athenian *politai*, this idea was as obvious to them as the air they breathed in the city.

We have already seen that Maimonides does not accept the dictatorship of the principle of identity as Aristotle does in his *Metaphysics*. As for the Greek's understanding of the eternity of the world, Maimonides only accepts half of it: "We agree with Aristotle with regard to one half of his opinion and we believe that what exists is eternal a parte post and will last forever with that nature which He, may He be exalted, has willed . . . However, that which exists has had a beginning, and at first nothing at all existed except God . . . We have already said and explained that this doctrine can be arranged in a coherent way only through a recourse to the law of necessity and that necessity contains a presumptuous assertion with regard to the deity."[124]

A city or a political association is one that has the capacity to obligate its citizens to comply with the law. Maimonides certainly gives importance to the need for imposing the law. There is a natural demand for authority that emanates from the need for some people to rule over others with the purpose of organizing the governance of body and soul. This is a natural need: "This cannot be achieved in any way by one isolated individual. For an individual can only attain all this through a political association, it being already known that man is political by nature."[125]

The law looks after the welfare of the body and soul, given the fact that the human being is a man of the *polis*, he has lived in a *medina* (a city), and he should be associated with other men of his kind so as not to be alone in the wild space of animal life. It is necessary to understand that, for Rambam, the law is not only a product of the *polis*, but it is also the product of that transrational bond expressed in prophecy: "The fundamental principle of belief in prophecy precedes the belief in the Law. For if there is no prophet, there is no Law."[126]

Humans domesticate their impulses and are not like wild asses in the desert. They tame their instincts and avoid turning into dangerous beasts like many of those animals that live in the wilderness.

Maimonides has been accused of being an expert moralist. Quite to the contrary, Leo Strauss emphasized his theoretical-political transcendence. Nevertheless, I believe that his work must be read with the constant background of that Islamic world in which he and the Sephardic world evolved in part. The ability to govern includes the ability to command and organize the efforts of one's subjects in an orderly fashion and be in tune with their needs.

The issue is that, in the Mediterranean rhetorical tradition, rational and sociopolitical aspects go together. Rhetoric helps us to understand political action and explains how practical discussion functions in public life. This is why Maimonides refers to being rational *in actu* as an essential ingredient for the government of our lives.

It is true that, thanks to the fear of the ruler who backs up the law, it is easy for the law to govern its citizens. This can be seen in daily life in the limits that the inhabitants put on their own conduct that are the result of that effort to create order. Maimonides illustrates this point with a parable about a citizen who is big and strong but poor. He comes up against a money lender who is small and weak, with a pile of dinars in front of him. In spite of the man's refusal to give him a small amount of alms, the big man respects him out of fear of the authorities. Maimonides concludes that "this is a proof of the fact that this city has a king."[127] Later on, however, Maimonides lets us know, "In all that we have said by way of parable there is nothing to give an indication of the ruler's essence and of the true reality of his substance in respect of his being a ruler."[128]

Within the realm of power, good judgment is needed. It is a necessity rooted in the seven original commandments of the law revealed, according to rabbinical tradition, to the "sons of Noah,"[129] in other words, the whole of humanity. Six of them are prohibitions against idolatry, blasphemy, killing, stealing, incest, and the eating of limbs cut off from a live animal, which Maimonides interprets as a prohibition against cruelty. The seventh commandment is the only positive one, for it demands the establishment of a judicial system to insure the maintenance of the other six. Nahmanides would broaden this to include the necessity and obligation of the powers to uphold the civil law of the kingdom.[130] Both Nahmanides and Solomon ibn Adret briefly opened the door to an appraisal of the Christian kingdom as an anointed entity with a certain sacred air anchored in divine command. Maimonides could never share this opinion.

The task of keeping a city together is not a question of an astute manager, as we would say today. It is a matter of a genuine political task with religious implications for the Jewish world.

Idle and Arrogant Teachers

Jewish teachers often devote a part of their work to the preservation and protection of *halakhah*, that tradition of oral discourse and jurisprudence that gives political and moral substance to the people of Israel. The very fact that these thinkers are rabbis (*rab*=teacher; *rabi*=my teacher) speaks of a moral leadership that combines theoretical inquiry and exegesis with the protection of daily practice. At times this concept comes perilously close to the idea of militancy, if it were not for the inexistence of an armed force or state to back it up. The reason can be found in the Torah itself, given that one of its clearest and most important mandates is to keep the people of Israel alive, which is not a simple task for a people without arms, their own land, or a secular state.

The Muslim *mutakallim* is the equivalent of the modern ideologue in charge of purity. In the case of Hebrew tradition, based on consensus and interpretation, he must oversee the correct interpretation of the sacred texts. This requires many hours of study, pious conduct, and the prophetic revelation that makes the interpreter recreate the written text in the same way that a brilliant musician interprets the *Urtext* of the great composers.

Maimonides also devoted a part of his work to this task. Leo Strauss was not far from the mark when he saw in him a *mutakallim* who was also influence by the political and religious tradition of the language in which he lived and wrote the *Guide of the Perplexed*, that is, in: medieval Arabic in Hebrew characters (*aljamiado*).

One of his concerns is "badly digested" teaching, which leads him to teachers who are lazy and arrogant. They are the pretentious scholars, in other words: "The students of small minds who have acquired an insufficient knowledge of the Torah, and yet seek to aggrandize themselves before the ignorant and among the townsmen by impertinently putting themselves forward and presuming to judge and render decisions in Israel—these are the ones who multiply strife, devastate the world, quench the light of the Torah, and spoil the vineyard of the Lord of hosts."[131]

In reality, the teacher should always bear in mind a central truth: "Much wisdom I learned from my teachers, more from my colleagues; from my pupils, most of all."[132] Study is vital to upholding the Torah and, by extension, the people of Israel. "Every Israelite is under an obligation to study Torah, whether he is poor or rich, in sound health or ailing, in the vigor of youth or very old and feeble":[133] Study is so vital for the preservation of Israel that "a bastard who is a scholar takes precedence over an Ignorant High Priest."[134] Because study is a sacred matter, teachers and pupils should always be respected: "Just as a person is commanded to honor and revere his father, so is he under an obligation to honor and revere his teacher, even to a greater extent than his father . . . As pupils are bound to honor their teacher, so a teacher ought to show courtesy and friendliness to his pupils. The sages said, 'Let the honor of your disciples be as dear to you as your own.'" [135]

The problem lies in the fact that it is not just a matter of only knowing the law just as it is written, but also the hermeneutic principles that allow us to translate and understand it. It is not a matter of executive knowledge based on the will to study and memory. The principles are the key to knowing what is permitted and what is forbidden: "this is termed Talmud."[136] Study is a lifelong necessity, "until the day of one's death."[137] It is a kind of knowledge that is different from that which can be identified with the power of knowing, and therefore, it is a deeper knowledge that touches not on our vigilant capacity but also on our lethargy, as we have said earlier.

Study is necessary to reveal the superstitions spread by the astrologists and other liars who sway people who are ill-informed. Maimonides reinforces human freedom: "Man's conduct is entirely in his own hands . . . Were a man compelled to act according to the dictates of predestination, then the commands and prohibitions of the Law would be null and void and the Law would be completely false, since man would have no freedom of choice in what he does."[138] This point is so important that Maimonides does not hesitate to confront tradition itself, even though he does so with his usual tact: "The theory generally accepted by people and found in rabbinical and prophetical writings, that man's sitting and rising and all of his movements are governed by the will and desire of God, is true only in one respect. For instance, when a stone is thrown into the air and falls to the ground, it is correct to say that the stone fell in accordance with the will of God, for it is true that God decreed that the earth and all its elements should be the center of attraction, so that when any part of it is thrown into the air, it is attracted back to the center."[139]

And he concludes his deduction: "[H]is nature was so determined that rising up and sitting down were to be optional to him, but they did not mean that God wills at any special moment that man should or should not get up."[140] Maimonides continues his main argument: "We do not agree with them, but believe that Divine Will ordained everything at creation and that all things, at all times, are regulated by the laws of nature and run their natural course in accordance with what Solomon said, 'As it was so it will ever be, as it was made so it continues, and there is nothing new under the sun.'"[141] This leads him to a vital conclusion for Israel: "Since it is an essential characteristic of man's makeup that he should of his own free will act morally or immorally, doing just as he chooses, it becomes necessary to teach him the ways of righteousness."[142]

The City: Lethargy and Knowledge

Maimonides' work had strong repercussions in Hispaniae and in the other Western kingdoms. The translation of his works into Hebrew and Latin marked a great intellectual happening. It meant a more open and tolerant understanding of life. It also helped to create a distance between the dogmatic and mystical visions that were leading the Jewish communities to have nothing to do with public life and to a feeling of persecution, when it was not anarchistic or Messianistic desperation.

Rambam signified the height of a pedagogical tradition that was very different from the Socratic and scholastic traditions of the religious orders of the West, given that the West is in large part Roman Christianity and would continue to be so until the Reformation.

As Isadore Twersky points out, "Maimonides was not only unshakably convinced of the indispensability of philosophy for religion and the general nobility of intellectual perfection but was also deeply concerned about the essential relationship or constant intersection of philosophy and *halakhah*."[143]

Rambam avoids seeing the city in the Aristotelian way, as a series of concentric circles. Thus he distances himself from the visual option that depicts the circle as the perfect shape, with its connotations of equality, equidistance, and absolute visibility. Maimonides is the spokesman for a world largely based on the ear, where plazas are replaced by patios and alleyways, and where one knows who comes and goes not because he is seen but because he is heard.

Learning by ear implies the idea that the *plaza mayor* (public square) and the agora are less prestigious as emblematic public spaces. In Jewish tradition the Temple of Jerusalem is represented as a meeting place for worship: it is not a transparent place, but rather it is divided into three spaces, one of which is dark and inaccessible to the majority. Perhaps because he belonged to a social minority that was always cautious and hidden, Maimonides emphasizes the importance of a more intricate, less geometric, and less visible public space.

Sephardic teaching, in this case, allows for access to other spaces that are only accessible by ear. These spaces are visually opaque but filled with sound. This is the same view of life that enables Don Quixote to fall in love by hearsay (*enamorarse de oído*).[144]

This tradition of learning corresponds to the idea that in order for learning to take place, it is necessary to count on certain flashes or minute intellectual visions that allow us to catch glimpses of truths. We do not know when or why these flashes come because they are beyond our control. The teacher should be aware of this and prepare his student so that when they come, he will be able to take advantage of this knowledge, even though he can never guarantee the results of the learning process. Thus, when a teacher resorts to a puzzle or parable, knowledge or his seed of stimulation appears like "an apple of gold overlaid with silver filigree-work having very small holes."[145] Of course that means that teaching cannot take place without the collaboration of the pupil. Nor should the teacher or sage attempt to interpret and explain to the student in great detail the meaning of the parables, dreams, or enigmas. Lethargy is an active source and, at the same time, offers a wealth of material for his interpretation, which in turn enables him to progress in the advancement of knowledge.[146]

But not everything is susceptible to interpretation: "The assumption of such an obligation would result in extravagant fantasies such as are entertained and written about in our time by most of the sects of the world, since each of these sects desires to find certain significations for words whose author in no way had in mind the significations wished by them."[147]

Maimonides seems to warn us against the temptation of the expert who thinks he is in full command of his subject or technique and dares to interpret the texts exhaustively or "to the fullest extent," as is sometimes said in a somewhat omnipotent phrase. This is because the person who proceeds as such will also dare to interpret us to others, whether he is dealing with our words, our dreams, or our acts, going even beyond what we ourselves would admit.

Maimonides attaches great importance to enigmas and parables. Of course he does not see them as material to seize upon in search of knowledge, but as data and inspiration to go beyond and reach a higher knowledge: "Your purpose, rather, should always be to know, regarding most parables, the whole that [through them] was intended to be known."[148]

Not all the elements of a parable, an enigma, or a dream are there to express a truth. And of course they are not accessible to will or accountable to entertainment of the teacher or his pupil. One should not learn simply by will or by orders.[149] For this reason teaching requires first that the teacher try to help his pupil and then to wait for him to glimpse those flashes that allow him to perceive "however lightly" new knowledge. Knowledge should never be imposed, and, in that, the pupil will always have the last word. The student will learn if he does so by his own effort: "This is the meaning of the dictum of the Sages: *able to understand by himself.*"[150]

In sum, because the teacher does not have the tools or the methodologies, to use a modern term, to allow him to access absolutely everything, he should approach the study material and its explanation without arrogance. Sometimes it is enough merely to perceive that a story is just a parable. As Maimonides himself remarks, that task is sufficient, "even if we explain nothing more." In reality, when a teacher tells us that a given story is a parable and that is how we should understand it, he is acting like "someone's removing a screen from between the eye and a visible thing."[151]

The Democratization of Power

Maimonides does not identify knowledge with power.[152] For him, knowledge should not be handed out as if one were handing out power to the people. True teaching has nothing to do with the democratization of power, and it cannot be done without the collaboration of the pupil. For this reason Rambam does not recommend "the instruction of the multitude"[153] in speculative methods because he thinks that this would be detrimental for teaching and give rise to error.

This would be a dangerous practice and one that could convert teaching into a marketable object. Teaching must take into account the pupil's aptitude, his enthusiasm, and his effort.[154] Far from fearing that knowledge should extend to everyone, Maimonides understands that the democratization of knowledge hides an omnipotent perversion that equates knowledge with power. It is a malignant identification that trivializes the true meaning of teaching. This distortion militarizes the educational process in the same way that it militarizes society as a whole.

It is true that, for Maimonides, certain kinds of learning should not be given to someone who is not prepared. Here he follows the example of the Torah, which offers one truth for simple people without any preparation and another type that would be available to those who can understand it. Some scholars interpret this as an elitist attitude. Others see it as a dialectical methodology. Of course they forget that the teacher also warns his readers that they should not read his texts if they have more preparation than that which is offered by the book itself, and he apologizes for that. It is not a matter of filtering knowledge through to a group of incredibly intelligent psyches, but to understand teaching *in the rhetorical way*, that is, taking into account the supply and demand both for the teacher and pupil and the author and his readers.[155]

Nevertheless, some interpreters of Maimonides insist on what they call "the dialectic nature" of his teachings, something with which, according to them, he would overcome the principle of Aristotelian contradiction. To overcome or leave to one side the principle of noncontradiction, which is the cornerstone of Aristotle's *Metaphysics,* was not a simple matter for an admirer of the Greek teacher. In this sense, the contradictions that Maimonides presents are intended to be justified on the part of specialists in his work, as calculated dichotomies. These dispersals or breakups are hardly understood even by some of the most renowned scholars of Maimonides such as Strauss, Pines, and Ravitzky. For them, these fluctuations in the teacher's thought can only be explained as contrasts on two sides of the same coin: Athens and Jerusalem, the multitude and the philosophers, the head and the heart.[156]

The fact is, they explain, that Maimonides tries, with his teachings, to protect the community and at the same time to promote knowledge in the direction of true learning, where we will find truth (*emet*) and peace (*shalom*). Of course, for many, this is not possible except in a utopia or in a Messianic period in which this harmonization of society would be possible.

These northern critics, however, perceive that in the Sephardic tradition, there is an awareness and treatment of this matter. This is the case of the Sevillian Yom Tov Ishbili ("Ritba"),[157] "an eminent fourteenth-century legal authority."[158] Ritba writes: "A cardinal rule for the diviner of secrets is that one should be aware of the frequent appearances of contradictions both in the scriptures and in the words of the Rabbis. [Moreover], as the secret becomes more profound so does the necessity of its concealment, therefore, only a few words [in such texts] represent the truth and most of them represent its opposite."[159]

The Ashkenazic tradition of the Middle Ages was seriously deficient in its knowledge of Greek culture from the very beginning. As we have seen, in contrast to the Sephardic teachers, they were ignorant of Greek or Arabic. Thus, their access to Aristotle's work was largely belated, as was the case in Christian universities. Abelard (1079–1142),[160] to cite a notable example, taught in Paris knowing very few of Aristotle's works. In the words of Étienne Gilson, he was "a mere dialectician."[161] And when it finally arrived, its absorption was hindered by the Reformation's battle, which ended in triumph with the annihilation of rhetoric. The rhetorical part of the life of the republic would be eradicated by a false dialectic, a dialectic swollen by Calvinism and designed by Petrus Ramus.[162] The political theory that arose from this was the product of the theoretical deterioration that took hold triumphantly in the twentieth century. The political theory consecrated by the Calvinistic victory would include such indispensable figures as Descartes (an indirect disciple of Petrus Ramus), John Milton, Jean Jacques Rousseau, Alexander Hamilton, Max Weber, Woodrow Wilson, and Michel Foucault, in addition to an occasional Catholic and Jewish thinker who assimilated this triumphalist philosophy.[163]

I believe that there is a transcendental error in all this, and this crucial point will be taken up in detail in the following chapters.

2

Moses Maimonides and the Politics of Dialectics

> If you wish to grasp the totality of what this Treatise contains, so that nothing of it will escape you, then you must connect its chapters one with another; and when reading a given chapter, your intention must be not only to understand the totality of the subject of that chapter, but also to grasp each word that occurs in it in the course of the speech, even if that word does not belong to the intention of the chapter.[1]
>
> —Maimonides

In his *Treatise on the Art of Logic* (*Maqala fi Sina' at al-Mantiq*) written in his youth, Maimonides maintained that political science is divided into four parts: the government of the individual, the government of the home, the government of the city, and the government of the nation (*al-umma al-akbira*) or nations (*al-umam*).[2] Later on in the second half of the twelfth century and in Christian territory, Domingo Gundisalvo, one of the most important figures in the School of Translators of Toledo, would enlarge the classification of the sciences "for the first time in the West."[3]

With this work, Maimonides makes a great contribution by distancing himself from the Aristotelian tradition of the Andalusian philosophers in which he had been educated.[4] This is important because his position takes him farther away from his respected al-Farabi (Alfarabi), whom he frequently mentions with admiration. For al-Farabi, political philosophy is divided into two types: ethics, which is concerned with "the moral habits of which beautiful actions and the capacity to acquire them are foremost," and political science, which includes "the knowledge of those things by which the inhabitants of cities attain beautiful things and the ability to acquire and preserve them."[5] The drastic separation of moral or ethical habits and public things led to a comprehension of the philosophy of government or the political regime (*al-fasafa al-syasa*) that understood the object of that science as something external to man and exposed to everyone's view. It is a science that, because of its marked visual nature, is inclined to understand judgment as a wise action or discernment, "given that philosophy can only be attained by the excellence of discernment, and this is achieved by the mind's ability to perceive what is right."[6]

While Maimonides had closely followed and admired the Aristotelian tradition, here he moves away from it and points toward a subject that will be central in his work, namely politics. Given the extent of this divergence, it is not unusual that Leo Strauss was immediately attracted by this great teacher whom he appreciated as an extraordinary innovator.[7]

An important aspect in this turning point is the value Maimonides places on contingency in human life. Strauss understood this very intelligently when he analyzed Maimonides' theory about miracles, in which the teacher "assumes the distinction between the enduring and the transitory, between what always occurs and what rarely occurs, as an ontologically relevant distinction.[8]

The importance of the contingent as opposed to the inherent, in the words of Harry Eckstein,[9] lies in the fact that judgment is necessary to elaborate that part of life in which feelings, desires, and human interaction are constantly following each other. In other words, this is the unceasing and unpredictable life that classical rhetoric considers to be the core of any political knowledge. It is also that part of reality that Niccolò Machiavelli (1469–1527) deals with under the name of Fortune and that belongs to the world of rhetoric and is the property of good judgment.

Thus, Maimonides differs from European tradition, which was in debt to the classical world preserved by the Andalusian philosophers. This was a world in which judgment would be shorn of its contingent content and where syllogism—the reason that links together causes and effects—and scientific analysis according to the rules of the philosophy of science would give us a kind of "pasturized vision" of public life. In this view, technical indifference or detachment is the product of a certain "sanitization of thought." The grave consequences of all this would be the manipulation of the idea of good judgment, in the usual sense of the word, and the resulting substitution of the figure of the judge for the prosecutor.

If judgment, as understood by Immanuel Kant (1724–1804) and his many followers, is the capacity to discern, then the judges, teachers, and we ourselves as judges of others, and all sorts of judges that we come up against in public life will have become virtual prosecutors that have nothing to do with the figure of the judge that guarantees the happiness and tranquility of every citizen.

This perversion of one of the pillars of politics has been the cause of deep anxiety in the modern world and became increasingly exacerbated during the romantic period. Friedrich Nietzsche was particularly upset about the downfall of the theater and poetry as a result of what he called the suicide of the Greek musical tragedy.[10] Starting with Sophocles, the theater begins to expel music from the stage and submerges the chorus in silence and shadow, thus plunging the art of tragedy into a superficiality of the mundane and lacking in transcendence. Cassandra's dialogue with a coryphaeus can never be horizontal or equal, as it is in the speech of the characters in the theater after that time. From then on the text and the plot of a work would be well explained and taken apart until the last detail. Everything would be explained and discussed according to cause and effect and motives and results. For that reason, Nietzsche, in his impotent exasperation, and perhaps because of his limited understanding of the problem, accused the "whip of syllogism" of having perverted the one and only tragedy—musical drama—the theater that presented life in all its rich facets. It was not the "simian-like" substitution that contemporary opera had made of it.[11]

Mutakallim or Philosopher

In the twelfth century Maimonides lived in a world where two great powers and organizers of politics—Christianity and Islam—sought to expand and impose their religion on whomever came under their sphere of influence. Forced conversion to a religion was common and occasionally a prerequisite to be able to enjoy the most basic rights and live in a particular territory. It was thought that religious knowledge would lead to the introduction of a certain morality, a code of norms and values that would help individuals to know how to behave in a constructive way for the kingdom.

As a result, there began to appear in almost all the spheres of the realms the figure of the apologist, and in the powerful Islamic world, the *mutakallim*,[12] the wise man with an interest in reinforcing the beliefs that shape society.

Maimonides is often obliged to distance himself from those apologists whom he accuses of violating the rules of Themistius,[13] given that, instead of seeking to adapt their ideas to what exists, they wish to shape what exists to the measure of their beliefs. In other words, the philosopher attempts to tie imagination to the intellect, while the *mutakallim* tries to tie intelligence to his imagination.[14] He writes: "To sum up, I shall say to you that the matter is as Themistius puts it: that which exists does not conform to the various opinions, but rather the correct opinions conform to that which exists."[15]

What is interesting about this distinction, precisely in someone so respectful about the lethargic capacity of the individual, is that Maimonides seeks to preserve good judgment. Good judgment is the key tool in constructing the tranquility and happiness of the kingdom. And this requires thoughtful consideration and avoiding phobias. While his entire masterpiece, *Moreh Nebukim*, is devoted to defending the metaphor and periphrasis of the prophetic vision, in other words, *the lethargy of the life of the individual*, in this chapter he makes an effort to distance himself from the invasion of the imagination. The importance of the balance between vigilance and lethargy now comes to the foreground.

Theory as Edification

Maimonides seems to vindicate the protection of good judgment against tyranny, whether it be pagan, atheist, or the missionary tyranny of the *mutakallim*. The *mutakallim* seeks to control the ability of the intellect to observe and understand life by tying it down to fantasies and partial opinions while at the same time introducing those rational abuses that impose disbelief on the lethargic part of the life of man. This second error often leads men into darkness and confusion, thus closing the way to happiness.

Leo Strauss perceives this aspect of the man whom he considers his true teacher very well when he rightly classifies the *Guide of the Perplexed* as a nondphilosophical book, far from mathematics, economics, ethics, physics, and metaphysics. For Strauss, Maimonides practices with the *Guide* a kind of *kalam*,[16] given that he is above all interested in defending the law of Yahveh against the opinions of the philosophers. Nevertheless, we should be cautious here about taking him literally because Strauss, applying his very personal method of study, gives us an exoteric reading of Maimonides at the same time as he also leaves us an esoteric reading of the same work.

This is why, in another place, he also comments that the *Guide* holds a kind of *enchantment*—a key word in the sixteenth-century Spanish world of *Don Quixote*—for the reader. Moreover, he adds that in the reading of this exceptional book, "progress in understanding it is a progress in becoming enchanted by it."[17] Strauss, with admirable intelligence, understands that, for Maimonides, "Enchanting understanding is perhaps the highest form of edification."[18] Finally he comes to the conclusion that the *Guide* "is not a philosophical book—a book written by a philosopher for philosophers—but a Jewish book: a book written by a Jew for Jews."[19]

Is Strauss suggesting, with his esoteric way of writing, that perhaps the *Guide* is a kind of enlightened *kalam*? Or is it something that, at first sight, Strauss admits to recognizing, hoping that the reader will find what is behind it for himself?

Reason and Transgression

Maimonides stands in opposition to his respected Aristotle and the Andalusian teachers in his country of origin in that, for them, the world is an eternal thing that was not created by a higher being, an idea that he rejects precisely to defend the revealed law.

Although this might seem like a clash between atheist and religious beliefs, it is not so. Atheist belief in the eternity of the universe transforms the world into a closed receptacle, a kind of gigantic corral, which can only be understood by an individual endowed with a microscopic-telescopic eye: a vigilant man. This point is dependent on a view of science and knowledge that Maimonides holds to be sadly erroneous, because for him it mutilates man's capacity to understand and seek the truth and happiness: "*Emet* (truth) refers to intellectual qualities, in that they are true and invariable . . . while *shalom* (peace), refers to those moral qualities thanks to which peace reigns in the world."[20]

Rambam is more in tune with the classical tradition of rhetoric[21] in which dreams, the ability to daydream, music, the creative imagination, and prophetic visions are all essential aspects of man together with his aptitude for programming, precision, punctuality, and the analysis of causes. Like Giambattista Vico (1668–1744), who lived in the Spanish kingdom of Naples, Maimonides is confronted with a polarization between vigilance and a lethargy moved by phobias. This is why the *Guide* devotes several pages to evaluating what he calls "prophecy," a reality that he explains through the concept of *emanation*, so rooted in rabbinical tradition.[22] He uses this idea to defend the working of a less omnipotent and more human intellect, much more capable of understanding and enjoying the reality of our own world.

Far from thinking that his religious beliefs, the Talmud Torah,[23] or the writings of the prophets keep us apart from the understanding of the world, Maimonides thinks that, on the contrary, they protect us from madness and omnipotent phobia, both from the lunatic and from the rationalist *mutakallim* who are leading young Jews of his time to painful perplexity. For Rambam, "Man is merely the most noble among the things that are subject to generation, namely, in this our nether world."[24]

Man is the way he is precisely because he is equipped with the necessary faculties to understand his own life and the world around him. But in doing so, he must not deprive himself of certain qualities that are essential in order to enjoy and understand his existence. If he does this, he runs the risk of being enclosed in a world in which matter hinders him from understanding the meaning of reality: "Matter is a strong veil preventing the apprehension of that which is separate from matter as it truly is."[25] Obviously Maimonides always took great care not to fall into these errors that, for him, were sterile because they would lead one into unreality.

He therefore tries to flee from those distressing outlets that lead to mystery or to the opacity of life, for this only avoids the problem by rushing headlong toward instant certainty. This is why he often demands precision, linguistic accuracy, or realism in observations—and above all, truth. But it is worth noting that at other times he defends the importance of allegory as a tool for achieving the truth. And he always does this with the public in mind, given that allegory allows many people to have access to the truth without overwhelming them or converting them. This is contrary to what often happens in the Socratic or Christian traditions, if we recall, for example, the Christian concept of empathy: "The parables of the prophets, peace be on them, are similar. Their external meaning contains wisdom that is useful in many respects, among which is the welfare of human societies . . . Their internal meaning, on the other hand, contains wisdom that is useful for beliefs concerned with the truth as it is."[26]

He alerts his pupils to the aforementioned dangers and gives them advice about the parables of the prophets: "In some of these parables each word has a meaning, while in others the parable as a whole indicates the whole of the intended meaning."[27]

Misgovernment and Contingency

The vision of Maimonides, "the Sephardic one," as he was known and called himself, implies a radical change in political science, as well as an extraordinary recovery of the interests and capacity of political theory.

The Reform Christian tradition, and in particular its Calvinist branch, carried out in the sixteenth century a very severe purge of the rhetorical contents of political science. In other words, it violently expelled from thought on the public sphere everything that had to do with contingency. Emotion, passion, sudden changes in life became devaluated as objects of deep thinking and were gradually eliminated from the chessboard of public science. They could only be glimpsed through general formulations, philosophical reflections on finely honed abstractions, and those well-worn universal concepts so often dealt with by philosophers. Little by little Calvinism would expel from the world of the public sphere the little daily details that would be eventually taken up by the novel, the theater, and the sciences that specialized in the private sphere.

The crucial point can be found in the extraordinary Calvinist reformer Petrus Ramus (1515–1572) who, throughout his notorious career as a religious thinker, educator, and Calvinist militant, went to the extreme of prohibiting the theater in the university.[28] This measure was the beginning of a theory that gradually began to transform science into an exclusively dialectical matter. At the same time, it condemned rhetoric to be a mere *ornato* or to end up being a simple *ars fallendi* or a strategy of tricksters.

With the work of Ramus and his followers and their denunciation of *manque de méthode*, the way was prepared for a new idea of *methodus* or way, a new way of dealing with matters and investigating reality. Beginning with Petrus Ramus and René Descartes (1596–1650) rhetorical *inventio* became an exclusive matter for dialectics and showed up as a part of the design of the investigation.[29] This design encompasses the art of planning, which, in turn, includes the elegance of definitions, conceptual accuracy, and ingenuity of the exposition prior to the development of the investigation. The rest is subject to scientific rigor, with the guarantee of certainty in the case of Descartes or the concatenation of causes and effects in the case of Kant.

From this time on the contents of lethargy would only show up in the world of thought as nutrients, somewhat vague, always indirect, and prior to the thought process. Thus the way was open for a vigilant thought that, from now on, would defend method, rigor, and system. This was the road marked out by Petrus Ramus, with his *manque de méthode*, to correct the vices of southern European humanism.

With this, the government of citizens remained largely under the control of moral and political law. The ultimate problems confronting the modern believer, the citizen of the reformed Christian republic—"*Of a Christian Commonwealth*"[30]—were looked upon only as something subject to the moral rules that inspired the community of believers, whose advance patrol would always be its secular saints.[31]

Any misgovernment of the Calvinist citizen would be exposed to the view of the religious assembly of the reformed republic. In the case of the Catholic believer, he also continued to be under the control of the judges appointed by the legally constituted power; and in its moral aspect, misgovernment that was not considered to be public was governed by the church as the administrator of a complicated system of carefully woven penalties, punishments, and spiritual rewards.

For the average person, the misgovernment of his life seemed like something that was depoliticized. It was a matter to be taken care of by ethics, morality, the church, doctors, and healers. This form of life continues to exist until the present day.

In the twenty-first century every time a citizen has a problem with the misgovernment of his body or his soul, he seeks out a social specialist for the symptom in question. If it is someone "possessed," a priest is called; if it is an outburst of violent rebellious behavior, the person is referred to a counselor; and for a personality disorder, a teacher, an elder, or even a specialist in alienation is consulted. If a vice or serious addiction is detected, a spiritual guide is called; if someone has an anxiety attack, chronic insomnia, or deep fears, he or she goes to a psychiatrist; and if there is dysfunction in family or social life, social workers are called in. There is a whole arsenal of experts available to repair the misgovernment.

In the case of scandalous misgovernment with an obvious public dimension, such as the humiliating use of power, tyranny, the theft of public funds, or treason against the will of the people, the solution can only come from the law currently in force, that is, if previous legislators had been able to foresee the problem. If not, that misgovernment will be left to chance at the risk of more misrule, which might touch off an uprising, a struggle for revenge, the picaresque, civil disobedience, or even civil war. Of course these forms are often ill-prepared to find solutions to the problems of misgovernment of individuals.

Distance and Secrecy

On many occasions political secrecy and the gap between the governor and the governed prevents corrupt acts from being brought to light. This is why the only hope citizens have of cutting off that evil lies in inculcating (*inculcare*)—the act of marking with something that is rubbed insistently—practices that, within their own internal space, can stop the abuse of office, of putting one's hand in the till when someone is not looking, of imposing one's omnipotent whims on other miserable people, or of using force as a way of taking pleasure from the suffering of others.

This pedagogy is unthinkable for Maimonides. Rhetorical tradition warns that it is impossible to do one's work without counting on the pupil.[32] Teaching is not only a matter of preparation and will, but also of good judgment. In the classroom the teacher can only hope that the truth he is trying to teach can be made credible.[33] For this, it is necessary to have the collaboration of the pupil,[34] and of course, it must take place in an atmosphere of contingent emotions and sensations. Moreover, the didactical sessions should not be held in one full meeting, nor in one day, but rather distributed over several days and nights in durable periods of time when both vigilance and lethargy are taken into account.[35]

For modern political science of Christian inspiration, above all, in the case of the American Revolution, the way of controlling the problem is through public inspection. This became institutionalized with the separation of powers and their mutual controls, or checks and balances. But it also counts on the fact that the moral programming of citizens within their churches has endowed them with a system of personal government capable of orienting them when they come up against secretive actions or hidden or unseen practices. Thus, the importance of the citizen as "church-goer," the believer who attends church.

The atheist—*anti-Christian*—version confides in pedagogy of revolutionary and secular values. Once the authority of God has been discarded, scientific logic appears as an instrument for finding a perfect government for each one of us. This is a government based on the rational, thoughtful, and positive study of the facts of life. Now the ideology that informs its citizens is no longer a product of divine revelation, but the work of the human intellect and reason. It is the outcome of the emancipating effort of a knowledge that has achieved a system of values and explanations that is entirely satisfying to us and has prepared us to be the true masters of our lives and to never again live under the yoke of tyrants.

Once we accept this explanation, the issue arises as to what tyrants are corrupt citizens subjected to. Revolutionary ideologies believe that the corrupt are victims of a contaminated society built on the violent repression of one group over another, or simply on the torture and exploitation of a few dominant elite groups over a powerless populace.

In any case, we assume that a person who has grown up with the principles of an ideology, whether it is secular or religious, is already immune to corruption, the fruit of moral evil, or malign ignorance. The emancipation of human beings contaminated because of the fall of man before a god who was disobeyed or because a society was blind to oppression and to the manipulation of the powerful would open the way to individuals who were free and incorruptible. This was precisely the proposal of the romantic revolution and the emancipating ideas that it brought forth.

Of course, today, in view of all the events of the past century, with its concentration camps, gulags, Maoist purges, red civil wars, and corruption of churches, this formative model has been called into question.[36]

Government of the Body and the Soul

The practice of good government is the last bastion of democracy left to us. Today political scientists would say that it is the habitat of democracy. But many would question whether or not democracy is capable of restraining those tendencies toward misgovernment, in spite of its guarantees that the rights of its citizens will be respected and an institutional framework that is prepared to curtail any deviation or inclination toward misrule.

Moreover, are those countries with advanced democracies still capable of turning out citizens who can resist corruption? Can citizens resist the temptation to accept illegal commissions, the practice of tax evasion, or the mafia-like dirty schemes to promote one's career? Can the widening of democratic channels deactivate the bacteria of urban corruption?

It seems impossible. Today it is generally recognized that a person can be a passionate defender of democracy, even someone who is known for his personal dedication or for taking risks to defend it. But at the same time it does not necessarily mean that at a given time he would not be above promoting the interests of his friends, lovers, relatives, or accomplices, abandoning the criteria of fairness and excellence, or seeking personal gain and substantial lucrative benefits by using his office to obtain benefits that he is not entitled to if justice were enforced.

Perhaps for that reason the figure of Maimonides and the tradition he represents are so important for the recovery of a lost political theory.

Probably because he was a physician, Maimonides gave such importance to the need to care for the body as well as the soul. For him, without a sound body, the rest would be unthinkable. The body and the mind must be cared for so that both may live peacefully.

Something similar happens with politics and religion. Religion is higher, but politics is earlier and basic. If the world was created by Yahveh, the nobility of his origin imposes on man the need to respect his fellow people who are also creations of the divine. It follows that humiliation, magic, and gratuitous violence are not acceptable for solving public problems.

The recognition of Yahveh that Maimonides recovers for rabbinical tradition is the equivalent of accepting the fact that *we cannot have access to omnipotence and that we are limited beings*. Yahveh is a *locus* of omnipotent power located beyond us. Consequently, His very existence signifies the renunciation of omnipotence in the world. Obviously this idea is very far from the Christian approach to the problem. But it is also very different from the anti-Christian or atheist approaches of abandoning God or the conviction that God does not exist, ways of thinking that are widespread in Western tradition. For Maimonides, these ideas represent a recovery of omnipotence.

Now then, is the ordering of our lives an individual matter, or should it be done at the same time as we organize the lives of others?

Enmity and Hate

Twenty-first-century political theory takes into account the idea that we must attend to the mind—our own and that of our fellow citizens—in order to achieve an orderly government. This includes public attention to the citizen from the moment we are immersed in *infantile*[37] impotence to the time of our coming of age in public. This leads us to the need to learn to govern and be governed. The famous *consolation of the soul*[38] mentioned in medieval tradition speaks of the therapeutic content of wisdom, which helps us to understand our anxiety and the need to embrace so many contradictory things at the same time.

We must take into account that during the time when we have no government of our own, such as infancy, we still experience command and control over our lives. Those who have gone through childhood are fortunate to have been controlled, dominated, and cared for mentally and emotionally. Nowadays we citizens are filled with implants, and even our immunological system is programmed with vaccinations. In this sense we are all survivors, for we have passed through that benign dependence that has enabled us to reach adulthood. If that relationship had failed, or simply not existed, we would have been left by the wayside. Something similar happens to us with the law later on during the rest of our life.

Of course it could be the case that the attention given to the child was minimal, inadequate, or bad. This would have left traumatic experiences and decisive wounds on the transcendental part of the government of our lives, a government that is necessary in order for us not to experience hunger, fear, terror, humiliation, violence, disdain, abandonment, pain, or death. Strangely enough, Niccolò Machiavelli (1469–1527) had already told us that the four basic fears in the life of man were boredom—what today we would call depression—conflict, poverty, and death.[39]

Our Sephardic teacher believes that it is necessary to do away with enmity and hatred in order for good politics to exist. And this is only possible in an environment where harm is avoided and progress is made in improving the welfare of our bodies. Enmity is not only the lack of friendship; thus Maimonides associates it directly with hatred. It is also a matter of avoiding situations that lead to war among human beings. Politics implies the eradication of war, or what amounts to the same thing, the predominance of the intellect over desire: "For when only the desires are followed . . . thus cares and sorrows multiply, mutual envy, hatred, and strife aiming at taking away what the other has, multiply."[40]

Necessity and Omnipotence: Maimonides and Aristotelianism

Rambam coincides with Aristotle in believing that humans are political animals.[41] They are that way by nature from the time they are born and because of the way they are born. But, while Aristotle attributes the peculiarity of human beings to the fact that they are in possession of the *logos*, the speech with which to solve their common problems, Maimonides attributes it to the way we are born. This idea is probably not expressed in his work as frankly as I do here, but it coincides in essence with the thought. The Jewish philosophy I refer to attributes to Yahveh the origin of the creation of the world, of man, and, of course, the exclusive possession of omnipotence. This means that, by recognizing his omnipotence, we manifest and accept the awareness of our limitation.

People are born helpless, in a position of zero power, and dependent on their family or surrogates for survival. They are also dependent on their city. They compensate for this with fantasies and a perception of the world seen as a collection of automatisms, levers and explosions, drastic and concrete sensations with immediate solutions. At the same time it is a real world where the life and death of the baby or child comes into play, the possibility of abandonment is constant, and there is a perpetual risk of death or madness.

In sum, the following is a résumé of the basic deductions that Maimonides' view of political science attempts to preserve:

1. Man is not self-sufficient. Man's sovereignty is an inaccurate image of himself.

2. This implies that man's primary problem is how to govern himself and others.

3. Man is characterized by his ability to govern and his need for government. His life is a continual progression toward resolving his helplessness. He never wants to return to that terrifying situation of being abandoned or constantly being on the verge of loss, madness, and radical abandonment that would leave him out in the cold.

4. For this reason, man needs to be governed; in other words, he needs someone with power to protect him and to guarantee that all the evil that he fears will not come to pass. He needs shelter, security, affection, food, order, and presence and represence.

5. Another possible solution would be for man to govern himself. In order to do so, he must control numerous resources and persons in order to assure himself that shadows will never appear in his curriculum. One must always be first in line, be seen by others, taken into account, always be first on the list, obtain the best resources, and accumulate wealth, heirs, property, and food. And above all, control, exercise power over others.

6. It is also possible to transform a desire or basic necessity into its opposite. For example, take care of everyone, serve everyone, or dedicate oneself to helping others.

7. Human beings are political by nature. We are all born in a situation of helplessness, and we will never lose the need to govern and be governed. Our ability to command and obey is also a necessity of life.

In view of the above, in the thirteenth and fourteenth centuries, some Jewish communities equated Maimonides with Aristotle and even accused him of being impious. They were mistrustful of his naturalization of knowledge. There were those who accused him of being a rationalist and even compared him with St. Thomas Aquinas (1225–1274) in later years, as if the *Guide* were the Jewish equivalent of the *Summa Theologiae.*

In contrast, there were other lines of thought in the Jewish communities of medieval Spain such as those headed by Nahmanides[42] and Solomon ibn Adret and his School of Barcelona, which reached its height in the thirteenth and fourteenth centuries with Ibn Adret and Nissim Reuben

Gerondi (c. 1310–1376).[43] This school continued along the lines of Maimonides although largely to modify his vision of political science, as we shall see in the following chapter.

In any case, we should not forget that in Sephardic tradition there is also a line of defense of Judaism that emphasizes precisely a certain rationalization of its faith in the face of the irrational trust of the Christians, as in these words by Isaac Pollegar: "And once you are aware of, and reflect on these words, the many sorrows and sufferings that have come upon this honored people, and its small numbers, will not be hard for you; for since the principles of its faith are more wonderful and holy and singular and different from the other people's faiths, since they have arisen and come from reason, which is remote from them and scorned by them."[44]

Broadly speaking we could say that, in spite of appearances, the thought and understanding of life that we find in Maimonides is completely separate from Aristotelianism. Moreover, this is probably his greatest contribution to European political theory.

Command and Obey

Everyone feels the need to be cared for, attended to, directed, and ordered about. We have seen that, for Maimonides, but not for Aristotle, it is not essential to have a *logos*, a very advanced speech. It is important as an instrument for understanding what is happening. But not everyone has it, nor does our whole self speak with that logos. There are people who are mute, parts of the city that are not able to speak during the period of wakefulness.

As we have already seen, the role of Yahveh is essential in this vision. It is not the belief in a god but the *recognition* of the existence of an omnipotent power and creator of the universe (Yahveh) that causes all the rest of the powers, no matter how great, to exist in the measurable world; in other words, to have their limits. Yahveh's world immediately becomes a universe free of omnipotence, an atmosphere cleansed of magic and fit for politics. The central problem of life is how to elaborate on and organize this real lack of power in practice in order to preserve us and live without becoming insane.

Naturally when a child grows up, he will gradually control his life, feed himself, protect himself, and mentally attend to his needs. Even so, he can never forget that incurable wound of the radical helplessness of his origin: to always be on the edge of a more promising life and an imminent death. This menace never disappears because much of the activity of the human brain functions *without a sense of time or space*, that is, without being ruled by Aristotle's principle of identity. This postulate was clearly expressed in the words of Aristotle himself: "Contradictions cannot be predicated at the same time."[45]

Today we know that, on the contrary, there are feelings, emotions, and fantasies that never expire and remain with us until the day of our death. The principle of identity does not rule in a large part of the activity of the brain, something that Sigmund Freud, Leo Strauss, and quantum physics came to know in their time.

Political apprenticeship includes how to avoid falling into the hands of indigence, hunger, cold, and fear of abandonment. It can also be learned through the accumulation of food, wealth, control, prestige, popularity, preeminence, affection, and submission. All the intentions of government are directed at guaranteeing that an individual will not fall back into that original state of absolute dependence with respect to others.

This dependency has also left good memories of pleasure, satisfaction, protection, and security. Changes in self-government are also open to domination, avarice, greed, and the need to give, as well as the need for affection, submission, protection, recognition, encouragement, and love.

Man never entirely resolves this problem because he is marked from birth and was born that way. For Maimonides, the matter of *to govern and be governed* is inherent to life itself. The domination of one person over another is a natural necessity.[46] In this sense, the temptation to be omnipotent is constant. Thus comes the inclination to ignore the fact that we are mortal, our intelligence is limited, and our health is fragile and will not hold up forever. We cannot take charge of everything, and our desires cannot automatically become reality.

It is hard to learn all this, but even so, we does not cease in our effort to make a fortune that will last a lifetime, to gain more and more power, fame, prestige, eternal health, and youth. All this insatiable accumulation of life, attention, security, and power is, at the same time, indicative of the fact that these needs are constantly changing and at times limitless: "For whereas all necessary things are restricted and limited, that which is superfluous is unlimited."

Perhaps Machiavelli was one of the few Western theoreticians to capture the importance of this variable to explain public life:

> Con che versi
> canterò io del regno di Fortuna
> . . . E comme iniuriosa ed importuna

. . . Sotto il suo seggio tutto il mondo aduna?
E benché in alto sopra tutti segga,
Comandi e regni impetuosamente,
Questa da molti è detta onnipotente,
Perché qualunche in questa vita viene,
O tardi o presto la sua forza sente.[47]

The City in Aristotle and Maimonides

I do not believe that Maimonides' thought can be understood from the Neoplatonic Byzantine tradition as some have suggested. Maimonides does not understand the citizen as the bearer of an inner city that must be in tune with the *polis*. This Athenian vision of the matter is not what the Sephardic teacher had in mind. For him, it was more a matter of internal public spaces, a *fuero interno* (inner space), a phrase that, curiously, is still preserved in the Spanish language.[48]

Nor is the city conceived like that medieval city built in the Athenian mode, inspired by Aristotle's idea of a series of concentric circles—the circle being the form closest to beauty and goodness—built around a square, the stronghold of a medieval fortress or marketplace—like the one in the palace at Knossos in ancient Crete—where trading took place under the watchful eye of the sentinels. Not all the medieval cities of Europe were the products of the evolution of earlier communities or villages; they sometimes arose as new foundations established by charters or communal civic oaths that gave them cohesion and replaced any religious connection. In some cases these cities would, for the first time, create the opportunity for a secular nonpagan republicanism.

In reality Maimonides' city is more like *a series of courtyards and alleyways* where law rules because it is feared and respected. This is a very different understanding of the city from the classical Greco-Latin model of Aristotle and Thomas Aquinas. Their city was imbued with a geometry that gives priority to visual public control, the sphere and the circle as perfect forms for living together. For the Thomists, the public square is a radiant element within the city, while for the pupils of Maimonides it was possibly something threatening.

For Rambam, a rabbi, the individual carries within him a public space, which is why self-government is such an important matter for political science. But this point must be clarified so as not to be misunderstood, for this science of the public does not necessarily have to intrude on private spaces, either external or internal.

Maimonides is undoubtedly close to the rhetorical tradition for which there were three ways of transmitting our life to others: through the executive, by means of a legislative, and with a good judgment. In the case of rabbinical tradition, where thought is always open to the transcendent by way of prophecy, man always receives the emanation of divine intelligence through dreams, daydreaming, or creative fantasies; in other words, through lethargy. Generation after generation this religious approach has prevented lethargy from being excluded from public experience. For this very reason, Jewish tradition—the one that Maimonides captures and synthesizes so masterfully—is naturally shielded against the tyranny of the dialectics that, with the defeat of civic humanism, began to take root so strongly in Western thought.

It is true that dreams were also a way of thinking for Aristotle, and for the inhabitants of the Greek *poleis*. It is well acknowledged that myth and tragedy contributed elements to incorporate the tragic substance of life into the common interest. But the predominance of the dialectics that took hold in Christian Europe caused the retreat of republican rhetoric, increasingly besieged by the authoritarianism of the executive, probably for reasons of convenience in the administration of the republic.

The republican humanism that blossomed in southern Europe from the thirteenth century on in a few medieval kingdoms and Italian cities did not take root. It was subjected to the imposition of dialectics as the only tool for thinking about and organizing the city, which also affected those *internal public spaces* symbolized by the Latin term *in foro interno* as used by the rhetoricians and by Thomas Hobbes.

Moses Maimonides was aware of the fact that, in order to achieve peace of mind and tranquility and avoid discomfort, perplexity, and painful confusion, it was necessary to gain access to that internal world and allow to exist within it a worthy government guided by wisdom. This included attending to specific factors such as health, inner peace, well-grounded convictions, and the control of emotions and feelings without violence or lies.

Naturally all this necessitates a more profound science than is usually applied to people's lives. It also requires greater knowledge of the links among all the forums, courtyards, and alleyways of our lives: "The true Law then, which as we have already made clear is unique—namely, the Law of *Moses our Master*—has come to bring us both perfections [the welfare of the body and of reason *in actu*], I mean the welfare of the states of people in their relations with one another through the abolition of reciprocal wrongdoing and through the acquisition of a noble and excellent character."[49]

In short, public law has much to do with the perfection of individual lives and the introduction of good practices, and it is also essential for the good government of the above-mentioned forums.

The laws of Yahveh, that is, those not subject to human omnipotence, have as their goal to always "abolish reciprocal wrongdoing, or urge to a noble moral quality leading to a good social relationship."[50]

It is true that this vision partakes of the Aristotelian idea that we are necessarily public, for we need others to achieve the satisfaction of our necessities. We are also capable of reflection, for our maximum perfection is to become rational beings *en acto*.[51] This implies that we can aspire to the knowledge about the world that is accessible to everyone. Neverthless, for Maimonides, a man cannot think if he is bothered by pain or suffering from hunger, thirst, heat, or cold. Nor can he be responsible for his feelings, formulate his ideas, and achieve perfection. This is why he has need of the law to live day by day. To be attentive to the search for happiness and eternal life will always be a daily human task.

The governance of our own life is thus linked by necessity to the governance of public life. Therefore any misgovernment also implies a public concern. All this immediately reveals a danger: if every matter dealing with self-government were a public matter, then would we not be on the verge of a totalitarian Platonic city? Would Maimonides be a Neoplatonic medieval author as Philo of Alexandria or Themistius were in their day?

Maimonides and Neoplatonism

The answer is simple. In principle, the matters of the government of each person are not of a public nature, and they only acquire that dimension when they collide with the Law of Yahveh given to Moses and upheld through the oral teachings collected in the Torah. The objectivity of Jewish tradition radically separates this view of the problem from the dialectical treatments of the Athenians: "As for my own belief with regard to this fundamental principle, I mean divine providence . . . I am not relying on the conclusion to which demonstration has led me, but upon what has clearly appeared as the intention of the book of God and the books of our prophets."[52]

Maimonides does not accept Greek philosophy's goal to pass from cosmogony to cosmology, or substitute theology for theogony. In other words, he disagrees with the idea that philosophers are not so interested in asking where things come from, but rather in inquiring about the underlying nature of all things. This is precisely why Aristotle regarded Thales of Miletus as the first philosopher.[53]

If a person is corrupt, it is because he has transgressed the laws of Yahveh as they were preserved and accepted in the collection of rabbinical *responsa* and the teachings of the prophets collected, treasured, and lived in daily life. There is no room here for the examination of people's consciences from the point of view of public power, but rather it should submit to the criteria of good judgment based on those practices and laws established in the external world shared by everyone.

Nor should it be allowed to segregate the ethics or filter the morality of our acts in order to set aside the political, for this would neutralize society and sanitize its emotions and feelings. The contingency is in the midst of the public space, and only by cultivating this wise tradition of teachings and laws, and the judicial tradition developed on a daily basis, can we attempt to give free reign to the needs of the political. But we cannot, nor would it be meaningful to look for moral happiness in the world if we did not recognize the kingdom of Yahveh.

Maimonides shows himself to be respectful of the established powers. He was loyal to Islam and worked for Saladin, but he did not believe that the city or the kingdom to which he was attached in order to achieve happiness was that of the Sunni caliph. He felt himself to be a part of the Jewish people united by the Law of Moses and the protection of Yahveh, the *locus* of omnipotence that guaranteed the cleanliness of public air and the safeguard of a citizenry limited in the time and space of their lives.

Respect for the law and constant work to maintain the good governance of our lives was not necessarily linked to a specific political faction or even to a language or a nation as such. For him, it had to do with the search for happiness through the contemplation of the truth and the understanding of our limitations and abilities. For this, it was indispensable to count on the emanation of the prophecy that, through lethargy, would have enabled us to gain access to some knowledge necessary to find the truth. When elaborated on through allegories that come to us through dreams or visions, this emanation obliges us to be open to those deep wells of the mind and sensitivity that are expressed with an ambiguity and ambivalence that Rambam claims are indispensable for human thought.

Is he in favor of mystic confusion? Certainly not. As we have seen, Maimonides tries to clarify in an intelligent way any doubts about the contents of rabbinical tradition, the exegesis of the writings of the Jewish people, the contribution of its sages and prophets, and basically, the Law of Moses given face to face to him by Yahveh.

For Maimonides, it is not a question of looking for confusion. On the contrary, his efforts are aimed at installing knowledge, the knowledge that was organized and experienced in daily practice. We should not forget that he is a physician. What he does not accept is the fantastic conviction that it is possible to get to know the entire universe and come to know everything about reality. In practice, many things can still not be known because we do not have the means or the knowledge. It is an erroneous triviality to attempt to talk about everything. This is why his books always set a good example by indicating at the beginning for whom they are written and, what is more curious, for whom they are not written. In them he sometimes indicates the reason why some people should not read them, either because they know more than the book in question can offer them, or because the contents of the book are beyond their education.

Dialectics and Rhetoric

In an attitude in harmony with Greek rhetoric Maimonides does not write syllogistically or for everyone. He writes for a specific person whom he knows or with whom he wishes to establish communication. He does not think it is possible to write for everyone at the same time, not because they are incapable of understanding him but because he must always count on an audience. In relation to rhetorical wisdom, what is spoken about requires a listener in order for it to become *dicere* and not only *loquor*, as the rhetorician Quintilian maintained.[54] Both Maimonides and his tradition were aware of this gap between speaking and saying.

Rational and political abilities are intimately linked together. Maimonides understands political rhetoric as a kind of musical consort. It should be the art of explaining the function of practical reasoning. Reason and the art of politics together should facilitate the government of the conduct of man. It is not enough to have true knowledge, but it must be made believable for others so that they will accept it voluntarily and without violence. The fact is that it must be integrated into their everyday emotions and passions. This is why Maimonides constantly combines the rational and sociopolitical aspects of the human being.[55]

Thus a citizen cannot be transformed only through teaching campaigns or educational plans drawn up by the executive and legislative powers. There is always an everyday view of politics in which all this is worked out through intense emotions, passions, fantasies, and dreams. It is a world in which fear alternates with knowledge and where necessities are malleable and change according to eventuality. For Maimonides, it is clear that there are objective needs such as those we might manifest today in questions such as the following: How many vaccinations are needed? How many kilos of wheat are needed to feed this number of people for a month? How many jobs are available? Of course they exist and must be taken into account. These are specific needs that must be attended to immediately. However, there are other, more *ancestral needs*—Maimonides does not use the term, although the idea does exist in his work—that cannot be placated by merely satisfying a demand, but that, once they are satiated, they metamorphose into adjacent and at times more virulent forms.

That which is public cannot be treated in the enlightened way as it is done by the *mutakallim*. It is an manner that runs counter to rhetoric and in the long run becomes profoundly authoritarian, even though those who transmit it may not see it that way.

If we have learned a lesson from Maimonides, we could say that the present-day approaches to eliminating corruption often resort to underhanded methods to confront the government of the very lives of its interpreters. On the one hand, they apply restraints and punishments, and, on the other, they sometimes confuse judges with prosecutors, thus increasing the impunity of the powerful. Deception and the double law—with its gap between what I say and what I do—are the norm. This is the citizens' misfortune, for they see those false prophets "castrated"[56] in their imaginative capacity by a falsely enlightened commitment. They see how the mutilation of the public and the expulsion of lethargy from their reasoning incapacitates them from finding an outlet to a profoundly political subject.

The end of the tormented reflections of those moralistic and ideological texts lies in darkness, despair, and depression, even if it does not threaten us with evil omens. These disturbing premonitions come down to us precisely from those who are immersed headlong in their own misgovernment. They propose one thing to their constituents and do the opposite in daily practice.

The importance of Maimonides in contemporary political theory is deep and greater than recognized. His study of political wisdom begins with the conviction that the greatest suffering of man is incurred by living together, thus, its cure is in the hands of political science. As we pointed out in the previous chapter, one of his closest pupils, although probably unknowingly, was Sigmund Freud. For Freud, there are three constant and inexhaustible sources of suffering: (1) our body, with its illnesses and aging process, the producers of pain and anxiety; (2) the external world, "which may rage against us with overwhelming and merciless forces of destruction"; and (3) "our relations to other men." To which he would add in order to avoid doubts that "the suffering which comes from this last source is perhaps more painful to us than any other."[57] These statements are clearly echoed in the voice of the teacher, Maimonides, "the Sephardic one": "The evils of the second kind are those that men inflict upon one another, such as tyrannical domination of some of them over others. These evils are more numerous than those belonging to the first kind [those produced by their original natural disposition, in other words, those produced by their being endowed with matter]."[58]

A Forgotten Figure

It is not easy to understand the oblivion—Christian as well as atheist—of a tradition of thought so rich and suggestive as the one represented by Maimonides. What is true is that European anti-Semitism banished or ignored a theoretical tradition that deserves to be recovered today, especially in the Europe of the south, where its seeds were sown and where its echoes can still be heard in its cultures, traditions, and art.

Unfortunately Catholic fundamentalism has cooperated blindly and with a complex about it, together with Lutheranism and particularly with political Calvinism, the most modern and progressive of all. The outcome has led to an evolution of Western democracy that is somewhat questionable. The Calvinist thinkers—John Calvin (1509–1564), Theodore de Bèze (1519–1605),[59] Petrus Ramus, Thomas Hobbes (1588–1679), John Locke (1632–1704), Alexander Hamilton (1757–1804), Woodrow Wilson (1856–1924), Max Weber (1864–1920), Michel Foucault (1926–1984)[60]—found the shortest and most expedient way to back up in one way or another a vigilant vision of politics that today has led many democrats, and much of their political theory, to extenuation and confusion.

The politics of the vigilant society is based on a fundamental axiom that establishes categorically that "knowledge is power." In fact, the advance in *knowledge*—translated loosely by some as *science*—is posed in the first place as a cleansing with extraordinary guarantees of asepsis against error and followed up by posing knowledge as a predatory work of conquest. The recovery of the world gives way to an appropriation, or simply to the command and control of the physical and the human—curiously—by laws! These include laws of the atom, the stars, chemical reactions, and the iron laws concerning behavior.

This is a true "triumphal march" in a major key that alarmed the admirable Vico in his time and that he wisely called "the barbarism of reflection."

Moses Maimonides stands among the great thinkers as a wise teacher who, having suffered all this in his own life, clarified this error *ex-ante*. This virulent mutation, in view of what was still to come, had wide-ranging consequences. For Rambam, there is no room for error, in this sense: "for the notion of knowledge is in us other than the notion of power, and the latter other than the notion of will."[61]

His position probably had something to do with having always lived between two great religious and ideological powers that sought to convert everyone else. He had to live in a dangerous divide in which the two great empires of the time, Christianity and Islam, were in mortal combat. He knew and admired Aristotle, but he lived and wrote in Arabic, and he worked for Saladin in Cairo. Apart from that, we should not forget that he had to flee because of political oppression on several occasions and that in Fez he was even obliged to convert to Islam.

3

The Gothic World Comes to the South

"Di Provenza il mar, il suol,
Chi dal cor ti cancellò?"[1]

—*La Traviata*

The Government of Our Lives

Beginning with his *Treatise on Logic*, an early work written in Arabic, Maimonides understood political science as the knowledge concerning he who commands and he who obeys, as well as the ability to do away with corruption.[2] Strangely enough, among the ingredients that made up this science, he included *the government of the life of each person*. In order to understand that life more fully, human beings are the only ones capable of governing their lives according to the art and knowledge of the political. It is essential for them not to lose control over their lives for, if they did so, they would fall into the same category as animals. Maimonides' critics have interpreted this very advanced and, at the same time, vexing definition merely as a youthful step designed simply to digest the teachings of his Muslim masters.

Nevertheless, this underestimates the Hebrew education of Rambam. During the cultural apogee of the tenth century it is known that the Jews of al-Andalus spoke Arabic while still preserving their Hebrew language.[3] Medieval Jewish thought flourished under the influence of Islamic civilization from the ninth century to the thirteenth century: Maimonides' "language was Arabic [and] his concerns were determined by matters arising within the context of Islamic thought."[4] As a young man, Maimonides studied with his father and his teachers from Lucena,[5] and it is logical to assume that his knowledge was distilled by the quality of his teachers.[6] To state that this vision of political science is a mere transposition of Aristotilianism[7] is, to say the least, to simplify matters. This implies an ignorance of the depth of the internal world that Maimonides had already perceived and valued.

It is not unusual to try to depoliticize Rambam's statement, given that, for political science, and more specifically, for Calvinist positivism, it is forbidden to speak of the *misgovernment of persons* outside the matrix of the modern sciences. Thus, when a dysfunction is detected in the life of a child or an adult, he or she is referred to a priest, teacher, psychologist, social worker, psychiatrist, or psychoanalyst. The cause of this dysfunction may be due to hyperactivity, malign phobias, sleep disorders, compulsive addictions, or antisocial behavior.[8]

Among the few who dared to propose openly the importance of controlling every aspect of a person's life was Sigmund Freud, a figure close to Maimonides in this sense. Freud approaches the world of the government and misgovernment of an individual from a medical standpoint. His initial position is that of a young, progressive Jewish scientist assimilated into the Viennese culture of the Austro-Hungarian Empire. As one of his biographers says, he is a rightful "heir of the eighteenth-century Enlightenment."[9]

His strategy of assimilation into Viennese society is to resort to a radical scientific pose that is both atheistic and positivist. This manifests itself openly in his reluctance to follow Jewish traditions and rituals, as he had already done in his father's house. Later on, and in spite of the fact that his wife, Martha Bernays, was very observant, he would also impose this ban categorically in his own home. Professionally he would lean toward medicine, which, at that time was seen as a hard science of the laboratory and experimentation in its strictist materialistic version.

With the passage of time, Freud retraced his steps, passing from materialistic science to what he called "psychology," to end up recognizing that his work was neither in medicine nor in psychology but really in philosophy. But given the fact that Freud's training in philosophy was limited to the teachings of Franz Brentano,[10] and little else, we can infer that he is referring to *political philosophy*, which, in the long run, is what his work will deal with in a very innovative way. Thus, Freud's philosophy is perfectly clear when seen in the light of Maimonides' wise vision of political thought.

But returning to Maimonides, we have already said that he should not be considered merely as an Aristotelian. He is not a Sephardic philosopher educated in the memory of Greek culture that sees in man the animal whose species, different from the others, possesses the logos. In this line of thought man is an animal of the *polis* whose public activity extends in concentric circles that spread from the family to the kingdom of kingdoms. We should not lose sight of the fact that political science and philosophy in the Sephardic world were very complex and their orientations multifarious.

Nahmanides, for example, believes that something else differentiates man from animals: "The only difference between them is that He bestowed upon man this known distinction that each individual person has a guardian angel, while the individual beast has no such protector although the species as a whole does. Therefore, there are certain times when a certain species fares well and another fares badly."[11]

It should be noted that Maimonides attaches a great importance to the government of our lives and links it to the essence of man, which implies something more than the logos or man as a rational human being. Rambam sees the political man not only as a thinker but also as someone who has insight into governing himself, for which, in the long run, he has to count on divine revelation. In other words, he has to rely on wisdom given by God in the Torah, the indispensable law in dealing with human government and from which are derived certain precepts accepted in a mutual covenant between Yahveh and his people. The term "human" here seems tautologous.

It is not a matter of the rule of wisdom but rather of the government of the law. This opens the way to revelation and the prophetic perception of that revelation. Both are needed to initiate a public life that cannot be attained by wisdom or scientific knowledge alone.

Politics, therefore, has some natural bases in the sense that Strauss[12] would read it later on, but it has nothing to do with Roman or Christian natural law. It does, however, have much to do with the prophetic function and the recognition of an omnipotent god, Yahveh.

Edicts and *Halakhah*

I commented earlier that Jewish culture in southern Europe experienced a true golden age from 900 to 1300.[13] It was "a secure asylum . . . the home of the cultivated sciences and arts, the leading spirit in European culture."[14]

From the tenth to the fifteenth centuries a series of *responsa*, or rabbinical decisions, that gradually evolved into a corpus of public law began to be accumulated in territories included in present-day France, Germany, Poland, Spain, and North Africa. Medieval Christian tradition, in contrast, regularly tended to mistrust Jewish legality because of its lack of concision, obstinacy, and dependence on the Torah. As Suzanne Last Stone has pointed out: "With the ascendance of Christianity and under the influence of the theological debates, Western culture, all too often, portrayed the halachic mentality as obsessively literalist, excessively formalist, crassly particularist, and preoccupied with the idea of law as coercion."[15]

The Jewish neighbor was always suspect of having a dual loyalty, one to the government of the king or caliph of his country of asylum and another to Israel. This same intimate conflict continues to be present in the State of

Israel today.[16] Although it is true that the Talmudic law (BT Bava Kamma 113a–b), formulated in the third century, says that "the Law of the kingdom is the Law," it was not easy to apply in later centuries. What would happen when a Christian law in the thirteenth or fourteenth century infringed on the precepts of the Torah?

As medieval Christian cities advanced it became necessary to develop the idea of a Jewish community as a legal entity capable of formulating rules and negotiating agreements with sovereign powers. The *aljama* or *kahal*[17] (the Jewish community) had the power to collect taxes for the Crown, administer justice, regulate the internal life of the ghetto, and apply restrictions whenever necessary. Thus special legal procedures were created with the purpose of controlling these transactions. We should bear in mind that the Diaspora generated a very wide variety of confines in which the Jewish communities had to live according to this law. These were associations or neighborhoods that, in many cases, lived a very harsh exile.

This situation would produce a transcendental leap. When confronted with the Greek tradition of the *politai* (citizens of the *polis*, the people of the city), the Jews affirmed the idea of the *kahal ha kaddosh*, the sacred or holy community.[18] The term "*kahal*" is a biblical one meaning a congregation for religious worship. It gives politics a biblical content that enables the various Jewish communities to maintain a common identity in spite of being very different and disseminated throughout the world. It is a kind of metaphysical feeling that connects the *kehillah* (local congregation) with all Israel (*kelal Ysrael*).[19]

During the thirteenth and fourteenth centuries the evolution of communal law reached its height, particularly in the *responsa* of Solomon ibn Adret (c. 1235–1310) in Spain and Meir of Rothenburg (c. 1215–1293) in Germany. This idea of community would be forged parallel to the way it would be forming in the Christian kingdoms and would be reflected in the *responsa* of the rabbis. These *responsa* are actually questions and answers. The appearance of a body of public legislation is a fundamental point in the European political tradition that would lead later on to the appearance of the modern state.[20] It is obvious that this also applies to Jewish life that lived embedded in the Christian kingdoms. There was a difference, however, in that the Jewish *kahal* would make as its own a legislation in rapid evolution at the same time as it had to preserve its integrity as a part of the people of Israel. In difficult situations there is always a deep-seated doubt: can a community committed to the law revealed by God recognize as valid the law of a human state? How does it account for laws concerning education, religious worship, conscription, trade with foreigners, or taxation? In such a delicate situation the internal debates in the ghettos can tell us a great deal of what must have been the advance of the Christian monarchies toward the modern state.

An example of this can be found in the matter of loans. From a Jewish point of view, according to divine law, it is forbidden to charge interest among the inhabitants of the kingdom or city. What comes into play here is the idea of "charging your neighbor interest." Nevertheless, the *kahal* could charge interest on its own funds because they had been donated to or invested in its treasury by private individuals. As Ibn Adret argues in one of his *responsa* concerning the donation of a sum of money to the *kahal* treasury: "In line with the strict law, it would seem that there is [no prohibition] of interest in such a case. For the Torah only prohibited interest coming from the borrower to the loaner . . . while this principal has no owner and the [*kahal's*] treasurer does not take the money for himself. It is akin to the case of a donation to the temple, where interest is not prohibited [because it is not considered a case of 'your neighbor']."[21]

As for the authorities of the *kahal*, they are considered as agents, not as citizens, and their acts are binding until after their death. This suggests that the *tzibbur* (that which is public) does not die. The money collected for charity is considered to be the property of the poor. If necessary, however, it can be diverted to payments to the *kahal*, given that the preservation of the community is above all else. An example of this would be in order to avoid the bankruptcy of the *kahal*. The only requirement is that it must be for just causes, not for unlawful intent to take advantage of these funds by corruption.

Maimonides and the Authority of the Community

It is known that in Muslim Spain the rabbis had refused to recognize communal authority above that of individuals in the sense that the community had a juridical personality: "The community is not a legal persona distinct from its members, but rather a partnership of individuals."[22]

In accordance with the School of Lucena of Alfasi (c. 1013–1039), his pupil Ibn Migash (1077–1141), and later on, Meir Abulafia (c. 1175–1244), Maimonides also holds that the community enjoys a great deal of power and that it acts with a fair amount of independence, but he does not concede that it is a metaphysical entity on its own. It is only a community or neighborhood, a people united by its faith and practices that is aware that it is a part of all Israel.

The public, for Maimonides, is quite different.[23] As a global entity, Maimonides does not trust it, because he probably saw in the multitude a not very noble expression of the individual.[24] This idea gave some Ashkenazic commentators cause to speculate that Maimonides had authoritarian and centralist tendencies. In many cases the suggestion is implied—incorrect, in our opinion—that Maimonides was influenced by the centralist Muslim tradition in which he was raised and educated. This is unacceptable in the light of the teacher's thought.[25]

The Rambam refuses to recognize the great powers of the community, the *kahal*. What leads him to this resistance are his commentaries on the Talmud and the conclusions he reaches.

Of course there are differences in the Talmudic texts in this regard. The Bava Batra deals with the matter with the example of the division of a courtyard between its co-owners. Again we are dealing with the important Jewish question of the law of neighbors. There is no difference between dividing the courtyard and dividing the property of the *kahal*. A city needs a wall and a gate just as a courtyard needs a wall and a gate. It is a matter of quantity, not quality.[26] The problem of the division of individual property eventually touches on the idea of dividing the property of the community. It is a question of whether or not the community is recognized as a different type of owner with a different entity.

The evolution of the Jewish people throughout its existence signifies, in part, the biography of a collective of enslaved individuals without any property whatsoever on their road towards liberty and property. It was a pilgrimage from the march of liberation from Egypt to the reception of the Torah in the Sinai in five days. The law of the Torah served the community at the very beginning, but it also had to be useful later in very different situations.

City Space

In reality, the courtyard or patio is common property, just like the narrow side streets that connect various patios and the space of each quarter. Thus, there will be the people of the courtyards, the alleyways, and the city.

The Jewish neighborhoods had the capacity to regulate prices, weights and measures, and wages. Workers guilds existed in the cities. But these organizations needed some type of religious ties to help them collect money, care for the temple, and purchase the necessary material for religious worship. It was necessary to build synagogues, carry on the cult, and pay the expenses. Moreover, the Jewish communities knew what it was to have to pay contributions to the Christian monarchs.

Thus there appeared a concept of public domain which refers to those places of worship shared by the inhabitants of the city, places where neighbors carried out their lives in a common space. Prior to this there was another idea of common property open to everyone but which did not belong to anyone in particular.

Maimonides proposes the idea of a government of individuals not as something reduced to the realm of morality but as a matter of politics and religion, that is, of divine law. He envisions a law that is, in essence, natural and in accord with divine law, not because man is a part of nature—an idea that makes no sense in the Jewish tradition that he keeps—but because the world and man were created by Yahveh that way, with the need for a government, to govern and be governed.

The Rambam perceives political life in a more Jewish way; it is neither as centralized nor as powerful as in Islam,[27] nor is it the way the Ashkenazic rabbis perceived it with their tradition of openness toward the authorities of the feudal lords and Christian monarchs.

In order to understand the public philosophy of Maimonides it is important to understand that he is following the Mishnah when he considers the city to be "merely a large collection of courtyards and alleys."[28]

But the city is not of a different nature from the patios or side streets. It is merely a matter of scale.[29] The city is an aggregation of courtyards, alleyways, and spaces that are joined together. It has its own needs: walls, highways, water supplies, and synagogues. Maimonides limits himself to discussing these matters, without entering into the question of legislation for the city. He doesn't seem to consider the cities as essentially different units from patios and side streets.[30]

What is certain is that he does recognize that the residents of a city can obligate others to build walls, close off the city, build a synagogue, and purchase a Torah scroll, or buy the text of the prophets and *Hagiographa*[31] so that any member of the public may have access to them.[32]

The people of the city can obligate one another to buy the scrolls or carry out the necessary public works. And those whose animals graze on public lands must pay the community for it. But Maimonides avoids extracting from these precedents the specific ability of the city to create and enforce laws. It seems that he had serious misgivings about accepting the city as an entity that could pass laws and carry them out by itself.

It has sometimes been said that Maimonides is a monarchist. This is admissible if we refer to the monarchy in the traditional Jewish sense, in which a central authority is needed to have a source of legality apart from divine laws: it is a transmitter of rules that are adequate and appropriate to assure the safety of the city. It should be a person who would know how to command respect and awe with his edicts to insure a proper response to the daily needs of the community. That which is public is a value that becomes operative between neighbors once the law comes into effect. In other words, it is valid when the common space is guaranteed for everyone and the rules of behavior have been established as such. Without these political safeguards, it is possible that the *aljama*, and even the people of Israel—both of whom have need of law and order to be able to survive—can disappear.

It seems that Maimonides distrusted the behavior of the professional guilds. This is why he refers to the mediation of a well-known scholar in the community, a student of the scriptures who could contribute his good judgment to the resolution of disputes. Maimonides is always wary of the regulations and practices carried out without the supervision of the community.

It doesn't occur to him, however, to give control to the executives of the community, to the governing councils. He looks for authority to the judicial courts, where one should go to find a solution to these problems.

The judicial courts are the ones who must establish and deliberate on matters of prices and taxes in order to avoid abuse by those merchants who are moved by their all too ambitious interests.[33] The city, however, has the authority to fix the price of basic commodities such as meat or bread. As for the activities of the guilds, he is confident that they will always go to a prominent scholar (*hakham*) to resolve civic matters and maintain the high standards of community life. If there is a famous scholar in the city, the guilds' agreements are not binding, nor can anyone be punished for not carrying them out. Here Maimonides probably wished to introduce some control over the interested parts as a corporation, and in order to do so, he looks for a judge who will maintain those high standards of excellence.

It must be taken into account that the Jewish people of the Diaspora must always live in collusion with local authorities and their social practices. In such a social environment, to accept a verdict ad hoc, without the guarantee of a scholar who is familiar with the Torah and the Talmud, is an indication of an unlawful decision.

The appearance on the scene of a wise and pious man does not mean that the decision is based on a strict adherence to religion, but rather it is an attempt to avoid a banal decision or to give in to non-Jewish political practices that were constantly inundating the environment. The norms should be practiced by those citizens who shared a common religious and political tradition, but the presence of a local scholar implies a special safeguard against superficiality, anxiety, or attempts at assimilation.

This wise man was already mentioned in the Talmud as a person of renowned moral and religious stature. Maimonides refers to him as an eminent scholar or learned man, in other words, one who is familiar with religious tradition and the sacred scriptures, but is also *a scholarly and learned man* in the other disciplines. This is a new turn.

It is not entirely accurate to explain these measures as a symptom of Jewish Neoplatonism in the Sephardic world. The pursuit of learning here is always something intimately connected with the quest for the respect for the law of the Torah, for the value of the political wisdom that emanates from it.

Maimonides wants to prevent the people of the city from giving orders that are partial or motivated by isolated interests and current fashion, or dependent on chance. For this reason, the Talmudic figure of an eminent man is a safeguard against those excesses and curbs an eventual outburst of anger within the neighborhood. The needs of the city that require public works and other properties form a continuum just like the one that makes up their courtyards and streets. It is logical that the city should seek to satisfy its needs, but this should always be carried out with the supervision of the wise man, a prominent administrator who is in accord with the city and keeps watch over it.

In any case, the matter of buying and selling, so important in the life of the *aljama*, always falls under the jurisdiction of the courts. It is never in the hands of the citizens and their legislative or executive advisory body. In regard to the trade or transport of merchandise, the Torah carefully outlines the conditions under which one must exercise good judgment. For example, "It is forbidden to deceive people in buying or selling,"[34] or to sell damaged goods or deceive the buyer through tricks; it is forbidden to deceive the people "even by words."[35] And in these dealings "a heathen and an Israelite are to be treated alike in this respect."[36] Not only is it important not to commit improper deeds, but the law also teaches us how we should exercise our own judgment and how we should protect the way we do it.

We also find a particular concern with what the Latin world would come to know as aid to the poor (*de subventione pauperum*).[37] Contrary to the Babylonian School, for Rambam, the Talmudic protection of donations to the poor in wills is legitimate, and he takes this position in opposition to other less generous traditions.[38] Donations with pious or sacred purposes are also protected in a similar manner.[39]

Maimonides shows a particular concern for shoring up the pillars of justice within the politics of the city. He always takes special care to see that public affairs are controlled and evaluated wisely, simply, and without sectarian interests. It is a matter of a rhetorical understanding of public life. Maimonides is greatly interested in the current situation of everyday decisions and the oral ingredients which these judgments must necessarily draw upon.

The subject of donations, subsidies, and public corruption also concerns him, undoubtedly in line with his idea of politics as an antidote to corruption. Here again, slander is worse than the acceptance of bribes or cheating those who trusted a person as pupils, clients, or collaborators. "Oral deception is more heinous than monetary fraud because restoration is possible in the latter while no restoration is possible in the former, and the latter concerns one's money while the former affects his person."[40] Basing himself in the law, for Maimonides, deception with words, which includes lies, slander, destructive criticism, and scandal, is not a moral fault but causes oppressive harm to our own kind. In this regard he wisely refers to Leviticus (25.14 and 25.17), where it is forbidden to cheat ("neither of you may exploit the other."), and to Exodus (22.21), which speaks clearly of not oppressing ("You shall not wrong or oppress").[41] His position once again recalls the rhetorical tradition of Quintilian. When he refers back to the figure of that man who is knowledgeable in civic, scientific, and religious matters, he does so in order to guarantee good judgment and the application of laws with reasonably good moral standards for government. This idea touches on the deepest part of the Jewish religion. Maimonides concedes that the citizens councils can issue decrees concerning the laws of neighbors, that is, if one should pay something to someone else because of having done such and such, but always with the aforementioned controls. It is amazing that Maimonides states over and over again that good judgment is an essential part of the government of the city and, as such, protects its quality of life. It is a life that, for him, should encourage truth (*emet*) and peace (*shalom*).

While Maimonides distrusts the civic action of the masses, of the group that moves by necessities altered by working as a crowd, this does not mean that he relegates citizens to a passive attitude. Rather, his understanding of civic action always leads to the idea that the citizen must study from the first to the last day of his life in order to learn things for himself. Each person must become a righteous citizen opposed to all forms of tyranny, whether they are derived from slavery, economic abuse, monetary power, or the manipulation of ignorance. Rabbi Maimonides has no idea of freedom obtained only in an external and vigilant way by resorting to new metaphysical entities such as the people, the homeland of modern Christians, or the fraternity of the masses. The judicial councils and scholars of Jewish law are merely the guarantee that judgment in the *aljama* or the *kahal*—the elaboration of daily life in the street as well as in the internal world—is respected, not destroyed by the populism of collective mobilizations. What is strictly forbidden is that a Jew should enslave another Jew, even though he may have bought the man because he had incurred a debt to him. "You will not make him do the work of a slave" (Lev. 25.39), he sums up. And whether it be "man or woman," he should treat him as a brother:

> You shall not eat white bread and the servant black, nor drink old wine and he new wine, nor you sleep under feathers and he under straw, nor reside in the city and he in the country . . . as the wise men said: 'For him who would buy a Hebrew slave it is as if he had bought a master for himself.'

In this mixture of categorical and conceptually precise proposals with specific everyday details so typical of the Torah, Maimonides reveals his real political concern: tyranny as corruption and the harm men can do to others.

The Arrival of the Ashkenazic *Halakhah* and Nahmanides (Ramban) Who Introduced It into Spain

Rabbi Nahmanides[42] is another of the great figures in Jewish philosophy. Born in Gerona at the end of the twelfth century, this eminent scholar was a man of great intellectual and religious stature throughout the Jewish world.

This Sephardic teacher was one of the portals through which the Ashkenazic *halakhah* entered Spain, given that Ramban was partial to the French Tosafists and their innovative way of studying the Talmud.[43] In turn, this led the way for a new vision of the public to arrive in Gerona. Ashkenazic influence reached its height with the arrival in Catalonia of Asher ben Yehiel (c. 1250–1328),[44] a pupil of Meir of Rothenburg.

The arrival of Ashkenazic public philosophy was the result of the strengthening of the Christian kingdoms and the increasingly harsh repression mobilized by the Crusades[45] on the Jewish communities of the Rhine.[46] Moreover, the inclusion within the kingdom of Aragon of some of the territories of Occitania—Catalonia, Majorca, Saragossa, and Valencia—offered many possibilities of communication among them. Thus, it is simply anachronistic to speak of the teachers of different countries in reference to the rabbis of Montpellier, Barcelona, or Saragossa.

Nahmanides, whose Catalan name is Bonastruc Sa Porta, was a major figure in the kingdom of Aragon. He was a member of a prominent family, although there is a question about whether or not he belonged to the great Saporta family.[47] He was an eminent exegete of the sacred texts, a follower and scholar of Rambam and his teachings, a highly reputed commentator on the Talmud and the kabbalah, and a very prestigious rabbi who lived in times of great transformations. Like Maimonides, although at the end of his life, Nahmanides was also forced to go into exile from his country by those very authorities whom he had tried to please.

Ramban—not to be confused with Rambam (Maimonides)—writes with a heartfelt conviction that distinguishes him from his contemporaries. In spite of being a strict interpreter of the Talmud, his prose is very suggestive. His theological precision reveals a thorough scholarship, but he always expresses himself with a view to reinforcing the importance of the imagination in his study.

Early on, the central point of his thought was the firm belief in the importance of the Torah as the greatest testimony of God, far superior in any case to the evidence of the grandeur of the universe. "[The Torah] removes all doubts from the hearts of the wise and the injudicious more than do the movements of [the spheres in] the heavens and the arrays of the stars . . . The Torah is the most precious and honored object of all things extant in the world and is hidden from all wise men and all the prophets . . . We must necessarily inquire into and elucidate [the nature of] this preciousness and this honor and [we must understand] this great wisdom that is concealed in the Torah."[48]

In referring to wisdom, Nahmanides recalls Job's words: "She cannot be seen by any living creature,/She is hidden from the birds of the sky."[49]

At an early age he came under the influence of those texts of the prophets that were filled with the most mysterious and evocative imagination. He perceived divine law in a very Sephardic way, as medicine for the soul: "The Law of the eternal is perfect, restoring the soul."[50]

Ramban is the defender of a universe created exclusively for man, and he understands the Torah as the key to Messianic teaching. The Messianic era culminates in the arrival of the political leader, the Messiah King,[51] who would reconstruct the temple physically and give Israel its sovereignty.[52] And, of course, the original land of Israel would be recovered.

For this reason he is very critical of one of his Sephardic colleagues, Rabbi Abraham ibn Ezra (1089–1164),[53] who held that the universe is too large to have been created for man alone.[54] Ibn Ezra's reflections often take on a somber tone, full of common sense, which Nahmanides turns against on several occasions.

In a line that shows his inclination toward the kabbalah, Nahmanides rejects the naturalistic explanations that he considered to be an influence of Greek science in the culture of his colleagues of al-Andalus. He did not like that tendency to demythify a part of what, for him, is the realm of the spirit. And undoubtedly he was not pleased at all with the way Maimonides reinterprets the law by resorting to a more erudite and informed viewpoint, even though the stature of his teacher from Córdoba is so great that he does not dare to contradict him very often. His attacks on Ibn Ezra, however, do seem to go against that erudite and scientific view of life that, at the same time, is said to be compatible with religious orthodoxy.

Nahmanides is annoyed at Aristotle, whom he sees at the bottom of this philosophical tendency rooted in the Judaism of the south:

> It is from this standpoint that you can come to realize the ruthlessness and stubbornness of the principal Greek philosopher Aristotle—may his name be erased from memory—who denies the truth of a number of things which many people have observed . . . things which have become publicized throughout the world and known to all in those ancient times . . . A certain individual [Aristotle] believed only in the physical sciences. In seeking to establish the physical sciences, he denied the realm of the spiritual, declaring that there are no such things as demons and deeds of sorcery, for the world is subject only to natural law.[55]

A Mysterious World

In order to discredit Aristotle, Nahmanides resorts to astronomic and geographic arguments that today are erroneous, such as his curious mistake of calling Rome the capital of Tuscany.[56] But this should not detract from the scope of his criticism toward that naturalism of Greek origin that had arrived through Arabic and its translations into Latin,[57] which he saw as a menace to Jewish spirituality, so charged with reverie. It is true, however, that Nahmanides agrees with Maimonides in defending the importance of dreams as vehicles of knowledge and the intervention of angels as intermediaries in the transmission of prophetic wisdom. Nevertheless, he rejects the opening of the teacher from Córdoba toward Greek science that he considers excessive.

For Ramban, there exists a profoundly esoteric world in which the Torah should be interpreted. Life is much more mysterious than what the philosophers and naturalistic rabbis would have us think. In his reflections he is in agreement with the *philosophers*—as the rabbis of the south were called in Catalonia and Occitania—concerning the existence of "the *Separate* Intelligences that dwell in the heavens . . . others reside in the atmosphere within the spheres of the [four] elements; they are called demons."[58] But other popular practices also exist that, although harmful and deceptive, nevertheless achieve their objective.

An example of this would be those who practice sorcery as a means of communication with the dead. Nahmanides gives importance to this type of knowledge that causes people to consult "a ghost or familiar spirit" as a way of furthering their knowledge. They do it through enchantments that they recite at the tomb of their deceased family member and, in popular practice, it is usually done by a man and a woman. This form of sorcery exists, although it is harmful. What Ramban does not accept is that its existence should be denied with such offhandedness by the philosophers: "The nations also consult the enchanters, [and the] augurs who interpret omens afforded by birds. This practice, too, has persisted in these generations because of its sensory nature, but men of speculation, philosophers, deny this practice also, calling it mockery . . . It is clearly established that there are those among the enchanters who do foretell some future events."[59]

Nahmanides makes it clear that this type of knowledge in the name of philosophy cannot be dismissed lightly, and he concedes that there are birds that say things through the sounds they make or the way they beat their wings. Undoubtedly, he is on the side of those who see the world as a more complex place and where esoteric knowledge exists and is effective. As he is aware of the terrain on which he stands, he concedes, in the long run, that even though he explains all this, he does not know "whether I am doing the right thing."[60]

His defense of the existence of that lower world of demons, enchantments, and sorcery is established with the conviction of being more realistic than the rationalist philosophers, who are too "affected" by philosophy. It is interesting to observe the effort with which he tries to separate these occult realities, however negative, from the concept of idolatry, one of the three great sins for divine law.[61] Nahmanides takes great care in demonstrating that these practices are complete realities that one has to count on, not mere empty idolatry.[62]

Naturally the highest form of knowledge is prophecy, whether it is in direct form, as in the unique case of Moses, or by means of an angel. It can also be attained with the help of the Bath Kol (Divine Voice), as during the time of the Second Sanctuary, although this voice was only audible to those who possessed the gift of prophecy. But these are exceptional situations that do not occur at all times. This is why people resort to other alternative means of prophecy, which, while not pious, are certainly real.[63]

Nahmanides warns of the possible influence of other peoples with whom the Jews are in close contact: "We should not be mistaken with respect to those peoples who are settled near the center of the civilized world, such as the Christians and Arabs. They believe that they, too, are inheritors of the Torah, but make no mistake on that. It is only that they translated the Torah and studied it when Rome extended its power to some of these remote regions."[64]

For Nahmanides, God is "One, active, omnipotent, omniscient, and providential"[65] and does not admit *intermediaries* in acting on the world, for that is precisely the evil of idolatry. The same is true if we were to call upon our guardian angels to intercede for us: All of these [types of idolatry] have been forbidden to us by the Torah. It appears that it is forbidden even for us to pray to them in this manner."[66]

This Jewish perception of omnipotence, which places it outside of our world and sealed in the beyond, is accentuated in Nahmanides. Creation as a supreme act, creation ex-nihilo, is an essential element; thus, he flatly rejects any Greek suggestion of an eternal world. The existence of an omnipotent creator is the crucial part of this comprehension of life and, in this he coincides in general with the *halakhah*.

Philosophy and Knowledge

Nevertheless, things are different when one attempts to explain the regularities observed in life. For the *philosophers*,[67] among whom Ramban certainly places Maimonides, the eternal law pervades the universe and is what makes it move according to intelligible laws, obviously leaving aside miracles.

Nahmanides recognizes that, like him, Maimonides also accepts the existence of miracles, exceptional events that are the products of the intervention of the providence of Yahveh,[68] and he even admits that there are also hidden miracles.[69] The latter are happenings that seem normal to us because they are due to natural forces, although, in reality, they occur because providence has made them that way.[70] In spite of it all, Maimonides considers that the world functions according to preestablished divine laws, not as a continual miracle of the will of Yahveh. Obviously, this is not the way Ramban understands it.

He is prepared to debate this point cautiously, but with decided intention: "Most people think that God does not always work through miracles but instead the world [or nature] follows its laws. Many philosophers, the Rabbi [Moshe ben Maimon] among them, likewise subscribe to that opinion."[71]

What bothers him is that he cannot accept the idea of nature as an independent entity with its own laws and autonomy from the power of God. This is not the case of Maimonides, but Nahmanides thinks that the teacher from Córdoba can mislead students with his ambiguity and invite them to assimilation.

A little later on Ramban declares the existence of continuous miracles. The miracles of life occur constantly, although they are not always evident; it is a question of hidden miracles. Thus, many daily occurrences "are not recognized as being wondrous because they are covert miracles; man is not aware that a certain person's recovery from illness was due to the charity he gave, while another healthy person's demise was due to the forbidden fat which he ate."[72]

Occasionally his Gothic tone becomes more evident when he declares the unpredictability of the world in opposition to its possible philosophical adversaries, which are nature and fortune: "It is not [in nature] that man should be rewarded for performance of a commandment or punished for committing a transgression but by a miracle. If man were left to his nature or his fortune, his deeds would neither add to him nor diminish from him. Rather, reward and punishment in this world, as mentioned in the entire scope of the Torah, are all miracles, but they are hidden. They appear to the onlooker as being part of the natural order of things, but in truth they come upon man as punishment and reward [for his deeds]."[73] This is the point of confrontation between his world vision and that of Maimonides: "Therefore, we are at a loss to understand Rabbi Moshe ben Maimon, of blessed memory, who tended to minimize the covert miracles and augment [the importance of] the laws of nature, and who further stated that the miracles are not of a permanent nature but are only temporary."[74]

Nahmanides accentuates his understanding of the world created by God as a strongly voluntaristic entity in a very interesting way. It is a space in which Divine Providence intervenes constantly and unceasingly, producing many of the daily events we live in such a way that they occur exclusively through the direct intervention of will, wisdom, and action—all qualities that are identified simultaneously with divine power—and produce numerous covert miracles. Although we are not capable of comprehending this concept, miracles do come to us and affect our lives. Rain, a successful journey, an accident, or any situation can be due to an act of God that brings with it logically his judgment and, in many cases, rewards and punishments for our acts. We are dealing here with an extraordinarily vigilant vision of the public and the private, in which the will of the Creator shines with a dazzling splendor. This world contains a powerful executive charge that accumulates both good and the brilliance of evil, accentuating those negative powers that, at any moment, could take control of life, were it not for our confidence in Divine Providence.

This world, so inclined toward memory and will, clashed head on with the philosophy of al-Andalus. It also clashed with a Jewish tradition stemming from the same theological origins—the creation of the world by an omnipotent and omniscient God—which saw creation established at a particular time and was devoted to an exemplary body of laws that could not be altered except in very exceptional situations.

Just as Nahmanides believes that it is harmful for the Jewish faith to think that the world has existed eternally without the intervention of a creator, he also rejects the idea that there is a nature of things that is eternal. For this reason he repeats that, if such natural laws did exist, they would be worthless, given that they are based on direct miracles of God.[75]

In the case of Maimonides, the teacher from Córdoba accepts the existence of regularities in the world, models that can be studied and used as a means to knowledge. He says that he agrees with Aristotle, "but only in regard to one half of his opinion."[76]

The danger here, from the point of view of the great Hebrew conquests, lies in the fact that omnipotence could again slip back in through some laws of nature that were artificial in their Greek origin, given that law is an artifice created by the *polis* as a supreme creation of man. This would also be applicable today. If law is an artificial invention, to sustain that there are laws embedded in biology, astronomy, or fluid mechanics is, to a certain extent, an act of omnipotence to be rejected. This was how the Athenians understood the laws of the city that were supposed to govern the gods, men, stars, and particles of nature.

Naturally Nahmanides' extremely voluntaristic position gives us a view of the public and private world dramatically open to direct leadership, to the constant updating of divine power. In the public sphere, he leans toward versions of government in which man's good judgment, based on his meager sensible experience and on the regularities he learns with effort throughout his life, is diminished. Thus, it becomes less possible for good judgment or for judicious men to act as a counterweight or antidote to executive power, an executive power that may be legitimate, but that may also become absolute when it lacks the possibility for correction.

On this point Maimonides sensibly recognizes that Aristotle puts forth the opinion that the universe is eternal and therefore does not admit creation: "Aristotle . . . thinks that just as the world is eternal a parte post . . . and will not disappear, it is also eternal a parte ante and has not been produced.

Now we have already said and explained that this doctrine can be arranged in a coherent way only through recourse to the law of necessity and that necessity contains a presumptuous assertion with regard to the deity."[77]

For Rambam, creation becomes the expression of wisdom and the power of God: "That which exists has had a beginning, and at first nothing at all existed except God. His wisdom required that He should bring creation into existence at the time when He did do it, and that what He has brought into existence should not be annihilated nor any of its natures changed except in certain particulars that He willed to change; about some of these we know, whereas about others that will be changed in the future we do not know."[78]

Culminating in a line of thought in a coherent form, Maimonides explains that, when we are confronted with the universe and man, scholarship can provide us with explanations through a knowledge of those laws and regularities handed down by God, with the assurance that they are valid and eternal. The only exceptions are those miracles that can happen on very few and very special occasions. This vision, both humble and aware of the danger of opening the door of omnipotence, presents a more intelligible view of the world. Study, science, and revealed knowledge can open the way to wisdom with stability, thus avoiding the unnecessary vertigo of a universe perpetually and unceasingly beyond human rationality.

Maimonides does not accept the idea of a world always waiting for a miracle or a science knowledgeable about physical or political laws that come to be merely the fragile covering for hidden miracles. His view is in contrast to the *vigilant vision* of life that Calvinism would formulate radically in the sixteenth century, with the idea that *life is a war* in which people must live as if they constantly had a knife at their throats.[79]

Will, Truth, and Order

For Nahmanides, the voluntarism of his conception of the world is compensated for with the counterweight of kabbalistic predictions or prophecies. This ingredient was lacking in the sixteenth-century Reformation, where it was hated and persecuted by the reformed Christians. A good example of this is the torture and condemnation of another Sa Porta[80] from the kingdom of Aragon, in this case, Miguel Servet (Michael Servetus), a young Hebrew scholar who was also a physician, astrologer, and theologian. Servet was condemned to death in Geneva, where he was burned at the stake along with his books by the city fathers, while his supposed friend, Philipp Melanchthon, and John Calvin, in particular, called him contemptuously "*bonus rabinus*."[81] In addition to this disgraceful fact, Calvin had also received the support in this case of his friend and admirer Théodore de Bèze, the moral inspirer of Thomas Hobbes.

For the Disputation of Barcelona of 1263 the Dominicans intentionally chose Nahmanides to debate: "The rabbi of Gerona justifiably commanded the respect and admiration of all Spanish Jewry for his erudition; if many Jews could not respond effectively to Christian polemic, they all believed that *Nahmanides could. Pablo (Paulo) knew very well that, were the rabbi discredited publicly, the Jewish community would lose much of its ability to withstand Christian missionary efforts.*"[82]

It is sinister to see how the topics that arose in the Disputation of Barcelona of 1263 between the apostate or *converso* Paulo Christiani[83] and Nahmanides are very similar to those confronting Servet and Calvin in Geneva. In particular, there was the question of the Holy Trinity, something inconceivable for a Jewish child, much less for an intelligently prepared scholar. When one of the friars asks Nahmanides about how he understands the Trinity, he answers: "What is this Trinity? Is God composed of three compact bodies like those of men?"[84] This point touches on the very foundation of the Torah, on the basis of the entire Jewish faith. The Trinity is such an obvious idolatry for a Jew that it must have been unbearable for Ramban even to debate such a horrifying and stupid thing. Likewise, Servet would also clash with Calvin on this topic. Servet believed that the Christian faith should get rid of the dogma of the Trinity in order to restore it to sanity.[85] Today this Hebrew vision of Nahmanides is criticized even by his translators and editors. Nevertheless, this is not entirely fair, in our opinion, given that he is trying to elevate the ultimate principles of his faith to the highest degree of purity. He knows very well that these are the same principles he shares with his teacher Maimonides. Nahmanides' principles, then, cannot be evaluated without understanding that, given his Sephardic upbringing, his theological position is balanced by his education within the great Mediterranean tradition. It is precisely this element that is missing in some of the scholars who used his radical position later on to open the way to a Gothic Christianization of public Jewish philosophy. It was a philosophy that, in this case, would gradually lean toward a view that was more open to accepting collective entities, and as a result, to a public law that would include new juridical public persona such as the king, the city, the corporations, and in particular and above all, *la patria* (the homeland). This *patria* would gradually but relentlessly be imposed—and this is the great leap forward—above and beyond religion;

this is precisely the line that Niccolò Machiavelli would adopt so blatantly in the sixteenth century.[86]

It is obvious on reading Nahmanides that there is an agitation in his thought that suggests that he is avid for the new. He lives in a world in which what is known as Christianity is clearly establishing itself in Hispaniae. The capture of Toledo (1085) was a crucial turning point in the struggle between the two great empires, Christianity and Islam. Urban II had preached the First Crusade (1097), and Ramban lived, at the age of forty, the impressive conquest of Córdoba, the great seat of the caliphate of the West and the birthplace of his teacher Maimonides. Europe wavered between an unstoppable reinforcement of Christianity under which he and his family were living, because Gerona was, moreover, a border town that had hardly been touched by Muslim domination. In this situation, his thought shows the same air of increasing growth and expansion that was being experienced by the kingdom of Aragon.

Nahmanides is very rigid in regard to ethical questions. He agrees with Rabbi Abraham ibn Ezra, in that he holds that man is superior to woman[87] or in conceding importance to palm reading to divine the future of a person or other acts rooted in popular culture that he considered to be true.

It is curious that he tends to reinforce the significance of Noah—an important figure in his own right—within Jewish tradition. Noah is on earth alone, without parents; he is the only one who appears like Adam on earth but, contrary to Adam, he was abandoned by his parents. In one sense, he is a new Adam. Nahmanides seems to present him as a second creative opportunity for mankind: a new possibility for procreation, to produce a mankind equally rooted in the Torah, but with a wider base. Of course we can speak here of the Diaspora of man, mankind throughout the world and with different languages.[88] According to him, only three generations have gone by from Adam to Noah, but Noah was a witness to God's punishment of mankind from which he was saved because he was a righteous man. In this remaking of the world, Noah is the just man who became the foundation of the world.[89]

The existence in Talmudic tradition of a *Noah Code* refers to a series of laws or obligations for all human beings, not only Jews, that make up a kind of natural law for all mankind. Nahmanides, of course, does not detach himself from the Torah, and he believes that everything is in it, implying with it that there is much more in it than what we have found. If we complain that we do not find the necessary replies, the fault lies in our incapacity to perceive how much we are given in the Torah. In fact, we are given everything, and if we do not find it, it is because we do not know how to listen: "The Torah is complete in everything . . . [N]othing is lacking in it."[90]

With this declaration, Nahmanides clarifies his hermeneutic position. The task at hand consists of improving our meager capacity for perception in order to receive what we have been given here in the Law. The task of the teacher is twofold: to undertake the thorough and tireless study of the texts and commentaries of the scholars and to prepare capable pupils, attending to the individual, in the Sephardic manner, so that they become receptive and take advantage of how much they are being given. Curiously, this emphasis on receptivity, especially *ex auditu*, "to hear, and sometimes having the meaning, to accept,"[91] is found in both Maimonides and Nahmanides.

This, then, will be the foundation for the kabbalah, the line of knowledge in which Nahmanides inscribes himself. With all his prestige, he will be a staunch guarantor for the kabbalah as an essential part of the preparation of the individual to attain knowledge. The kabbalah is based on the desire for knowledge. In the search for true knowledge, learning occasionally is beyond our effort and individual achievement. Concerning the broader themes that Nahmanides dealt with at a given moment, such as why evildoers triumph while the righteous suffer, or why knowledge does not advance by sheer will or effort, he seems to believe that knowledge does not progress only by means of courage and willful discipline, but rather something else is needed, almost a concerted effort throughout time: "There is a great secret contained in this matter which cannot be known except through tradition . . . no man can attain a knowledge of the truth of these matters and their like by his own reasoning; it can only be achieved by tradition."[92]

In important matters the talent of an individual wise man is not enough to elucidate the questions. In case of doubt about an interpretation, particularly if it is by a philosopher, and especially if it is by the great Maimonides, Nahmanides opts for the rabbis: "I believe only in the words of our Rabbis, for in such similar matters, a mere opinion of one wise man will not suffice to attain the truth."[93]

Nahmanides is suspicious of the idea that several southern teachers, and in its original form, Maimonides put forth: that the world is a reasonably comprehensible home for people, if only we make the effort to observe and study it. This habitability of Maimonides' world is based not only on its accessibility through reason, but also on favorable living experiences. If a learned man is pious and makes an effort to know the law of God, no matter what his level of learning, he can, within the limits of his possibilities, find a reasonable explanation for his life and the world around him; and he can live in peace feeling that he has been fully accepted. For this reason Maimonides speaks in his texts using different levels of understanding, something very consistent with the Mediterranean rhetorical tradition, the key to understanding the scholars of al-Andalus. Those who have some education, are pious, and sincerely seek to know the law of God do not have to accept everything from memory and willfully in a purely executive and vigilant relationship with their piety. But rather, it is through what they can learn that they will arrive at some reasonable explanations that will help them to live not only with a certain understanding of truth (*emet*) but also to enjoy peace (*shalom*). This is an understanding of life that sounds like the Latin *temperies* of the rhetoric of humanism. Knowledge should give truth and peace.

God Is Not Lethargic

One point that divides these two great Sephardic teachers, Rambam and Ramban, is Maimonides' idea that the teachings of the masters should not be limited to transmitting the truth per se. The teacher must help his pupil to attain the truth by himself, but teaching must also give his students a feeling of tranquility. This very beautiful and incredibly modern idea of teaching is not taken up by Nahmanides, who seems to have overlooked this aspect of pedagogy. Nahmanides is wary of this advance in learning that has confidence in the power of science and human reasoning. For him that logic is a valuable but dangerous tool if it separates human beings from their submission to the omnipotence of God.

Nahmanides stands against the excesses of that attitude that is so favorable to human knowledge and typical of a land such as al-Andalus, at the height of culture and the scientific advances of the period, and he retreats to a position that links human contingency to God's will. This position is closer to what we have termed the "Gothic" position of the Ashkenazim.

Man must not trust his belief in the rationality of the universe. He should not think that by cultivating science and study, even with pious practices, he can ever feel comfortable in the world. The Gothic vision to which he suscribes maintains a very vigilant version of a life in perpetual vigilance. In this vein, Nahmanides recalls the constant vigilance of an omnipotent God that never sleeps. Ramban warns of the danger of lethargy considering that Yahveh never stops watching us: "I am present with you always and see you in private and in public."[94]

Likewise, the commandment to remember the Sabbath to keep it holy also means "to remember it continually every day."[95] But this means not only during the day but also "at night"[96] because, as Nahmanides summarizes, "the main sanctification is at nighttime."[97] Curiously, the night to which he refers does not seem to include sleep, obviously alien to the mandates of will, in other words, beyond our control. Logically, starting from that vision of life and for the government of our person, sleep—jointly with daydreaming, and fantasies—becomes an uncontrolled and suspect ingredient. Lethargy is only permitted in its minimal expression. As for sleep, it is only minimally necessary for the body's rest.

We find ourselves in a world in which any appearance of rationality is superficial and often erroneous because the cause that underlies it is a divine will unintelligible for philosophy.

This type of argumentation is compatible with the executive vision of life that had gradually been imposing itself on the feudal tradition of Christianity and Germanic law. This is a vision of politics that imposes submission to a prince or a monarch as the supreme symbol of power and will end up embodied in the *cuius regio, eius religio*[98] of Martin Luther. As Jewish tradition knows very well, the appearance of these national entities in Europe and their public law announced the rise of a grandiose actor who brought with him, by means of a massive transference, the omnipotence of the papacy; we refer here to the national state. This task, by no means casual, would reach its height at the hands of juridical theologians.[99] These thinkers articulated the faith in order to create an omnipotent apparatus that was not subject to anything or anyone, not even to the law, given that the only existing law is that which the State promulgates and sanctions. At the head of the State, as in God, the three powers—executive, legislative, and judicial—are inseparably united.

Nahmanides' idea of a world that is intelligible only to a certain extent, of an environment that is never peaceful, is rather unsettling. This space of life, always subject to the unexpected will of its creator, immediately brings to mind that very precise expression of John Calvin that man should always live on earth as if he had a knife at his throat.[100]

If the philo-Gothic position of Nahmanides and other Sephardic teachers points, on the one hand, toward an updating of other learned predecessors such as Ibn Ezra or Maimonides, on the other hand, it incorporates a *magnificent compensation*. We will not find the lethargy of life in the teachers of rhetoric or in the tradition of Maimonides, but in the kabbalah. It can be found in the kabbalistic wisdom and teaching that would be kept discretely hidden from surrounding eyes. Naturally this development would never reach Calvin or his long list of followers.

This knowledge, understood as a treasure, must be protected from the incomprehension of those coreligionists who were not versed in such matters. And, of course, it must also be protected from a Catholicism in the grip of dogma where the way was closed to freedom of thought from the time of the first civil wars with the Protestants. The papists would be increasingly partial to an executive and dogmatic world, while the reformers would opt for an equally executive world, but more "modern," more astute, where will and memory are illustrated with the manipulation of *knowledge* articulated scientifically. Now its conviction is that *knowledge is directly power.* The shameful sectarian trial of Miguel Servet (1511–1553) in Geneva in 1553 is a fundamental example for understanding this great transfer of power in Renaissance and Baroque Europe.[101]

To what extent was Nahmanides open to this Gothic vision? The teacher from Gerona undoubtedly accepted the political transformations that were taking place in the Christian world. Referring to knowledge, however, he was open to the kabbalah as a formidable counterweight. In this sense, a pupil of Nahmanides, in whom the teacher had instilled the notion that he cannot attain knowledge by his own reasoning, would not be left out in the cold or driven to depression, because Nahmanides opens the way to a higher road—the kabbalah—that will allow him to attain the knowledge encompassed by the Torah. This is a very fragile and vulnerable tradition that must be cared for, a knowledge preserved from time immemorial to which he alludes in his writings in code with the expression "by way of the truth."[102] The proper method of the kabbalah would be this protection that we find in our teachers who, one on one, very much in the Sephardic tradition, will continue to pass on the truth: "The subject is elucidated in the Torah for all who have properly heard the rationale of the commandments according to the mystic teachings of the kabbalah. One kabbalist hears it from the mouth of another kabbalist, thus extending the line of oral transmission back to Moses our teacher, who heard it from the mouth of the Almighty."[103]

It is an attempt to lead the pupils along the path of truth while, at the same time, they are advised not to divulge a knowledge that can only be learned orally from *teacher to pupil.* An inadequate transmission of knowledge can, in itself, be an obstacle on the path to truth. This is a very Sephardic point in which he coincides with Maimonides.

Kabbalistic compensation for the imbalance that was occurring in the interpretation of Jewish law in the thirteenth century is neither capricious nor accidental. This is why Nahmanides transmitted it to some of his disciples and, in particular, to the School of Barcelona during the thirteenth and fourteenth centuries: a scientific lineage that acquired exceptional prestige with the financier and chief rabbi of Aragon, Solomon ibn Adret, "Rashba" (1235–1310). In fact, Ibn Adret illustrated this apparent contradiction between what is acceptable outwardly and what is practiced inwardly *in foro interno* in his controversial edict of 1305, in which he prohibited the reading of scientific books or having access to to the works of the philosophers for Jews under twenty-five, with the exception of medical students. The penalty for those who violated this edict was excommunication. It should be recalled that Ibn Adret was one of the most important Talmudic scholars of his time, and his advice was sought throughout the world. In contrast to his teachers Rambam and Ramban, he was a leader who was born and died in Barcelona, his native city. Fortunately, Ibn Adret did not live to see the terrible happenings of 1391 when the synagogues of Catalonia were attacked and burned.

There are aspects in which Nahmanides stands out in his own right at the height of Sephardic tradition, as in the case of his subtle inquiry into the inner needs of man. For the teacher from Gerona, these needs are not merely the product of the insatisfaction of a function and, therefore, it is not enough to placate them in order for them to stop. There are some needs that cannot be easily satisfied and others that become transformed even when they are satisfied: "The eye is not satisfied with seeing . . . nor is the ear filled with hearing because of the constant transformation of things. Not one of the sounds which are heard fill the ear satisfactorily before the particular sound is silenced and another sound replaces it."[104]

Nahmanides explains with admirable depth that the dynamism of the human being can never be condensed in a set of inherent mechanical formulas. Now, when we are still so close to the pedantic excesses of romanticism, we see this subtlety as astonishing in the thirteenth century.

In spite of his reticence toward "his teacher," Maimonides, as he frequently speaks of him, there are points in which Nahmanides literally adheres to the thought of the Cordoban in a true communion of ideas as, for example, in his understanding of charity. Ramban believes that "Harav Rabbeinu Moshe [ben Maimon] is not among the authors who unduly enlarge upon a theme; in fact, he has censured those who utilize an overstatement of language. Nevertheless, he wrote an entire chapter on charity." With this reflection, Nahmanides, in this case, appropriates the entire text as his own, merely limiting himself to transcribing it.[105]

Nahmanides versus Maimonides

In order to avoid misunderstandings, we should clarify an important point in relation to Nahmanides and his teacher, Rambam: Nahmanides was a decisive actor in the peaceful resolution of the great controversy within the European Jewish communities concerning the two books of Maimonides, *The Guide of the Perplexed* and the "Book of Knowledge" (*Sefer Hamada*), the first of fourteen books that make up his *Mishneh Torah*.

The appearance of these two great works raised many objections in the Ashkenazic world. Soon the controversy spread to the heart of the Jewish world, which, in the twelfth century, was centered in France and Spain. We should note that Maimonides finished writing the *Guide* in 1191 and that it took nine years for news of this book to spread throughout Western Europe. Early on, it was necessary to translate it. Finally it was done by the very competent rabbi Samuel ben Judah ibn Tibbon of Lunel in Provence. Nevertheless, given the fact that Ibn Tibbon's translation was difficult because of its terminology, some leaders in the community of Provence commissioned a more accessible translation from the poet Judah al-Harizi. In spite of the fact that this translation was not as accurate as Ibn Tibbon's version, it was the one that was used to debate the work publicly in study groups throughout Provence.[106] Soon it gave rise to a virulent controversy between the partisans and detractors of Maimonides.

The quarrel was touched off by the eminent Rabbi Solomon ben Hehar of Montpellier, together with his disciples Rabbi Jonah ben Abraham, a cousin of Nahmanides and the father-in-law of his son Solomon, and David ben Saul. All these scholars considered Maimonides' work as a menace to the Jewish religion. Contrary to these learned men, the reaction in Provence was clearly favorable to the Cordoban, and the majority of the rabbis of Provence began to criticize Rabbi Solomon and his disciples so harshly that they were obliged to travel to northern France to seek support. As a consequence of all this, some prominent northern Ashkenazim proclaimed an edict forbidding the study of the two works by Maimonides.

The reaction of the Jewish communities of Provence and Aragon was not long in coming. It was so severe that protests were made to the Jewish and Gentile authorities against Rabbi Solomon and his group.

Nahmanides made his entrance into this difficult situation to make peace between the two factions in the south and north of France, where an ideological and moral battle of important consequences was being waged for the future. His first initiative was to send a letter to the Christian authorities in Aragon, Navarra, and Castile proposing a meeting between the two opposing factions—the rabbis of northern France and those of Provence—so that they could expound their views before a group of Spanish rabbis. With this move, Ramban tried to avoid an abrupt exit from the conflict that would have divided his coreligionists.

At the same time, and in order to avoid a hasty and harmful outcome for the Jewish people, Nahmanides wrote a fascinating *Letter to the French Rabbis* in which he advocated a peaceful solution to the conflict.[107] But in spite of his efforts, he could not prevent the Jewish authorities from excommunicating Rabbi Solomon and his disciples in an edict promulgated in Saragossa in 1232.

In this *Letter* Nahmanides makes use of an extraordinary ambiguity in which he tries to find a way to heal very serious wounds. His strategy consists of the use of fragments of the Torah that he takes out of context, even though he takes into account that his readers would know how to complete them with the rest of the quote. Thus, the readers would give them the intention that, at first sight, he does not want to reveal. For example, when he refers to the situation of the Jewish faith in Sepharad, he does so in a humble tone. His voice alludes to the corruption of Israel and the contamination of its customs and to a people whom he sees as

> Children who have been exiled from their Father's table,
> and then defiled themselves with the king's food
> and with the wine they drank;
> They mingled themselves with the nations[108]
> and learned from their work.[109]

Initially Nahmanides addresses his French colleagues in obvious agreement with them in the face of a troubling situation for the people of Israel and, in particular, the Jews of Sepharad, where he clearly sees an emergency situation. The mendicant orders, whom he calls "the sword of apostasy,"[110] are enslaving the Jewish communities with their preaching, using those apostate Jews that the Christians call "conversos," whenever possible. Ramban implies that this political strategy is wreaking havoc within the Jewish community. The situation is very serious in *"the captivity of Jerusalem that is in Sepharad,"*[111] undoubtedly because of the grave sins of its members.

But Nahmanides also attempts to explain to his northern colleagues that they should not have excommunicated the southern Jews as a whole, including "the fortress of Montpellier, the bitter and impetuous," with the rest of the communities. He clarifies this for them:

> In our area, since there are no dissensions,
> neither desolation nor destruction within our borders,
> we do not bear the responsibility
> of adhering to your excommunication.

> Our communities are concerned for the honor
> of the great Rabbi [Maimonides]
> and are jealous for him with a great jealousy[112]
> in honor of his learning, his saintliness,
> and the glory of his excellent majesty.[113]

Nahmanides points out that he does not want to avoid the issue by maintaining a comfortably neutral position. Instead, he tries to convince them by reminding them that, even if the scholars of Provence might withdraw the *Guide of the Perplexed* and prohibit its reading, how could they do the same with the *Sefer Hamada*, if its content is the very word of God transcribed by Maimonides?[114]

Ramban then goes on to defend his teacher openly with a sincerity that, for one who is familiar with his writings, not only leaves no doubt, but is also very moving for its honesty and profound nobility. For this, he uses bits of phrases from the Torah in such a way that, if the reader is learned, as it is assumed in the case of the French rabbis, he will complete this absence mentally, thereby composing a formidable argument. Thus, when he says that Maimonides "instructs sinners in the way,"[115] he is alluding to Psalms 25:8, which says, "Integrity and generosity are marks of Yahveh . . . judiciously he guides the humble, instructing the poor in his way."[116]

Maimonides—synthesizes Ramban—teaches "in calmness and peacefulness"[117] and "without questions or prolonged discussions, he brings forth gems."[118] His defense of the *Rab* is extraordinarily truthful, almost emotional. For Nahmanides, what Maimonides compiles in his "Laws of Repentance" even exceeds the contribution of the Talmud:

> In the Talmud, we have found nothing
> [comprehensive] on the theme of Repentance . . .
> This is our clear opinion
> concerning this book [*Sefer Hamada*].
> We have therefore borne it upon the shoulders,
> and placed it in [our] sight;
> we did not thrust it away, as you [did],
> with [the force of] both hands.[119]

Finally, Ramban provides very learned data indicating the extent of his information about the matter. He reminds them that his venerated French rabbi, Isaac ben Abraham, in one of his *responsa* to Rabbi Yonathan Hakohein of Lunel, shows that he has read Maimonides' works and felt blessed with them and with their author, whose name he mentions: "for praise, for honor, and for glory."[120] The expression is taken from Isaiah 13:11 in the context that Yahveh rejects the pride of Israel and the entire house of Judah before something sublime that is offered to them, and they do not take advantage of it because "they do not listen."[121] In writing this way, Nahmanides seems to be giving us only the melody, indicating, at the same time, the place in the Torah where the harmony can be filled in by the reader.

If Nahmanides' respect for his great teacher Maimonides is obvious, it is also true that there are disagreements between the two authors, particularly concerning matters of ritual. We should take into account that Nahmanides lived in a Christian city with a frontier spirit at a time when the Reconquest was advancing inexorably toward Christian preponderance in Europe. At the age of forty he had lived to see the Christian conquest of Córdoba by Ferdinand III in 1236, and one might think that, while the rabbis of Andalusia mourned the fall of a magnificent world, his native city of Gerona, where he was living, probably celebrated joyfully the conquest of the seat of the former caliphate. Living alongside Christian society was an actual fact in his life, the reality of "my native land"[122] from which he would be exiled because it was decreed by the king of Aragon and in perpetuity by the pope. He was exiled from his native land of Catalonia, which he longed for in the words of Jeremiah (12:7)—"I have forsaken my house, I have cast off my heritage"—and which he would only leave to die "in the lap of my mother," Jerusalem.[123]

The Christian Front Line

While the southern border of the Christian advance was in the kingdoms of Spain, its protecting rear guard was in the north. For this reason, although Nahmanides admired the great rabbi philosophers of a sophisticated al-Andalus, his ritualistic education, the vehicle of his daily piety, was oriented perhaps more towards the Tosefta,[124] to which he constantly refers.[125]

He writes that his education was with "the French rabbis, before Harav Rabbi Moshe ben Rabbi Shneiur and his brother Rabbi Shmuel, and before Rabbi Yechiel of Paris through my relative, Harav Rabbi Jonah, who studied there."[126] He is, therefore, the importer of new ideas brought to him by his cousin Jonah Gerondi. As a resident of the kingdom of Aragon, he is under the political jurisdiction of the same Christian king as his coreligionists in Montpellier and Roussillon, which would clearly orient him toward a ritualistic education and customs influenced by feudal Germanic law. His city, Gerona, belonged to the Marca Hispánica, the Christian frontier with Islam. Thus, when he refers to certain ritualistic practices, he mentions the difference between what he has seen in France and "the customs we have established in Spain."

This was a Christian world more prone to asceticism, in which there was no place for Jewish polygamy, which would be abandoned little by little. It was a society whose highest rewards to which a man could aspire were "peace, riches, possessions, and honors."[127] However, the figure of God as "the great Judge who will appear to sit on His throne of justice to pass judgment on the world,"[128] which is still mentioned in Nahmanides, will gradually give way to that of an omnipotent Prince, who is astute and, above all, invincible. It is no longer a matter of a judgment in which the judge applies the Law so that there are precisely no victims or victors. What is looked for now is an executive leader who is endowed with charisma and can establish an undisputed domination over an increasingly stable territory with pride in its homeland.

A new ethical environment leaning towards asceticism was also installed in which man "should not resort to luxuries but utilize only necessities."[129] This suspicious idea is reinforced that because "there is no death without sin, nor is there suffering without iniquity. Man should not be biased in his own favor; he should examine his conduct and confess even the unknown sins that he may have committed."[130]

The Jewish communities gradually came to accept as their own the figure of the prince or king whose protection they came under, just as they did with the corresponding national laws that would also be the laws of the Jews. The Talmudic idea that "the law of the kingdom is the law of Israel" would also be understood in such a way that a law would be higher, if necessary, than the Torah itself. Divine law would gradually be relegated to the inside of the home or enclosed within the walls of the Jewish quarter, otherwise obedient to the Crown, which would begin to be their Crown. The idea that "I love my country more than my soul,"[131] voiced by Niccolò Machiavelli a century later, would begin to project its shadow on the horizon of European Jewry.

Of course this idea clashed head-on with the public vision of Maimonides and with that Sephardism in which everyday good judgment was an immovable pillar of public life. At the end of his life, in exile in the land of Israel, Nahmanides' disagreements with his admired Maimonides tend to be more focused on certain excesses of ritual practices.[132]

Communal Decrees and Oaths

Nahmanides began to study a major topic in the thirteenth century: the question of what legal technique should be used to enforce the obligations of communal charters that would have a coercive effect on the inhabitants of the city. Ramban recalls that, in its origins, the *herem* was a binding oath taken by all the inhabitants of a place on establishing a charter of founding rights. Later on, this oath was transformed into an obligation of voluntary acceptance rather than submission to it.[133]

Christian society followed a similar process: the oath articulated the fact of coexistence (*convivencia*) with the binding moral and psychological force that it contributed to society.

When used by a *kahal*, these citizens' charters opened the way for Jewish groups to be inserted in Gentile society, together with their aspirations, loyalties, and values. Nevertheless, this incorporation had as its counterweight the consequence of relegating Judaism to the private home and the internal world of each individual. Naturally, the Jewish quarter, the *kahal*, and the Catalan *call jueu* would also find themselves at the mercy of the ideals of nationalistic integration in the societies that absorbed them.

The new cities of the eleventh and twelfth centuries were, in reality, religious associations that practiced diverse rituals and shared common values, including religious oaths. The Christian parishes are a good example of this concept. This common bond provided the necessary cohesion and intimate acceptance on the part of the inhabitants of a power recognized as such to command, reward, and punish. They were legal associations in the sense that each inhabitant was aware of the obligations acquired and shared concerning deeply rooted practices and values. Nevertheless, even when we take into account the religious nature of the cities and towns, "[it] is not to say that they were ecclesiastical associations. They were wholly separate from the church."[134]

It must be clarified, however, that the European cities of this period were, in some cases, new cities, newly founded, in which the legal and religious factors were essential: "If one examines . . . the circumstances of the emergence of modern cities and towns in Europe . . . then one must take into account two factors often neglected by social, economic, and political historians: the religious factor and the legal factor . . . In fact, it was by a legal act, usually the granting of a charter, that most of the European cities and towns came into being; they did not simply emerge but were founded."[135]

The *aljamas* enjoyed a great deal of autonomy within the city. Their inhabitants maintained "a rule within a rule . . . a society within a society,"[136] since they normally contained their own law courts, temples, schools, authorities, businesses, laws, cemeteries, and very clearly differentiated social practices. These norms were respected by the Christian or Muslim powers under which they lived.

Nevertheless, we should recall that the Jewish community lacked arms, territory, and sovereignty. It was a community always accustomed to living under a foreign power and, as such, its laws and public morality necessarily had to reflect that situation "for Judaism and its *halakhah* are essentially the products of exile and exclusion. They reflect the experience of being ruled by the *others*."[137]

We should clarify the fact that these *aljamas* or *calls* were secular associations, not ecclesiastic communities. For Harold Berman, they were the first communal entities of secular origin, "the first secular states of Europe."[138] They were legal associations, given that each one felt itself linked by an urban conscience and by distinctly differentiated urban institutions.

Nahmanides bases his argument on the Tosefta,[139] where he sees support for this communal view of the law. The authority to impose a ban, a prohibition, lies with the power of the community to impose these obligations. Nevertheless, if the community already has the authority to make and enforce laws, what is the reason for this new precision and this special power? Nahmanides suggests that the *kahal* invests a ban with the magical power of the religious oath that penetrates the criminal and can destroy him. The ban contributes a religious power that holds one back through fear, dissuades the criminal, and reinforces the prudent decisions of the community.

If the prohibition is broken, it can harm the life of the community and its safe and ordered existence. This is why the *kahal* can issue a ban to threaten the possible transgressor with the loss of his belonging to the city.

This procedure is ideal to give great power, in part magical, to the *kahal* on important occasions such as its foundation, in special situations, or on the occasion of especially important decrees. And it would also serve to assure the existence of the *aljamas*. It was believed that the transgressor of the prohibition was, to a certain extent, already outside the community and that his expulsion or excommunication was merely the culmination of a process that the transgressor had already initiated and deserved.

This ban had only one condition to be imposed: it had to carried out by a council of at least ten men: "Because [less] is not considered a *tzibbur* [a public], nor are they considered a court which stands for a public. Such a group has no power to impose a ban. It can only demand an oath [which must be verbally accepted] of each individual."[140]

The mention of a quorum underscores the religious nature of the *herem* (oath). It undoubtedly reinforces the idea of the *kahal* as a charismatic unit in which this oath is rooted, and as such, it is the reflection of the people of Israel as a whole. The court, says Nahmanides, is convened in public: "And if the ban was imposed by a king of Israel or the Sanhedrin, in the presence of the majority of Israel, the transgressor is liable to the death penalty and the king or Sanhedrin is permitted to execute him in whatever they choose. This is the role of Joshua, who tried Akhan as a capital case [for breaching the *herem* of Jericho, see Joshua 7]."[141]

Thus, the authority of an executive power to impose a ban is derived from that public entity.

In his *Commentaries on the Torah* Nahmanides discusses or reviews the legislative activities of Israel's political leadership. In the *Book of Exodus* he already tells us that Moses wrote a statute or ordinance before receiving the Torah at Sinai; and he recalls that, when Moses went with his people into a dry land without water,[142] he established customs for them referring to how they should regulate their lives and their business "until they reached inhabited country."[143]

This guaranteed the way for the adaptation to the world of the new cities founded in the West: cities in which, time and again, the problem arose of the demands of loyalty to the king and to the civil authorities. All this was pressured by the perennial urgency of generating a more practical legislation that was rapid and capable of facing up to the *needs of the moment.*

The Weight of Religion

Nahmanides analyzes the ban or communal edict as a type of oath. These demands of the community carry a heavy burden of prohibition, such as the one mentioned in Leviticus on the obligation to set aside a certain amount of the community's wealth for God. The individual is not always the actor present in everything. Sometimes the city itself issues these demands in order to protect communal life. Thus, whoever does certain things or tears down a fence or wall will find himself under that communal prohibition and, as such, liable to punishment.

There is an important difference between an edict and an oath. An oath requires that it be accepted or sworn voluntarily and explicitly. The prohibition of a ban can fall on a person without his having accepted it and can be applied by a foreign body that imposes it on him. A ban can be something of an oath. It has the power of a religious oath, but within a civic environment. Thus, anyone who commits an act that goes beyond the limits of a particular matter comes under this prohibition. Although this type of prohibition did not exist in Moses' time, among other things, because Moses led a band of slaves towards freedom and property, it gradually began to appear with tradition and became operative on that individual to whom it applied. The *herem* involves the individual and obligates him to the community. If anyone breaks this obligation, he commits a sin; he is banished from the city and, in extreme cases, is excommunicated.

In contrast to the oath, which binds only the individual who takes it, the edict can operate on a person who has not accepted it but on whom it has been imposed from outside by an external legal body alien to him. This method was used by the councils to issue binding decrees for the people.

There is a fundamental difference between Christian and Jewish tradition. In the history of *halakhah*, "the Jewish legal and moral discourse,"[144] always takes into account that the original covenant that unites the people of Israel under their God is based on an alliance that generates an obligation.

While in Christian law the ideas of self-reliance, freedom, emancipation, sovereignty, kingdom, and State were taking shape around the concept of individual rights, in *halakhah,* the basis of coexistence and the foundation of the existence of the Jewish community lay in an essential pact with Yahveh, an alliance that obligated them as members of the chosen people to obey the law. The law of the *kahal* or *aljama* could hardly be justified as an advance in human rationality, or even as a product of a rational coherent system that is justified in itself, as in Hans Kelsen's view. For the strictest rabbis, the law was given completely at Sinai,[145] and this was where the experience of the search for freedom and human fulfillment originated. When a young man reaches the proper age, he does not receive the rights for his emancipation; rather, what identifies his entrance into the Jewish community will be *the acceptance of his obligation*—this is the meaning of bar or bat mitzvah—as a member of the people of Israel.[146] It has nothing to do with achieving any kind of rights that would curtail the way to abuse and tyranny.

This difference is essential and it is why, within Judaism, there have always been tensions concerning the idea of citizenship and civil society. This concept, intrinsically foreign to *halakhah* and, of course, to the Torah, has been the object of criticism by philosophers such as Leo Strauss, among many others. There is a tense coexistence between universalism and particularism that has been, at the same time, the problem of Judaism and its most intimate definition.[147] In reality, and as Suzanne Last Stone points out, "There is no term, much less a theory, that defines civil society in classical Jewish texts . . . The Jewish tradition has few resources from which to build a modern, liberal conception of civil society."[148] If this difference is not understood, everything can be misinterpreted. This is not infrequent today, given that Judaism's understanding of modern political philosophy has largely assimilated the Calvinist influence of Geneva.

In this same sense, the idea of nature, so important in the Roman and, in general, in the Christian tradition, carries little weight in *halakhah*.[149]

For Nahmanides, the city can make decisions by majority that obligate all of its inhabitants to comply. Of course Ramban says that these decisions must be made in the presence of the wise men of the city, as the Talmud requires, so that they can oversee the event and, with it, avoid any populist aberrations. But these ordinances become obligations for everyone and can permit the application of communal punishments on all the inhabitants of the city. Therefore, the people of the city, not its councils of rabbis or the law courts, are the ones who can impose these prohibitions or bans.[150] As Lorberbaum points out, with the recognition of the right of the civil authorities to impose bans, Nahmanides bases himself in the Tosefta to reinforce the ability of the city to impose restrictions and punishments unilaterally. In this way, he reinforces the authority of the community.[151] Even so, the individual oath continues to contribute a religious weight that invests the communal decree with an almost magical power to penetrate and destroy the criminal from within.[152]

Nahmanides mentions Nehemiah's decrees against mixed marriages between Gentiles and Jews. As a leader of Judea, Nehemiah found a way to impose these measures with the power of the law and by means of legal punishments. Later on, this authority was transferred to the law courts. Nahmanides insists on the idea that it is the inhabitants of the city, not the courts, who have the power to inflict these punishments, to impose the *herem*.

Therefore, if the inhabitants of a city decide by majority to impose a ban, they are authorized to impose it and oblige all those who are affected by it to follow their instructions. Thus, the citizen who transgresses a ban is, in the long run, transgressing an oath and is excommunicated from the people of his city.[153]

Some scholars have interpreted this as a democratic advance at the moment of legally constructing a city, because it refers legal power back to its political roots and, ultimately, to the inhabitants of the city. Following the echoes of Germanic law, it is in the city as an entirety where Nahmanides seems to place real power and legal authority in order to issue bans, edicts that later will become decrees and, in time, will eventually acquire the status of law when applied by the tribunals.

Nahmanides is responding to a new situation: the increasing influence of the Ashkenazim in the *halakhists* of the Iberian Peninsula. Ramban seems to have played a prominent role in the task of disseminating this influence in Sepharad. This process would be reinforced with the arrival in Spain of Asher ben Yehiel, a pupil of Meir of Rothenburg.[154]

We often find in specialists, usually non-Jews or Ashkenazic Jews, the historical interpretation that Nahmanides and his successors in Gerona and Barcelona point toward the modernization of public Jewish philosophy. It was a modernization that, in the retrospective words of Martin Heidegger in the twentieth century, would come to be understood as the Europeanization of the world. This process carried along with its turbulent waters the expulsion of the Jews, first in France in 1182, crossing over to England in 1290, arriving in Catalonia in 1391, then in Castile and Aragon in 1492,[155] Portugal in 1496, and finally Navarra in 1498.[156]

Here there is an important difference between Rambam and Ramban. We should take into account that Maimonides wrote his *Guide of the Perplexed* in Arabic,[157] and that, because of his education in that language, he was very familiar with Greek philosophy. It is also obvious that he knew Greek science and particularly the philosophy of Aristotle very well, by way of Averroes. The Jewish teachers of Catalonia, however, lacked this training.[158] They had absorbed Muslim wisdom through translations, but they were reticent to accept the line of the *philosophers*.[159] The Hebrew translation of the *Guide of the Perplexed* and the influence of the entire oeuvre of Maimonides had such a great impact on the knowledge of European rabbis that it would be the cause of a real internal schism in Judaism that would only be resolved after a tremendous trauma.[160]

Disputations and Autonomy

We should not forget that Jewish identity does not include in its basic precepts the idea of the individual, autonomous, and vigilant in his own life. To belong to the people of Israel is not a voluntary matter. The idea that the individual has rights of his own that separate him from his fellow citizens does not enter into the *halakhah*. One of the principles collected in the Talmud is that all Jews are responsible for each other. As the teacher Ritva paraphrased it: "All Jews are responsible for one another. They are like [parts of] one body and like a guarantor who repays the debt of a friend."[161]

The late Middle Ages was a period of great social changes, with newly created cities, settlements in the lowlands, and the appearance of thriving markets. Languedoc and Catalonia also enjoyed great prosperity during this time."Socio-economic factors added to this diffusion, given that, Jews and non-Jews in the south of France and Catalonia achieved the necessary economic prosperity for the evolution of their thought and, as a result, a fair degree of stability. When new cities emerged, thanks to this flourishing economy, they were able to play their role in favoring mutual encounter and suffocating the fire of religious fanaticism that had prevailed until then."[162]

The idea that the public philosophy of the Jewish communities of Provence and Catalonia was moving toward democratization begins to appear again. Provence and Catalonia were intimately linked, given that King James I of Aragon was also the seigneur de Montpellier. Provence also had a distant past with feudal ties to the counts of Barcelona and, in any case, its proximity to the other side of the Rhone, a natural frontier with Languedoc, lent itself to constant mutual influences. Later on, in the sixteenth century, Montpellier was a center for a great deal of activity by the Huguenots. Their siege and submission by Louis XIII of France in 1622 would provoke a massive flight of its inhabitants. Some of these emigrants fled to Roussillon and Catalonia, itself. The *ugonaus*, in Catalan, gathered in massive public *pretxas* and had *diacres*, or very charismatic religious leaders. They initiated a kind of Protestant banditry, including trafficking in arms, which destabilized the entire region for many years.

Nahmanides must have been very aware of the dangers of living together with the Gentile world. This proximity was sometimes fraught with temptations for the Jews and always exposed to the specters of assimilation and apostasy. This was the case of Fray Paulo Christiani,[163] of the Order of Preachers, a Jewish apostate who would achieve notoriety in a famous disputation. As the assistant of Raimundo de Penyafort, his superior and confessor to the Pope, Christiani was ordered to preach against the Jewish community in Montpellier. Subsequently, he would come up against Nahmanides, in the presence of James I, in the Disputation of Barcelona.[164] The *disputation* was a common practice in Christian universities of the period:

> It was a kind of dialectical contest that took place [among students] presided over or under the responsibility of one or more teachers. A question was proposed and each one sustained, according to whatever arguments were most convincing to them, a solution in favor or against; then . . . a teacher would collect and put in order the various arguments in pro or in contra and determine the solution . . . They were usually held on weekends or every two weeks . . . On the other hand, some disputations were held . . . at Easter or Christmas . . . The memories of these

> disputations gave rise to the *Quaestiones quodlibetales*, like those of St. Thomas Aquinas or William of Ockham."[165]

These disputations carried over into the streets. They were staged as veritable local happenings in an open public space, and the actors were well-known persons, Christians as well as Jews. The Paris Disputatio of 1240 is a famous precedent. Others would follow after the Barcelona Disputatio of 1263.[166]

The phenomenon of the Disputatio speaks to us of a public event, presided over by a judicial authority that, in the case of the Disputatio de Barcelona, is none other than King James I. A setting is created with all the ingredients of a trial: (1) it is open to the public; (2) it is an open confrontation of the parts in litigation who are guaranteed the freedom and the time to prepare their arguments; (3) no weapons are allowed in the room or place where the trial is to be conducted; (4) the safety of the witnesses is guaranteed; and (5) it is not carried out in a vigilant way in a single day, but rather in several sessions and for several days, that is, with lethargy.

Obviously, even though this *disputatio* pretended to be a trial, it was not so in the sense that Maimonides would use the term, but rather a simulacrum that was in fact a performance of prosecution and accusation. In the *disputatio*, a dialectical word that implies an aggressive confrontation, one does not seek to reveal the truth, but rather to carry out an act of political propaganda incarnated in a politics of conquest. The participants are dogmatic partisans a priori, and the judge is not a judge. In the case of Barcelona, the king, himself, attempting to shore up the Christian theses, intervened in the middle of the trial to speak without any consideration for the opposition. It was a definitive fact that, on one of those sessions, King James came to the Barcelona synagogue with Raimundo de Penyafort to preach to members of the Jewish congregation.

The Barcelona Disputatio of 1263, was, therefore, a political happening of major consequences. It cannot be compared—as one critic has tried to do—to the present debates on television, since, in this case, the judge is the public television viewer, and the verdict is pronounced by the audience. In the Barcelona Disputatio of 1263, the highest judge in the kingdom was on the presiding throne and expressly guaranteed the safety of both parts and their freedom of speech. But he presided over the happening in such a way that, while wanting to give the impression of a trial in a rhetorical sense, he ended up by transforming the judge into a prosecutor, an act that has predominated in the evolution of the dialectic of Western Europe and would soon be established as one of the most profound characteristics of our culture. The Barcelona debate was an open discussion, but it was not a trial. As Martin A. Cohen has pointed out, it was "an encounter that could only lead to a public defeat in order to aid the king of Aragon in his purposes."[167]

These acts can be framed within what we might call *the illusion of conversion*, a kind of crusade of the internal public spaces of the individuals directed against the Muslim and Jewish minorities. The new mendicant orders of Franciscans and Dominicans showed themselves to be very active in these initiatives. These efforts spread from Morocco to China, and the first objectives at home were the borderlands of the kingdom of Aragon. This matter was especially virulent in the Jewish *calls*, for several reasons. First, the Jews spoke a Romance language, in this case Catalan, and, as such, were more accessible to preaching. Moreover, there were precedents of previous debates on the subject. Finally, the friars thought that, by manipulating the Talmud, they could break down the solidarity of the Jewish communities and attract many of them to conversion. The Jewish communities, without the status of a defeated people, were in the ascendance economically and socially, while the Muslims were in constant retreat.

In contrast, the relationship between the Christian population and *the Moors* was always more sharply defined. They were clearly identified by their appearance, and there was a military front line against them; they were the secular enemy of Christianity. This, however, was not the same relationship with the Sephardic Jews, for they could not always be easily identified.[168] They spoke Romance, there had never existed an armed confrontation between them, and as such, there was no military front. For the most orthodox factions of Christianity, they were the enemy inside, at times, undetectable, but very powerful and on the rise.

This was why, in addition to the charges of anti-Semitism and stereotypes, or the annoying restrictions imposed by civil and ecclesiastical decrees, the Jews of Catalonia-Aragon would have to fend for themselves in the face of a disorienting invasion of their most intimate psychological space and their most recondite autonomy.[169]

It is evident that the Jewish minority was comfortably installed within the Christian society of the kingdom of Aragon. During the reigns of James I the Conqueror and his son, Peter the Great, from 1208 to 1285, the kingdom enjoyed a period of imperial expansion that extended to Sicily, Sardinia, and as far east as Athens. The wealth of Aragonese Jewry attracted many emigrants and refugees from other places, bringing about a significant rise in population. Likewise, their influence at court also increased to the extent that it provoked a reaction among the Christian notables who, in 1283, sought to curtail their influence in the different levels of royal administration.[170]

It should be recalled that these were the times of the first Crusades, of intense anti-Semitism in Christian Europe, with the subsequent consequence, as we have seen, of the expulsion of the Jews from England in 1290.[171] This situation would give rise to a Jewish public philosophy adapted above all to the flourishing urban society that was becoming more powerful.

Within this climate of prosperity and the firm establishment of the Jews in the kingdom of Aragon, Nahmanides found in the prophets Isaiah and Jeremiah the basis for his grave warning to his fellow citizens in whom he saw—just as those prophets had seen—the downfall of Israel: "because of how in exile they have put all their thoughts into mundane interests, each one thinking only of himself, his family, and his own affairs."[172]

In the midst of all these contrasts and threats, it was not unusual for the Catalan commentators of the Talmud to try to assure the existence of their people. On the one hand, they tried to do it by cultivating a good relationship with the Christian kings who were becoming richer and more powerful and, on the other, by preserving their coreligionists from an excessive adaptation to a desperate exile without any idea of return or redemption.

For Ramban, the recovery of their land of origin is essential for the recovery of the true Israel. The importance that Nahmanides attaches to the original land of Israel and the need to recover it has earned him the title of a pioneer of Zionism.

In political terms, the entrance into the Gothic world brought with it a relegation of the rabbinical courts, those heirs of the ancient Sanhedrin, to a secondary status. It would also open the Jewish quarters to new forms of life. This would lead to a greater ritualistic and administrative tolerance, which, to a certain extent, implied the dismantling of the strict and, in part, obsolete rabbinical control over the conduct of their people. In this sense, the acceptance of the Gentile authorities and their administrative mechanisms not only implied a certain rejection of the power of the rabbis and the guardians of the orthodoxy of the Torah and the *halakhah*, but it also brought with it a bold commitment to the predominance of the executive, a specific characteristic of Ashkenazic political science. This would ultimately bring about the deterioration of good judgment.

The culmination of the executive for pragmatic reasons assuredly reinforced the rebellion against the power of the rabbis, just as the kabbalah did, in its own way. This blind enthusiasm for efficiency, charisma, and leadership that perhaps did not see the dangers of exalting an increasingly despotic and economically powerful executive, was precisely a factor that had always worried Maimonides and his colleagues in the south.

4

Kabbalah and Political Power

In the Sanctuary [of Jerusalem] there were windows broad within and narrow without.[1]

—Nahmanides

One of the problems in the transmission of knowledge is the difficulty of transmitting what one has acquired through experience. How can we pass on to another person a portion of our own life? Western pedagogical tradition has always tried to convert knowledge into digestible fragments through systems of the transmission of data or knowledge. Nevertheless, while all it takes is a trained mind to understand the content of a concept or evaluate a situation based on our desires and satisfactions, illusions, and pleasures, we still run up against the problem that its intensity and quality are unrepeatable. Although the world is inherently stable, eventuality speaks to us of the changeability of our lives.

Jewish mysticism presents special characteristics due to the fact that, in the Diaspora, it has always had to live embedded in other political regimes. Kabbalah (a word meaning "tradition")[2] appears as a Jewish school of mysticism that has hardly been studied until our time. In the nineteenth century, when romanticism stirred up historical interest in this spiritual tendency, prominent Jewish scholars "had little sympathy—to put it mildly—for kabbalah."[3]

As Gershom Scholem points out—and we shall follow his line of thought from here—it was uncomfortable for Jewish scholars who showed their "lack of adequate knowledge of the sources or the subjects on which in many cases they venture to pass judgment."[4] This led to the peculiar circumstances that Christian scholars were the ones who showed "a real insight into the world of kabbalism."[5] As a consequence of these doubts and ambivalence, the study of the subject was neglected, and "all manner of charlatans and dreamers came and treated it as their own property."[6]

The search for the *unio mystica* with God in order to know Him has been cultivated in Europe for centuries. Its existence is so ancient that St.

Thomas Aquinas called it *cognitio Dei experimentalis*, alluding to the form of knowledge where neither reason nor intellect directs the search for the proof and existence of God, but one's own personal living experiences, that is, those extreme feelings, capable of ecstasy, of escaping from one's being, in order to make the leap and bridge the abyss between man and his Creator.

Judaism and Omnipotence

Judaism has distinguished itself in the construction of Europe through its capacity to understand the strange omnipotence of the life of man, who, by contrast, is born destitute and with the genuine impotence of the baby. Its contribution to political theory consists of placing this omnipotence in the locus of power that is Yahveh and then projecting it far beyond, where omnipotence remains sealed off and inaccessible.

Eric Voegelin[7] very intelligently saw that this expulsion of omnipotence evolved through the idea of an alliance or covenant between God and Israel. It is a people that is alluded to as the chosen people, but in reality it is the only one who has recognized its God and to whom will be given the divine law. The Torah was given to Moses, its prophet and leader, in which its most eminent commentators would find at least 613 *mitsvot* (divine precepts). The Talmud, or scholarly commentary of the Torah and the precepts that Yahveh gave orally to the founders, contains the political and moral wisdom that articulates the life of the Jewish people.

The fact is that such omnipotence will not remain forever isolated in a world far off, for Christianity proclaims and acknowledges the coming of Christ as the Messiah who brought with him God's omnipotence.

When seen from the perspective of Jewish life, the return of that longed-for omnipotence that will rescue them from the painful limitation and vital impotence will only happen with the coming of the Messiah, the victorious leader and liberator. Jewish existence always has something of a hope and longing for the true Messiah who will set them free.

As we have seen in the previous chapter, the chessboard of Europe was clearly being dominated by Christianity. The Western world began to leave behind the bipolarity of two powerful empires, Islam and Christianity, and open its doors to the increasingly evident hegemony of the latter. The center of the political sphere had gravitated to Charlemagne's empire, with intervals when the papacy also migrated to Occitania.

Throughout the thirteenth century the hegemony of Christian politics and culture was reinforced, and by 1300 it had completely triumphed over Islam in the West. This does not mean that Islam lost its power entirely, but in the lands of Western Europe, Christianity had completely imposed its domination. The Christian advance and recolonization took place at such a pace that it was easy to foresee the definitive end with the expulsion of the last of the Muslim regimes in Europe. This, too, would bring with it a few decades later the decline of Sepharad: "The decline of Spanish Jewry that began in the middle of the fourteenth century became intensified with the anti-Jewish uprisings of 1391 that ravished the Jewish communities throughout Castile and Aragon. Many Jews perished at the hands of the rioters, and numerous others were baptized, either voluntarily or under duress."[8]

Sephardic Judaism would undergo a profound adaptation. The rabbis and congregations of the peninsula gradually began to understand that their future lay with the sign of the cross. In this sense we have seen the importance of the confrontation between two visions of the political and the moral: the one that lived in northern France, the territory between the Rhine and the Elbe, and part of Poland, and the other in Sepharad. The arrival of the Christian troops in Seville in 1248 may have seemed in its day the beginning of the end, the consolidation of an unstoppable military, religious, and cultural advance.

It is not strange, then, that the Jewish quarters of the cities of Sepharad began to plan for their adaptation to the new times. Thus the debate began in the meetings between the Ashkenazic and Sephardic rabbis from the twelfth century on with the emigration to the south. The Ashkenazim sought refuge from the anti-Semitic attacks in 1097 with the First Crusade,[9] intermittent outbreaks in France, and the continual assaults and slaughters in the Rhine. Eminent Ashkenazic rabbis sought asylum with their prosperous coreligionists and often occupied privileged positions in Sepharad. An example of this was the arrival in 1303 of Asher ben Yehiel (Rosh), who became rabbi of Toledo in 1305.

These meetings between figures of the two cultural environments gave rise to the cross-pollination mentioned in previous chapters. A professor at the University of Paris or a school master from Metz or Cologne could not communicate with the pupils of Averroes, but the rabbis of Córdoba and Erfurt could do so in Hebrew. Many exchanged ideas in personal meetings either because they came to study in Barcelona or because they took refuge in Toledo, but others did so by means of the *responsa*. Hundreds of these consultations were sent to the great rabbis of Sepharad, such as Solomon ibn Adret, asking for advice and orientation on legal, ritual, or moral matters.

A very visual case of this phenomenon occurred in the Hispano-Jewish emigration to North Africa beginning with the 1391 persecutions. According to the *responsa* of Rabbi Simon ben Zemah Duran, the Spaniards became integrated into Algerian Jewish communities with customs and legal traditions very different from their own. The Spaniards were used to a very democratic organization in the *aljamas*,[10] in contrast to the almost dictatorial authoritarianism that prevailed in the Algerian communities.[11] The local Jews took off their shoes in Muslim fashion before entering the synagogue because of the influence and by order of the local authorities,[12] and in many cases were governed by Muslim laws,[13] and even assimilated local superstitious customs.[14] The immigrants from the Iberian Peninsula introduced the figure of the rabbi dedicated solely to performing his duties as a rabbi, rather than having many professions such as teacher, ritual slaughterer, or merchant, which was very common in Algeria. The newcomers also introduced new taxes such as the *sisas*[15] and brought with them other pedagogical and legal practices.[16] This same exchange of ideas, practices, and customs also took place between Christians and Muslims that both religions absorbed as their own.

What would happen in the political life of the fifteenth century in Western Europe had already begun a century and a half earlier in the heart of the Ashkenazic and Sephardic communities. In the midst of upheavals and perils that threatened their very survival, these communities became involved in wide-reaching bellicose situations such as the Crusades and ruthless persecutions such as those provoked by the Black Death of 1348–1351, that forced them to flee from both Christian and Muslim territories. On the other hand, the evolution of the war provoked strong political and religious reactions in those lands of Hispaniae under Muslim domination. The changes in political regimes with the invasion of the Almoravids in 1086 and the Almohads in 1147 brought about harsh dogmatic reactions that had immediate consequences for the Jewish population that lived in those territories and resulted in their being forced to abandon their homes overnight.

This meant that they had to emigrate hastily to other lands. Many of them were very familiar with Arabic culture and ended up going to North Africa.[17] In most of those cases, however, their emigration did not stop there but continued on towards other Eastern lands and occasionally ended with the long-desired return to Jerusalem.

Jewish Contributions

The evolution of Jewish culture in medieval Spain made two great contributions to the West. The first is the philosophical and spiritual tradition inspired by the extraordinary level of Muslim philosophy in al-Andalus, whose high point is Maimonides' *Guide of the Perplexed.* This current spread throughout the Jewish world and made inroads into the education of the rest of the *aljamas* in the peninsula and Occitania. The other contribution is the kabbalah, which offers a different way of thought and a very different view of the world.

Both the height of the philosophical current and that of kabbalah correspond, in large measure, to a period in the Christian world that has been called the renaissance of the thirteenth century and that took root largely in the reign of Alfonso X the Wise (1221–1284) in León and Castile.

Kabbalistic tradition respects the Torah, but it looks for hidden meanings in it that will only become evident to those who acquire the necessary preparation.

The origins of kabbalah lay in the scholarly centers of Babylonia, Egypt, and southern Italy before arriving in the north of Spain. Once in Spain, they took root first in Catalonia, and in Gerona and Barcelona in particular, and later in Castile, around the cultural wealth of Toledo. The highest point in Castilian kabbalism, and perhaps in world Judaism, is the *Zohar* (*Sefer ha-Zohar), Book of Splendor*, by Moses de Leon: "the great medieval Jewish compendium of mysticism, myth, and esoteric teaching. It may be considered the highest expression of Jewish literary imagination in the Middle Ages."[18]

According to Moses de Leon, a text written in a rather crude form of old Aramaic—a fact that has led many scholars to assume that the original document never existed—was found in Palestine and is attributed to an ancient teacher. It is the very pretext, oddly enough, that Miguel de Cervantes uses to introduce his novel *Don Quixote.*[19]

The origin of kabbalistic studies seems to lie in a few brief texts from Provence,[20] but it was consolidated with the creation of the school of Gerona that centered around the figures of Rabbi Azriel (1160–1230)[21] and Nahmanides.[22] Both were pupils of Rabbi Isaac the Blind (1160–1235) of Provence,[23] who strongly urged his students not to divulge their knowledge to just anyone and to keep it hidden from the public. This prohibition was still enforced until recent times. Knowledge should be transmitted only from the teacher to a pupil who is especially trained and capable.

Strictly speaking, kabbalah is not actually a form of mysticism. Although Christian mysticism may have had some influence on the Aragonese kabbalah, the two tendencies are not assimilable. Kabbalah takes science into account; moreover, it believes that, with science, individuals can understand the universe in all its splendor. The kabbalists believe that the sciences are necessary to understand the Torah, although it should be remembered that the sciences are considered to be lower levels of knowledge. This lower knowledge of science is the vessel where a person can contain the light of celestial wisdom or kabbalah. The kabbalists prepare their students to receive the knowledge and intuitions necessary to understand life and the universe.

Far from centering on the objects to be captured, kabbalah is concerned with the capacity for *reception* of the person who wishes to understand life. The kabbalists believe that this desire stems from an erroneous assumption if it is posed as a decision of the government of the individual himself and not as something that goes beyond the executive potentials of the intellect, memory, and will. In short, the sciences are necessary for the revelation of wisdom. In effect, the *Zohar* poses the revelation of truth as something that will happen by natural means through the wisdom of science. Moreover, there is a necessary interrelationship between science and kabbalah. An example of this is Baruch Spinoza (1632–1677), whose kabbalistic training served as a platform for his research into the formulation of a new methodology of mathematics and geometry. In sum, *the sciences are necessary in order to gain access to kabbalah.*

Contrary to what might seem a schism in Jewish thought, kabbalistic literature does not imply a reaction against philosophical orientation. In Spain, kabbalah, to a certain extent, is intertwined with the school of philosophy and *halakhah.* Nahmanides illustrates this point because he was an exceptional teacher of kabbalah and, at the same time, a scholar of Maimonides and strict commentarist of the Talmud. He was also a very well respected rabbi and a serious leader of the entire Jewish community of Aragon. In short, he was a person who was very aware of his political reality. Kabbalists and philosophers are, in reality, both anchored to the sacred texts, and their personal and public lives are completely given over to the interpretation of the Law and how it was transmitted to its people.

It is not surprising that some thought that even the *Guide of the Perplexed* contained concealed meanings far beyond the enormous wealth of wisdom that can help everyone. The kabbalist Abraham Abulafia[24] held that Maimonides' *Guide* concealed a web of secrets that the author never revealed to his pupil, Rabbi Samuel ibn Tibbon.[25]

Kabbalah undoubtedly contributed its exceptional airs of interpretive and imaginative freedom to breaking up the control of *halakhah* by the fundamentalist rabbis. The kabbalists benefited from the exceptional opening of the world of Hispaniae while absorbing, at the same time, a considerable amount of humanistic knowledge brought by rabbis from other lands.

As we have said, kabbalah became strongly rooted in Gerona and later reached its height in Castile with Moses de Leon and the *Zohar.* This work arose within the great cultural sphere of Toledo and its magnificent work of cultural synthesis. The kabbalist movement speaks to us of the serious conflicts that were happening in Judaism as a result of a new public philosophy that was emerging in Europe. The case of Isaac Abravanel (1437–1508), a wealthy and illustrious Portuguese Jew,[26] is very significant. As a member of the court at Lisbon, he was influential in the highest levels of politics, but when his patron, Alfonso V of Portugal, died[27] he was obliged to flee to Castile because of intrigues over power. In Castile he was renowned for his financial and administrative abilities, in addition to being a great learned man within the Jewish community of Castile. Although he served again at the highest levels of administration at the court of the Catholic Rulers, Isabella and Ferdinand, he was obliged to leave Spain because of the expulsion decree in 1492. From there he went to Naples and eventually ended up in Venice, where his brother was a physician.

Abravanel was a true humanist and a well-known writer in this line.[28] He was an admirer of Cicero and Seneca and was familiar with translations of these writers in Catalonia, Portugal, and Castile. He was very much influenced by the works of Petrarch (1304–1374) and shared his conviction about the almost medicinal, healing properties of words (*medicamenta verborum*) in dealing with the illnesses of the mind (*animorum morbi*); and that, like mental illnesses, their remedies are also invisible.[29] He finds a great deal of sense in Petrarch's rhetorical orientation. For the Italian poet, a philosopher should not only seek the truth, but he should also be a kind of therapist of the mind, or, in the literal Catholic translation, a healer of souls (*medicus animorum*),[30] which is slightly equivocal, because what he attempts to translate has no translation.

Mystics and Heretics

Mystics are usually followers of a great and often monotheistic religion. The mystic tries to gain access to God through an existential abyss, which was established in these religions between man and the Divinity. The mystic naturally needs to have an intimate awareness of that abyss.

In pagan religions, the gods mingle with the people, and their "presence can be experienced without recourse to ecstatic meditation."[31] In monotheistic religions, there was a historic revelation that the faithful and their leaders have preserved as their own particular treasure, which they care for and administrate. But, for the mystic, this is merely a historical circumstance. The temerity of the mystic consists of searching for a direct alternative, no matter how difficult, of access to that Divinity that is in principle inaccessible. Nevertheless, if the mystic knows that the way is inaccessible to him, why does he even attempt it?

The Jewish mystic believes that his religious commitment to his people and their covenant with God, which he has assumed as a believer, is based on the fact that he has accepted it consciously as a governor of his own life. He has assumed it with knowledge: with the memory of the teachings of his childhood and a firm will. His ego, in other words, the chief governor of his life, has accepted that way, and has committed itself in the name of his entire being.

There are, however, other forces in a mystic's personal life beyond his vigilant conscience. Thus he tries to gain access to the Divinity, not through will, but through a search given over to waiting for something to come up on the other side that will give him an outlet that would otherwise be impossible. The conscious and labored way of the human being, which is guided by the *executive power* of will and memory and the *legislative power* of thought, does not reach these regions of the knowledge of God.

The mystic has made his moral commitments from the government of his own life, and he knows that the key to directing his religious life lies in divine law and, in general, in any revelation. But he hopes that this Divinity is accessible through other means which can be accessed in an unpremeditated way.

It goes without saying that, although all the mystics coincide in this approach, each mystical tendency will have its own peculiarities according to the religious faith in which it appears. In this sense: "Jewish mysticism . . . concentrates on the idea of the living God who manifests himself in the acts of Creation, Revelation, and Redemption. Pushed to its extreme, the mystical meditation on this idea gives birth to the conception of a sphere, a whole reality of divinity, which underlies the world of our sense-data and which is present and active in all that exists. This is the meaning of what the kabbalists call the *world of the 'Sefirot.'*"[32]

The mystics differentiate between a God that reveals himself through revelation, acts, miracles, creations, and magnificence, and another God who remains completely inaccessible, a *deus absconditus*.[33] That is why one cannot count on words or intellectual reasoning, the language of words that moves according to the rules of grammar and logic, to have access to that God.

The Spanish kabbalists referred to that God with lengthy paraphrases that, rather than determining a substance or being, evoked an ample space in which each person could place his feelings and diverse experiences and find his own way. If one thing is clear to the mystic, it is that his way to

God is unique, personal, and untransferable, The Spanish kabbalah alludes to the Divinity as Ein Sof or, as Isaac the Blind would say, "that which is infinite" and "that which is not conceivable by thinking."[34] An important step in kabbalah is its separation of a personal vision of God from the biblical sense of a God who frequently behaves with his followers like a father, governor, friend, or judge. In this case the believer evokes an imaginary anthropomorphic figure to convey the idea of God, even if it is just for practical matters or teaching purposes.

The kabbalist is concerned with reaching that hidden, withdrawn, and unknowable God who remains "in the depths of His nothingness."[35] This God cannot be visualized, depicted in images, analyzed, or understood. Naturally the kabbalist does have his own perception of a living God of the Torah, a God whom he will understand "from the mystic's own scale of moral values."[36]

The search for God as the source of all things prepares us to look for, in that "everything," all the evil that everyone sees in the world. The kabbalist has to face the fact that the absolute unity of God is a complex series of heavenly spheres and stages in the universe. From the contemplation of these *sefirot* or spheres, he hopes to perceive that infinite unity of the divine.

The God of the kabbalah must always be unique, given that Jewish mysticism can never deviate from its point of departure, the unity of almighty God as the Creator of all things. And in the center of all things lies always the *radical rejection of idolatry*. This is why the kabbalists do not distinguish between a creator God and one that shows himself in the continual process of becoming in the world. God is infinite without technical or theological foresight. In this sense, for the kabbalists, the inappropriateness of philosophy, grammar, or even creative philology is absolute.

Insomnia

The kabbalists approach the Divinity with their deepest experiences and starting from their emotional discoveries.

There are two central elements in this relation between man and God: fear and desire. The fear of God is a biblical element, and it is found at the center of Jewish tradition, but the kabbalists would transform it into an incessant factor, or in their own words, a "constant,"[37] which means that it functions continually twenty-four hours a day, every day of the week. The advantage of fear, as far as the moral schema is concerned, is that it does not need the permission of will to operate; it is transrational and therefore valid for both wakefulness and sleep.

Its moral companion is desire. The latter is also a factor adaptable to Gothic morality, given that it seems to have a dual origin: earthly desires based on the body and its necessities, and perverted desires (evil inclinations) that sprout from and operate disconnected from bodily functions. Those evildoers "have not been coerced by their evil inclinations; nor have they been seized and driven to sin by the working of earthly, physical desire. Their actions proceed from no other source than perversity of the heart."[38]

Desire and fear fight each other and sometimes clash precisely because of their proximity. Occasionally perverse desires cause men "to cast off the yoke of Heaven from their necks."[39] In this view of society, desire is the motivator of human action. It is a cause that works on every man without exception: "No one leaves the world having realized half of his desires. If he has one hundred, he desires two hundred. If he attains two hundred, he desires four hundred (Koheleth Rabat 1: 34), as it is written, 'He that loveth silver, shall not be satisfied with silver' (Eccles. 5:9)."[40]

The value of repentance, a purely executive action of man *in foro interno*, acquires its price according to the desires it confronts. As if it were a personal epic, repentance acquires its price in the world according to the actual power of the desire of the enemy it defeats. Thus, the most honorable repentance is the one achieved when one is young in the face of very strong desires: "When one becomes old and his inclination to evil is weak, he is not rewarded for repentance as for perfecting his heart in his youth."[41]

However, with age, our will loses its strength to resist and its ability to defend itself: "During old age, when one's senses lose their intensity, one cannot summon up enough strength to blaze new trails in his heart and to put forth thoughts with which to war against his evil inclination."[42]

In this all out war between desire and fear, the greatest incentive of will is undoubtedly the *fear of God*. This should be the *fons et origo* of all the strategies of human governance. *Fear by day and by night.* Human fear is oriented toward death, not because of what this natural act has in itself, but because death points to the soul's submission to God's judgment. In the Gothic view, death is a natural fact that is very devalued and leaves a bad taste if one plays around with it. The body loses its value as is seen as a mere shell or prison of the soul.[43] But the real terror is transferred to the judgment of the soul, and that is where the real death, the spiritual death lies: "One who does not constantly have the day of death in mind supposes that he has time and leisure to attain his ends."[44]

This is an absolute judgment[45] in which the qualities of a terrestrial judgment have become blurred. This is the first step in the public transfiguration of the judge into prosecutor.

In order for this fear to be more powerful and constant, the unpredictability of death, or what amounts to the same thing, the judgment of the soul, is emphasized. By staking everything on this one moment and not being able to predict when it will happen, man is perpetually equipped with a very powerful weapon with which to discourage one's own or others' desires. In fact, the fear of death is a human capacity that differentiates man from the beasts. Now what differentiates humans from the beasts is not the capacity of the *logos* as a specific human trait, but their constant fear of death and God's judgment. "There are those who are not impelled by the thought of death to lay up provisions for the way or to correct their deeds, and into whose heart the thought of their day of death does not enter until its arrival. They are likened to beasts, who are not aware of death until the day of slaughter."[46]

Fears are central to the public life of the Gothic world that was making inroads into Sepharad: "The reward for the *mitzvah* of fear is very great, in respect of many *mitzvot*, whose foundation it is."[47] Fear is a very useful ingredient in civic education.

Receptivity

A wise teacher passes on his approaches to the divine (*Atziluth*) to an exceptional pupil, one who is endowed with unusual receptivity in order to absorb this knowledge. As Nahmanides reminds us, "If one teaches the Torah to one's fellow man, Scripture accounts it to him as though he had begotten him."[48] Receptivity is fundamental for the kabbalists, given that true knowledge *remains outside of time and space*, and outside of all cognitive programming and technical objectivity. In the words of Rabbi Yose in the *Zohar*, the Highest only speaks to "those among you whose ears have been penetrated by spirit to listen, whose eyes are open to see, heart receptive to know!"[49]

The Jewish mystics, beginning with the Therapeutae in the time of Philo of Alexandria (20 BCE–c.50 CE), have always taken the Torah as their point of departure as their golden link with God. The Torah not only is the expression of the law of the Jewish people, but in itself is the expression of the divine. Just as the Greek icons are not only depictions of sacred images but are also themselves divine objects, the Torah in itself is "the living incarnation of the divine wisdom which eternally sends out new rays of light."[50] The Torah is alive, and as a divine work, it emits divine light. It is not merely an expression of the historical law of the Chosen People, but it is also "the cosmic law of the universe."[51] Scholem has expressed this masterfully: "Each configuration of letters in it, whether it makes sense in human speech or not, symbolizes some aspect of God's creative power which is active in the universe. And just as the thoughts of God, in contrast to those of man, are of infinite profundity, so no single interpretation of the Torah in human language is capable of taking in the whole of its meaning."[52]

This is why Nahmanides finds that the verses of the Torah "are in methodical arrangement,"[53] for that order is a sacred expression in itself, what the wisdom of the kabbalah relies on to find its hidden meaning.

With this evaluation of the Torah, the sacred scriptures contain within them much more than what their theological or philological study can give us. They are, in themselves, a living expression of the divine being. This is why the meaning that successive generations can find in them is far superior to their content as a mere text. When seen as an expression of divinity, these texts offer us extraordinary access to the spheres of Atziluth or proximity to the Ein Sof. What we find in them becomes more valuable that their original meaning although, as Scholem concludes: "Who knows what their original meaning was?"[54]

A paradox in the mysticism of the kabbalists is the need for expression, their urgent desire to express themselves even though they are aware of the incapacity of language to do so.

Is it possible for the individual to express his contact with the divine through words more or less worked through and freed from the usual servitude of language? How can one express in words the mystical knowledge that excludes language by its very nature?[55]

The kabbalists complain bitterly of the incapacity of language to express their experiences. Perhaps Scholem is mistaken when he believes that the kabbalists play around with words and "indulge in rhetoric."[56] The kabbalists have a background in Mediterranean humanism in which the expression of life begins with silence, as in a musical score.[57] It is not that the Sephardic kabbalists indulge in slightly sterile linguistic games because they feel themselves incapable of expressing what they *mean*. This interpretation—what we might call the veiled accusation of hysterics against the kabbalists—is unfair and, in the long run, denotes the lack of understanding of the northern commentator toward the meaning of Greco-Roman rhetoric.

It is too simple to sum up the problem of the kabbalists by saying that they are the first ones to recognize that it is inexpressible. And in the midst of it all there is a misunderstanding of rhetoric.

In his instruction manuals for meditation, the kabbalist Abraham Abulafia speaks of three superimposed planes: thought, writing, and articulation,[58] which brings to mind the three basic parts of rhetoric: *inventio*, *dispositio*, and *elocutio*. This is an understanding of the logos inherited from the Mediterranean rhetoric of Isocrates, Cicero, and Quintilian.

The kabbalists probably thought that what they wished to transmit, and what they had achieved in preverbal spheres, needed new ways of being told. In my opinion, more than one must have realized that language is not a game of presences of symbols and associations of agreed upon meanings; it is a gift of mankind that, starting from silence, enables pieces of life to be passed from one individual to another.

It is not strange, then, that they are proud of their "striking reserve"[59] in regard to their supreme experience, nor is it surprising to find their very positive evaluation of language as "God's own instrument."[60]

Peculiarities of Kabbalah

There are some aspects unique to the kabbalah that are not found in other mystical schools. For example, the kabbalah is a *school of men*; there are no women kabbalists.[61] This does not happen in Spanish mysticism, as is well known. Perhaps it has something to do with what the *Zohar* tells us: "Torah was given only to males . . . demonstrating the superiority of male over female."[62] Given the importance of divine unity in the kabbalah—it is enough to recall their hatred of the idolatry of the Christian Trinity—the kabbalists make a great effort to keep within that orthodox vision of the unity of God, without leaving any room for misinterpretation.

Divine unity is difficult to sustain for some mystics whose search for truth is based on the ecstatic experience of each individual. By definition, ecstasy implies a division of an individual's being; he literally goes out of himself in order to gain access to a way that is clear for the soul to reach God. The kabbalah was always aware of this problem of the dissociation of the individual as a way of opening up to new sensorial experiences of God's being. It can be a multiple experience, but the object of his search—the Shekinah or Divinity—is unique.

Nevertheless, Jewish mysticism cannot leave aside something that is the very heart of mystical life: the ecstatic experience as a way of entering into contact with divine reality in the depths of our soul. What happens is that the Jewish mystics are reluctant to tell of that experience in public. They do not resort to autobiographic confessions that are so typical of Christian mysticism. This fact is an obstacle to knowing the inner workings of the kabbalistic phenomenon. It is very rare that we find details of the personal life of the kabbalists and how they progressed in their journey that is, in itself, a biographical road.

Why do Christians express their confessions by giving an account of their mystical experience, their arrival at ecstasy and its discoveries? Is it perhaps a question of exhibitionism or a lack of modesty? In line with their morality, in Christianity it is a matter of an effort to find God. This work can in part be erudite, but in another way it is always experiential and can be attained by any individual. Christian mystics write their memoirs or confessions to give an account of a process of which they feel themselves to be personal authors, intimately responsible, and always in communication with God, and thanks to the mercy of his aid.

The kabbalist does not see it that way. To begin, he resorts to a new way as a part of the pious wisdom of rabbinical tradition. And he receives it first from a teacher who, in due time, will pass on his hidden knowledge. This knowledge will come to him "from mouth to ear"—or face to face as it is said in *Exodus*[63] and in other languages—handed down from the first sages who received those truths directly from God and later passed them on to their pupils on a *one-to-one basis*.

What the kabbalist will gradually find will be (1) the outcome of his work, (2) the results of the teachings that his teacher wished to transmit to him and that are the fruit of an intergenerational *choral labor*, and (3) the result of divine help, if this help sees fit to come about by means of that emanation, from which the prophets also benefited and, to a certain extent, suffered.

The result of this knowledge is not the fruit of a personal feat, a kind of epic poem of internal public spaces, as happens with mystics of other religions. On the contrary, what the kabbalists store up is an impersonal knowledge, and thus they are proud to present it and "glory in objective descriptions and are deeply averse to letting their own personalities intrude into the picture."[64]

This is a curious phenomenon in that the writings of the kabbalists concede a great deal of importance to language, and they have a brilliant narrative style. It is not a matter of their being unable to express a complex experience, but of a firm and uncompromising decision not to involve personal experiences and, more specifically, biographies in explaining their findings.

The protagonism of the individual is incompatible with the perception of a God that is unique, absolute, and almighty. It is as if this protagonism exacerbated beyond the experience of the average mortal were looked upon with suspicion as a manifestation of idolatry or one's own omnipotence. Or perhaps it is an attempt by the kabbalah to remove human measure from the understanding of life and refer it all to great cosmological forces.

In sum, very few of the known kabbalists have left us autobiographical writings. One of the few exceptions has been the recovery of the personal correspondence of a few of them. Where it exists, it allows us to recompose their biographies parallel to the evolution of their kabbalistic writings.[65] In the case of Spain, the most outstanding example is that of Abraham Abulafia.[66]

As we have mentioned above, the kabbalists also have a very special perception of language. For them, it is not merely an instrument to express themselves. It is not a matter of joining together a group of signs that are simply conventional.

Language and its use in Revelation are, in themselves, divine objects, a part of that Divinity, and therefore have a "mystical value."[67] They are words that emanate from God, they are the word of God, but in a literal sense, as we mentioned in the case of the icons. They are not representations of the word of God; *they are the word of God*, and for that reason their exegesis is only applicable to the Hebrew language, not to translations. An Englishman may believe that the King James version of the Bible is the word of God, but for a kabbalist, this is erroneous. The word of God is God's own word. Because it emanated that way from him, it contains a great many meanings and an expressivity that is there before us: it is almost a direct contact with the divine. The arrangement of letters, its word play, its connections of all kinds are not casual. They are *divine* as a product of the Divinity. All creation is the expression of a hidden knowledge as is the language of God and its revelation.

This, then, is the origin of the kabbalists' enthusiasm for the concept of truth that is central to their efforts and study. Kabbalah is a knowledge of truth. When Nahmanides alludes to the kabbalah, he always uses a somewhat mysterious expression: "by means of the truth."[68] Simon ben Zemah Duran is also an admirer of that "Wisdom of Truth."[69] Language will always be the object of great respect for them because it is the means God used for Revelation. Through the exclusive use of Hebrew, we have been left with a unique product emanated as a part of that Divinity with which it tries to connect.

The kabbalists, and the mystics in general, seek contact with the divine. Their communication is direct and very powerful. The individual achieves this without taking control of the process and, although his search may be voluntary, his effort is reduced to cultivating and opening human receptivity as much as possible. The kabbalists have faith in their perseverance to produce what the Greeks call *kairos*, an opportunity that can be granted to us. Just as the alchemist spends many hours with his preparations waiting for the transmutation of the ingredients, the kabbalist prepares himself with knowledge so that his receptivity can take advantage of the opportunity when it comes. Like the prophet, he must be prepared and be wise, so that if intuition comes to him, he will be able to develop it.

The Search for Truth

As we saw at the beginning of this chapter, kabbalah literally means "tradition," in the sense of received tradition. Scholem was right when he saw a certain initial contradiction between kabbalah and mysticism. On the one hand, the mystic seeks an intimate and personal contact with God, while what characterizes kabbalah is precisely its choral sense of knowledge, ethnocultural and impersonal.

However, the understanding of the divine as something preverbal does not mean that it necessarily has to be inaccessible. I believe this can lead to a misunderstanding. The experts in the texts and kabbalistic works start from those writings as the obvious object of their investigations. Nevertheless, this is only acceptable if these writings are understood as musical scores in which *the primary matrix of the expression is silence*, which acts as a support for the sounds and the written notes.

The kabbalists' search for access to the divine, as given in the revelation to the Jewish people, always implies the participation of hermeneutics and incorporates much of the rhetorical understanding of life. The kabbalists had always denied the bad influences of the Greeks, with Aristotle at their head. But, in spite of themselves, they understood that in the leap to understanding or contact with the Divinity and his attributes, it is indispensable to rely on preverbal aspects such as the value of silence or the capacity of imagination, an *imaginative faculty*, "that increases through habitual contact and grows with the growth of the child."[70] This is the same faculty that Maimonides refers to in his writings and is similar to the *inventio* of the rhetoricians.

Even the *Zohar* presents its knowledge in the setting of a peripatetic school, with a group of friends who converse and walk while others teach peacefully, enjoying the fresh air in the country in a mild and sunny climate.[71]

On this point it must be said that rhetoric is a public tradition in the Mediterranean that reached young Sephardic men who were more or less aware of its significance. They were aware of the writings of the Greek philosophers, historians, geographers, and physicians, but they probably knew very little of the tradition of the very oral understanding of life that takes into account the feelings, emotions, and passions that arise from the contingency of the Latin *temperies*. In order for these experiences to be understood, they must be imbued in a human being, man, woman, or child, with their body and soul, the human being that moves about in the courtyards and alleyways of the city. It is a civic world in which all those matters and mechanisms function in their true entity.

The kabbalist's knowledge, then, is not a product of a personal epic but rather a part of knowledge always close to the "original stock of knowledge common to all mankind."[72] The kabbalists did not consider themselves outside rabbinical tradition. Moreover, some of the great kabbalists were noted commentators of the Talmud or prestigious authorities on the tradition of *halakhah*, such as Nahmanides and Ibn Adret.[73]

By no means did they feel they were outside the tradition of Jewish scholars, but rather their successors. Many mystics must have seen themselves as successors of the teachers in the rabbinical tradition. This is why, at the end of the thirteenth century, Rabbi Moses of Burgos was angry when he heard the people praising the philosophers, and he scolded them, saying: "You ought to know that these philosophers whose wisdom you are praising, end where we begin."[74] Aside from revealing the popularity and affection the works of the philosophers were for many and how irritating they were to others, the incident expresses something very typical of the kabbalah: that its knowledge is, in part, complementary to that of rabbinical wisdom. This is why the kabbalah can be understood as a tradition that will never be far from the root of Jewish wisdom.

I do not think it is fair to see kabbalah as a knowledge that arose as a reaction against the defense of the propagation of philosophical ideas. Scholem was correct when he pointed out the close connection between the kabbalists and Judah Halevi. He was one of the most Jewish of philosophers, and the mystics are "the legitimate trustees of his spiritual heritage."[75]

It does not seem appropriate to understand the kabbalah as a desperate outlet to stem the advance of the rationality and scientific knowledge of Revelation and existence, much less as a result of the weakening of the Jewish people and expression of its decadence.

In reality the kabbalah was not a false or easy outlet for the problems of public life created by the opposition to the Jewish people. On the contrary, it was probably a torturous and anguishing outlet.

Perhaps we should direct our understanding to the rise of the movement in the thirteenth century in Sepharad, a borderland that, like all frontiers, was open to new trends and advances in the development of language and culture. This happened precisely at a moment of drastic change in political equilibrium. The Christian world was advancing headlong toward hegemony in Sepharad. Moreover, a new vision of the public, of politics and the government of the life of its citizens, came along with it. Sometimes the Jewish communities joined together in fear during political difficulties: "We have seen the weakness of the communities and that each acting alone cannot achieve what is essential for it to succeed in sustaining itself. If the communities will not help one another to heal the sick of their wounds, then we fear that we shall become defenseless."[76]

If we understand political science as the art of government, including the governance of each one of us, there is no doubt that in the thirteenth century the *aljamas* and the *calls jueus* of Sepharad faced transcendental changes in their view of the world. A new public philosophy appeared, and with it, a remodelling of the life of the Jewish communities. The Christian understanding of life, with its consolidation of leadership, efficiency, and understanding of *knowledge as power* introduces its view of *life as war*. Meanwhile, in the external forum, the battlefields, trade routes, current laws, constitutional order, the organization of institutions, fusion of fiefdoms and noble families under the figure of the Crown, and the reinforcement of the metaphysical idea of the territorial homeland are establishing themselves unopposed and in the Gothic manner. This is a new world that will impose its hegemony and absolute validity. Thus the Jewish faith becomes a hindrance that merits a drastic treatment in order for the normal order to be restored. At most, it would be tolerated as an anomaly that, in any case, would have to be dealt with politically and, in time, administratively.

In this situation perhaps the kabbalah is, as we have pointed out above, a compensation for the adaptation of the *juderías* to a very regimented and secure power and to an authority that, through its imperial connections and territorial security, would become ever more unquestionable and present. This controlling power would soon discover the value of knowledge as a powerful weapon to conquer, sell, colonize, and organize Christian supremacy in the West. The idea that "knowledge is power," coined by Francis Bacon in the sixteenth century, merely expresses more precisely a reality that has existed since the fourteenth century. The thirteen century, then, saw this accelerated transition head toward the new public philosophy that is going to articulate Western Europe. It is a type of politics based on the unity of faith and the articulation of a State morality: *cujus regio, eius religio*. The religion of a territory becomes a matter for the one who governs it.

An essential and distinctive point in the Jewish religion and its faith is the belief that the world did not exist eternally but was created by God from nothingness: "[T]he world was brought forth from nothingness."[77] Obviously this nothingness is a difficult idea to explain. To a certain extent, this *Nothingness* is easy to understand if it is included in the idea of a Divine Creator, given the fact that, if creation began with God and the world arose from nothingness, both concepts are disconcertingly similar.

The Arabic philosophers also spoke of "creation *a nihilo*, where by 'nothing' they meant the One beyond being and attributes."[78] This God is incomprehensible and ineffable.

The kabbalists attribute to the educated scholars with access to philosophical tradition the fact that they have not known how to integrate in a harmonious way the legal Jewish tradition with *aggadah*, that is, the elaborations in the form of illustrations, stories, or legends, properly speaking, that have been passed on from father to son, and in which much of the wisdom given by Yahveh to his people has been preserved.

The philosophers feel uneasy with these legends that they treat as something out of their sphere of investigation; it is a material that does not concern them, even if they had been trained and brought up in an atmosphere where these contents had molded the consciences of individuals. Scholem believes that the philosophers had failed to synthesize those two pillars of Jewish life.[79]

The kabbalists felt that when the philosophers attempt to explain historically the reason for being of the *mitsvot*, the religious commandments, they are illustrative, but they do not encourage young men to practice the religious life. They do not move men profoundly to the point of promoting an identification with Israel and what it means when it comes to living. The kabbalists understand the precepts as something inserted in the vicinity of the divine, something like cosmic precepts beyond what they can indicate as guides of the life and government of the people of Israel and the government of each individual. The kabbalah sees in these precepts part of divine emanation, but it also sees them as a part of that Divinity in which to delve deeper and connect with the great truth of God.

For the kabbalists, the traditions and popular legends have great value. It is not a question of lesser wisdom or simple interpretations that have a cultural and rather functional value. On the contrary, they are a very direct expression of a genuine Jewish world: "The whole of *aggadah* can in a way be regarded as a popular mythology of the Jewish universe."[80] What happens is that the kabbalists will read it on a cosmic horizon with popular mythological depth on a large scale.

Aggadah, the legend, and its *aggadot*, the expressive narratives and stories of Jewish life in depth, are very much linked to a popular wisdom that reads its daily life imaginatively in the light of its revelation and takes from it those stories as their own cultural and moral treasure. They are the expression of the most profound everyday wisdom.

The kabbalists read these stories as if they were a compelling treasure that expresses very deep realities. These legends are elaborated on by the Jewish people and implied by Revelation, which gives them their intrinsic value.

These sources of revelation are similar to the *intellectual agens* of the commentaries of Themistius and other authors on Aristotle's *De Anima*. This is an intelligence that emanates from the One and our minds participate in. Thus "the universe is rational and knowable because the same cosmic mind that determines its order (the laws of nature) illumines human intelligence."[81] It is curious that, in this Neoplatonic version of that actor, we are dealing with an "Agent Intellect [that] is separate, pure, and impassive, and it thinks incessantly."[82] In other words, an agent that never sleeps, without any lethargy whatsoever.

The kabbalists do not extract the *aggadot* from their everyday life, moreover, they receive them and use them with great respect. They live very narrow lives, more and more limited to the life of their *cahal* or Jewish quarter, within a disciplined Judaism administratively locked into Christian society.

Sephardic kabbalism is, therefore, a counterweight, a magnificent compensation for a world that is becoming ever more disciplined and given over to a public view of life in which leadership, efficiency, and the existential vigilant clarity will bring order to the ambiguity of Sephardic lethargic tradition.

The kabbalists are never ashamed of the *aggadot* or of any earlier *aggadah*. They don't think of rejecting them because they do not look to them for logical coherence, mental discipline, or historical connections. To a certain extent they see them as an expression of those internal public spaces of Judaism over which the Aristotelian principle of identity has no control. Here no one demands any type of order, coherence, or systematization from them. In this space one can say anything and its opposite, be in two places at once, or simply allude to things that may never have existed.

This acceptance and estimation of *aggadah* has, therefore, more value than can be assigned to it a priori. The kabbalists withdraw into this wisdom, the true way to truth because they hold that the other way—the road taken by the rabbis and experts on *halakhah*—is not sufficient. It is, to say the least, incomplete. Following this line of reasoning, it wouldn't take much to admit that the kabbalistic investigations into the divine and the truth of the life of the Jewish people in the world created by Yahveh are relevant today.

What happens is that this magnificent withdrawal is based in part on a rather dangerous renunciation. The acceptance of a new vision of the public and refusal to protect contingency in the daily life of the *calls* and *aljamas* creates a vacuum within the civic responsibility of the Jewish communities. The way is open to a more turbulent world because of this retreat from those public spaces where the quality of everyday good judgment was guaranteed by its wise interventions of reputable men based on the Torah. It is open to a city given over to a Gothic view of life, one that no longer has the measure of man and where contingency gives way to inherency.

With the appearance of the Christian Gothic kingdom and the metaphysical stars that have come with it such as the homeland and the future State, rabbinical wisdom must confront a world of great forces and concepts larger than life. Now cosmological influences arise that give us an explanation of public life while, at the same time, doing away with the smallest interpretations, rooted in the courtyards and alleyways of neighborhoods. In this idea of the city, one does not look for grandeur through magical omnipotence. Rather, it can be found in the elevation of the human being through a wisdom worked out through the intellect, the simplest experiences, and the strongest passions. This vision of public life recovers something of the political rhetoric of Greece and the contribution of the Mediterranean lethargy of Jerusalem. It is a night that is rich in intelligent and intelligible content—non-Wagnerian—a world of the constant night, filled with great astrological influences and mysterious forces unattainable through human intelligence. In this sense, chapter 19 of *Don Quixote* offers us a magnificent reflection on the Gothic night and lethargy in the Sephardic tradition.[83]

This new world is governed by its dependence on God's constant creativity, in other words, His leadership,[84] active, always up-to-date, and, instant by instant, perpetual. It is a divine dominion in which man is always immersed in an emergency situation. It is an idea that reaches its height with Calvin's expression: "[M]an should live as if he had a knife at his throat."[85]

In this sense, the world of Maimonides is smaller, and in certain ways, it is also much larger. The intuition that leads him to dismantle the magical and omnipotent roots of astrology is interesting. This was a daring step for his time, given the attraction that it had for many Jews. His position was very risky, given the fact that, in moral questions, rabbinical tradition showed a great consideration for astrology, while at the same time it looked for a way for the Jewish people to free themselves from the decisive role of the constellations.[86] Nahmanides himself did not hide his interest in palmistry.

As for the Islamic world, "astrology was widely accepted by intellectuals," and they even applied a "judicial astrology which assessed the astral influences on human destiny."[87]

As Langermann points out, "astrology is categorically rejected [by Maimonides] without any reservation."[88] Rambam's explanation for the inadequacy of astrology, the worship of the stars and magic is not just a whim. He delves deeply into the problem because he understands the dangers of finding this fast and direct way of obtaining things. Today as well as yesterday we would call this "the omnipotent solution" that is constantly being offered to the individual. Omnipotence can be found in the despotism of passions, compulsive sex, pleasures dissociated from the growth of the soul and body, and lack of moderation in inquiring into the truth of life. Idel rightly called him "the most anti-magical thinker in Judaism."[89]

Maimonides' pages on circumcision are both interesting and exemplary. Some of his detractors think that they are directed against man's natural inclinations. The truth is that, in order to understand them, it is necessary to return to the Talmudic idea of the circumcision of the heart. This action does not devalue or diminish man's strength or demonize pleasure. It does, however, avoid the temptation of turning to the great central themes of life—passion, fear, faith, and prophecy—in order to look for the rapid road that characterizes omnipotent solutions. Rambam criticized this type of behavior that wants to leave man's intrinsic helplessness behind in a terrifying way by going to the other extreme and embracing omnipotence.

Some kabbalistic schools *equate knowledge with power*. This was something that Maimonides opposed outright and thought of as an intolerable barrier for the adaptation of Jewish life to the demands of the sovereign Christian kingdoms of Western Europe. This is a point scholars do not usually think about.

The kabbalists happened on the idea of finding a way to manipulate celestial forces for man's benefit by looking into esoteric wisdom[90] and did so with an increasingly blatant practicality. In their reaction against the great Cordoban teacher, whom they considered a real obstacle to their modern drift, they went so far as to look for reasons for the kabbalah in Aristotelian philosophy itself. Some turned to a commentary of Abraham ibn Ezra, the twelfth-century philosopher: "Know that when the 'part' knows the All [*kol*], it conjoins with the All, and through the All it creates signs and wonders."[91] By means of fusion with the Active Intellect, the door would be opened for "the human to know the natural order and manipulate it."[92] Nahmanides himself refers to "*the statutes of the heavens*"[93] and recalls that Rabbi Simon said, "There is not a single kind of herb that does not have a constellation in heaven which smites it and says to it, 'Grow' . . . [because] all planets have their foundations in higher [forces]."[94]

Likewise, each nation has its corresponding constellation.[95] This knowledge implies prohibitions, such as mixing seeds improperly because it would alter the forces of nature, but it would also allow a transforming intervention.

The possibility of this fusive power leads directly to the belief that "humans can know how nature works and they can intervene or manipulate natural processes by virtue of the spiritual power they possess."[96] These are clearly Gothic powers that open their eyes to the possibility of the existence of "thieves of the minds of other men,"[97] something that Jonah Gerondi thinks he has already read in the Torah. This leads directly to what Ibn Ezra thought, that if a prophet can work miracles, then why can't the kabbalist do the same?[98] On this point Tirosh-Samuelson sums up the kabbalists' point of view very well:

> Moses was able to overcome the Egyptian magicians, because he was a superior astrologer. His intellectual perfection included the knowledge of astrology, culminating in the conjunction between his intellect and the Active Intellect. He was a practicing magician who correctly understood the causal link between earthly and celestial powers. The knowledge of astrology enables the intellectually perfect to extricate themselves from an astral causality. Moreover, the uniqueness of the people of Israel is explained by its ability to transcend the impact of astral causality through mastery of the astrological sciences. Most importantly, the commandments themselves function as tools in the manipulation of astral forces. The commandments either manifest the influence of a given celestial body or are given as techniques to draw spiritual energy from the celestial spheres in the corporeal world. In this regard the commandments mitigate the destructive forces of the corporeal world that are regulated by the celestial bodies. Observance of the commandments thus has an instrumental value, for the more consistently one performs them, the more one can extricate oneself from the impact of the stars.[99]

Eventually the influence of Gothic Christianity will be revealed behind this intellectual attitude. The convictions of the kabbalists lead to a collective idea of omnipotence that now becomes incorporated into a collective subject that looks similar to the Christian idea of homeland. The fact that some of the teachers of kabbalah have been seen as pre-Zionists is not merely coincidental: "The primary purpose of the commandments is not the betterment of human social order as the philosophers held, but the restoration of the imbalance within the Godhead. This metaphysical imbalance is manifested historically in the exile of the Jewish people and their subordination to the Gentiles. Therefore, when Israel performs the commandments correctly, linking each one to the sefirotic world, Israel could correct the imbalance in the life of the individual, the community, the cosmos, and the Godhead."[100]

It is not surprising that the romantic historians were the ones who connected straight away with this idea of the kabbalists. Romanticism, with its inner *motus* of the search for the final solution, was extremely sensitive to this aspect of the kabbalah, which turns up often and for some has gone unnoticed.

Prayer and Evil

It is odd that the kabbalists were the first mystics to compose prayers addressed to God. In contrast to the intellectuals or scholars, the mystics have always gone beyond ritual and have personalized it. They transformed it into a way of communicating with God and orienting behavior toward the Divinity.

The kabbalah has been very intense in this sense, and this is why the authors of the first prayers of a mystical type arose in Provence and Catalonia,[101] taking into account that the kingdom of Aragon extended as far as the Rhone, the natural border between the Aragonese dominion of Montpellier and Provence.

Prayer is a way of relating to the Divinity that adopts an oral form that is almost conversational or narrative. This assumes that *God has a language,* and he understands us. Obviously there is always the possibility that he may or may not answer our prayers, either with a sign or a change in circumstances in our lives.

Kabbalah is a phenomenon oriented toward contingency, in which it wants to intervene to help govern the individual and the world. There is always an element of rebellion in the kabbalist against a world that dissatisfies him. Thus he undertakes a more profound and ambitious search to help him fit more easily into life once he has achieved a more direct relationship with it and has overcome an unsatisfactory everyday reality.

An important characteristic of kabbalah is its acceptance of evil as an integral part of the world and an important presence in our lives. We accept evil because our feelings put up with it every day, which means that we put up with it in our inner self. The kabbalist does not aspire, as in Socratism, to a world of knowledge that can pulverize evil, but he simply accepts the fact that evil will always be around. The knowledge of evil cannot be reduced to dismantling and destroying it, if possible. The kabbalist confronts it as something mundane through whose experience we can learn and free ourselves. As Leo Strauss would say, "vice emancipates us more than virtue."[102]

Evil appears naturally in popular wisdom, for it has its origin in daily life. It is also reflected and assimilated in folklore. The kabbalah leaves itself open to the experience of evil as a way of delving into the most hidden part of the world, something that is a considerably important pursuit for evil. This is how kabbalah basically approaches popular wisdom, which it hardly ever scorns, even in its most violently magical, escapist, or mythical aspects. In the sordid and the occult, in that sea of fantasies uncontrolled by the intellect, and in the popular delirium of the multitude, the kabbalist finds the mythical expression of very profound truths, albeit in a very distorted way.

Thanks to that public attitude, kabbalah has always been close to the Jewish people in their search for the living God, the one we experience daily in our sorrow and happiness, but it also runs the risk of losing itself in the labyrinth of popular mythology.[103] The kabbalah has always managed to maintain a certain enthusiasm among simple people and a notoriously close connection with the anxieties of the common man; but, at the same time, by emphasizing the experiential, the personal aspect of our contingency that is intransferable and unrepeatable, it has seriously dedicated itself to destroying the objectivity necessary for the intellectual transmission of knowledge.

The kabbalah does have recourse to abstraction. In spite of their search for firsthand experiences, the kabbalists' quest for the Divinity will escape from humanistic control and advocate a cosmological understanding of life and what goes on in the world. In this view, the forces are gigantic, greater than anything measured by man. Thus it is perfectly clear that a comprehension of divine acts does not allow for any type of conversion to a human scale.

It is not unusual, therefore, for the vision of God the Creator in the medieval Ashkenazic mystical stories to be enormous and of an obvious and inconsequential unreality. Some Ashkenazi scholars, including Scholem, the most unique and outstanding of them, are so perplexed by such dimensions and depictions that, no matter how hard they try, they cannot find any rational explanations for the phenomenon. As for the Sephardic sensibility, this dislocation of the human dimensions by which the Sephardim were accustomed to relating to the vortex of mundane acts and perceptions caused them to become disoriented. The youth of the south feel lost; they are offended by this mystical Ashkenazic strategy—what we have called the Gothic world—in which the human element is directly annulled and broken down. This will give way to another view of the public sphere and the world in general. The way is open for another confrontation of those young men whose lives will no longer have recourse to the Mediterranean humanistic rhetoric of their ancestors. They can no longer use the measure of man as the regulator and assimilator of the many demands that are being made on their very existence.

The Penitence of the Body

An example of all this is the appearance of exaggerated penitence as a form of paying compensation to God and the Divinity for our sins. The Latin tradition of the German Rhineland, as the heart of Ashkenazic Jewry, introduced a very violent and antihumanist element: the injury and migration of the most contingent part of our lives, our own body. The disdain for the contingent as opposed to the inherent of our existence (the soul) is reflected in the assumption of some brutal and contemptuous practices of our small humanity. It is illogical and insane for the penitent to see the need to pay for an immense guilt with such a limited and worthless frame in spiritual terms as our own body.

The Celts and Franks absorbed these practices with their mystical and hyperbolic visions full of gigantic obscure forces and recorded them in the penitential books of the Christian Church. The result was a depreciation and humiliation of the body as a means of paying for the errors committed against that world of giants in which the soul was moving about. Guilt encourages persecution.[104]

This point merits a few comments. The concept of guilt is obviously a theoretical-political one. "Guilt" is a term that comes from the language of the law courts, from one of the three rhetorical pillars of politics. Moreover, its treatment here is clearly omnipotent. The intervention of redemption from guilt by means of penitential suffering results in two extremes: (1) it turns the body into a public instrument with which this improper conduct can be annulled; (2) it also allows for complete control of the individual over those judgments in which the individual came out badly in the first place—he turned out to be "guilty," or in today's popular idolizing language, he was "blamed" for or "accused" of something.

The advantage of penitence is that we as private persons can set our own punishment and thus avoid action by the civic courts. In other words, we can privatize those judgments very skilfully and reduce them to a question of personal morality.

If we have been blamed or accused of a guilty act, we can propose our own personal penitential technique, for which there are even manuals available on the market, and thus succeed in neutralizing and dissolving the guilt. If the offence is a small one, it will be enough to offer some embarrassing prayers, fasting, and some little punishments for the body and its comfort; if the offence is more serious, it could involve whiplashes, unhealthy practices that might even bring on chronic illness or mutilation; and if the guilt is very great, it can bring about voluntary exile, with the uprooting of our body from its usual habitat or, in an even more drastic measure, suicide, understood as the ultimate removal or exile of our life.

The extermination of the soul is to be avoided at all costs. This in itself is a healthy objective, albeit at the cost of the deterioration and denigration of man's body and its integrity. All these acts, such as sleeping on a bed of fleas, putting one's feet or hands in icy water until they are frozen, flagellation until the body is inflamed, exposing one's body to the bite of insects, and even the most benevolent ones hide behind them a truly despotic attitude. The "spirit of fanatical earnestness which animated the zealots,"[105] in the words of learned Ashkenazi sympathizers, is seen from the point of view of political theory as an example of tyranny over an *in-fant* part of man's life, the human body that cannot *say*, or speak for itself, in the rhetorical sense of the word.

The control of judgment in the city, therefore, is reduced to a private practice that is dependent on our red memory and our own will. In reality, it is a form of omnipotence. I believe that this is the key to understanding many of the aspirations of the kabbalists and mystics. Omnipotence is behind those attitudes with which any judgment in the city—whether it comes from our teachers, neighbors, friends, or lovers—can be appealed and sent to a private court. This private court is precisely the one that guarantees everything, including annulment, in an exact, mechanical, and regimented way. For political theory, this approach is equivalent to a spurious and hidden return of omnipotence to our lives. This is difficult to defend in Jewish tradition. This is why the kabbalah will have to make an effort and bend over backwards to get rid of this danger.[106]

If seen from a political perspective, these practices come close to idolatry. But they are presented in such a subtle and sophisticated way, with so many popular allies and abilities of their own, that it is not easy to unmask them. Nahmanides' rejection of idolatry is very sincere, and he applies it to all the commandments of life: "'Ye shall make you no idols.' Scripture is speaking with reference to this person [mentioned above] who sold himself to an idolater, that he should not say, 'Since my master is immoral, I too will be dissolute; since my master does not observe the Sabbath, I will also profane the Sabbath.' Scripture therefore states, '*Ye shall make you no idols . . . Ye shall keep My Sabbaths and reverence My Sanctuary.*'"[107]

Nahmanides and his Gerona colleagues accepted the Ashkenazic public view that came down from the Latinized Frank and Celtic world, the Ostrogothic world, loaded with exorbitant mystical visions. This was very alien to their life in the south, more educated and developed, more comfortable and peaceful, more open to science and knowledge. But they would have to accommodate themselves to that world that was triumphantly victorious. They were educated in part by absorbing the influences of a Talmud read by way of the Tosefta, particularly in matters of piety and ritual.[108] And in opposition to the south with its great sages, a south in imperial and military decline, they must openly pact with the feudal lords and Hispanic monarchs, so they did. But their withdrawal into kabbalah, the glorious peak and surge of the Sephardic kabbalah in the thirteenth century, can probably be understood as a magnificent compensation, as we have seen above.

We are not dealing with a necessity brought on by the desperation introduced by the Crusades and the malicious anti-Semitism of the Christians. The Ashkenazim never wanted to recognize this maliciousness (*malum signum*), for deep down they were afraid of it. Their suffering, however, is not the fertile soil for such a rich and brilliant development as the *Zohar*. Moreover, the kabbalah always preserves an element of Mediterranean rhetoric. The very dialogue in the open air where the *Zohar* takes place would be unthinkable in the Rhenish or Polish world. It is more sensible to think of the kabbalah as the phenomenon of a rich and prosperous world that was obliged to reconvert its height and evolution in view of the new circumstances.

This society welcomed and protected the frightened Askenazi refugees who were fleeing from a very violent world, where the Christian wars pushed on toward the east in the hope of extending their might for thousands of miles. The Ashkenazim brought with them great novelties that would alter the life of the political sphere. They would change the experience of the city, and the *good judgment* of the Latin *temperies* would be eradicated. Soon the simplicity of the teaching that sought not only knowledge but also peace, where knowledge is not identified with power, would no longer have any meaning.

The Classical Period of Kabbalism

This is the period between the end of the thirteenth and beginning of the fourteenth centuries.[109] The kabbalists were always looking for a way of entering into contact with the hidden God in the hope that he would reveal himself as God the Creator. Logically this did not involve waiting for the miracle to come but rather a constant preparation of receptivity. This receptivity could be increased by a more pious and moral life, as well as by a progress in theological and scientific knowledge, but above all by a personal preparation that, with its own techniques, would prepare the individual for his opening up to a more profound reality.

The kabbalists were not in favor of cultivating outlandish or demented behavior. Nevertheless, mysticism has always been described by its most rebellious aspects, which might lead us to think that all the kabbalists were looked down upon or at least observed with mistrust by the guardians of *halakhah* or traditional wisdom. This is not the case. As we have pointed out before, some of the most prominent kabbalists such as Moses Nahmanides, and Solomon ibn Adret, teacher and pupil respectively, were also respected as outstanding rabbinical authorities.

In the light of what we now know today, we can say that the normal education of a kabbalist was that of a rabbi or, at least, a man familiar with rabbinical tradition. In Sepharad the thirteenth-century kabbalists were familiar with the teachers of the south and in particular, the work of the great rabbi Maimonides. Nahmanides and Ibn Adret had been educated in the wake of those teachings and maintained a high level of knowledge largely thanks to the teachings of Rambam. In the thirteenth century, however, the winds were clearly blowing in the other direction thanks to the way events were unfolding, the arrival of the Tosefta, and the Gothic vision of the city and the kingdom.

Throughout the thirteenth century it became difficult to maintain the orientation of good judgment—very humanistic, to a certain extent—that had been implanted and cultivated by the teachers of the south while the basic requirements of Christian politics were making inroads into its territory. Nahmanides opted for the imported version, which, as we have seen, he compensated for with his kabbalism, although at the end of his life he clashed with those very powers he had tried to accommodate. He had accepted their vision of the public, which included accepting the idea of monarchy and the feeling for a homeland that had begun to weigh on the consciences of Christian countries. His brother collaborated closely with King James I as an important civil administrator of finances, and he himself was the most respected rabbi in the kingdom of Aragon. Because of his close proximity to power, he must have been very conscious of how the Jewish people should behave in a world that was rapidly leaning toward the Christian vision of the public sphere.

To a certain extent it must not have taken much for him to adapt to the situation, since he had already distinguished himself as a rabbi who was open to the Tosafist Talmudic ways of the north. Perhaps he felt like a leader for having received from his cousin, Rabbi Jonah Gerondi, the knowledge he had learned from the rabbis of Paris and northern France.[110]

Strangely enough, Nahmanides would be humiliated by the ecclesiastic and political authorities, the pope and the king of Aragon, and obligated to go into perpetual exile from his beloved Catalonia as a consequence of the Barcelona Disputation of 1263. It was as if he were dealt a bad hand because he opted for secularization and for that new and more modern way of seeing the life of the city as a community, an approach to public life that carried along with it a very idiosyncratic legality. This view was the legacy of the Franks and Ostrogoths, with their bellicose notion of life, their view of law as a result of their communal, migratory way of life, their exaltation of the elective monarchy and, by extension, a charismatic and executive political leadership.

These northern political elements had little to do with the tradition of Sepharad, where the *aljamas* had collaborated with Islam against the Visigothic monarchs. Upon their Christianization, the Visigothic authorities had carried out very severe anti-Jewish policies. These warlike nomadic monarchies exacted a heavy price for reinforcing a dogmatic Christianity in the service of a uniform political identity.

The thirteenth century was a long way off from the initial origins of these peoples; now the imperial worlds that are taking shape are quite different. A part of Occitania is the sister of Catalonia and, although it sympathizes with the Sephardic tradition, it is open to the influence of the Tosafists. However, the world of the south showed worrying signs of an excessive assimilation of the Jewish population due to its prosperity. The very prominent role of the southern Jews allowed them to posses weapons, occupy public office, hold military posts, and own property. This was a world that worried Asher ben Yehiel upon his arrival in Toledo from northern lands. One part of Sephardic Jewry must have been very unnerved by this significant incrustation of Ashkenazic rabbis in the rich cities of the south. The assimilation of young Jews into a brilliant and comfortable society must have caused a good deal of distrust in that Golden Age of Judaism (900–1300).[111] The philosophy and cultural advances of the teachers of al-Andalus, who were undoubtedly a source of pride for all Jews, began to be a serious source of concern as one more example of that excessive assimilation. While it was admirable in itself, it threatened to undermine the identity and loyalty of a Jewish people that had wandered about Europe for centuries. Assimilation would be the silent death of Judaism. The danger lay in falling into the trap of the wealth and tolerance of the emirate of

Córdoba or its *taifa* kingdoms.[112] The violent reaction of the Almoravids to the loss of Toledo[113] in 1085 must have confirmed the ideas of more than one rabbi, as in the case of the School of Gerona, who looked upon the excessive identification of the *aljamas* with a wealthy and plentiful regime that was not theirs as reckless indiscretion.

Only if we look at it in this context can we understand why prominent sages, learned and educated in philosophy, law, astronomy, medicine,[114] and political science, men of proven common sense and known for their discretion, turned against the philosophy they had admired and now looked toward the north. They were wary of the trap that some Jewish leaders saw in the philosophical school because they believed that ultimately it would cause young Jews to lose their faith and push them toward assimilation into a society in which—they should never forget—they were living only temporarily.

This self-protecting reaction, while not opposed to advancing knowledge, would reach its high point with the decree of Ibn Adret. As the rabbi of Barcelona and an internationally known eminence, he prohibited access to the books of the philosophers, including those of Maimonides, by students up to thirty years old. Ibn Adret did not consider the books to be bad or evil; on the contrary, he valued them very highly for their exceptional worth. This is why he permitted the medical students and other adults to read them. If he had thought they contained something bad, the students would not have been allowed to read them. Although they were good books, the general public could not be allowed access to them because it was in danger of taking refuge in the fantasy that the Diaspora had ended.

The Jewish leaders of the pro-Ashkenazi band began to size up the extent of the seduction of a Sepharad full of enchanting attractions. They were also frightened of the extraordinary advance of the Christian Church with its aggressive campaigns of Christianization. These campaigns were based on two fundamental points: (1) to show that Christ was the long-awaited Messiah and that Judaism, which had performed a historical service of incalculable value, was no longer necessary and should be dissolved; (2) to undertake campaigns to enlist people in the ranks of Christianity by advertising the fiscal, commercial, and social advantages of conversion. This is the way the prestige of the social figure of the *converso*, the Jewish convert, will be enhanced. The *converso* is a good citizen, open to progress, and a person whose great social value will open the doors for him to respect and social prestige. The very efficient and aggressive campaigns of the Franciscans and Dominicans reached into the heart of the Jewish quarters where they preached in the synagogues. The pope took special care to single out those young converts who dared to make the leap but in reality were actually Jewish apostates. They took new names, Christian names not tainted by the Jewish question, and began their way to the most important posts in administration, teaching, and the church.

The Crusades preached in France and England during the eleventh and twelfth centuries fortified the efforts of the preachers, and, in view of the success of the friars, the Jews responsible for the communities of Catalonia convinced themselves that it was necessary to reaffirm rabbinical tradition and reinforce popular identity. Moreover, they mobilized traditional customs, strengthened rituals, and protected orthodoxy, to the detriment of those open and educated views of the humanist teachers who were one step away from living together with the secularization of knowledge. Later on, in 1309, Pope Clement V moved the papal court to Avignon in Provence, a territory belonging to the kingdom of Naples.

This was a time to extol the customs of the Jewish people, their simplest beliefs, and their folklore as important elements to firm up their religious and public identity. The Catalan rabbis tried to keep up a *halakhic* tradition refined with the use of the *responsa* as a way of strengthening their own tradition and opened their arms to that type of religiosity that gathered up the expression of the faith of its elders. There was no need for more scrutiny or self-criticism in a world in which Christian dogmatism was so effective on a military plane.

Unfortunately this doctrinal and political movement did not save Nahmanides from exile. He must have been torn apart by his love for a peaceful constructive tradition, typical of a world filled with knowledge and wealth. This tradition stood in opposition to a much more convulsive one that was given over to the values of new metaphysical entities such as homeland, a territorial king, and Christian universality so alien to the Jewish people. He undoubtedly found compensation in his kabbalism, but it must have been very sad for him to live in his own flesh that Christian wave that would carry him away without his knowing why and, what was even more anguishing, without being able to anticipate what was coming behind the eye of the hurricane that was blowing from Burgundy.

Solomon ibn Adret, Nahmanides' favorite pupil, would continue a policy of adjustment and strengthening of Jewish identity along with an adaptation to the Christian world. Although he did end his days in Barcelona, the city of his birth, he must have seen some of the symptoms of the great devastation of 1391, when the Catalan Jewish communities would be massively struck down. Until then, these attacks had occurred only occasionally, but now they would be carried out on a large scale and with a vehemence that speaks of the changing times. Who knows what would have happened if there had been another type of Jewish leadership? What is true, however, is that the Sephardim felt that it was necessary to accept the Christian public way of life. This explains the important role of the egalitarian masses, inflamed by the new metaphysical concepts of homeland, a new tool of the Christian monarchy consecrated in the Reformation as an omnipotent engineering apparatus, and the European franchise of the State, which has been so successful until now. The results of this adjustment by the Sephardim would have poor results for some and disastrous consequences for others.

This sudden historical change is often confused with the modernization and secularization of Western Europe. It is assumed that the ideas it brought with it contributed to a more efficient political administration, the separation of politics and theology, and the secularization of university and government. Obviously these ideas contributed to advances in man's rationalization.

The contrast between different types of Christians is usually given as proof of this historical change. First, there are the sober, well-trained administrators of the secularized sovereigns such as Ferdinand the Catholic or the princes à la Machiavelli and, second, the dogmatic inquisitorial rulers, clinging to the old identification of church and society. In sum, the result of this historic struggle ended with the two protagonists of the European civil war of the seventeenth century: the Habsburgs, with their dogmatic centralism and reactionary morality, and the new independent secular nations, open to the progress of a science liberated from dogma and to the expansion of Atlantic commerce.

Nevertheless, this may not be the proper approach to the problem. There was another alternative, particularly if we allow ourselves to go beyond the exclusive Christianity of Europe outlined above.

The Design of the Vigilant Society

In the thirteenth century southern Europe still preserved a rhetorical tradition, which implied a politics open to its inhabitants and to the contingency of life. It was a public vision of life where good judgment had not yet been undermined by the threat from or surrender to the executive. It was the model for a city that might well have tried to block the militarization of life that would soon bring with it the blueprint for a vigilant society.

Wherever the executive and military elements overran that society, they destroyed important components of European society that were against dogmatism but in favor of the advancement of the sciences, including political science. This is the same public vision that we find in Quintilian, Maimonides, the Republican humanism of Italy, and the great later works that resisted with all their strength that unstoppable advance of the vigilant society. This view was present at that time and did not represent any of the reactionary or dogmatic sectors of society. The fact that Arabic was the host language of many of the Jewish thinkers caused the works of these authors to be destroyed in part with the military defeat of the Muslims in the West. Nevertheless, there were incidents where the rabbis were able to protect that vision as a more advanced and peaceful way of viewing the life of the Jewish people. Thus the admirable reaction of the Jewish congregations of Provence who had opposed the campaign against Maimonides' work in the first great attempt to suppress it under the pretext of saying that the *Guide* went against the faith or was harmful to Israel. It is worth noting that the rabbis of Provence, who were on the borderline between Tosefta and Sepharad, were the staunch defenders of its popular value.

Nahmanides concedes a great deal of importance to the need for leadership; in other words, "men who are capable of leading a great multitude of people."[115] They must be "Men of *chayil*."[116] "Each assembly or gathering is called *chayil*, and it does not only apply to soldiers who are going off to war."[117] He also clarifies that *chayil* can also mean wealth, power, and many resources. Ramban also transfers the figure of the leader to executive spheres, referring to the administration of the kingdom. His perception of the authority figure underlines his vigilant qualities: intelligence, capacity for staying alert, and honesty. Justice is beginning to be understood as another public service, a function that must be administrated correctly with adequate techniques and competent officials: "Thus an *ish chayil* in the administration of justice is one who is wise, alert, and fair; in war, an *ish chayil* is one who is strong, alert, and who knows the art of arraying forces in battle. A woman is also an *eisheth chayil* (a woman of valor) when she is alert and knows how to conduct the management of a home."[118]

Setting himself apart from rhetorical tradition, Nahmanides sees the function of judgment as a public task linked to leadership. In this way good judgment vanishes with the rise of the efficient executive: "Jethro[119] . . . told Moses to select people with powers of leadership in the administration of justice for this great people . . . [T]hey should fear God, be men of truth, and hate unjust gain, for it is impossible for them to be 'men of *chayil*' in judgment without these qualities."[120]

Good judgment vanished in the Gothic world that came in through Gerona. Magic has always had a direct connection with omnipotence, with the tumultuous desire to obtain our objectives automatically. Thus it introduces us into a world of springs and automatisms in which there are only two positions: total success or frustration. This is an environment where "the magician's dream of power and lordship over nature by mere words and strained intention" imposes itself on the moral and public sphere.[121]

The Notion of Authority

In the tradition of Sephardic Jewry there are three ways of understanding public life, and the world in general: the Talmudic, philosophical, and kabbalistic.

Until the thirteenth century most Jews were governed by the guidelines set down by the commentators of the Talmud and Torah. Often they were rabbis who had devoted many years to deciphering the content of the divine precepts (*mitsvot*), both those expressed directly in the Torah and the oral commentaries compiled later on.

Although Jewish communities were dispersed throughout the world, they preserved their identity and unity and maintained contact with the rest of the people of Israel through this rabbinical tradition. The reason for this was the institution of the *responsa* and the appearance of nonlocal authorities who were consulted on widely diverse subjects in all the Jewish congregations.

The philosophical tradition arose in the wake of the Greek language fostered in Alexandria, Constantinople, and the Mediterranean cities where this culture had been preserved. It was also continued in the *aljamas* of Islam, where this knowledge was transmitted in Arabic. The rise of the Umayyad emirate in Córdoba (756–1031) and its political power contributed to the emergence of an important center for the diffusion of Mediterranean philosophy based on the teachings of the Greek schools.[122]

Finally, there is the position of the mystics. While this tendency been very much alive throughout this period, the appearance of the kabbalah became more specifically rooted in Provence, in the kingdom of Aragon, and in the thirteenth century in Castile. As we have seen, the objective of the kabbalist's religious experience is contact with the Divinity.[123]

For the Talmud scholar, the idea of God is that of a legislator and father who guides his people through the teachings given in the Torah. By means of his revealed precepts, the Un-Nameable educates man through his primary attributes: justice and mercy.

As Henoch points out, the Jewish philosopher conceives of God as the ultimate foundation, wisdom, and source of every being in a world in which he is the Active Intellect and Creator of All Things.[124]

The kabbalist does not accept a dualistic vision of a God that is (1) the source of wisdom and mercy and at the same time is (2) a strict and inaccessible legislator. Confronted with this dialectical separation, the kabbalist looks for an alternative way of knowing. This method consists of gaining access to the knowledge of God through a contemplative and intuitive effort that goes beyond the logical and moral capacity of the individual and, as such, differs from the Talmudist and philosophical ways of knowing Him.

The kabbalists always work with the idea that the soul and thought are united and cannot be separated by analytical or logical procedures. The two are inextricably entwined, which calls to mind the rhetorical stance of Aristotelianism concerning the complementary union of dialectics and rhetoric as inseparable elements.[125] Thought can never rid itself of intimate feelings, or of the contingency of life and, if it were to do so, it would be at the cost of losing certain abilities. This is unacceptable if one is prepared to inquire into the highest levels and accept the most profound challenges.

The source of the Divinity is the ultimate goal of the kabbalist's inquiry into the nature of God. The principal object of his search is the Ein Sof, the limitless, that which cannot be grasped. The Ein Sof is hidden and cannot be reached by thought because it is unthinkable. It is beyond description. It is not revealed directly in the Torah or in its *mitsvot* (precepts).

A second aspect of the divine source is the ten emanations of Atziluth, the proximity of the divine, an intermediate sphere between what is hidden and what has been revealed of the Divinity. This Atziluth emanates from the divine source of Nothing, the sphere of Kether (Highest Crown), which is sometimes identified by the kabbalists as the Ein Sof. Thus the idea emerges in the kabbalah of Nothing as the origin of all being.[126]

When the kabbalist decides to cross the divide that separates the Hidden God from the Revealed God, he will find that the limitless brightness of divine light comes with its own limitation. If it were not that way, it would cause immediate and absolute blindness. This limitation of divine light occurs in the realm of the sphere of emanation, or *sefirah*, of the Kether, and is the cause of darkness and void, which brings about the emanation of a second *sefirah*, wisdom (Hokhmah). From wisdom comes forth understanding (Binah), which completes the upper part, the head of Atziluth. From there on, the *sefirah* of understanding becomes the base for the emanation of the following seven spheres or *sefirot*: grace, power, beauty, victory, splendor, foundation, and kingdom. These seven *sefirot* are also known as the body or constitution of the divine Atziluth.[127]

The kabbalists know that it is impossible to gain direct access to "that which is inconceivable by thinking," the Ein Sof, or the primordial Nothing.

For this reason their efforts to approach the Divinity are centered on the *sefirot*, the powers or spheres that emanate from the Ein Sof. Their options consist in taking advantage of the mystical link of the soul with what is given in the world or as a part or direct reflection of the Divinity—an idea that vaguely recalls a kind of pantheism. Their aim is to provoke an intuitive approach to the Ein Sof by stirring up their capacity to activate those powers. At this point the kabbalists' task becomes unique.

The Talmudists study the Torah in order to extract the fundamental teachings for governing their lives, given that the Torah and the Talmudic commentaries contain the lessons they must follow in order to act wisely and piously. The philosophers, on the other hand, cultivate the study and the capacity of the human intellect to have a deeper and more accurate understanding of the revealed teachings.

The kabbalists, however, do no such thing. The kabbalist's action, no matter how individualistic it might seem, has a choral component that shows up in the effects he wishes to produce. Kabbalah attempts to activate the resplendent emanation of the Divinity in its manifestations in the higher spheres where the unthinkable, inaccessible, and the unimaginable Divinity is reflected. Its action seeks to *agitate the splendor of the world* by activating the powerful stimuli of those spheres or *sefirot*. Parallel to this action, it leads the individual, personally and intuitively, to be more receptive to that resplendent truth of the Ein Sof, as shown in its *sefirot* in the form of divine emanations.

If something characterizes the kabbalists, then, it is their dynamic vision of the world and human existence. For them, the Divinity reveals itself by way of its emanations. Its powers or spheres are susceptible to being stimulated from below, precisely by the creative power of the human soul in its intuitive search for that Divinity. There is a kind of "pattern of creative synchronization of two powerful stimuli,"[128] the spiritual agitation of the soul below and the reciprocal exacerbation of the divine sphere above. This possibility of exacerbation by the divine powers that eventually come into contact with intuition is the basis for the kabbalist's dynamic receptivity in his attempt to gain access to truth. In any event, this access to God can only be attained through His manifestations in the spheres emanating from the Divinity that make up Atziluth.

The importance of the intuitive soul is specific to the way of the kabbalists, for it is the protagonist of their extraordinary effort in the quest for the Divinity. This is what differentiates them radically from the Talmudic scholars. For the latter, the heuristic instrument is the analytic, disciplined, and observant mind; and for the philosophers, it is their attitude toward investigative research based in the logical observation and thought of the mind.

The kabbalist's soul plays very thoroughly with that intuitive soul that he never sees as separate from thought and in which he confides for his great crossing. It is not a matter of shutting one's self off from objective knowledge, but rather of understanding that human knowledge has a much more complex and deeper aspect to it. It has an inner core that cannot be explained away by practical or scientific simplifications, particularly when one is attempting to embark on a voyage that is so long and hazardous that the ship needs all the sails it has at its disposal.

To appreciate that mystical bond means accepting the idea that the soul is also a divine emanation, like the Torah, the *mitzvot*, and the world itself. Although the soul also has a connection with the Divinity, the Ein Sof, or the primordial and inaccessible Nothing, it is not an obvious connection. The leap cannot be made just like that. The connection is in the soul of the individual because it is a sacred part, an expression of the divine emanation. Therefore, if we let it play that intuitive part of divine origin, there is the hope that it can go farther, perhaps even to the divine itself.

It is not clear if the kabbalah dares to confirm that, thanks to that intuitive part, the individual succeeds in making that leap beyond. This affirmation would bring the kabbalist to the edge of heresy, for what characterizes Judaism—what is, in fact, its great contribution to the Western mind and its political life—is the eradication of the omnipotence of the world, the omnipotence deposited in God as the locus of power that remains sealed in the beyond and inaccessible to man. To try to gain access to this omnipotence would be very problematic for a Jewish thinker.

It should be said that the kabbalist considers his knowledge as an assault, or perhaps lets himself be assaulted, as an access that he cannot arrive at in a conscious and voluntary way. But we are not dealing with the kind of knowledge that will guarantee access to infinite power. Man cannot benefit from this access in terms of power because it is not a real public access. Rather, it touches divine truth in order to achieve the peace and pleasure of human surrender to a higher truth.

The kabbalist who arrives at this contact does not achieve it solely as a product of his work or efforts. It is not as if he discovers a treasure that he benefits from through the possession and ultimate administration of that wealth. His contact with the Divinity will only succeed in activating his individual nature. He is transmuted spiritually in order to better his human nature but without his being able to control the process at any time or control it for his benefit in terms of the *government of his own life.*

With such an extraordinary journey, in this aspect one can speak of the kabbalist the same as one speaks of a theoretician. The divine spheres that mediate between the primordial Nothing and the Jewish people are altered. We have to take into account that those *sefirot* operate upon the force and transforming capacity of the divine emanations. In sum, the action of the kabbalist can bring about a profound transformation of the world. Likewise, through the changes in the *sefirot* or emanations of the Divinity that mediate between the Jewish people and their God, there will be a transformation in the real life of individuals, in their living conditions, and in the existential possibilities.

Naturally all this refers to the Jewish people for whom this relation of intermediary with omnipotence is applicable. It would be a different matter if we were dealing with a world of idol worship of multiple gods mixed in with men. This would be an inconceivable political situation for which the abyss that the kabbalists assume exists between the Divinity and the individual makes no sense. This sealing off of the Almighty and the existential abyss only exists in the world of monotheism. This, then, is where the task of the kabbalah makes sense.

But if we add to this the Mediterranean vision of politics, that is, the art of governing the life of each one of us, what we would obtain would be a profound restatement of the concept of government. The kabbalists are wary of public engineering; instead, they confide in the renovation of our existential foundation. They are in favor of the change in the position of the individual in opposition to power, authority, and true knowledge.

There is in all this a very Sephardic instrument for transformation that is not based in the conscious, executive individual, in other words, the individual in a state of wakeful governance. Sephardic culture does not nourish that supremacy of the executive power of the wakeful individual, nor does it give itself over to the powers of magic or daydreaming. It is more in the line of Cervantes and his expression of life as the substance of dreams as told by men who are awake.

It is an attempt to transform society and existence, not only by the analytical, legalistic, or scholarly individual who uses an exclusive logic, but by someone who has these qualities and knows that there are more capacities that one cannot renounce.

They believe that the individual is something more than that. This is why it is not possible to destroy the link between the soul and thought without throwing man into a well of isolation and blindness, in other words, into a life without hope. Perhaps this is the origin of his insistence on revaluing popular wisdom, no matter how awkward or limited, or even erroneous, given that this essential link has never been cut off from them. The simple man may be clumsy or disoriented, but if he is pious and uses his simple popular wisdom, he can still maintain an indestructible capacity to embark on the journey to higher knowledge. Or, at least he does not close himself off from the possibility, unlike others who are perhaps more well versed in the subject but go off on more arid paths of uncertain destinations.

The kabbalists imply an anthropological criticism of Western power. While there is no outward evidence for this, their criticism of the philosophers is derived from the differences in their spiritual and pedagogical activity. Their disagreements with the rabbis are not so obvious, since they themselves are rabbis. Thus they try to get around the issue by living a dual life. On the one hand, they participate in local public life in which they accept the legalism and living together with Christian rationalism as a means for survival. Nevertheless, at the same time, they cultivate their own hermetic knowledge. They accept that *entente* according to the basic principle of the Talmud that guarantees first and foremost the existence of Israel, while at the same time they continue to devote themselves to the search for another world in which the truth they discover and its actions will transform the identity of all Israel. We could say that it is a question of the duality between (1) a local public life that defers to the host power under whom they live as if they were parasitic entities or a symbiotic colony and (2) the theory of public life of the greater Israel that lies at the bottom of this thought. As we have pointed out, it is not unusual that some of its most eminent followers were perhaps the most convinced figures in the forefront of Zionism.

For Nahmanides, the conquest of the land of Israel is a major issue. First off, it is a biblical mandate for every generation (*sefer Ha Mitzvot*). Moreover, there is the matter that the land of Israel has a sanctity inherent from the day of Creation that cannot be canceled or annuled.[129] Moreover, this position had its antecedents in Judah Halevi (Tudela 1070–Egypt 1141), who insisted on the importance of living in the land of Israel.[130]

There is only one reference and one aim in the kabbalists' task: the life of the people of Israel. Of course the kabbalah sees life as an individual task. As we have seen, however, this is also a choral effort with a few collective aims: the life of the people of God to which this action is applicable. In other words, a kabbalist like Nahmanides is guided by "the profound sense of responsibility for the physical and spiritual well-being of the Jewish community throughout his life."[131]

In relation to the society of the period, the action and political foundations of the Catalan kabbalah seem to suggest several points: (1) a broader view of the individual, (2) the negation of the vigilant man, (3) the closing of the way to Christian omnipotence, and (4) a different understanding of the possibilities of the people of God in their existence.

Loving and Knowing

A point of discord between Rambam and Ramban is the idea that in order to love God, one has to know Him, for the love of God is sustained by the knowledge of Him. Obviously, behind this understanding of the love of God lies the Socratic idea, and beyond that, the Mediterranean idea, that good attracts love. In other words, the good is beautiful and arouses the desire for one to understand and enjoy it. There is a profound connection between desire and the lasting moral goodness.

Maimonides pays attention to the emotions that sustain that love, which he compares with the love for his wife, whom he continues to think of night and day, and whom he loves with his heart and soul in the manner of the Song of Songs. For Rambam, the love of God is a matter for the mind. From here on we arrive at the conclusion that if we follow the *mitsvot*, the precepts, we do so to make public that love and seek to share it with other loved ones, friends, and coreligionists. In this vision, obedience and authority originate more from love than from fear.[132]

Nahmanides detaches himself from this idea of power and authority. He probably does not need to do so since he sees it from a more traditional and religious vantage point. The *mitsvot* that deal with the love of God do not need to be analyzed since it is not an intellectual matter or a matter of the knowledge of God's magnificence and goodness, but rather the total surrender to His love. It is an unconditional surrender by our whole being.[133] What then, is the meaning of all this?

Nahmanides refers to a continual willingness to give one's life over to our Creator. This means an intimate and perpetual will to surrender everything one has: life, property, heart, and soul. It reveals a total and perpetual dependence of the creature with respect to his Creator. Nahmanides cites Abraham as an example of this disposition.

Nahmanides does not admit the interpretation the love of God as the result of his knowledge, nor does he see love as the basis for human actions. On the contrary, he alludes to fear and distrust as motives for many acts and as an explanation for behavior transmitted by the Torah. An example of this is his controversy with Rashi[134] concerning the obligation not to humiliate or shame foreigners because they were not natives of Israel. Rashi reminded the Israelites that their ancestors had been foreigners in Egypt and because of this they should be aware of the suffering and insults that these people had endured and therefore should not be repeated. Rashi believes that the Talmudic exhortation not to oppress strangers comes from the reasoning and historical and cultural explanations of the past. Nahmanides, however, does not see it that way. For him, the reason for this admonition was much more pragmatic: the Israelites did not oppress foreigners simply because they were in the minority and did not have any allies to help them, and that was the end of it.[135]

Another point of disagreement between Maimonides and Nahmanides is the question of self-sacrifice, something that is important for Ramban and is associated with the idea of complete surrender. In Jewish tradition the idea of sacrifice had been relegated to the background after the destruction of the temple in Jerusalem and was treated very carefully by the exegetes. Nahmanides seems to be open to the possibility of self-sacrifice as a way of voluntarily accelerating or intensifying that surrender.

Nevertheless, there is an element here that contradicts his anthropological view of the believer. Is surrender something that can be done through will and ritual memory—in other words, through the executive power of our government—or is it something that corresponds to our entire being and goes beyond voluntary acceptance?

If we admit that self-sacrifice is possible in a voluntary form, or at least induced by the mind—perhaps by the legislative power of our internal government, that is, our thought—then the reply would be that Nahmanides moves about in a vigilant world. And this would take him farther away from the roots of Sephardic Judaism of which he is the protector to a certain extent.

Could it be that Nahmanides dangles between a Gothic vigilant vision, where moral intensifiers to foster the union of the individual with the authority are utilized, and a wider kabbalist approach where such a union is impossible by definition?

Before answering this question we should perhaps try to understand his ambiguity. Nahmanides presents himself as a defender of the entrance of those Ashkenazic novelties that he says he received from studying with his cousin Jonah Gerondi in northern France and Occitania. Nevertheless, it is also true that, as a Sephardic rabbi, he finds himself anchored in the lessons of his teachers, Ibn Ezra, Judah Halevi, and Maimonides.

We can understand his position if seen through the example of Abraham. This is the idea of surrender to God through a love based on the fusion of divine authority and the absolute acceptance of his power. It implies a fusion or total identification, something like erasing the outlines of one's own self,[136] in the face of his commandments or precepts. Curiously, some commentators interpret this as a demonstration of humility and the virtuous search for the knowledge of God. For others, however, the idea is not so clear, given that fusion is a passive strategy in the world of human relations; and with fusion, one can absorb or enjoy the virtues he admires of the source. Fusion always implies a high degree of disorientation, although we might think that, given the difference in the level between the omnipotent source and the creature who approaches it, there is nothing more than a sacrifice of love. We should not forget, however, that behind that kind of relationship there lies a certain type of omnipotent fusion that is passive and submissive.

If this is seen as a human aspect that comes with the surrender to and knowledge of God, if, with it, one wishes to express the component of omnipotent fusion, but elaborated on at the level of a more subtle and higher relationship that transcends it, then that is another question that we will continue to investigate throughout this work. But we should not forget that the negative aspect of omnipotence—its misfortune—is that beyond the satisfaction we receive from putting it into practice, in the long run, it makes us sterile: "The idolater is *void of counsel, he hath no counsel and no understanding*, but only walks after his idol and forever denies *the Glorious Name*."[137] In reality omnipotence amounts to the other side of the coin, which is helplessness.

If we study Nahmanides' approaches from the point of view of helplessness, we may find other things that will come to light. Perhaps we will see a pious attitude, an approach to religion that compensates in an exaggerated way for a position of real disempowerment. Once again we return to our idea of *magnificent compensation* that leads the kabbalah to a vulnerable political position and perhaps with no way out.

The Harmony of Creation

As a kabbalist, Nahmanides frequently touches on the musical concept of harmony. In this explanation, the act of creation takes on the significance of a harmonious transition in which the Divinity is present in the created world and manifests Itself within it. But with Adam's sin, this introduced a serious disruption of that harmony by altering the original design of the world. As seen through his kabbalistic system of symbols, Nahmanides studies in depth the idea of a lack of harmony in a world that was harmonious in its origins.

When Adam cut a divide between the plants in the Garden of Eden, he caused a considerable change in the created world. Moreover, with this act, he "disturbed the harmony in the divine world of Atziluth,"[138] or the closeness of the Divinity, since the Divinity itself is unthinkable and inaccessible by any means. Ramban's interpretation goes more deeply into this mystery:

> "The fruit of a beauteous tree"—this is the "fruit" linked to a lot of passion, and with it sinned Adam (Leviticus 23:40). Applied here, it means: This refers to the Tree of Knowledge above [*Atziluth*], because the *sefirah* of knowledge is Beauty, *Tiferet*, and "Tree" relates to Foundation, *Yesod*, and the "fruit" is the Assembly of Israel [Knesseth Ysrael]; the "fruit" is next to the Tree, and the Tree of Knowledge (manuscript Jerusalem 8:597, p. 128a). Therefore, by taking and eating of the forbidden "fruit" from the Tree of Knowledge . . . Adam disturbed the harmony in the Divine world of *Atziluth*.[139]

This harmony sometimes appears linked to an idea of correspondence between the upper world of the Divinity, the heavens, and the earthly world of creation or the Garden of Eden. Ramban tells us that "God created everything down here parallel to what is up there. So He created the Garden of Eden down here in the land, with all the configuration of the Garden of Eden of above."[140]

This provocative way of seeing the earthly Eden as a projection or duplicate of the heavenly Eden seems to be a version of the Western Platonic perception that the city we live in is also like that internal city that each one of us carries within him- or herself. This conviction would amount almost to the idea of dogma in the Republican expression that the city is man written *in extenso* (*man writ large* in the English Baroque version) or perhaps a little like the idea of that *foro interno* (inner public space) of the Latin rhetoricians that each one of us carries within himself. It is an inner world which is not limited to being a private space kept hidden from the curiosity of others.

Nahmanides explains all this to tell us that God did it that way so as not to leave the soul completely lost after its violent separation from the Divinity. The rupture of primordial harmony *dia-bolized*[141] the world because, during the time the world was being created, the Divinity inhabited the world and its manifestations. This meant that there was a harmonious presence of the Divinity that was still fused with His creatures.

This reasoning was taken up by Rabbi Joseph Gikatila,[142] of a generation younger than Nahmanides, when he refers to Adam's sin as a sin both of action and thought[143] that profoundly altered the harmony of the world. Before then, and during creation, divine energy flowed without obstacles from the Divinity to its creatures, a situation that was characterized by a total absence of walls and fences between God and his creation.[144]

There is an interesting consequence of this reasoning. Human acts can change the balance of the world here below and there above. Man's action can, therefore, exacerbate and alter very profound harmonies, which makes the kabbalists think that someday they will find that still unknown way of stirring up the *sefirot* of Atziluth. This is a hope that seems to be perpetuated in the *Zohar*.

5

The *Zohar*

Wherever gold is found, scoria goes unmentioned.[1]

—The *Zohar*

The *Zohar* (*Sefer ha-Zohar*), *Book of Splendor*, represents the highest point of inspiration within medieval Spanish kabbalah.[2] This book, with its unique structure, appeared in Castile at the end of the thirteenth century. From its very beginnings it appeared as a mysterious work because it was presented as an ancient text that its author says he had found on a journey to Palestine. As Gershom Scholem sums it up, it was a book "which was destined to overshadow all other documents of kabbalistic literature . . . and for a period of several centuries actually ranked with the Bible and the Talmud."[3] Its authorship is attributed to Shi' mon bar Yohai or Simeon ben Yohai, a venerable sage of antiquity who lived in the second century and wrote in Aramaic, the vernacular language of the Jewish people of that time.

The literary device of presenting a text as if it were of another author, usually a mysterious author or a renowned authority, is known as pseudo-epigraphy[4] and was fairly frequent among the kabbalists. It was a way of attracting the attention of readers. The Spanish world, of course, has the sublime example of *Don Quixote* (part 1, 1505).

According to the most knowledgeable experts, the real authorship of the text can be attributed to Moses de Leon, a scholar who resided in Guadalajara for a part of his life. De Leon was a member of a circle of Castilian kabbalists, among whom was his friend and fellow resident Todros Abulafia. In the *Zohar* he proves to be a brilliant writer. In addition, he wrote other works and hundreds of pages on Jewish topics consisting mainly of commentaries on the Torah. It is not difficult to see him as a man of broad culture and knowledge. As a young man he already had in his extensive library his own copy, surely costly to obtain, of Maimonides' *Guide of the Perplexed*.[5]

The *Zohar* is an extraordinarily imaginative work, and its influence in Judaism is universal. Its content is clearly kabbalistic,[6] but he is oriented toward a Castilian branch of its own[7] rather than following the line of Gerona kabbalism. In this respect, we should recall that the original school of Gerona was founded by the followers of Rabbi Isaac the Blind (1160–1235) from Provence. Around 1250 the Gerona-Barcelona kabbalistic school became the continuation of the earlier one. This school, headed by Nahmanides, with the help of his cousin Rabbi Jonah Gerondi, lasted for three generations but produced fewer literary works of note.[8]

Among the many interesting features of this extensive and irregular work is its narrative technique in the line of the *aggadah*. By means of its numerous twists and turns, the author gives proof of his creative freedom to express himself in a unique form through legends, narration, biblical commentary, or simply his own invention. His initial intention is to comment on the sacred texts as just another exegete, but his literary style "where possible avoids theoretical, let alone systematic disquisition; preference is given to homiletics."[9] He opts for the free narrative style, interweaving little stories with intriguing anecdotes, all of which are submerged in a wealth of details and superb descriptions. One of his abilities is to interpolate stories within a much larger framework. The book appears to be asystematic, but it flows along with a wealth of exceptional thought. As Scholem points out, the *Zohar* "does not so much develop an idea as it applies it in a homily."[10]

The book is composed of very diverse works collected in five, grouped in five volumes in which he narrates the wanderings and conversations "of Simeon ben Yohai and his companions (including his own son Eleazar) with whom he shares his mystical experiences and knowledge about divine subjects he had acquired from them."[11] The book also includes other insertions and additions that, in the case of the *Raya Mehemna* and the *Tikkunim*, are deliberate and inferior imitations of the real *Zohar.* [12]

The *Zohar* is presented in uniform, limited, and anachronistic language: "The Aramaic of the *Zohar* is a purely artificial affair, a literary language employed by a writer who obviously knew no other Aramaic than that of certain Jewish literary documents, and who fashioned his own style in accordance with definite subjective criteria."[13] Moses de Leon's Aramaic corresponds more to a version learned in texts that he probably consulted in his time and also shows traces of the Hebrew language of the thirteenth century.[14]

The Zoharic texts that have come down to us apparently include some forgeries or copies of little value. We will not go into the structure of the book here, but we will follow the thorough and knowledgeable exposition by Scholem.[15] We will, however, discuss in more detail the work in reference to the theoretical political evolution of the Jewish world. Our goal is to look for the significance that, in this sense, the kabbalistic school had in thirteenth-century Spain.

To begin, it is striking that De Leon was not a philologist, nor was he interested in the analytical philological technique so proper to Nahmanides. However, he could count on certain stylistic devices well-rooted in Spanish rhetorical culture. This is evident, for example, in his use of two opposing adjectives to express something entirely different. Thus, to call something "cooked and uncooked" can mean something "half-baked." As Scholem points out,[16] this technique appears in the Talmud, but here his imagination takes flight with a much more daring use:

> "It split and did not split its aura."[17]
> "which touched and did not touch this point"[18]
> "purities of Torah, impurities of Torah"[19]
> "*Darkness* does not shine unless it merges into *light*."[20]

To say that something is and is not means that it is being attributed to a spiritual entity that is difficult to describe with realistic words. His sublime and grandiloquent style encloses an extraordinary concretion, like those individuals who are good conversationalists and speak fluently but hide inside them an implacable observer of the external and the internal, a perceptive talent of the first order. What is true is that the *Zohar* succeeds in creating a "declamatory, pathetical, and sonorous" prose[21] that comes down to us from a tradition of life more oriented toward the ear and the oral and sounds this way to us:

> Which is the serpent that flies in the air and walks alone, and meanwhile an ant resting between its teeth has the enjoyment, beginning in community and ending in isolation? Which is the eagle whose nest is in the tree that does not exist? Which are his young that grow up, but not among the creatures, which were created in the place where they were not created? What are those which, when they ascend, descend, and when they descend, ascend, two which are one, and one which is three? Who is the beautiful girl on whom nobody has set his eyes, whose body is concealed and revealed, who goes out in the morning and hides in the day, who puts on the ornaments which are not there?[22]

Another aspect which brings to mind *Don Quixote* is the use of an imaginary landscape, the natural setting of a Palestine never visited by the author and in whose description there appear some mountains that "accord far better with the reality of Castile than with that of Galilee."[23] It is a kind of pseudo-realism in which detailed and rich descriptions do not attempt to describe specific situations in the external world. Nor is the *Zohar* concerned with chronological accuracy in fixing the times of its characters and the appearances. It is obvious that the author is not bound by the Aristotelian principle of identity and that he moves in a world where *vigilance* and *lethargy* come together to achieve an expressive capacity of the highest order.

Curiously, both in the *Zohar* and in *Don Quixote* a book is found by chance. Rabbi Yosef, one of the peripatetic friends and rabbis who participate in these dialogues, finds a book when he enters a cave, and "in its recesses he found a book wedged into the cleft of a rock . . . As soon as he opened it, he saw seventy-two engravings of letters originally transmitted to Adam."[24] Nevertheless, the atmosphere in which this happening occurs is very different from Cervantes' novel. In the *Zohar* everything occurs in the course of a conversation in which Rabbi Yosef and Rabbi Yehuda are walking like wandering nomads and when Rabbi Yosef recalls an enigmatic premonition by his father. In it, his father tells him in an almost magical vision about some flames that would touch off his memories, something that he says he knows because he has seen it and tells him of the omen of "these two birds passing over your head."[25] The scene is completely magical: memories loaded with symbolism, omens, unexpected sayings, surprising encounters, and in the background, the massive divine revelation, instantaneous and automatic. Rabbi Yosef enters a cave that just happens to be in the place they are wandering about. After a while he emerges from the cave: "He came out with it. As soon as he opened it, he saw the seventy-two engravings of letters originally transmitted to Adam, through which he discovered all the wisdom of holy supernal beings and of all those behind the millstones revolving behind the curtain[26] among supernal dazzling demons and everything destined to come about in the world—until the day when a cloud will arise in the West, darkening the world."[27]

Rabbi Yosef quickly calls Rabbi Yehuda, and they "began to study that book,"[28] which means in this pre-Gothic ambient that "they found themselves contemplating supernal wisdom. As they began penetrating the secrecy of the book."[29]

The literary incident reveals a technique similar to that of the *Quixote*, but its resolution and what these techniques initiate is very different in both cases. In *Don Quixote* the manuscript with the title "Novel of the

Man Who Was Curiously Impertinent"[30] is kept by the innkeeper in "an old travelling case, locked with a small chain."[31] It is found by the priest at the inn and taken out to be read slowly and listened to; from it will come forth a wonderfully human story, like an unusual piece of music. On the contrary, from Rabbi Yosef's book will come forth definitive and total visions with final explanations. The *Quixote* narrative will suggest evocations, down-to-earth and human-sized wisdom without any definitive solution. These are just suggestions, feelings, and facts of fiction very close to our lives. With them, those who are listening can nourish their good judgment. In the *Zohar*, Rabbi Yusef's book would vanish: "a flame of fire and a whirlwind burst forth, striking their hands, and it vanished from them."[32] The text manuscript of *Don Quixote* would remain lethargic among the men and women of the inn waiting for other hands that might want to open it.

One very interesting and revealing difference between *Don Quixote* and the Gothic world is the feeling of *enchantment.*[33] Don Quixote occasionally calls on the idea of bewitchment when he feels he is surrounded and wants to get out of a difficult situation. When he claims he is the victim of an enchantment, he is telling us that his enemies have used omnipotent mechanisms—magic—against him. Thus he alleges that he couldn't defend himself and was defeated by trickery. What Don Quixote is telling us is that his enemies used "borrowed" forces, powers that did not belong to them, since they took them from cosmological instances to defeat him or besiege him irresistibly. From his point of view, his enemies have a malevolent connection—we don't know with what dishonorable compensation—with those forces that they benefit from.

What is curious is that, in this way, those very malevolent forces that his adversaries have used against him are now used by him in his own self-defense. An omnipotent trick like bewitchment is mentioned in an almost ridiculous way, precisely to protect him from a situation of mental abuse. The key to all this is the mechanism—tenderness and humor—by which Don Quixote turns the situation around in his favor. In a gently humorous way we see how a defenseless person is attacked by others who are much more vigilant and take advantage of his daydreaming to besiege him and try to *steal his mind.*[34] A good example of this is the episode in which the priest, the barber, the niece, and the housekeeper burn Don Quixote's books in the corral and wall up his library, "the room of books,"[35] while the poor man is convalescing. When he wakes up and looks for his books, they convince him through an insidious lie and conspiracy that his library never existed. In other words, they implant in him, by means of violence, a conviction previously agreed upon and *force him to believe* that it never existed. In his helplessness, as is almost always the case of lethargy in the face of vigilance, Don Quixote resorts to the explanation of bewitchment, which works out in his favor.

Contrary to the world of Don Quixote, the enchanter is, for the Gothic world, the synonym of diviner. The Gothic universe automatically associates the enchanter with the diviner, as if they were almost the same thing. And it does so to reject both of them: "[T]here is no enchantment or divination in Israel."[36]

The enchanter or the diviner has direct connections with gigantic cosmological forces that reside outside the human-sized world. But Don Quixote puts those powers on his side, given that they serve as an explanation that calms him down and enables him to explain calmly a situation of perverse abuse. His real enemies, those who pass for his friends and benefactors, are the ones who organized the plot. They wove a conspiracy through lies in order to provoke his madness and crush his mental stability.

Thus Don Quixote himself becomes an *enchanter*, and the work he does in the course of his adventures gradually begins to enchant us, the readers. But the spell Don Quixote casts on us is the opposite of that of the snake charmer. He is not a diviner or sorcerer. What he explains to us with his conjecture over what happened, what he is completely convinced of even though we readers know it did not happen that way, reveals to us a deeper reality that will, in the long run, unmask his attackers.

With this rhetorical turnaround, the enchantment that wanted to harm him and made his beloved library—his noble and humane wisdom—disappears forever, has now been transformed into a proper gift; he himself is now an enchanter. Don Quixote is a tender and kindly character even if, with this change, his intelligent ingenuity leads us to a more cruel and intimate revelation, a less evident truth, in that the vigilant characters who interpret the scene cannot have access to that world.

This vision of life and intelligence is curiously akin to the one we find in Maimonides' *Guide of the Perplexed*, the same book that, as Leo Strauss so admirably saw, also charms us with its *enchantment*.[37] Both books are aimed at persons who have lived in a world that which has always wanted to convert them.

Another characteristic of the *Zohar* is its rejection of idolatry, which is obvious in a Jewish work, but also of astrology, a knowledge that is equally inadmissible. The book does not even accept some stray popular wisdom that might contain some sort of knowledge. Nahmanides, for example, did consider popular knowledge as valuable; De Leon follows Maimonides on this point by adhering to the southern rhetorical tradition, a fact that seems strange for someone who has read his Gerona predecessors.[38] His inquiry into the internal world and the depths of the Divinity does not cause him to reject the sensible rhetoric of the Mediterranean tradition with which Maimonides was imbued.[39]

The *Zohar* is a work in which its characters' dialogues are not orchestrated by one single conductor who controls and directs everything like a meticulous director in the theater. Figures appear and disappear like individuals endowed with a spontaneity beyond the control of the know-it-all teacher in perfect control of the scene as in Socratic dialogues. Here conversations are interwoven in a daring and dynamic form with stories inserted in the course of the dialogues that have nothing to do with the suffocating orchestration of the Socratic teacher. It is a more open and fractured dialogue in which whoever wishes to speak does so without need of having the director give him the cue to enter. However, these are peripatetic dialogues, with the characters in movement and in which their development and content are clearly in the orbit of the rhetorical *oratio* and far from the Latin *sermo*. This *sermo* would take hold in the Gothic world, and in the Sephardic world it found a worthy spokesman in Juan Luis Vives (1493–1540), the Valencian scholar and humanist.[40] This is one more similarity with *Don Quixote*, an exceptional bastion, like *Hamlet*—the Horatio character—of the rhetorical *orare*. The *Zohar* is a good example of how imagination and literary talent can go beyond the bounds of disciplined discourse and commentary subject to philology.

Far from trying to speak through the sacred texts, something typical of the Gothic Ashkenazic or Spanish scholars—in other words, the exegetes—De Leon delves freely into the sacred metaphors. He lets some of his own take off in flight, reworking those of the Talmud and reconstructing realities by means of repetitions and changes in rhythm worthy of a musical score. As Scholem has seen with great sensibility, De Leon "displays a sovereign contempt for the literal text, using it freely as plastic material for his own constructive purposes and giving free rein to his imagination."[41]

Nevertheless, it is obvious that Ashkenazic influence reached the *Zohar* by way of the *halakhah* of the north that was gradually imposing itself throughout the peninsula. We should not forget that the social penetration of *halakhah* was particularly deep because "in contrast with other political and legal systems that emphasize human rights and legal remedies, the Jewish *halakhah* is characterized by its emphasis upon human duties."[42] It was also pointed out that it also arrived by way of Rabbi Dan Ashkenazi, an occultist from Cologne.[43] The Tosefta (Addenda) that appears included as enigmatic revelations addressed to the traveling companions perhaps better illustrates this opening to the violently mysterious, like urgencies that demand submission to the mysteries revealed unexpectedly out of the blue.[44]

The People's Feelings

Within the lack of system of the *Zohar*, there can be seen in this work an intent to free oneself from well-versed knowledge and wisdom that is the product of intellectual study. However, its aim is to attain knowledge of the highest thing that is sought after by human curiosity: the Divinity.

Of course its point of reference is the scholarly teachers of al-Andalus who expressed themselves in Arabic and undertook the explanation of the political and spiritual world, a task that they carried out without renouncing the civic courage of the individual believer in man and God. This was a tradition that inherited the advanced knowledge of the Mediterranean. It was a vitality gathered up in the literature and science of Greece that had been reflected in the rhetorical experience of life.

This rhetoric was very close to Jewish tradition. Until the Mishnah,[45] in both the Jerusalem and the Babylonian versions, was written down, Jewish life was governed by a powerful oral, almost choral, tradition. It was transmitted and preserved from one generation to another by the rabbinical academies that studied and commentated customarily on this tradition that included a judicial part (*halakhah*) and another ingenious and inventive part (*aggadah*), with its histories and little clarifying narrations.

The downfall of Muslim Spain and the consolidation of monolithic Christianity in its Gothic version would unleash strong reactions against that so-called philosophic school of Jewish science. Christian predominance brought with it important changes. In the thirteenth century Christian power in the West grew and acquired its structure. Islam, the external enemy, was in retreat. The moment had come to control Judaism, the enemy *in foro interno*.

In order to carry out this task, one of the strategies of Christianity consisted in showing publicly that the Messiah awaited by the Jews had already arrived in the form of Jesus of Nazareth. These medieval practices were based on a very old tradition of writings *contra Iudaeos*, the name of a famous work by Saint Isidore of Seville.[46] There was a particular style for this type of work that repeatedly insisted on two basic arguments: (1) to prove the truth of Christian doctrine and (2) to attack Judaism, its false beliefs, fallacious literature, and in particular, the Talmud.[47] The twelfth century was especially productive for this type of literature that, as we have seen in previous chapters, had an unequivocally military aspect to it. In contrast to the rhetorical tradition, where words had the power of healing (*medicamenta verborum*), in the dialectics of the disputations the word is used as a lethal weapon. The Christian authors who devoted themselves to this work did so with a zeal that sometimes transformed the very nature of their authors. This is the case of Peter the Venerable, a man considered to be moderate and a great abbot of Cluny for more than thirty years (1122–1156). Petrus Venerabilis, a humanist by education, although the quality of his Latin was not first rate, did not hesitate to attack those "obstinate Jews" with epithets such as "beasts," "animals," or "pigs." His zeal must have been exemplary, or at least it seemed that way to his secretary, Pierre de Poitiers, who, as we can see from the following commentary, was a great admirer: "You are the only one of your generation who, with the sword of Divine words, slaughtered the three greatest enemies of holy Christianity, the Jews, the heretics, and the Saracens . . . in order to humble the satanic pride and arrogance which rise up against the greatness of God."[48]

Peter the Venerable probably saw himself in a saga as a conquering warrior who sought to hand over the empire to Christ: "He shall have dominion from sea to sea and from the rivers to the ends of the earth."[49] The climate of the moment was so violent that, in his extreme irritation *contra errores Iudeorum*, the abbot of Cluny acknowledged, "Who would contain the hands of our people from your blood, but for the commandment of the Scriptures."[50]

Given the evolution of the military situation in Western Europe and in view of the systematic and well-organized attacks against it, the Jewish population was left without hope and without a future of its own. The Christian assault rendered meaningless the concepts, so intimately lived by the Jews, of exile and redemption.[51] However, with the stroke of a pen, Jewish piety was transformed into something useless, while the identity of the Jewish people was obliged to dissolve into the innards of Christian society.[52] The Barcelona Disputation of 1263 is a perfect example of that attempt by Christian authorities to prove to the people that the beliefs of the Jews were no longer valid and were contradictory to their own beliefs. The awareness that these attacks were becoming more dangerous probably radicalized many rabbis in their defense of Messianism. This would explain why "the normally conservative Rabbi Moses ben Nahman [would] take such a public and strident position on the imminent advent of the Messiah."[53] Rabbi Meir ben Simon of Narbonne and Rabbi Mordechai ben Jehosapha of Avignon were also affected by this concern and published dialogues and sermons to counteract the increasingly strident Christian assault.[54]

It is almost certain that Moses de Leon had learned a lot from Maimonides, and therefore, from the school of Lucena and its achievements. We have seen that De Leon had read him in his youth,[55] and it is easy to imagine the impact that *The Guide of the Perplexed* must have had on such an imaginative young man. But Moses de Leon would go farther in his approach, not so much in the details of the Cordovan's knowledge, which was unquestionable in most cases, but in adhering to a new anthropological vision that was coming into the peninsula and one that the author of the *Zohar* found more to his liking. De Leon would opt for a kabbalistic stance in which Maimonides' *unquestionable renunciation* of omnipotence was called into question in a new way.

The kabbalistic schools of Provence and Gerona had already taken the step towards the nonintellectual comprehension of the Divinity—direct contact with God—and His understanding through mystical means. We should not forget that the Jewish communities of Languedoc and Provence belonged to the western Mediterranean and "had more in common with the Jews in Spain than with their brethren in northern France (*Zarfat*)."[56] De Leon also joined in the search for that primordial Nothingness that so attracted the kabbalists. But in his case the search would not be systematic or academic but rather open to the wisdom of daily popular experience.

The Divinity cannot be double—much less triple, as in the Christian Trinity—we already know that this is off bounds for the Jewish mystic. Thus, God the Creator and God the Unknowable—the Greek Demiurge and the *Nous* are one and the same. The recovery of the unity that sometimes is lacking in the Gnostics is achieved here with the coming to the foreground of the Ain, the Nothing, that Nothing from which, according to the Torah, everything emanates. That Nothingness, which in itself can only be divine, is the origin. From it, and in a process of self-knowledge, the dark being—the Ein Sof—reveals itself in all its splendor. The Nothingness is, then, the Supreme Crown of God, the most difficult and farthest away from man's comprehension, and can only be perceived by the most extreme and radical experiences in his own life.

The world emerged from that Nothing through creation, while God reveals himself as the Creator who, at the time of the creation—this also appears in the Gerona kabbalists—can be found at the center of the universe. From the time of man's creation until he sinned, the harmony of the universe was complete. This is the reason why the Ein Sof reveals itself in flashes of light throughout the work of creation. Thus God's revelation to man is not only that which is given specifically as the *motus* to begin reparation as the result of the sin. This means that flashes of the light of the divine occur throughout creation and in all its manifestations, and that they are real parts of the revelation that man has received. This idea comes dangerously close to pantheism, or at least, to panentheism, the assurance that God lies behind all that is created.

God's opening to man is completed with the sacred texts that are in themselves direct revelation, and as such, they contain a part of the Divinity. Of course the Divinity can not be understood as a fact or an object, thus the insistence that the Highest Crown of the Ein Sof is precisely Nothingness. This guarantees that we will not fall into the dichotomy of the God that creates, on the one hand, and what is created, on the other. There is no such thing. All things are manifestations of an Ein Sof that is observed or an experience on ten different planes or spheres, the *sefirot*. The *sefirot* are very active realities and not apprehensible as such in themselves, for they partake of each other and nurture each other mutually. This is why the image of the tree or the human body is used to show the different spheres or realms that give us access to the Divinity. Man must be well prepared to capture those flashes of the light of the divine whenever he may be permitted to accede to them. Likewise, he must be alert to the effect that it can have on his life and the life of the people of Israel.

Perhaps the intellectual evolution of De Leon, from his philosophical learning to his fondness for the kabbalah, lies in having put aside his efforts sustained and guided by good judgment in order to devote himself to recouping a knowledge anchored in popular wisdom. Far from the steady hand of Maimonides' thought, De Leon makes use of that substratum of beliefs and wisdom, with its fears and instability. He starts from those elements and the experiences he has gained from them in order to find a way to sense the action of the *sefirot* in the most direct way possible. This implies breaking the mold of the intellect in such a way that it will release the torrent of passion, feelings, and visions—often the product of daily fears—in which the original flash of light of the world can be found exactly as it was produced by God.

One of the key points in the center of all this is *the existence of evil*. Evil exists because people suffer it day by day and generation after generation, and they cannot neutralize it. In contrast to the sages, the people are not capable of understanding this concept. There is no explanation for why God allows it to exist. Nor is there any way to predict it or avoid it by means of effective psychological or political engineering. Evil is a part of the world and, as such, a part of creation. Of course it is not a part of God, but it does exist in the realm of the *sefirot*, in other words, the powers of the Divinity. We meet up with it because it exists, just like death, madness, or chronic, if not eternal, injustice. Popular feeling perceives it clearly and counts on it to survive. De Leon speaks of the various souls nurtured in man: the vegetative, animal, and rational. But when he deals with the sacred soul of the individual, De Leon does not attribute it to man as a substantial part that belongs to him. *The soul belongs to the Divinity.* This means that if man sins and is condemned to hell, his soul will not accompany him because it is not rightly his, but is a part of the Divinity. This is why his soul goes away and leaves him when he is punished. It could not be any other way because if it were so, God would be punishing himself.

This recuperation of popular faith is seen by some as a return to the democratic, the nonelitist. This is highly unlikely, given that the kabbalistic way expresses itself in a very complex and hermetic manner and prides itself on doing so. It is difficult to see in that supposed appropriation of the popular intent to recover the popular faith. Rather, it seems to us that it is more of a zealous search for an alternative outlet to rigorous Talmudic inquiry and the ever-increasing systematic codification of the *halakhah* that the Gothic Christian world brought with it to the southern part of Western Europe.

The kabbalah came to be a kind of compensation, an extraordinary counterweight. To a certain extent this compensation also plays with the exaltation of the mysterious, the ineffable, the inapprehensive. That unknowable Ein Sof is understood not as something that is there and should be respected but as a fundamental cause that sustains the entire kabbalistic edifice. The affirmation of Nothingness as negative omnipotence presents less of a problem within Judaism than God's omnipotence, because "nothing" is more accessible to human recuperation. However, it is easier to realize because it is not as scandalous as recovering the connection with divine omnipotence by such cryptic methods as magic and Christian mysticism. The astonishment or bewilderment that will be seen later in Christian mysticism is very close to this strategy of identifying the primordial One with that all-powerful and all-comprehensive Nothing from which everything emerges. For the kabbalists, within that everything lies the Ein Sof.

The entrance on stage of Nothingness and the frenetic quest for it in the *Zohar* led man to the discovery of his solitude and his limitations. It was presented in an amplified version in terms that are always enormous and larger than life. Later on this esthetic will be taken up by the Enlightenment in its most omnipotent manifestation such as Hegelianism or romanticism in the music of Carl Maria von Weber (1786–1826) (*Der Freischütz*) or Richard Wagner (1813–1883) (*Die Götterdamerung*).

Thus we have a gigantic stage setting in which Nothingness, as the matrix of all that is fractured and terrifying, coexists with the splendor of the world where the kabbalist, in light or faint flashes of light, can feel and meet up with the Ein Sof.

The elevation of Nothingness to a relevant existence and with existential significance produces a disruption of all kinds of values. Life and its achievements become smaller and insignificant. In this way, freedom will appear in tiny and fleeting flashes in the midst of contact with the creative Nothingness—this calls to mind Sheldon Wolin's *fugitive democracy*[57]—and where beauty and mercy are shown as ephemeral instants. Man is left to chance in the face of those dense, interchangeable, and inconstant forces. These forces do not even have the backup of any kind of mythology, for they dissolve and change shape, in addition to playing at will with the clumsiness and insignificance of the human intellect.

The Shadow of the Splendor

Is the *Zohar* a viable democratic way of kabbalistics? Does it signify a turn toward popular values and the daily life of the Jewish people as a source for gathering transformative and revolutionary wisdom? I do not believe there is any room for such an intensely popular interpretation of the *Zohar*. Certainly we can find in it extraordinary values, both in the widening of freedom of expression and in its distancing itself from the constrictions of the Talmud, as in the brilliant introduction of freedom of association *in foro interno*, something that can also be found in Maimonides. Nevertheless, its novelty with respect to conventional exegesis is that there is an assault on the boundaries, the blurring of separations and limitations that the rhetorical world finds necessary to be able to think in a nonsterile way in life.

With the appearance of Nothingness on the stage of thought, we have a situation of "thinking about the unthinkable."[58] This indispensable "nothing" that begins with the emanation of the divine until the formation of the Ein Sof, eliminates the essential rhetorical idea of looking for a way out of omnipotence. With it, the possibility of *good judgment* is shattered. This means closing the way of access to *the government of one's life*. In order to attain it, the inclusion of good judgment is essential. Man cannot live in public without the public experience of his knowledge, which requires both vigilance and lethargy.

Maimonides saw the subject of the governance of one's self as a part of political science, and it was a key element in his vision of life. The idea came from Aristotle, but it acquired a central place in his thought and was not distorted by ethics. This is one of the most important and transcendental aspects of Rambam's work and will be carried on by *Don Quixote* and can also be found in Giambattista Vico.

In the kabbalah, however, the subject of the government of the life of the individual will not be sustained as the primary aim of politics but will be postponed *sine die* as something unimportant.

In spite of Moses de Leon's divorce with respect to the Sephardic rhetorical tradition that would culminate in the *Quixote*, it is astonishing to see how much Sephardic wisdom the *Zohar* did absorb. This is shown in its negation of the principle of identity *in foro interno*, its adherence to teaching on a one-to-one basis, its recovery of the night and all the knowledge hidden from the conscious mind, and its respect for silence as the basis of thought. Its rejection of the Aristotelian principle of identity would elevate it far above the Christian tradition of logic or, perhaps we should say, removes it from that tradition. Rabbi Eleazar comments: "[T]here are three who fear without knowing what they fear."[59]

But De Leon also contributes some tendencies in the opposite direction. Two very revealing indications of this are the inundation of lethargic knowledge with a fantasy activated to the point of exacerbation and the reduction of the human almost to an insignificant scale. The human becomes minuscule in the face of the apotheosis of fantasy and its huge cosmological feats. On these occasions the anonymous epic of the universe establishes a world where men become very diminished.

To a certain extent it is not by accident that the *Zohar* presents a world that is not only entirely masculine, but it is also a world where woman is absent, banished, and expelled in a radical and inflexible way. She only appears in magnificent roles as mother, lover, wife, queen, or an erotic suggestion in stories filled with enthusiasm or insinuation. Of course women are notably absent, in contrast, in Simeon ben Horay's group, where men are handsome in body and soul and lend their physical, corporeal, and existential support to the work. This absence is so absolute that it again brings to mind the maddening and sterilizing shadow of omnipotence.

Nor is it a world of normal children. Occasionally child prodigies appear in a show of infantile omnipotence as a way of extracting exceptional interpretations from the mysteries of the Torah. In a broader sense, the world of the *in-fantes*, in its rhetorical meaning, does not appear.[60]

The work takes place in an inland setting without any marine references. The sea does not lend its immensity to the author's imagination.

Contrary to the *Quixote*, the *Zohar* gives itself over to a dizzying search for fusion with the Great Unknown. It sets out to approach a cosmic scenario of transcendental force and reality. Maimonides and Don Quixote, as well as Franz Kafka (1883–1924), never lose the conviction of their insignificance. In them, there are no superhuman displacements of forces and powers that go from the impotent to omnipotence in a flash. Nor do bodies throw off the soul, nor does the soul shed the body like a useless shell. Both respect and need each other for a human life full of limits, and they react to transcendental protagonism.

It is not unusual that Scholem, a noteworthy defender of the *Zohar*, tries to convince us *ex ante* that the absence of women is, in the long run, a case of a kind of misogyny. He suggests that, while it doesn't settle the matter, it is actually something found throughout kabbalism, as if that excuse serves to lighten the negative balance of the work.

The appearance of the idea of Nothingness—a problematic term in itself, given that it denotes something that cannot be designated—substantially alters the human possibilities of its installation in this world. It should be clarified that this Nothingness does not designate a nonbeing, nor is it a substantive concept. In kabbalistic tradition it is more like a sigh that accepts the immensity of our insignificance. It is the idea of surrendering to new possibilities of life that are not based on the capacities of individual workers and thinkers alone. Rather, it relies on the transmutation of man in order to acquire an opening of his receptivity and passivity anchored in the confidence and absolute devotion to the divine.

Around 1300 Joseph ben Shalom of Barcelona held that, in any transformation of reality or any change of form, the abyss of nothingness is crossed and "for a fleeting mystical moment becomes visible" and that "nothing can change without coming into contact with this region of pure absolute Being which the mystics call Nothing."[61]

The Existence of Evil

An important problem in both politics and mysticism is how to explain the existence of evil. In other words, we need a reason for why man can enjoy doing harm to his fellow man by destroying and creating unnecessary pain or humiliation gratuitously. Likewise, it is painful for the ordinary man to see how the most depraved, the opportunists, or those who resort to polluted moral arms like slandering their neighbor, lies, robbery, or violence are favored by fortune and lead a better life than those who are kind. How can we explain this to those faithful who live in a world governed by God? How can we respect a human ruler who finds it difficult to maintain the respect and affection of his subjects in a kingdom full of corruption of this type? How can we respect or even love God in the midst of so much injustice that life shows us and makes us suffer?

It has always been difficult for political theorists and theologians to answer these questions in any period. These questions about life are often incomprehensible, especially for those sincere believers in good government, filled with naivety and benevolence. Injustice upsets those who believe in authority and are ready to collaborate in attaining a just world, and cases of flagrant injustice drive them crazy. This is even more true for those persons who are given over to the understanding of a religion or a political theory, who are constantly reminded of a kingdom of justice, peace, and occasionally of love.

The *Zohar* takes up this question and anticipates an explanation that implies a complete vision of the public world, that is, of the powers that govern and order our lives. Its reply is that evil undoubtedly exists. In this, the book is in the same line as Yitzhak ben Yacob Hacoen of Soria, Moses ben Simon of Burgos, and Joseph Gikatila. In the *Zohar* we can perceive what we saw before in Maimonides and will see again in the twentieth century in Sigmund Freud, the existence of suffering that comes from three sources: illness, natural disasters, and especially, moral evil with which men do harm to others.

Why is there so much injustice in a world that puts its trust in the capable hands of our rulers or God? The reason for that evil seems to be attributed to a kind of residue that was left in the world. It is assumed that, since Creation, a negative remnant expelled by the Divinity because of its corrupt nature has remained among us since then. This explanation, which sounds inevitably like the Gnostics, sees evil in its origin as a force originating in the sphere of the Divinity. In reality, everything in creation has its origin in God. In the case of evil, however, we are dealing with a product of divine creation that, because of its perverse transformation, has become something unfortunate. Some scholars have speculated on the possible Cathar influence and the drastic repression of this heresy in the heartland of Christendom near Albi in Provence around 1200–1220. It was during these very years that the kabbalistic school of Gerona was coming to fruition. Moreover, the influence of the Cathar emigration that took refuge in Catalonia fleeing from repression in Provence is well known.

Evil, therefore, is something that is denaturalized and perverted and something that was dysfunctional from its very beginning. Nevertheless, this original dysfunction eventually became functional in the future because its very existence has brought to the foreground man's capacity for choosing freedom.

The *Zohar*, with its motley idea of freedom that occasionally borders on anarchy, sees human evil as a kind of bark for the tree of life. It is something very much alive and embedded in human life. At the same time, it is a provocative but necessary ingredient, even if it originally burst forth like a rupture in the harmony of the universe and is the product of a separation or division in it. Rupture by division, as indicated in the Greek prefix *dia*, is the cause of a brutal dissonance that produces much sorrow or pain—never presented as a tragic pain, something that the kabbalah tends to reject just like the mystics of Gerona—a cosmic pain that provoked man's isolation. Neither birth nor death is very important except as a corporeal biographic marker. In this situation, if man tries to repair the harm done in the world, he would probably fall into the substitution of the divine for magic. As we can see, the problem of omnipotence is always present in the public anthropology of the medieval Jewish communities inserted into the Christian world. In the face of a buoyant Christianity, obviously triumphant, and in rapid and productive expansion throughout the entire West, the Jewish communities begin to feel inundated with the Christian vision of power and the articulation that the Christians make both of the government of their lives as well as the known world.

Set apart by sin from the Tree of Life and the Tree of Knowledge, man becomes isolated, and this opens him up to the temptation of trying to replace the divine capacities of regeneration on his own or, if not, he becomes anxious to manipulate those powers to reconstruct the lost unity. It is a matter of nothing less that resorting to magic or to the omnipotent behavior of pride. In short, he resorts to an intellect that is scattered about or elevated to a position of exaltation and hypertrophy.

Ultimately, that man who is sometimes glimpsed in the *Zohar* is one step away from the abyss of European romanticism. From the fifteenth century on he will want to continue to be a part of that now perverted world initially created by the Divinity, and he wants to be a part of its regeneration as a tiny collaborator of God. Or, as God's great collaborator, he hides behind that larger group called the nation in order to recompose the lost harmony he has desired for so long.

Even if seen from an Ashkenazic point of view, Scholem calls this an act of apostasy because it allows man to attempt "to take God's place and to join what God has separated. Evil thus creates an unreal world of false contexts after having destroyed or deserted the real."[62]

In the *Zohar* "a river issues from Eden to water the garden."[63] The flow of divine emanation comes from the highest Sephirah to the garden, or Shekinah. Below the Shekinah the unity of the divine produces multiplicity. Contrarily, the serpent, the impulse of evil, divides. Samael comes down from heaven riding on this serpent "and the form of the *serpent* is

Satan; all is one [and he inflicts death on the world] and through wisdom Samael brought curses in the world, destroying the primordial tree created in the world by the blessed Holy One."[64]

The Left Hand

Evil is associated in the *Zohar* with the left hand of God, symbolizing His wrath, a power of God that has need of His right hand symbolizing Mercy. When the balance (or dialectic) of this tension is upset, evil comes forth, and all that was divine in its origin disappears. Evil becomes a dead or half-dead residue like the shell of a nut or the bark of the cork oak. These are the protecting tissues of the inner life of those living beings, but in any case, they are the result of the death of cells that were alive in the past.

Thus the existence of evil appears as a constant and almost necessary ugliness—every cloud has a silver lining, in popular wisdom—and is accepted as something negative, unpleasant, and frightening. It is something to be avoided at all costs even though *it is there and always will be there*. We have no choice but to accept it and live with it. The interpretation of scholars who hold similar ideas to this Gothic vision of evil, so disheartening and somewhat morbid, is that this idea of evil belongs more to the common people. With this they almost mean something like it is *more democratic*. The Sephardic kabbalists—Nahmanides, Jonah Gerondi, the influential Solomon ibn Adret, Gikatila, and Moses de Leon, himself—none of whom were illiterate or naïve self-taught men—attribute man's public and personal misfortune to the existence of a Kingdom of Evil, of the dark side of life that, in its origin, was created by God. What they accept is that awful part that is dominated by evil. It is a sinister part that, because of man's sin and the perversion of the original harmony, has prevailed over us and ended up having its place in the world.

The place of evil in our lives is consolidated in the kabbalah in accordance with the popular perception that the misfortunes caused by evil can never be expelled from the world. These depressing perceptions of injustice, corruption, violence, and disloyalty alternate with peaks of exalted optimism. But these perceptions also establish the existence of these human misfortunes as necessary evils in order for man to be free in a society that is *always at war*. The idea that corruption partially fuels the economy of societies, that war, to a certain extent, favors the progress of history, or that treason makes one free opens the way to the theoretical axiom of politics that injustice is profoundly human.

Naturally all this can have a very disturbing consequence for power, as we see later on in Miguel de Molinos (1628–1696), a Spanish mystic and thinker. In his *Guía espiritual* (1675), this Baroque moralist proposes to his Quietist followers that they resign themselves to experiencing the evil of sin and not offer resistance to its effects, but they should not let its lies take hold of their soul. In this work—a true study of the *government of the individual*—Molinos preaches that the soul should surrender itself to the Divinity and let itself be entirely absorbed by it without offering any resistance. Molinos was detained by the Inquisition and tried in Rome in 1685. A gentle, peaceful man who acted according to his beliefs, he did not offer resistance to the Vatican's accusations. He confessed his errors, and in 1687 he was condemned to prison, where he spent the rest of his life.

Kabbalah and Public Life

The assessment of the kabbalah as an explosion of individual and moral freedom is guilty of an essential deformation. In the light of political theory, and once we review the moments when it emerges and its political and religious antecedents, serious doubts arise about its ability to protect the dignity of the people. To a certain extent, its answers to the great questions of the Jewish people make one think of a solution of compromise, of an escape from an irresistible world in which the philosophy of the great Maimonides becomes a defective formula. Rambam's city of courtyards and alleyways, quest for the protection of everyday *good judgment*, rejection of the ethnic argument, denial of the sinister as sterile and pompous omnipotence, and opening toward a public space shared with dignity has no place in the Gothic Christian settlement with its inhuman scale and gigantic dimensions. An example of this that can be understood by modern-day standards is the sprawling city of Seville with its enormous cathedral, one of the largest in Europe.

None of this can be sustained in the face of the advance and public protection of territorial Christian patriotism and the affirmation of national unity. National integrity becomes firmly established in the internal public spaces by religious identity integrated with the political power—*cujus regio, eius religio*—of Martin Luther. The Christian homeland is incompatible with Jewish identity, which has its origins in the Torah, the written law given by Yahveh to his people in a covenant established "face to face" with Moses to escape from bondage. This homeland is built around an identity of political engineering based on the *principium segregationis*. This new identity brings with it severe anthropological impositions that subordinate knowledge to power and establish a public kingdom in order to triumph. Everything revolves around the power of knowledge, the leadership of the articulating power, and the perpetual vigilance that leads to victory: "Who is *mighty*? A virtuous person, someone who engages in holy Torah day and night."[65]

At this point Maimonides′ ideas are no longer valid. The world is in a hurry to take up positions, and Sephardic Jewry, too, will be forced to become integrated into the definitive expansion of Gothic Christendom in Western Europe for many centuries to come.

The ambiguity of the kabbalah may have its roots in the acceptance of the new political panorama. Western Jewry now has to open the gates of its Jewish quarters to royal notaries; it has to accept their fictitious money instead of gold and silver and allow their preachers to enter the synagogue along with their police, school masters, and scholars.[66] Moreover, this is all done with a certain conviction, given that it is seen as a way of getting rid of the threat of philosophical knowledge. Western Jewry must separate itself from the sciences of the south, tainted by the sensibility of Greek and Mediterranean rhetoric and the progress and pleasures of intellectual scholarship. The misleading idea that to inquire into nature with the assurance that what lies beneath it is something knowable to a great extent is no longer sustainable. They must renounce their opening up to the transmission of knowledge and the idea that man can become installed rationally and happily in a world that does not reject him in a convulsive and inexplicable way. They must abandon the conviction that things happy or unhappy can have—although not always, as Maimonides clarified—a reasonable explanation, if one looks for it and studies without pride. Life is not a perpetual war.

Beginning with the fourteenth century the rhetorical world was taken by surprise and became easy prey for what Vico called "the barbarism of reflection."[67] Loquacity overwhelmed *dicere* (to say or tell). *Loquor* and *dicere* become confused, bypassing the important distances that separate them—differences that come to light in expressions such as "the president spoke, but what did he say?" The sound of speech and its semiotic overtones diminish a public thought that, like music, begins with silence as its original matrix.

The fear of the rational world, the enjoyment of a pleasant and hospitable life, was considered highly dangerous by the Spanish Tosafists. They accused it of weakening Jewish identity, with the consequent rise in conversions to Christianity that were occurring everywhere. According to these scholars, to feel comfortably installed in the world debilitated those sentiments that we had mentioned earlier of exile and redemption, which are so central to the Talmud and Jewish sensibility. The fear of that philosophical inclination became so violent that it unleashed a reaction against its representative figures, and in particular, against Maimonides, the great teacher who embodied these tendencies. The problem was further aggravated by Maimonides' brilliant exposition of the question and because he was a maximum authority as an exceptional codifier of *halakhah*.

We have already seen that the first assault against Maimonides occurred in the thirteenth century from the domain of Montpellier, which belonged to the kingdom of Aragon. It was launched by Solomon of Montpellier and perhaps instigated by Jonah Gerondi, Nahmanides' first cousin and a mediocre but strict and loyal Talmudist. He was backed up by several others[68] but, as we have seen, the attempt failed because it was rejected by the Provençal faction and the subsequent reaction of the other Spaniards who were, to a certain extent, aloof from what they must have seen as an excessively conservative mania. But, in out opinion, the most serious and definitive reaction would be carried out years later by Rabbi Solomon ibn Adret (Rashba), Nahmanides' best pupil. Ibn Adret, a highly esteemed authority among Aragonese Jewry, was an important financier, well-versed in law and politics. As an expert on legal questions, he knew both Christian civil law and Roman law and obviously, Jewish *halakhah*. As a prominent member of the community, he served as its rabbi for almost fifty years and taught in the synagogue in Barcelona. Moreover, he was a protégé of the king of Aragon, a prestigious judge, and a rabbinical authority who was widely consulted throughout the Jewish world.[69] Whenever he appears as a public figure, he gives evidence of his extraordinary practical intelligence and first-rate talent in political diplomacy. Yitzhak Baer calls him "the foremost rabbinic authority of the day."[70] A truly great man of his time, he was "the great spiritual leader who guided the Jewish communities of Spain through these troubled times with firmness and discretion."[71] In contrast to many of his coreligionists, he died in his native city. Ibn Adret never went to Jerusalem, either by choice or necessity, as did several of his predecessors.

In Spain Ibn Adret seems to have exemplified the pragmatic leader, concerned for the preservation of Israel, who must have reached the conclusion that it was imperative to make the necessary adaptations to the Christian advance. As a responsible leader he understood that, if the Jewish communities did not adapt to the new Christian world, they would endanger their very existence. It was a matter of recognizing the power of the Christian advance realistically and making adequate adjustments for living in this new world. This was a higher world, specializing in institutional dogmatism, to which they had to adapt. This was a new public life that, in turn, would bring with it many options for the Jewish community, providing they knew how to take advantage of them.

It was a question, above all, of living well connected to Christian society so as not to disappear as a people; it was a primordial divine command. This was why the Jews of the time had to make a drastic turnabout in their way of viewing public life. An example of this was transcribed by Lorberbaum in a particularly revealing incident about the intervention of eminent Jews in a trial ordered by Peter III of Aragon. [72]

It is not surprising that such a practical and experienced man as Ibn Adret was also an outstanding kabbalist. The simplest explanation is that Adret was Nahmanides' most worthy pupil. But I think it is more fitting to understand that Ibn Adret, like other kabbalists, combined a practical life of adaptation—and occasionally of apparent submission—with that great compensation *in foro interno* that was the *way of truth* of the kabbalah.

Evil, for the kabbalists, like corruption for many Gothic or romantic democrats, has its place in life. It is an essential part of life, but it is not the result of the fall of Adam or an odd residue of Creation that can easily be discarded. There is no place for this. Moreover, evil is there to accustom us to experiencing it on the road to freedom, to make human freedom possible. Evil is necessary for man to attain dignity. To live with evil, to know how to deal with it is, therefore, a common and meritorious human virtue. The vision of the Sephardic kabbalists opens the southern mind to a dark and sinister world that increases man's possibilities.[73]

This dark side that threatens living things from within "exercises a peculiar fascination upon the author of the *Zohar*."[74] But what is astonishing from the point of view of the twenty-first century is that, far from being a mere passing fashion of the religiosity of the time, it is still present as a seed of public philosophy that has endured in Western tradition until now. This sinister side, which is at the same time spiritually sublime, is clearly visible in the still refined and hypersensitive Spain of the thirteenth and fourteenth centuries. We are dealing with a Gothic component that will effect important changes in political theory. This wave that came into the peninsula had already passed through other European lands with similar results. Nevertheless, it did not produce the heightened awareness with which it was received in the Iberian Peninsula, a Mediterranean land, but also with an Atlantic vocation, a frontier, but also a land open to multiculturalism. These lands were the periphery and the battleground, but they were also a place for fruitful exchanges between Christianity and Islam.

This Gothic world where the State was being born as an internationally accepted European franchise—with everything that it entailed of territory, sovereignty, vigilant society, efficient leadership, homeland, hypertrophied dialectics, judge-prosecutors, executive administrators, and astute princes—is an original production of Western Europe that appeared with exceptional virulence in the Iberian Peninsula, as happened on other historical occasions.

Reflections from the Point of View of Political Theory

It is difficult to encompass the entire meaning of the kabbalah within a single historicopolitical concept. This is why we should think carefully about the extraordinary popularity of this Jewish mystical ideology in the Iberian Peninsula. Even if we concede that its foundations and seed came from outside Spain, its extraordinary creativity and force within Sepharad undoubtedly merit further analysis. The appearance of centers like Gerona and its Catalan school of kabbalah or the wealth of Castilian kabbalism that reached its brilliant peak with the *Zohar* speak to us of an extraordinary creativity, and at the same time, it is a significant phenomenon of what was happening in Western Europe during this period.

We should recall that the beginning of the thirteenth century witnessed the extraordinary boom of kabbalism in Gerona, but it also signified the end of a period. It was a time of splendor in international Judaism that had flourished during three centuries and had found its second renaissance in Sepharad.[75]

In the light of everything we have said until now, it is necessary to comment on a few interesting questions from the point of view of political theory, without intending to interfere with the work of historians or theologians.

The first disconcerting point about Spanish kabbalism—whether it is Catalan or Castilian—lies in its continued *depreciation of lethargy* in man's life. This deterioration opens the way for the exaltation of vigilance (*vigilia*) in such a natural way that it does not need any explanation: "King David was vigilant all his days never to taste the taste of death, for sleep is one sixtieth of death . . . This, King David guarded against, so as not to taste the taste of death, not to be ruled by the Other Side."[76]

The protagonists of the *Zohar* are radicals in this respect. They have no doubt that the time we spend sleeping is something like a waste of time in our lives: "Woe to those who sleep, slumber in their sockets, unaware, unmindful! Eventually they will arise in judgment, for reckoning is exacted when the body is defiled and the soul drifts through the atmosphere of the noontime sun . . . Woe to them! Who will plead for them?"[77]

A good existence is one in which we continue to practice executive control over our lives, in other words, wakefulness, a condition in which the powers of memory and will that distinguish our executive being are the ones that govern in the majority. "At midnight all the truly virtuous awake to declaim Torah and proclaim praises of Torah . . . King David would rise at midnight. For if he sat or lay in bed, singing songs of praise, how it is written: *At midnight I rise to praise You* (Psalms 119:62).[78] *I rise*, literally, standing to engage in song and praise of Torah."[79]

Night is always subordinate to vigil. During sleep we pass through a kind of experience or second-class time of life, if not a time of risk and anxiety. When we sleep at night our life diminishes in dignity or loses some of its essential traits, undoubtedly degrading it. In fact, "when a man is dreaming—not in control of his body, his body lulled—an impure spirit comes and settles upon him."[80] True midnight is that which is inundated or invaded by a special vigilance where the virtuous are awake.

During the time of sleep, the predominant idea is that the soul abandons the body. In other words, the individual loses his soul or, if not, he remains split, in a position of dependence and extreme vulnerability: "the soul departs, and in the body remains nothing but a trace of a pint of the heart's vitality . . . She drifts this way all night long until the person awakes and she returns to her place."[81] Independently of whether or not the soul can perform transcendental tasks during this time, we are left with some clearly defined ideas among so many imaginative allusions: (1) the soul does not sleep; in other words, sleep is the function of the body; (2) the soul governs by night,[82] and (3) important acts require a wakefulness that can be interpreted here almost as an awakening of life.

During the night the soul comes before God and even testifies about the entire life of a person, which explains why, in terms of divine or spiritual life, the soul is almost completely responsible for the entire person.[83]

Sleep is held up as an example of wasted time for the most profound consciousness of our lives, to the extent that the completely unconscious person is compared to "someone roused from sleep."[84] This vigilant position is similar to and compatible with triumphant Gothic Christianity. It is not unusual that Baer finds that an occasional *responsum* of R. Solomon ibn Adret "resembles the opinions rendered by the Christian theologians in similar cases."[85]

As Rabbi Hiyya, Rabbi Yehuda, and Rabbi Yosef comment in their conversation: "Because a dream contains falsehood and truth, and the word controls all, so a dream needs favorable interpretation . . . Because every dream is of the rung below, controlled by Speech, so every dream follows speech . . . Since a dream includes all, as we have said, all dreams of the world follow oral interpretation . . . A dream uninterpreted is like a letter unread."[86]

In this view of the matter, dream becomes a kind of executive weapon involved in the action and its development. It is a kind of seed of each action or fact that, when interpreted, will enable us to alter the development of the phenomenon that it announces or introduces. Without the interpretation of the dream implicit in an event, things remain incomplete or unfinished: "Nothing in the world, before arriving in the world, is independent of a dream—or by means of a herald, for as has been said: 'Every single thing, before arriving in the world is heralded in heaven; whence it spreads throughout the world, transmitted by a herald.'"[87]

This is a Gothic vision of the world of dreams and their interpretation that could have been fabricated by the young Sigmund Freud in his initial search: "Our best hope for the future is that intellect—the scientific spirit, reason—may in process of time establish a dictatorship in the mental life of man."[88] But it is not true of the more mature Freud, who is closer to Maimonides, the teacher. Perhaps it is not by accident that the adolescent Freud became interested in Miguel de Cervantes, only to arrive much later at positions closer to Sephardic rhetoric.

Bernat Metge (1340/46–1413), a prominent public official and great writer from Barcelona, expressed this idea of Christian culture categorically: "Men were born to work, but they flee from work as if it were poison. And if they thought a little about it, they would embrace it, because work dissipates the superfluous humors in the body. They spend a third or more of their lives in sleep, which is first cousin to death, and the rest in the service of their bodies, of which they are slaves and captives."[89]

It is firmly established that "when a person sleeps in his bed . . . souls have to wander the world—leaving his body."[90] When the body is submerged in the need for sleep, which is a kind of basic tribute to our animal nature, the soul wanders off because it does not sleep and occasionally, although "not every single soul" ascends, "soaring to gaze on the splendor of the Countenance of Days."[91]

For medieval Judaism this is a complete reconfiguration of human government. At the same time as the body is discredited, the human figure as a whole is diminished as a measure of being. This would bring with it a change in the idea of the government of the person. Now those forces that move the lives of men, both from within as well as from the objects around them and from the lives of others, are no longer situated in man's inner being but in the cosmos. Maimonides intuited that the forces that govern us are within reach of political science. But from now on this idea could hardly be expected to advance in this world. As it happened with the rest of the sciences proposed by the so-called philosophers, political theory would no longer make any sense. This is true particularly if the great motives of the world—at this point it is impossible to speak only of causes—are located in the universe of astrology and are very far removed from man's rational or conscious capacity. It is no accident that astrology was an irreducible point of friction between Maimonides and Nahmanides.

Now the great protagonists of the drama of the world are the stars, the celestial characters, abstract entities that bear the names of public agents, unapproachable angels, in other words, all those forces that hover around our lives. Also present are the demons and manifestations of the Divinity that, in reality and when the authors are sincere, reveal themselves as divine powers.

The kabbalists do not perceive life as a tragedy. In their writings there are no deaths or births. And if they do appear, it is merely as biographical milestones.

An important point of public vision that can be distilled from Spanish kabbalism is its almost obsessive interest in power,[92] which is always out of the reach of mortals. Of course there is always the remote possibility of gaining access to the great superhuman powers by exercising influence on that world of celestial forces. The Spanish kabbalists insist on the idea that the sublunar world corresponds to the heavenly world, and with the appropriate human action those divine powers can be activated, a notion that comes perilously close to the Christian vision.

It is shocking that, in the *Zohar*, man is the piece that completes Creation: "Through Abraham the world was established."[93] It is even more astonishing if we take into account that this very man is denied the possibility of his own self-government. In the *Zohar*, Maimonides' very advanced idea of seeing *the government of each one of us as the aim of political science* is banished from the realm of the rational or even reasonable.

The time for sleep takes on somber overtones in the *Zohar*.[94] When an individual sleeps, which means in itself the division of his being, he must submit to a series of transcendental proofs that affect the judgment of his own worth. To begin, "while human beings sleep, the soul goes forth, offers testimony, and is found guilty."[95] It is clear that sin is inevitable, and everyone is guilty, which is one of the strongest points in Gothic religiosity. All this allows us to speak of "the age of culpability"[96] in the life of an individual. On the other hand, in the words that Rabbi Eleazar says he has heard, "Night is royal judgment, entailing judgment universally,"[97] the judgment of omnipotence. Night is the moment of a profound divine judgment out of bounds for man. The Gothic night appears in the *Zohar*.[98] In this context Maimonides' idea of *good judgment* is almost obsolete, a useless fossil, and diminished in the face of the Gothic grandeur of this cosmic plan, which is much closer to Richard Wagner than Giovanni Paisiello. The rabbis of the *Zohar* coincide in this vision that "at midnight the Kingdom of Heaven arouses . . . Night entails judgment universally, as we have already established."[99]

This description of the extraordinary imagination of the *Zohar* provides us with a premonition of the Gothic advance: "At midnight, when birds arouse, the side of the North arouses in a wind. A sceptre from the side of the South rises erect and strikes that wind, so it subsides, turning fragrant."[100]

Judgment as a part of public life, as the foundation of politics, is gradually being eroded as a result of our reading of the *Zohar*, to the point where preeminence gives way to action. Yahveh commands Israel: "to perform an act in order to evade being dominated by the one who must not dominate, to evade being dominated by judgment, so that they all may emerge innocent on earth through the compassion of a father toward his children. All depends on action and words, as we have established."[101] Had he known it, this melody would certainly have pleased and inspired Niccolò Machiavelli.

Rhetorical judgment, the *good judgment* that Maimonides looked upon as a guarantee against despotism or urban conspiracy, was completely dismantled in what we have called the Gothic vision. For Gothic Christianity—and that is something that vigilant democracy will appropriate for itself—the human being should not think so much about confronting and digesting contingency in a political way, an objective that is the aim of the human search for good judgment and its rules fashioned in the measure of man. It is true that, for the Gothic mentality, the individual is already involved directly in a trial before the Holy, before God. It is a trial by night, spiritual, cosmic, and omnipotent; a supreme act carried out without the obstruction of bodies, the Greek *soma* that precisely represents contingency. The constant counterposition between judgment and compassion is extremely disturbing, for the "paths of judgment and compassion radiate and diverge."[102]

Throughout the book, and as a result of this inclination, the identification of the judgment with the sentencing punishment is almost automatic. This idea is drastically removed from the world of the rhetoric of good judgment and the view of the judge in Maimonides.

The fact that bodies do not participate in this daily judgment means that *lethargy*[103] as an ingredient of political theory remains cut off from the human capacity for judgment, from that lethargy that Maimonides, *The*

Celestina, and *Don Quixote* can count on to deposit and elaborate on their sentiments. It is a lethargy that helps develop man's intellectual capacity but, in this case, is disjointed. The body does not participate, but rather it lies about like a useless shell. It is only the soul—the spirit, as it will be known later on in Europe—that enters into a public trial before God and at such a high level that the political potential of the judgment is annulled: "Every single night when a person climbs into bed, his soul leaves him to be judged before the King's Court of Justice. If deserving to endure, she is restored to this world."[104]

The soul will be judged not by its earthly king but by the King of Souls, which indicates that the real majesty of monarchy has passed over to the spiritual world as far as future happenings are concerned. In this regard, the text reveals an opportune declaration. Knowing full well that in the spiritual world—a realm alien to wakefulness—neither time nor space exists as such, the author specifies here that judgment will not be passed on good or bad or future or past actions: "A person is not judged for wrongdoing he will commit in the future . . . But do not say that he is judged only for the good deeds he has already performed . . . Rather, also for good deeds he will eventually perform, on account of which he is saved, even though now he is guilty."[105]

The author is clearly aware of the fact that, although he is using images of the world of souls to express himself, he is also touching on very specific public elements. He is dismantling ancient civic structures from the rhetorical world of Mediterranean politics from which the Jewish philosophers had spoken. The time is near when it will be possible to speak directly of *executing a judgment*. Soon the judge will be replaced by the arbitrator or the prosecutor. It can be said of this fundamental transmutation of the public, to use another extraordinarily expressive image from the *Zohar*, that "fire entered water."[106]

The idea of everyday good judgment, such an important activity for the personal government of each one of us, and that incessant activity with which we judge and are judged constantly, is going to be altered: "When judgment prevails in the world, that Court of Justice is like a pregnant woman undergoing hard labor—once she gives birth, agitation subsides. When judgment prevails in the world, it does not subside or rest until judgment is executed; then tranquillity—as She stands in position, perfect and firm, as is written: when the wicked perish, jubilation!" (Proverbs (11:10).[107]

6

Toward a Vigilant Society

Minds, however, are not conquered by arms, but by Love and Nobility.[1]

—Spinoza

Ashkenazim and Sephardim

In Spanish-speaking countries discussions about Judaism are often marked by ideological suspicion, guilt, or a settling of scores. It is not often that we think carefully about the subject about to be considered under this heading. Unfortunately, it is a matter in which misunderstandings are often accepted as truths. In reality, it is an accepted fact that "[m]ost books of any sort on the Jews in the modern world deal in the main with Ashkenazim."[2] It is as if, in the modern era, the Sephardim have become, even for the rest of the Jews, an almost folkloric minority, destined to become extinct on their own. Some scholars even label the Sephardim as extra-European, meaning by "Sephardic" a North African and Eastern phenomenon.[3] It is not surprising that those Sephardic Jews incorporated into Israel have felt themselves to be "in a subordinate position within a society offering two dominant models of European Jewish responses to Modernity—a secular national type and an Ashkenazic religious type."[4] Leaving aside the author's rather presumptive statement, it is obvious that the Sephardic world has not had the attention or respect that its splendid past deserves. Spanish-speaking culture, in particular, is not only indebted to Sephardic Jews, but it also has an enormous duty to study this great cultural tradition.

The two great branches of Judaism in Europe are the Ashkenazic and the Sephardic, the Jews originating from Ashkenaz and Sepharad. Initially until the Middle Ages, the Ashkenazim were from the Franco-Germanic territories, which included the Rhine basin and the Elbe, the inhabitants on both sides and the lands between them and the inhabitants of their tributaries, the Main and the Moselle. Jews had also settled along the Danube, particularly near Buda. In northeastern France the Jewish population was largely concentrated on the banks of the Seine and the Marne. Dijon, Troyes, Paris, and Touques had important Jewish communities.[5] In the sixteenth century this was broadened to include the Jews of Poland, the emigrants, and their descendents.

The term "Sephardim," referred "exclusively to the Jews of the entire Iberian Peninsula before their expulsion from Spain and Portugal in 1492 and 1498. Subsequently it is used for the Jewish exiles from those countries and their descendents."[6]

We should add that, although they have followed along different paths, these two Jewries "have always been united in their desire to serve Judaism."[7] Nevertheless, it is obvious that important differences have existed between them, contrasts that scholars have attributed to factors of origin, geography, anthropology, and politics. Although there are no differences in basic Jewish beliefs, "there are many differences in matters of custom and outlook."[8]

Beginning in ancient times there were already important divisions between the Babylonian and the Palestinian traditions in the Jewish world,[9] probably on account of their different political situation. The differences ranged from the use of Aramaic, more proper to the poorer classes and the Hebrew, used by the aristocratic class, to the liturgy, but the greatest discrepancy lay in their theological orientation. In Babylonia the study of the Talmud prevailed, while in Palestine, due to its situation of repression and persecution, including by the Byzantine Empire, the Jews tended more toward the cultivation of literature and poetry as ways of keeping up their tradition (midrash and *piyyut*).[10]

Because of the political circumstances mentioned above, the Jewish communities of central Europe came under the influence of Palestine, while the Sephardim were more influenced by Babylonia on account of their connections with North Africa and the spread of Islam.

Also put forth for this theory were racial, or as some scholars have termed, anthropological factors. According to this hypothesis, the Jews who emigrated from northern Israel mixed with the Aramaic, Mongol, Alpine, or Nordic population, while those from the south, the more refined and educated Jews from around Jerusalem, mixed with the eastern, Bedouin, or Mediterranean groups. An even earlier explanation was put forth by Rabbi Menahem b. Aaron ibn Zerah (d. Toledo, 1385): "It is well known that the appearance of the people of Germany is different from that of the people of Spain and that of the Ethiopian is different again by reason of the climate, the varying length of the sun which affects the air, and consequently the plants and the fruits vary. Those partaking of them change accordingly. Hence the difference in language and appearance."[11]

Babylonia and Palestine

These two schools of Judaism spread out and were transplanted to Europe in different ways. Both traditions had different pronunciations, a factor that, in turn, had its effect on the development of ritual and liturgy. These differences also affected the ways in which the sacred texts were studied, forms of marriage, transcription of texts, and preservation of certain customs. For example, the Palestinian school was more advanced than the Babylonian in matters of punctuation[12] and in ritual and matrimonial laws; in sum, in almost all aspects of daily life.

We should not forget that the Jewish communities have always been exposed to their host cultures and, in many cases, open to absorption by them. As Rabbi Judah the Hassid summed it up: "The usage of the Jews is in accordance with that of the non-Jews. If the non-Jews of a certain town are moral, the Jews born there will be so as well."[13] Naturally, when this phenomenon reaches inadmissible extremes, the alarm sounds, and they begin to talk of assimilation. This is one of the most serious and perennial phantoms of Jewish life in the Diaspora.

However, "The contact with Gentiles in the economic sphere caused some of their legal conceptions to be adopted by the Jews."[14] It is obvious that political circumstances also had important effects on Jewish public life. In the Sephardic world of the Middle Ages it was thought that the Ashkenazim had little knowledge of civil Jewish law because they lived under feudal law. In reality, however, the reason why this type of law was not practiced in feudalism was because it was forbidden by the feudal lords. This is precisely the explanation offered by Maimonides.

As seen from the point of view of the Ashkenazic Jews, the strict observance of the liturgical practices of the Sephardim and its demanding ritual, so careful in its details, was attributed to the influence of the Arabic ambiance in which they lived. Likewise, polygamy, a practice historically accepted in Judaism, would be rejected by the Ashkenazim due to Christian influence.[15] The first great advance in this matter was the *takkanah*,[16] or ordinance, promulgated against polygamy by the eminent Rabbi Gershom ben Judah (c. 960–1040),[17] the founder of the Ashkenazic school of theology, although it would take several centuries for this decree to become recognized in other parts of Europe. Strangely enough, polygamy would not be accepted either "among the Jews of North Africa, who were essentially, like the ancient Greeks, monogamists."[18]

Gershom of Mainz's ordinance would ratify the practice of monogamy that was already established among Ashkenazic Jewry, contrary to what was happening in Sepharad. Ibn Adret tells us that in Spain and Provence bigamy was a common practice even among educated and pious Jews around the middle of the thirteenth century.[19] Around 1300 it seems that monogamy began to spread among the Jewish population of the kingdom of Aragon, and Gershom's ordinance, backed up by Adret, would at least begin to be respected. There were communities that already allowed bigamy only in cases of infertility of the wife during ten years of marriage and with the consent of the majority of the community.[20] Initiatives began to appear in favor of women's rights to request divorce, although this practice hardly had any acceptance in Jewish Spain. The king himself had to intervene at times to force the *aljamas* to obligate the husband to accept the demands of his wife.[21]

In any case, Ibn Adret is very flexible—really ambiguous and adaptable—in his *responsa.* In a question from Castelló d'Empuries he softens Rabbi Gershom's anathema: "Everything leads us to believe that this teacher did not intend it to be valid for every type of circumstance,"[22] because there are cases in which it is not a question of "sitting around and doing nothing."[23] In some cases where the husband cannot legally retain his wife, or when he has lived with her for ten years without producing a son, "he may join together with another woman by virtue of the precept of to grow and multiply."[24] In sum, Adret considers in his response: "This ordinance is not wide-spread in our lands, nor in those of Provence, which are adjacent to France. In our towns there have been cases of wise men and saints who have married a second wife, even when they already had one, and many other people who have done the same, and no one has been mistrustful about it."[25]

Zimmels enumerates eight periods in the relationship between the two branches of Judaism:

1. From the beginning until the death of Maimonides (1205),
2. from Maimonides' death to the emigration of Rabbi Asher ben Yehiel from Germany to Spain (1304),
3. from the arrival of Asher ben Yehiel to 1391, a period of the predominance of Ashkenazic teaching in Spain,
4. from 1391 to the expulsion of the Jews from Sepharad, (1492–1498),
5. from the expulsion of the Jews from the Iberian Peninsula to the publication of Isserles' *Glosses* (1571, 1578),

6. from the publication of the *Glosses* to the establishment of the "Science of Judaism" (1819),
7. from the "Science of Judaism" to the foundation of the State of Israel (1948), and
8. after the foundation of the State of Israel (1948).[26]

Relations between Ashkenazim and Sephardim have fluctuated throughout the centuries. In reality, their mutual influence—always very intense for religious or linguistic reasons—frequently changed its meaning. If, in the twelfth century, Maimonides considered the culture of the French rabbis to be of a very low level, in the thirteenth century Nahmanides called them teachers and mentors, whom he considered the saviors who would rescue the peninsular Jews from their backwardness.[27]

In the fourteenth century a Sephardic rabbi, Isaac ben Shesheth, recognized, "For out of Zarephat (France) shall go forth the law, and the word of the Lord from *Ashkenaz* (Germany)."[28] This same rabbi holds that the great luminaries of Talmudic wisdom are Rashi[29] and Rabbi Tam,[30] both of whom are from the north, the very region that Maimonides and his colleagues accused of being so backward in legal and scientific knowledge in the twelfth century. For Rabbi Shesheth, these two prominent Ashkenazim are a blessing, thanks to which it has been possible to approach the wisdom of Jewish tradition properly. Referring to Rashi, he is convinced that "without his commentary the Talmud would be a sealed book."[31] For Nahmanides, Rashi is also a key figure as an exegete and R. Tam "in dialectic (*pilpul*) there has been none like him since the close of the Talmud,"[32] by no means an insignificant point coming from Ramban.

Rabbi Shesheth speaks very clearly of his own intellectual orientation and understanding of the Talmud. For him, the Ashkenazic teachers, Rabbi Tam and Rabbi Isaac of Dampierre (Ri ha-Zaken), are of greater intellectual stature than Maimonides. Moreover, he shows his enthusiasm for and adherence to a pedagogical orientation that, from now on, would be predominantly dialectical. This step toward dialectics, with its consequent rejection of rhetoric, will be an extremely important point in the transformation, not only of Jewish politics but in the whole of Europe in the fourteenth and fifteenth centuries. As José Gaos pointed out, dialectics originally prospered and, at the same time, degenerated with the Greeks. And from Greece, "[i]t passed to the first Christian dialecticians, who proposed the defense of their faith against the philosophy of the Gentiles by using those same dialectical arms of the Gentile and the Arab philosophers.

From those first dialecticians it passed on to the Arabic dialecticians who, in an analogous situation to the Christians, imitated these Christians, and from the Arabic philosophers and dialecticians, it finally and respectively passed to the Jewish philosophers and dialecticians."[33]

Vigilance and Lethargy

The validity of Ashkenazic wisdom is obvious, according to R. Shesheth. As we have seen, he expressed his enthusiasm for the teachers of the north. Thus, in opposition to Maimonides' learning by hearing—as we find later on in *Don Quixote*—he looks for another way of learning associated with the light that penetrates and reveals, in other words, the apotheosis of the dialectical and the visual:[34]

> The great luminary R. Solomon, his memory be for a blessing, has shed light on the darkest depths of the Talmud: no hidden matter was obscure to him. Without his commentary the Talmud would be a sealed book. The second luminary was R. Jacob Tam. In dialectic (*pilpul*) there has been none like him since the close of the Talmud. The Talmud was well arranged and fluent in his mouth, he was a *Sinai* uprooting mountains and grinding them one against another (i.e. an erudite scholar and a dialectician). All the wise must tremble at his *pilpul*, his depth of insight, and breadth of understanding. All the other French sages are great stars; on what comes from their mouth we live, and their water we drink.[35]

This is a world of light necessarily associated with *vigil*, wakefulness, never with the darkened world of lethargy. It is a life oriented toward analysis and minute scrutiny, controlled by a mind that is aware of itself, and where the greatest goal is "good or useful for preserving our being and enjoying a rational life."[36] This view of the external world as seen through the association and imagination so typical of the Jewish tradition is understood and confronted now by a reason that, as Baruch Spinoza (1637–1677) would write later on "God is without passions, and is not affected with any affect of Joy or Sadness."[37] It is an active and vigilant man that never sleeps and lives by the *dictate of reason*: "A free man, i.e., one who lives according to the dictate of reason alone, is not led by Fear, but desires the good directly, i.e., acts, lives, and preserves his being from the foundation of seeking his own advantage."[38]

In the sixteenth century Spinoza is probably the Sephardic philosopher who perceives most radically the consequences of that Gothic world that had made its way into Sepharad three centuries earlier: "I call him free who is led by reason alone."[39] It is a moral environment in which the Christian identification of knowledge with power had already been consummated, and one that Francis Bacon (1561–1626) had expressed so well. In addition, Spinoza remarks, "From what has been shown, it is clear how much the Wise man is capable of, and how much more powerful he is than one who is ignorant and driven only by lust."[40]

In order for this Gothic transition to dialectics to take place, it had previously been necessary to discredit lethargy. Dreams were completely devaluated and alien to the supreme truth of reason. When we dream, the mind is deactivated, unfeeling; dream appears here as we have previously seen in the *Zohar*, as a residual activity that cannot be trusted because it is lacking in any type of freedom: "For when the Body is at rest in sleep, the Mind at the same time remains senseless with it, nor does it have the power of thinking, as it does when awake."[41]

Lethargy is alien to thinking. In order for the mind to become free, it must work under the executive direction of memory and will[42] (what contemporary political theory has called *red memory*) to produce piloted thought. What it cannot do, however, is become inundated with images and fantasies that go and come without anyone evoking them, over which there is no control and can lead the individual to think erroneously that he is acting with autonomy when he is actually being carried along irrationally: "When we dream that we speak, we believe that we speak from a free decision of the Mind—and yet we do not speak, or if we do, it is from a spontaneous motion of the Body . . . We dream, finally, that, from a decision of the Mind, we do certain things we do not dare to do while we wake."[43]

The Sephardic Spinoza[44] was aware of how little control man has over his memory. In fact, his Sephardic background enables him to understand, in spite of everything, that there exists what today we would term a *green memory*. Moreover, what is surprising is that he shows an interest in forgetting and oblivion. However, this trait of Spinoza, an exceptional thinker totally assimilated into the Gothic world, still preserves a wonderful remnant of his southern education. This makes him one of the very few modern theoreticians who do not consider forgetting to be a negative memory but as a creative function in itself.[45] Fortunately for us, Spinoza "betrays" himself on this point:[46] "We can do nothing from a decision of the Mind unless we recollect it. E.g. we cannot speak a word unless we recollect it. And it is not in the free power of the Mind to either recollect a thing or forget it."[47]

Nevertheless, his Gothic education in Amsterdam would end up imposing on his thought. This is obvious in Spinoza's harsh disparagement of those who, in the rhetoric of the south, are the *in-fantes*:[48] "So the madman, the chatterbox, the child, and a great many people of this kind believe they speak from a free decision of the Mind, when really they cannot contain their impulse to speak."[49] Those elements that are not within the absolute domain of the mind are obstacles to freedom, unless they are duly controlled by dictatorial reason. Reason is the only road to freedom and happiness: "Postulate 52: Self-esteem can arise from reason, and only that self-esteem which does arise from reason is the greatest there can be."[50]

It is worrying to see the coincidence between this postulate and Freud's declaration that the intellect may in time "establish a dictatorship in the mental life of man,"[51] even though he spent his whole life trying to overcome this conviction. Spinoza's reason, as the reader will have surmised, is the equivalent of the *executive power* of the citizen's mind, that is shaped—as Hannah Arendt saw very well in the twentieth century—by memory and will.

All this brings us fully into the Gothic world that has come down to our time with its vigilant society and the apotheosis of action. It appears in two variants, as Michel Foucault so aptly analyzed: (1) vigilance and punishment, typical of romanticism and continuing on in the twentieth century, and (2) vigilance and a step toward action, proper to the postnuclear society.[52]

Rabbi Asher Arrives in Sepharad

Rabbi Asher ben Yehiel,[53] "Rosh" (1250–1328) arrived in Spain in search of asylum with his entire family after experiencing many hardships in his native Germany, where he was considered one of the most eminent authorities in Jewish law. Upon his arrival it seems he was welcomed by Solomon ibn Adret,[54] a noted rabbi of the kingdom of Aragon, whose rulers consulted him on important matters, and a dominant figure in the Jewish community of Barcelona. A pupil of Nahmanides, he had also attained a position of enormous prestige in the Jewish world as seen in his numerous *responsa*.

Asher's arrival would have important repercussions for the orientation of Sephardic Jewry. He came at a moment when Christianity was beginning to reveal itself as a powerful hegemony in Europe and the consolidation of the Christian monarchies was a fact.[55] Their advance was coming to an end, and European Judaism had no other way to survive than by adapting to the Christian world in some way, a culture with which it had already become impregnated.

It hardly seems possible that Rosh would have arrived in Spain without mentors who prepared the way for his visit. Nor is the explanation convincing that he ended up in Barcelona by accident. It would be interesting to investigate the preparations for his journey. Given its scope and the persons who intervened, it would seem to be the work of the Tosafist and pro-Ashkenazic sector, in favor of a change to "Europeanize" the Sephardic population.[56] We have already seen the serious conflict that arose in the twelfth century with the culture of the southern philosophers, undoubtedly more cultured and capable, a movement that largely failed due to the opposition of the Occitanian and Spanish rabbis. It is not strange that this opening to such an important figure in the Ashkenazic world would be a political movement favored by the pro-Ashkenazic sector of Sepharad. The difference probably lay in the fact that, instead of being promoted by persons of intellectual probity and religious zeal like Jonah Gerondi and Nahmanides, it was now patronized by Ibn Adret (Rashba), who was, moreover, also a political and diplomatic talent of the first order, and arguably the major political figure of Sephardic Judaism in the fourteenth century:[57] He was a great communitarian strategist, but not a particularly brilliant Talmudist.[58]

Asher arrived in Barcelona and was immediately appointed chief rabbi of "The Great Synagogue" of Toledo in 1305.[59] His appointment was made from one day to the next. Without having any knowledge of the local culture and without being open to a cosmopolitan outlook, Asher saw himself in Toledo as the head of a vital center of Sephardism. It seems, however, that the reaction of the Jews of Toledo was positive, which speaks for the tolerant attitude of this *aljama* and the trust in Asher's patrons. He immediately began to act as rabbi and judge, apparently with everyone's respect, even though this point has not yet been properly investigated.

It is possible that, for some people, Asher's arrival was a reinforcement of Jewish piety in the face of the increase in Christian proselytizing in Sepharad. The activity of the preaching missions must have done great damage in the Jewish communities of the kingdom of Aragon, with the consequent alarm of those responsible for their welfare. The flourishing Christian society must have pressured the Jewish population toward a conversion—feigned or real—that would have frightened its leaders. If young Jews were confused by the tension between the philosophical explanations and those given by the more mystical and imaginative rabbis at a time of

Christian social and demographic advances, the arrival of a more demanding Talmud rooted in the most sober piety of the Tosafists must have presented a good option for many of them. This it was necessary to combat in any way possible "the assault from the outside, from a powerful and aggressive Christendom now deeply committed to the propagation of its belief system everywhere and among all peoples."[60]

Upon his arrival, Asher found himself in a special religious environment. German Jewry, where he came from, was more united, perhaps because of the harsh persecution they had been subjected to, and much less integrated into the local society. He found differences in liturgy and marriage. In the Ashkenazic world Christian monogamy had imposed itself completely. In Sepharad it was widespread, thanks to the good offices of Ibn Adret, but polygamy had not completely disappeared. Moreover, the German Jews brought a stricter observance, with special insistence on virtues such as attendance at synagogue, honesty, frugality, and the idea of sacrifice.

Coming from very different lands and a climate that made living together or coexistence difficult with a very warlike Christian world, Asher found himself in Provence and Toledo with a more relaxed environment in its religious practices. This was particularly worrisome, especially in what he perceived as an abandonment of Talmud reading, something that in Germany was strictly established and that, thanks to the method of the Tosafists, had been able to spread with a certain uniformity. In Toledo his attention was called to the multiplicity of interpretations and attitudes. In any case, Asher made a great effort to overcome the obstacles of language, and in time he adapted to his new home, so much so that his two daughters married Sephardic men.[61] The fact is that Asher began to work at the top of the Sephardic community as its maximum leader and as the supreme judge in charge of trying matters that could not be resolved in the usual courts.

Moreover, he became the head of a *yeshiva* where, as it was to be expected, he used the Tosafist method of studying the Talmud, a method that was already known in Spain through Jonah Gerondi[62] and Nahmanides. These teachers were always staunch partisans of importing methods from the north of France, and from the Ashkenazim in general. As Lorberbaum points out: "Nahmanides was very instrumental in disseminating the Ashkenazic tradition in Spain."[63]

Asher began his task with a zeal that speaks to us of his leadership ability and his effort to implant this pro-Ashkenazic movement in Spanish lands. He ended up producing his own method within the Tosafist line that would spread throughout the Iberian Peninsula and other places in Europe. This line of work and progress in exerting his influence was undoubtedly seen with approval by those in favor of extirpating from Sepharad the peculiarities of its philosophers and its rhetorical humanism, clearly beyond the line that prevailed in the Christian world. This was expressed very well by a rabbi and faithful disciple affiliated with Asher's school: "In the year 5065 (1305) the Lord inspired the great teacher R. Asher b. Yehiel—his memory be for a blessing—to leave his native country Germany and to immigrate with his sons and his whole family into Toledo, to enlighten our eyes and to bring us out from darkness and backwardness to the light of wisdom and understanding."[64]

The idea of all the followers of this tendency coincides in expressing through these visual metaphors of light and opening what they believe is an updating of the societies in the peninsula. It is a matter of adapting a new public philosophy in consonance with the ways of life of the Christian world that was clearly overpowering in its expansion through Western Europe. The main argument is that, thanks to Asher, the Sephardim will come back to the ordered and systematic readings of the Talmud as a way of educating themselves in the faith and tradition of Israel.

From here on it seems that the adaptation of the Spanish Jews to Ashkenazic pedagogy is unquestionable. To a certain extent this movement reminds us of attempts to Europeanize the peninsula, an idea that comes up at certain periods later on in Spanish history.

While Rabbi Asher searched throughout his life for a synthesis between the Ashkenazic position and the Sephardic tradition he found in Toledo, his son, Rabbi Jacob, sought the integration or unity of the two. He was proud of a strict Talmudic purism and would not accept the use of non-Talmudic sources or substitutions for direct sources, something that he accused Maimonides and the Talmud scholar Isaac ben Jacob Alfasi (1013–1103) of doing. He would also fault Maimonides—always the prime target, more or less covert, of the attacks of the Ashkenazic faction—for not making use of hundreds of pages of the Talmud. In contrast, we should not be surprised at this point to learn that Rabbi Jacob Asher devoted a great deal of attention to the *responsa* of Solomon ibn Adret and his own father, Rabbi Asher.[65] In this he again united the names of those who seemed to have been the executors of a political program of enormous importance for the transformation of Spanish Jewry.

One of the Ashers' most frequent reproaches, that eventually became the reason for doing away with such a monumental and extraordinary work as Maimonides' *Code*, was that Rambam organized his *Mishneh Torah* according to obsolete procedures. For Rabbi Jacob, the organization of the code should take into account above all the usefulness of the precepts and the solutions for the present moment. In other words, he inclines toward the *modus hodiernus* that he would use to reorganize his entire version of Jewish *halakhah* in an extraordinarily new way for the Sephardim. However, he considered Maimonides too dense and too difficult to digest because of the way he synthesized his knowledge. Agility, efficiency, and updating were the three points that this rabbi opposed to "old" Maimonides and his obsolete knowledge.[66]

In his interest in those laws that had current applications, Rabbi Jacob praises and sets as examples the Tosefta scholars, whom he follows and frequently cites. Nevertheless, it was not all that simple and monotonous. Soon there would appear the first reactions against this orientation.

Sephardic Reaction against the Asherites

In spite of the operation to bring Asher to Toledo, there were also reactions contrary to the significance of this maneuver. After the death of Rabbi Asher in 1327 his son, Rabbi Judah, succeeded him in the High Synagogue of Toledo. But it seems that the son did not have his father's diplomatic talents or tact in relations with the community. These disagreements seem to have motivated his resignation from the post and his move to Seville.[67]

Other important discrepancies centered around matters of ritual where, leaving aside the details, two traditions, Sephardic and Ashkenazic, opposed each other, in addition to the validity of their different teachers. Asher signaled the massive entrance of new norms and ways of understanding the community, which was expressed constantly in changes in ritual or in the imposition of new texts and references. Sooner or later this implied a confrontation with the philosophical orientation of the Sephardic scholars and, of course, with Maimonides at its head.

Rabbi Asher, the father, succeeded in imposing certain interpretations in lieu of Maimonides' criteria, which indicates the widespread range of his modifications. Nevertheless, little by little the old opinions began to surface again, particularly in the second half of the fifteenth century. Isaac de Leon, the rabbi of Toledo, openly discredited Asher in favor of Maimonides on the controversial use of *tefillin*[68] that had caused problems for many years;[69] in this sense the *Zohar* is in favor of its usage.[70]

A good point of contrast can be found in the use of the Turim, a code written by R. Jacob Asher as a critical alternative to that of Maimonides. It seems, however, that this code, riding on the prestige of his father, Rabbi Asher, has not been preserved or mentioned in important works by contemporaries, nor is it cited by particularly relevant authors such as Hasdai

Crescas and Profiat (Perfet) Duran.[71] These absences are especially significant because Crescas, on the other hand, showed his admiration for the work done in Toledo by the Ashers. Possibly this rejection was specifically aimed at Rabbi Jacob Asher's code. This also seems to be confirmed by the fact that such a prestigious Ashkenazic author as Rabbi Solomon Luria chose to ignore it.[72] At present the question is still unresolved.

Another point of dissent seems to lie in moral questions. The arrival of the Ashers implied, to a large extent, a clash between two moral traditions. The Asher family's contact with Sephardic values probably took place through the faction headed by Jonah Gerondi and Solomon ibn Adret that was more sympathetic to Ashkenazic views.

For their part, the Ashers—the father and his two sons, Jacob and Judah—were consummate moralists, with written works to prove it. It appears that they themselves were devout examples of piety, obedience to the commandments and religious precepts. In this sense they seem to have imported a German piety based on austerity and honesty.

For the Asher family, piety and the fulfillment of religious duties must have been a truly divine obligation. The strict regimen of German Jewry, so encapsulated in that stern and adverse Germanic Christian environment that they brought with them, caused them to be almost scandalized when they saw the situation of the Sephardic communities in the peninsula who lacked their ritual and moral severity. An example of this rigorous commitment was exhibited by a grandson of Rabbi Asher, Judah ben Asher II. In 1392, in the midst of the wave of anti-Semitism that devastated the Spanish Jewish quarters to the cry of "baptism or death," he decided to put an end to his life and that of his entire family.[73] This example of radical Gothic moral did not fail to impress his Sephardic coreligionists.[74]

Modern Times

Some present-day scholars recognize the importance of the thirteenth century in the evolution of European public philosophy: "The thirteenth century was a critical time for the development of Jewish communal life in Spain and the Christian West was then undergoing a profound structural change."[75] This same period also gives evidence of "the major bifurcation in medieval Jewish *halakhah*: that between the Ashkenazic and the Sephardic."[76] Nevertheless, we are missing a few nuances to round out this matter.

For example, it is more than questionable to consider Meir of Rothenburg (c. 1215–1293) and Solomon ibn Adret, respectively, as representative leaders of the two divergent tendencies for, as we have already seen, Ibn

Adret was clearly in favor of introducing the northern vision of the public sphere in Sepharad. It is not strange, then, that with this erroneous basic supposition, these same scholars are astonished at "the strikingly similar lines of their legal and conceptual framework."[77]

Another objection that can be made is that, on evaluating the Sephardic influence in Ashkenazic schools, the presence of authors who were clearly in the pro-Ashkenazic band is counted in with these schools, as is the case of the aforementioned Jonah Gerondi in Gerona and Isaac ben Shesheth in Saragossa and Valencia, where the latter had his school until 1391.[78] There are isolated cases of Ashkenazic students from Provence who came to study with rabbis of the same orientation in Barcelona in the school of Rabbi Perez and Rabbi Nissim.[79]

In view of the data that has come down to us, everything seems to indicate that throughout the thirteenth century there was a massive entrance, encouraged by Solomon ibn Adret, of Ashkenazic influence in Spain. Surely the purpose was to introduce a kind of modernization, to use a term we can understand today, or perhaps an adaptation to a world that was imposing itself—the Christian world—with all that it signified politically and socially. The Reconquest had advanced to the point where it was in a phase of definitive consolidation, and the Christian kingdoms did not hesitate to take control of and colonize the newly won territories. The politics of the Catalan rabbis, more so than that of Provence, was oriented primarily to living together with the new circumstances and purging themselves of a local past that was often written in Arabic, a defeated language and a past that they had to do without. They could no longer hope for an existential outlet to European Judaism if they were anchored in a pedagogy taught in Arabic and a view of the *aljamas* that lived in Arabic.

In his time Maimonides had taken a decisive turn in shaping the maturity of Jewish culture expressed in Arabic. With the translation of his profoundly Sephardic work into Hebrew and Latin, the Islamic world of philosophy and science was gradually transferred to the Christian societies of Spain, Provence, and Italy, to later pass on to non-Mediterranean Europe. This was how the European Jews became liberated from their dependence with respect to their coreligionists in Islamic countries. Thus Maimonides marks "the end of an era"[80] and the passing of authority in the Jewish world to Gothic Europe.

The Catalan leaders found their uniqueness and their prestige in their liaison with Ashkenazic Jewry, and in this way they made their pioneering contacts with them. There are indications that Ibn Adret may have been the key player in this entire movement aimed at accepting pragmatically and adapting to the Christianization of the Iberian Peninsula. With it, he probably sought an advantageous situation of living-togetherness from the social, cultural, and financial—he was an expert in this field—point of view. In sum, he looked for the preservation of the well-being that Nahmanides refers to on one occasion,[81] when he mentions the wealth and comfort of the Sephardic communities in contrast to the instability and hazards of the Franco-Germanic communities. Leaders such as Ibn Adret must have thought something of the sort when they considered the need to adapt to adverse circumstances so as not to lose the advantages they still enjoyed. While it is true that they did not hesitate to accept the fact that many things had changed for the good, they also had to concede the deterioration of a line of democratic rhetorical conduct that was very Mediterranean. This rhetorical public life, so full of influences of Greek culture and Roman Hellenism, implied at the same time—and this is the crucial test—the deterioration of the tradition of good judgment and the devaluation of its cultural summit as represented by Maimonides, "the Sephardic one."

In spite of everything, the culture of Sepharad would leave an invaluable legacy: "The arrival in Italy of significant numbers of manuscripts from Spain dealing with an amalgam of philosophy, magic, and astrology, influenced the early Florentine Renaissance . . . The Italian printers preferred to print both Spanish philosophical and kabbalistic writings over the literature in those fields generated by Italian thinkers."[82]

Custom and Leadership

For Nahmanides, custom is not a spontaneous or conventional local practice that contrasts with the law. Custom is equivalent to legal norm and is characterized by its regularity and the careful measure with which it is put into practice by the political leader with the highest authority. Custom, in this slightly Ashkenazic view, is interchangeable with "law" (*hok*) and "statute" (*Mishpat).*[83]

Nahmanides points out that Joshua made a convenant with his people and established a statute or ordinance (*hok u-Mishpat*) in Shechem (Joshua 24:25). These were not divinely inspired laws but "the customs and ways of civilized society."[84] Such were the conditions that Joshua established on arriving in the promised land, "which the Rabbis have mentioned," according to Nahmanides.[85]

Joshua united his people in a pact, a covenant that stipulated the conditions for living of the Israelites as a people who agreed to live in the land of Israel. This legislative action gave way to laws that were not those of the Torah, the existing legal code. Nevertheless they were imposed on the people and took on the nature of basic laws. By bringing this up, Nahmanides opened the way for the possibility of introducing new laws derived from royal or urban powers so that the Jewish community could begin to evolve with the times and respond to the new needs that might arise.

Both Moses and Joshua established the norms for living that they previously agreed on with their people, and they did so by virtue of their leadership. With it, they helped to set the living conditions for their people, making use of their positions as leaders.

Nahmanides sees leadership as something absolutely indispensable to public life. It is essential for establishing adequate norms of life, ways of living that are necessary for the environment in which the people of Israel are obliged to live.

This ability to direct and introduce norms, even though it is consulted with the people, reveals a very profound communication of political leadership with the capacity for judgment. It does not obstruct judgment, but to a certain extent it passes itself off as judgment because it introduces the idea that those norms that were set up by the executive leadership are calculated, meditated on wisely by a leader who is prepared and can reach a consensus. Between the wisdom of the leader and the covenant with the people, the everyday function of judgment is set up to be directed or later on invaded by the other powers of Israel.

Nahmanides refers to the instructions that Moses gave his people to help them to become a civilized society, even when they were living in that wild and uninhabited territory before they reached the Promised Land. They now need new ways of living. He gives them rules by which they must lead their lives: love one another, follow the advice of the sages, endure hunger and thirst by praying to God without complaining, be discreet in their tents in front of women and children, and treat those strangers peacefully who come to the camp to sell various things. He gives them moral instructions, warning them that they should not become "like bands of marauders who do all abominable things and have no sense of shame."[86]

All this seems like a compendium of moral dictates with which Moses wants his people, who until a short while back were slaves, to become a people with self-discipline. This interpretation is the one that the Jewish scholars of Ashkenazic origin have used to establish and justify the need for this political turnabout toward positions in which Sephardic good judgment becomes marginalized as being antiquated[87] and ends up deferring to the leadership agreed upon. This turnabout was probably influenced by French

Christian public ideology.[88] In this sense, Nahmanides took the idea from Rashbam[89] (c.1085–c. 1158) on the quasicontractual relationship between the Jews and the Christian king to explain the position of the Jews living in the kingdom of Aragon. As Novak pointed out, "Nahmanides was the first Spanish-Jewish or 'Sephardic' scholar to incorporate in his writing the work of Franco-German or 'Ashkenazic' scholars like Rashbam and his grandfather Rashi."[90] The interpretations of tradition were debated around the Jewish principle of the Talmud, "The law of the kingdom is the law." This command recognizes the need to count on a legal order in the city and how important it was for the *aljamas* to live harmoniously together with the powers in whose territory the Jewish community had settled. Implied within it is the idea that the very existence of the people of Israel in the Diaspora is at stake. We should also say that, although Nahmanides accepts the Ashkenazic view of the relations between the Jewish communities and the Crown, he elaborates on it in his own way: "When we say 'the law of the kingdom is law,' we mean specifically those laws recognized . . . by the king throughout his kingdom, matters which he and all the other kings before him have employed . . . We infer this from the wording of 'the law of the kingdom [*duba de-malkhuta*] is law,' not 'the law of the king [*dina de-malka*] is law.' So, it means the law recognized by all the kings."[91]

The consequence of this acceptance of a royal justice with the ability to impose its laws on the Jewish inhabitants was very significant. Would the Jews become the subjects of the Christian king? Even if Nahmanides wanted to be inspired by precedents he found in the Jewish kings, the truth is that the medieval kings were the rulers of a Christian majority and would never submit to the wishes of the Jewish people, who were always in the minority. No matter how much they tried to base their practical acceptance on *halakhic* tradition, it is difficult not to see it as a practical solution that reflected the *needs of the moment*, in other words, political contingency.

Nahmanides was very concerned about this matter and attached a great deal of importance to the norms that Joshua gave to his people when they had settled in the Promised Land. These were mainly property ordinances having to do with conflicts over private and public land, when questions arose about ownership or inheritance of land. He was interested in the limits between public and private, in other words, everything having to do with the establishment of a public space. This may have had something to do with the fact that the people of Israel had evolved from being slaves and wanderers to becoming settlers in a permanent land of their own. Its members were now free men and had new property that should be theirs or taken over by them.

In this regard, notarial practices and the use of royal registries in civil matters were becoming more accepted. The Latin documents registered by a Christian notary could annul or modify the validity of a Jewish document. This is why some residents of the *call* began to use these registries as a convenient way of protecting their property, wills, and other civil documents. Although there was a rabbinical prohibition against using Christian courts or registers—something that was never entirely respected in Catalonia—at the end of the thirteenth century the tendency to use Christian notaries was almost universal.[92] As a result, Ibn Adret would order an updating of the registries and notarial practices of the *call*. At first he was opposed to acknowledging the validity of the royal notaries because he felt it would diminish the authority of the Jewish community.[93] Nevertheless, many Jews were already using this type of document as a useful civil tool in cases of local contracts and wills.

The de facto situation must have been so serious that Ibn Adret would lead the movement for the rabbinical authorities to accept the notarial culture. In the long run he was inclined to accept the established practice and acknowledged the Christian notaries. By doing so he followed "Nahmanides' innovation" of 1270.[94] The religious argument put forth to concede this point was the aforementioned Talmudic statement: "the law of the kingdom is the law."[95]

Such an administrative change also signified the passing of the culture of the Jewish scribes who prepared the documents in Hebrew or Aramaic to the Christian notaries who wrote letters in Latin and had no need of witnesses, which speeded up the procedures considerably. It also meant an important break in the exclusive monopoly of the scribes or notaries, who sometimes transferred or leased out these prerogatives.[96]

Nahmanides was very familiar with Maimonides' *Guide of the Perplexed* and his *Code*, where the teacher from Córdoba speaks of the relation between "the perfection of the body" and "the perfection of the soul." The latter implicated "the governance of the city and the well-being of the states of all its people according to their capacity."[97] Nahmanides also holds that in each of God's commandments there are many benefits "for body and soul."[98] Nevertheless, and in spite of his familiarity with Maimonides' ideas, he is closer to *halakhic* tradition. This can be seen in his ruling that if a problem arises between two properties or if two co-property owners have to divide their property, they should build a wall between the two made of uncut stones or half-bricks, "everything should follow local use."[99] This is an example of the *principium segregationis* against good judgment.

This detail is important because it is one thing to follow the usage established by half-conscious daily practice, full of wisdom and practical knowledge. It is another thing to have to make decisions based on the *good judgment* that is needed in each contingency. In each case the way contingency is dealt with is very different. For Nahmanides, treatment is automatic; it follows a collective everyday wisdom accumulated by experience. Thus the bother and disfunctionality of having *to stop and think* can be avoided. Maimonides, on the contrary, would have advocated maintaining the solution of stopping and thinking.

In the case of Rambam and the tradition of public philosophy that he sums up, it is essential to have a wise man present when reaching these agreements. This sage is a representative of the study of and commitment to the most profound religion. This criterion guarantees that certain values are not transgressed by the fact that the contingencies of each case are taken into account. The more we think about Maimonides' philosophy, the more we are left with a *defense of good judgment in public life* instead of justice in the abstract.

According to Nahmanides, the Mishnah gives its backing to local custom. Where there is an established custom, and if the city has agreed upon a type of conduct and has done so in view of everyone, the citizens are obligated to each other to uphold it in accordance with that custom. The decree of the *cahal* gives publicity to *halakhah*. When a custom is cited to establish the responsibility of one inhabitant against another, custom becomes publicized and legislated. In the face of this type of custom, good judgment is damaged. Custom is definitively endowed with entity, not only as a regulator of conduct but also of law that has been politically established.

Local custom establishes its true value as having provided nourishment for the law and as a support for the network of regulations, in other words, as a civilized foundation. Custom is the element that lends rational stability, power, and practical wisdom to laws. This aspect is essential for the contrast between the line of thought of Maimonides and the political theory of southern Europe and the later development of thought in northern Europe.

Here the Gothic world sees a reinforcement of the activity of the political authorities in the implantation of laws and a necessary way of assuring social order. But whom do we call "authority," if we leave aside the judges—who are all of us—of good judgment? It is obvious that the activity of these authorities is there to back up *the establishment of executive activity* with the purpose of securing the social order.

There is an interesting precedent in Joseph ibn Migash who, in one of his *responsa*, refers to a place in al-Andalus where they had to apply an excommunication that did not follow Jewish law but rather the law of political order and the government of the town: "We issued the enactment years ago in one of the provinces of Andalus for [local] reasons that compelled us to act differently from our practice in our own home."[100]

For Migash, the judicial activity of the courts is an act of government and a way of putting into practice the ordinances of city life. Apparently the Andalusian *aljamas* viewed the tribunals as an essential part of daily politics and were rather distrustful of those executives who had the ability to ally themselves with the assemblies and dictate ordinances, statutes, and laws. The idea lying behind all this seems to be that the custom of the place is tainted by the contamination of the assembly, of perverse judicial power, or at least the rather clumsy or ridiculous solution of being a replacement for the political management or conduct of contingency. Contingency must be served through judicial activity, always anchored in the wisdom of sages who are learned in *halakhah*. Even if it is seen from a medieval standpoint, at the bottom of this attitude lies the idea that good judgment is a therapeutic activity.

The tradition of the *responsa* can also be felt in all this. We should take into account that this was an essential practice in the Jewish quarters to regulate and order daily life. The rabbis' replies were always issued at the behest of the interest of the citizens who consulted them because they were considered to be wise men, morally qualified, with wisdom anchored in religion and ample experience. These *responsa*, or consultations of the teachers, are the basis of the confidence of the Sephardim in the idea of good judgment as an indispensable element in daily political life. For this view, the Talmud scholars were not judges but spiritual teachers and jurists who advised the judges and other persons about any subject that was put to them.[101]

Nahmanides, in contrast, tends to emphasize political leadership as the power and enterprising capacity of legislative tasks. This is why he refers to the labors of Moses and Joshua when it came time for them to give their people rules and regulations reinforced with the aid of their power as leaders. Of course he presents it as the legislative authority of a capable leader. This legislative ability of the leader is the foundation of public life, and political leadership is the motivating force that introduces those laws connected to charismatic power. A common space emerges that begins to be something like the nation. Nevertheless, the use of leadership as the essence of the idea of the public sphere was something that would fall to his disciples in the school of Barcelona, and to his pupil, Solomon ibn Adret, in particular.[102]

At this point we should stop and think about some doubts.

Great Jewish thinkers, particularly those who meddle in weighty political matters, frequently have a dual voice. In some cases, it has been attributed to a kind of esotericism provoked by the material in question (Leo Strauss); in others it has been attributed to their incoherence as authors (Hannah Arendt and her recourse to an alter ego) or opportunism (Sigmund Freud and his radical changes in theory). This dual voice can also be found in Nahmanides at a different level of depth and sometimes in diverging directions that speak to us of subjects with apparent incoherence. In view of the criticisms elicited by this mode of expression, I believe that there is some confusion between contradiction and counterpoint.

Bernard Septimus mentions cautiously that Nahmanides is a poet and the author "of some of the most memorable prose passages in medieval Hebrew literature."[103] For this scholar, the poems that have been preserved and his great kabbalistic poem reveal his close ties to the tradition of the south, a tradition that does nothing more than continue the link of the "*nasi* Sheshet Benveniste, the dominant figure in the Jewish culture of Catalonia of the generation prior to Nahmanides."[104] In his great *poem of the soul* Nahmanides shows himself to be within that "traditional Andalusian genre."[105] If we read his work with another sensibility, there appears a Nahmanides who is very faithful to his southern teachers.[106] This is why, in the dispute with Maimonides, he suggests as a mediator Ramah (Meir b. Todros Hal-evi Abulafia) of Toledo ("Let us go to the land of *ma*'arav"[107]). Literarily, Nahmanides' work falls within the Andalusian genre.[108]

When viewed in this light, it is no longer paradoxical that Ramban insisted on not introducing into the Gerona ritual the phrase "God, the faithful king," that had entered Gerona at the end of the twelfth century with the return of the great Talmud scholar R. Zerayah ha-Levi, after a brilliant career in Provence. Maimonides himself would have understood this rejection. Nor is it strange that Nahmanides refers to the attacks that had been taking place: "In recent generations by 'hordes and hordes [of scholars], all clever, who roaring like lions bring forward their objections and arguments to lower the lofty ramparts, who hold a doubled-edged sword . . . to kill wisdom that ought not die and to give life to worlds that ought not live.'"[109]

Here Nahmanides adapts into his own style the Sephardic technique of writing as if he were creating a mosaic. With it he takes advantage of the wealth of subjects that arise freely *in foro interno* and opens the way for the incorporation of lethargy into creative production. With this in mind we can begin to understand how Nahmanides "identified strongly with the old Spanish *halakhic* tradition."[110] Thus there emerges a Nahmanides who never ceased in "his attempts to limit northern erosion of Spanish *halakhic* tradition."[111] In short, this is the Nahmanides whose extraordinarily wide range of subjects, interests, and versatility is given over to the cultural ideal of embracing several disciplines that can enrich each other without one completely dominating or excluding the other: “This was perhaps one of the finest gifts of the Andalusian heritage to the mind of Nahmanides.”[112]

Philosophers and Believers

A key point in the evolution of public life in Western Europe is the confrontation between philosophy, the rational sense of life in all its aspects, and faith, which cultivates revealed knowledge and is moved entirely by a basic feeling: the love of God.

In this sense, the principal reasons by which a person takes on the task of living true to his beliefs within a city are influenced by both types of knowledge. On the one hand, it is true that a person is born into a community in which from within we are given a language, we experience our first loves of our parents and those who look after us and where—as René Descartes knew very well—we are inculcated with certain indelible sentiments that orient us in our behavior, probably for the rest of our lives. This is why our most elementary ideas about good and evil, good and bad people, and our purpose in life are instilled within us in our inner world, what present-day political theory calls *internal public spaces*, and with which we are going to live most, if not all our lives.

Moreover, the idea of ritual will also be imposed or passed on to us. Individuals commemorate certain events of their people or circumstances in the life of human beings such as the coming of age or marriage that are governed by authorized standards through collective or individual acts. They do so by means of specific rituals that instill in them certain patterns of thought or ways of confronting the unknown factors in life. Ritual is directed primarily to articulating the contingency of life. In the face of the great ideas or sentiments that tie the individual to everything that goes on in his city, to what is inherent in public life, ritual helps him to cope with his day-to-day existence. This is a contingency that includes problems and doubts, feelings that overwhelm us, painful wounds, and uncontrollable fears and their consequences.

From the twelfth to the fourteenth centuries public life was based on a mixture of religion and philosophical or scholastic knowledge, with the balance frequently leaning to one side or the other. It is enough to observe, on the one hand, how the historians of philosophy ignore the theologians, and on the other, the ambiguity toward politics of the religious philosophers to comprehend the dissonances within that union of knowledge. In the years when the State was coming into being and when the seeds were being sown for the concept of modern freedom, it is also obvious that theologians and religious leaders had serious problems with philosophy. As Agassi has said, "The Medieval venture was thus to merge theology and natural science; the modern parallel task was lesser: it was to free science from theology."[113]

The evolution in the West of what the Greeks called *episteme* and the Latins translated as *sciencia* was considerably hindered by the breaking off of relations between what we have already called the two Europes: the Greek-speaking and the Latin-speaking. This breakup of the Roman Empire, more than its collapse, is a concept that is historically inadequate. From the fourth century on it caused a very serious political confrontation in Rome. A classic example of this crisis is the rejection of eminent figures in Roman philosophy because they had been favorable to the predominance of the culture or directly by posing the subordination of Constantinople. Boethius (c. 480–524)[114] is a case in point.

This breakup of the empire, carried out with such hatred and violence, supposed the isolation of the Latin world with respect to Greek and Hellenistic culture that were marginalized from Western public philosophy. The concept of "West" probably originated with this civil fracture in Rome. The height of the Gothic cultures and law, albeit Christianized, would produce much of what we now term the Western identity. It is easy to understand that the so-called Crusades, those great military campaigns undertaken with the pretext of recovering the Holy Places, must have been very much influenced by that difficult but, at the same time, close relationship with the Byzantine Empire or, what is more understandable, with Greek-speaking Europe. It is highly probable that the connection with the Greek world and its scientific, philosophical, and literary production was interrupted in the Latin-speaking Christian schools. Even today students in the West cannot understand why they are taught with so much enthusiasm the work of the Greek schools up until the rise of the greater Rome of Augustus (Octavian) in the first century BCE, and then suddenly information about it is cut off abruptly as if it had vanished from history. Students no longer know that the Greek schools remained open until 529 and that the output of the Greek-speaking world was very worthwhile, even in later centuries. Many students, and perhaps an occasional professor who is not familiar with legal history, still believe that Justinian was a Roman emperor. All these gaps and distortions in teaching, and consequently in the culture of Latin Europe, give evidence of the grave political schism produced in the Roman civil war in the fourth century between the sons of the emperor Constantine.

In this situation it is not surprising that the evolution of the culture and identity of Western Europe is deficient in Greek influence. That gap was filled by Western Judaism as an intermediary rooted in both Christendom and Islam. Greek science and the knowledge of the treasures of the Mediterranean would be transmitted from the seventh century on by way of Islam. We can say that the expansion of Islam toward Europe would bring with it all that Greek culture that had been transplanted to Constantinople and Antioch and would arrive in European enclaves like Sicily, southern Italy, the Barbary Coast, and the Iberian Peninsula. For Islam, the Greek is very different from the Latin. Moreover, that scientific and philosophical culture was very close to them because to a large extent it had evolved within their own lands.

The role of the Jewish communities would be essential in this transmission. The *aljamas* preserved within them the influences of the Hellenized Jewish communities; they spoke Arabic and read Aristotle and the Greek sages by way of the Arabic philosophers, or *mutakallimun*. This preservation of Greek culture and access to its great wisdom by Jewish teachers would be produced and assimilated in a special way in Sepharad, a territory very far removed from the cultural and scientific centers of the period. The Jews in general longed for Jerusalem and looked toward the East as the source of so much excellent knowledge of philosophy and the sciences such as mathematics, geometry, medicine, and astronomy. It is no accident that the Sephardic Jew, Judah Halevi, defined himself as an inhabitant of the extreme west, that is, what would soon be a Western European: "My heart is in the east, and I in the uttermost west. / How can I find savor in food? How shall it be sweet to me?"[115]

The arrival of all this culture and its knowledge was bound to meet up with Latin Europe sooner or later. Culture in the Latin language arose in isolation from that politically antagonistic tradition, even though it was its matrix. The clash would be very intense because Europe has forged an entire public life based on the Christian religion in its Western version, and on Roman and Gothic law. The anathema against paganism on the part of the Christian church of Rome signified an anathema against anything Greek after Christ. The idea of *polis* is outside the Christian calculations. With the pretext of their universality they open up to the Gothic world and cultures alien to the Greek world such as those of the Celts and Franks. The paganism of the western tribes is assumed as barbarian, and, to a certain extent, although it is not acceptable, it is seen from Rome as something primitive, a product of ignorance. For Christianity this problem was easily solved through preaching. But Greek paganism was not the same; it was observed with much more trepidation because of the power of its arguments and the weight of its extraordinary knowledge.

It is not unusual for this clash between the Greek and the Latin to appear again in the West at a time when the Jewish philosophers are beginning to absorb that knowledge and the philosophies of Arabic science and transfer them to Latin Europe, a task or enterprise for which they are eminently qualified. Averroes never had direct access to the university chairs of Paris or the English schools of the time, but the Jewish teachers did. They were able to translate, interpret, and paraphrase Greek science and comment on it to their coreligionists of Christian Europe. The work of cross-pollination of the Jewish communities in Western Europe is of incalculable value. And, in the whole process, the prominence of the largest, richest, and most cultured Jewish population, in every sense of the word, would be paramount.

Christian Hatred

Today the profound rejection and genuine hatred of medieval Christianity for the Jews has frequently been passed over lightly: "The reason that the church, emperors, kings, and princes permitted the Jews to dwell among them and with Christians, is because they always lived, as it were, in captivity, as it was constantly in the minds of men that they were descended from those that crucified Our Lord Jesus Christ."[116]

Logically, after having overcome the paroxysm of the Gothic Holocaust of the Third Reich, Christianity has succeeded in emerging from such negative and destructive feelings that often led to homicide. Fortunately, today a Jew and a Christian can reason with more freedom in this respect, although there are still attempts to "sweeten" the underling problems. If, on the one hand, Pope Benedict XVI speaks of *pentimento*, "repentance" for the recent anti-Semitic abuses, he immediately reaffirms and reclaims public acknowledgment of the Christian identity of the European project. In dealing here with a German pope with a broad philosophical background, it is again evident that European identity is presently held captive by that Gothic culture that we have mentioned in this book on several occasions.

The advance and affirmation of the Christian world was being prepared in the twelfth century. The frontiers of Europe were moving southward, and Islam was being defeated religiously and on the battlefield. Military might was organizing around the Christian monarchies. Christian law became an amalgam of Roman law and Gothic legal tradition. Public sentiments that rallied around the rise of Western Christianity emphasized the love of the homeland, efficiency, the leadership of the Crown, dogmatic unity, and territory. Territorial repopulation was carried out every which way by taking advantage of all the resources with a great sense of pragmatism and military techniques. The conquest of public spaces, external and internal, was gradually being achieved by way of fortifications such as castles, citadels, colonized towns, and in another way by sermons, temples, monasteries, preaching orders, and the equally militant Church.

Christian life in the West is an example of the transmutation of effective Roman militarization whose domination carried over to consciences, that is, to the internal world of the population. Success was marked by the close alliance and coordination between the king's troops and the religious orders, with their strategic churches. The existence of orders that are both religious and political, military orders such as the Templars, are fascinating examples for a Western European for what they contain of virulence and omnipotence in its purest form. In essence they contain the seeds of the mentality and politics of Western Europe.

There is, however, a very disturbing element in all this. In a large part of the West, perhaps the most advanced in the sciences, the most developed financially, and the most cultured in the field of philosophy and the experience of living together, there was a clash between the two great empires of the moment. For the Christians, Islam is the enemy with whom there is a clear counteridentification, in that it can always be found on a military front. This is not the case with Judaism, whose communities are on both sides, with no sovereignty and without arms, which they would never resort to as a political solution; they have no land of their own and are unusual, different neighbors. They are industrious, pay their taxes, and do not present any military risks; and on many occasions, because of their natural propensity for books and learning—for religious purposes—they make up a large part of the educated and scholarly classes wherever they live. Many were born in those lands before the kingdoms in which they lived existed. They reside in a particular place, but sometimes they cannot be acknowledged as "one of our own" because they pledge their loyalty to another authority; they belong to another people: the *kehillal* Israel (all Israel).

When the clash between Greek and Latin Europe began, the same encounter would take place between the Jews. Many Jewish communities were Latinized—in time all the Jews of the south would become Latins or Ladinos. But there were others who spoke Arabic and breathed Greek science and philosophy in Arabic, and not only the science of classical philosophers such as Socrates, Plato, Aristotle, and Epicurus, but also that of Philo of Alexandria and Themistius. They were familiar with Babylonian mathematics, classical geometry, and the theory of numbers originally from India that arrived with Arabic mathematicians. Ibn Ezra (1092–1167) mentions the number 0 in one of his treatises on numbers, a novelty for the West. Those rabbis would study the Talmud and would produce a philosophy of the city much closer to the idea of Greek *polis* than that of their coreligionists—but not compatriots—in the north.

This encounter was anticipated, as on so many other occasions, in the heart of Western Judaism. The arrival of the science of the Arabic *falasifa* masked what was in the background; the real problem was the Greco-Latin confrontation. What touched it all off was the translation of all that Greek knowledge into Latin via the Arabic language. It is significant that Maimonides wrote his *Guide of the Perplexed* in Arabic *aljamiado*, that is, Arabic written in Hebrew characters, something he insisted a great deal on as if to give it a symbolic nature of particular importance.

This knowledge first made its way into Europe through places like the Sicilian court, al-Andalus, and Provence, points of very active contact between the Christian and Muslim empires. We know that the arrival of philosophy and science at the heart of Christian Europe was a decisive happening. This was true in the twelfth century with the translation of Aristotle, but the definitive moment came in the Quattrocento, or Early Renaissance, when the slow collapse of Byzantium began to filter out a priceless emigration that would contribute to Latin Europe all its scientific and cultural advances in the widest possible meaning. Those emigrants and refugees brought with them all their sophistication, including aspects such as eating with a fork—which arrived by way of Venice—and not with one's hands, daily bathing, new artistic forms such as those reflected in the School of Siena, and the rise of classical Greek studies.

The arrival of Greek philosophy had a particular significance for the Jewish world for several reasons:

1. First, the structure of Jewish public life, with its organization in neighborhoods, *calls*, or *aljamas*[117] had a very fragile autonomy. Because they could not function as an entirely independent entity, they could only dream of the idea of a self-sufficient autarchy. Obviously this was an almost utopian ideal, but it is easy to understand that the Jewish communities, who sometimes lived in enclosed spaces isolated from the rest of the city—not by choice but by imposition of the political powers—would feel closer to the idea of *polis*.

There were also some Jewish sectors that thought of the monarchy as it was in ancient times when Israel had kings, but in these cases the monarchical idea easily tended to project itself onto the past with overtones of Zionism or of regaining lost territory. Israel is their only land, the Holy Land, without which it would be impossible for Israel to achieve redemption. The insistence on this idea made it almost impossible for the Jewish inhabitants to settle down in the land of their birth, for time and again they recalled the transitory situation of the Jewish communities in the Diaspora, in spite of the fact that, for Spanish Jews, it had taken place a thousand years earlier.

The fact that the Jews either leaned toward the idea of a monarchy or toward the city as a model of public life to shape the *cahal* had profound implications when expressing their preference for one world or another, either Latin or Greek.

2. The view of public life would be adjusted in some cases to a very democratic and rhetorical idea of civic life. Personal, physical participation in the agora appears over and over again in the evaluation of political action. Life is not only based on the sight of banners and celebrations, on visual pedagogical and commemorative devices to reinforce the new patriotic identities with ensigns, flags, and decorations. The idea of *polis* as understood from Jerusalem, that is, from the *cahal*, is valid for the rabbis of the south. They give importance to the aural and consider the city, as we have seen in Maimonides, as a group of courtyards and alleyways that reflect the complex internal world of the individual.

3. In this sense, and perhaps as a corollary, we can say that the identity of the *cahal* cannot be visual, centered around the idea of a square where everyone is seen by everyone else. It is an audible world, favorable to a musical understanding of life.[118] This implies the rejection of the principle of identity of Aristotle's philosophy, which, in his *Metaphysics*, was imposed as a dictatorial principle. This aspect of Aristotelian thought is the one that did come into the Gothic world. This is why we cannot state categorically that Aristotelianism arrived from the south in a pernicious way. Maimonides' Aristotelianism is like that of the other philosophers of southern Europe, and in general, the Mediterranean, which is their common cultural matrix. It cultivates an idea of *polis* in which dialectics and rhetoric go

hand in hand. This is an idea of rhetoric understood as *the art of saying*, not speaking, where the feelings and passions of its citizens, in general, the affects, as well as their *doxai*, their ideas together with their beliefs, are taken into account. Moreover, these beliefs cannot be assessed without their affective foundations that are not guided by their consciences. The citizen is not an essentially executive figure but rather someone who judges himself by his entire worth, with aspects that are equally important for intelligence such as passion, daydreaming, creative fantasies, dreams, unconscious desire, and enchantment, in sum, what we have called *lethargy*. In this respect, we should recall the biblical character of Ruben, the eldest son of Jacob.

In the thirteenth century the scholars of Paris were also Aristotelians. But their Aristotelianism was completely faithful to his *Metaphysics* and his principle of identity. This is quite different from Aristotelian logic, which holds that dialectics and rhetoric are inseparable and complement each other. One without the other becomes a dangerous monster. This is the Aristoteles appreciated by Maimonides and the other sages of Sepharad. Public life has a body and a soul, inherency, and contingency and, if each one is not given its proper place, we can go crazy.

4. The recovery of good judgment. The drying up of the lethargic components of life—we should say that they are an essential part of Jewish tradition—as represented by Joseph, the prophet Daniel and so many others, introduced serious alterations that were very pernicious for Jewish life. Maimonides was very aware of the fact and deduced that this could very well translate into a fall into omnipotence, whether it be magic, as in resorting to astrology or chiromancy, or Christian, with the idea that *knowledge is power*. In medieval Christianity, knowledge was detached from good judgment, and public life was militarized. This moral breakdown was sublimely expressed in the character of Hamlet, a rebel Gothic prince, burning with civic rage, who ultimately resorted to death, although the author leaves the Horatio character, the rhetorical *orare*, alive.

The encounters between Christians and Jews always took place in Christian territory and by royal mandate. In every one of these cases the Jews were obligated to accept a meeting that they assuredly detested but had no choice but to attend. In pre-Renaissance times those encounters were known as *disputations*, as if they were scholarly exercises concerning a subject of interest, although they were far from being the real thing. Of course they did not have the structure of a trial, nor even the minimum guarantees required for a trial. These were actions carried out by a system of arbitration in which the essential factor was the intervention not of a judge but of an arbitrator. It is interesting to note that this perversion of judgment has persisted in Western European culture. Today anyone is called the "judge" of a contest even if he is just a mere referee or arbitrator to whom it is not possible to reply or carry on a dialogue.

In the Christian *disputatio* with Jews it was not a matter of attempting to find out the truth or searching for a hidden truth with a combined effort. In other words, there was no collaboration in a joint effort to clarify anything. Instead, it was a dogmatic, harsh, and almost militarized imposition. A good example of this is the Tortosa Disputation of 1413–1414, which was attended by many dignitaries, including the pope himself. His words are categorical: "You, scholars of the Jews, should know that I have not come here, and I have not sent for you, in order to prove which of our two religions is true; for it is a known thing with me that my religion and faith is true, and that your Torah was once true but was abolished. You have come only because Gerónimo has said that he will prove from the Talmud of your Rabbis, who knew more than you do, that the Messiah has come; therefore, you must speak before me on this topic alone."[119]

Solomon ibn Adret and His Prohibition Decree

We have already spoken of this rabbi who held a prominent position in Barcelona for over fifty years. His fame spread beyond the borders of Aragon, and there is evidence that it reached many other countries. If there was one single figure who supported the entrance of new ways of interpreting the Talmud and a new vision of public life in Sepharad, it was undoubtedly Ibn Adret.

As an authority in Catalonia and the most respected rabbi in Barcelona, Ibn Adret, or Ben Adret (Rashba) promulgated an influential decree that prohibited the reading of works by Maimonides. There had already been a fierce attack from within Judaisim against his philosophy and his alleged pernicious rationalism.

In the process of advancing the Gothic vision of politics toward southern Europe, Rashba is a very special figure, who was both prominent and discreet. There is no known work of his of literary or philosophical importance. In the words of Baer, "He himself contributed nothing to the philosophy of Judaism,"[120] But he did occupy a key place in thirteenth-century Jewish life.[121]

Ibn Adret was a man of broad scholarly education. Experts agree on his solid legal background. Not only was he learned in *halakhah*, but he was equally versed in Roman law. He intervened in cases of social relevance, such as a judgment involving the inheritance of a minor,[122] or in royal commissions on matters of informers, trials that required long periods of time to be resolved because of their political complexities and social repercussions. In these cases Ibn Adret appears to be rather unenthusiastic, unwilling to be a protagonist, but carried along by the king's mandate, by the request of his coreligionists, or petitions of *aljamas* other than that of Barcelona, which he served for decades as an indisputable authority. In spite of this alleged humility and discretion, Ibn Adret achieved international renown, as evidenced by the numerous *responsa* addressed to him from many different places.

Ibn Adret also appears at the core of the Jewish questions of the moment. In this sense the expression of the necessities of the moment (*dina de-malkuta dina*),[123] which he was so fond of repeating, came to refer to the necessities of politics as a changing reality and with its contingent demands.[124] We should make clear that these are not affective and emotional contingencies of thought and daily judgment, something that was probably very far removed from his concerns.

Ibn Adret's interest lay in the ability of the Jewish community to direct its political trajectory in agreement with the grand strategic designs.

This estrangement from the teachers of the south and a move closer to a view of politics that answered to contingency, but not *in foro interno*, was a major step toward Gothic thought. It was more concerned with the historical transmutation of the collective, a supposedly more democratic idea than the elitism of Maimonides. He was one of the architects of the adaptation of southern European Jewry, that is, Sepharad and its great defender, Provence, to the Gothic world.

In this sense we should analyze two points in his biography that are key to understanding his political orientation and relevance in the changes that would take place later on. We refer to (1) his decree against the reading of scientific and philosophical works and (2) his participation as a judge in important cases in the Jewish community of Barcelona.

Solomon ibn Adret always followed the lead of his teacher Nahmanides, as his best and most distinguished pupil. Moreover, the implication of the rabbis of Gerona in criticizing and attacking the works of Maimonides is well known. A first attempt implicated Jonah Gerundi and several rabbis from Montpellier, but Nahmanides' shadow was present in the background. Nahmanides owed a great deal to the teachings of Rambam and Ibn Ezra, but it is also true that, from his conservative stand point, he clearly had an aversion to the rationalism of the so-called "philosophers."

Nahmanides also taught and introduced Ibn Adret to the mystical teachings and the kabbalah. We know of his presence in these areas, but in these, as well as in other intellectual or theoretical undertakings, he did not stand out as an author.

Like his teacher, Ibn Adret was wary of the attempts of the Andalusian teachers to interpret the Torah and the Talmud in the light of the new scientific discoveries and the Greco-Arabic (Mediterranean) philosophical tradition. He was at the forefront, in a more or less visible way on occasions, of those who wished to restore the *halakhah* and the *aggadah*, in their literal simplicity, to the luminous position they had previously occupied in Jewish life and culture.[125] "And if one should persist in his error and say, 'I love these foreign ideas which have come to my notice and I shall pursue them,' we will say to him, 'The words of the sages cannot be discredited—that is impossible: let him who would cite evidence against them, and a thousand others like him, be set at naught, for they cannot invalidate even one iota of that which the sainted sages of Israel have validated.'"[126]

As a historian, Baer maintains that Ibn Adret was implicated in the defense of Jewish tradition. It is true that, in view of such opportune quotes as the one above, it might seem that way. But, from the standpoint of political theory, there seems to be another nuance. Ibn Adret is in favor of a Judaization of knowledge and morals, even though this might implicate such novelties as the kabbalah of Gerona. In this case it is not so much a question of innovation as a reinforcement of Jewish identity by linking up with popular traditions and wisdom received in a purely Jewish way such as teaching from master to pupil and the preservation of the law and its rabbinical commentaries. This Judaization incorporates a pro-Gothic line of exaltation of the popular as an expression of the essence of a community and opens the door to narratives, stories, simple beliefs, and massive feelings of identification that they encompass. Here the idea begins to take shape of a people as a candidate to become a distinct collective entity.

Ibn Adret was aware of the controversy concerning Maimonides. Solomon of Montpellier, a rabbi from the kingdom of Aragon,[127] hurled an anathema against the great Rambam. It was an astonishing ploy for its audacity and motivation, since it involved nothing less than tarnishing one of the greatest figures in rabbinical wisdom and Jewish creativity. This teacher, with the support of the well-known rabbi from Gerona, Jonah Gerondi, Nahmanides' cousin, launched an extremely violent attack on the Cordoban. In the end, the anathema was not seconded by the other rabbis of the north, thanks to the decisive intervention of the Provençal rabbis who defended the learned Sephardic tradition more effectively and enthusiastically than those teachers from Saragossa, Toledo, and Seville. It is odd that Provence had become a pro-Sephardic bastion in the descent of Gothic political theory toward the south, while the major Catalan rabbis and a few of their pupils from Toledo were staunch advocates of the entrance of Ashkenazic public philosophy into Spain.

One important point in this confrontation was Maimonides' categorical discrediting of magic, including chiromancy, astrology, and those popular practices that resorted to the omnipotence of desire as a way of acceding to the transformation of reality. Nahmanides turned against this attitude of the teacher from Córdoba because he believed that it did considerable harm to popular convictions that he felt were effective and achieved their objective in many cases. Philosophers cannot explain these acts, but they do have a place in life and are a reality. Ibn Adret and other followers in this line, such as R. Nissim ben Reuben Gerondi (Ran, 1290–1380), merely maintain this line of defense of the popular contrary to Maimonides. Ibn Adret is perfectly clear on this point:

> All that is not forbidden in the Gemarah as pagan, should not be prohibited by us just because we are ignorant of its properties or because they cannot be explained by the most well-known laws of nature. There are properties that the men of science do no know how to explain, such as the amulet of roots[128] or the cool touch of the yellow stone called *estopaci*,[129] or likewise, certain herbs and enchantments that our teachers of the Talmud allow . . . we can also include in this rule the therapeutic treatments that include the use of figures . . . A propos of the coins that are applied to corns [with the figure of a lion on it] . . . I have heard it said that my teacher Moses ben Nahman, of blessed memory, used to put this figure of a lion [on top of his corns] . . . and had no qualms about doing so.[130]

Curiously, in another *responsum* Ibn Adret states that he had fought, with the aid of God, to eliminate certain practices that seemed to him like "pagan superstitions," customs that had been introduced into Barcelona and consisted in cutting off the head of an old chicken "in redemption for the child that had been born" and hanging its entrails at the entrance to the house. In this case his Sephardic blood rebels against an exacerbated Gothicism: "Even when I heard it said of many very worthy men from Germany who live among us and come to our houses of study, that all the rabbis of their land slaughter geese and chickens as an expiatory sacrifice on the eve of the Day of Atonement. I have also heard it said that the teacher Hay Gaon, of blessed memory, having been consulted on this matter, replied that it was customary to do it. Nevertheless, I stopped this practice."[131]

In the final analysis, the pro-Ashkenazic line initiated by Nahmanides and Jonah Gerondi sustained that the philosophers explained everything erroneously around the Aristotelian idea that nature was moved by ubiquitous necessity and not by perpetual divine providence. Nissim ben Reuben Gerondi, a pupil of Ibn Adret, stated in this respect that rituals that were merely pedagogical tools for the philosophers were, in truth, effective rituals to change the world. He is referring to "[t]he philosophers [who] believe that God has no interest in or providence over creation, and that all being follows necessity."[132] This recriminatory Gothic-Ashkenazic idea against philosophy was taken to its ultimate consequences by Calvin.

As we have already seen, Ibn Adret was instrumental in bringing R. Asher to Toledo and supported him in the reforms of 1281. These changes incorporated a strict and austere pietism into the life of the Jews of Toledo, and by extension, to all Sepharad. Ashkenazic asceticism made a forceful entrance into a milieu that accepted it with a certain amount of naïveté, but in time, would react with disgust.

Ibn Adret connected with popular feelings, with the idea of a people understood in the Gothic manner, with a nomadic tradition in their background. This concept was loaded with a political identity that led the way to a collective agent. This collective vision of identity, without the traditional Jewish cautions of good judgment that Maimonides had demanded so often, gave way to an idea that was close to that of a homeland. Beginning with the fourteenth century, a national homeland would emerge as a quasimetaphysical agent capable of generating laws and a sovereign public identity. Obviously, for Maimonides, this concept would have bordered on idolatry. To a certain extent it probably would have annoyed Nahmanides, for whom "[t]he idolater is *void of counsel, he hath* no *counsel and* no *understanding*, but only walks after his idol and forever denies *the Glorious Name*."[133]

Of course Ibn Adret is not in favor of many other popular aspects that, no matter how much they are to the liking of the Jewish people, break up the vision of a unified collective with the importance of *idolus modernus*. This is why it is not surprising to see his opposition to the Messianic enthusiasm of people like Abraham Abulafia[134] and the prophet of Avila. Ibn Adret opposed these popular movements that he sees are headed toward an anarchism that dissolves the idea of a civil homeland or modern protonationalism. It seems that his bent toward the popular is only touched off when the popular works in favor of the construction of a collective identity of homeland.

Ibn Adret, like Jonah Gerondi before him, played his hand against Montpellier with the aid of R. Abba Mari b. Moses b. Joseph (Astruc of Lunel). This opened the way for the second controversy over Maimonides' works. The battle began on the Ashkenazic side because they considered the life of the Jewish communities of Languedoc to be full of heretics and disbelievers. Perpignan and Narbonne were enclaves of intellectuals who were very close to Maimonides, including the prominent Ibn Tibbon family, the translators of Rambam and a nucleus of great intellectual activity.

The criticisms of the pro-Ashkenazim centering on the decadence of certain Sephardic circles were shared by Ibn Adret, as they had previously been with his teacher, Nahmanides. In a letter written in 1303 R. Abba Mari addresses him with respect as "the foremost leader of his generation."[135] "Today there are many who tear down the fences, who despise instruction and scoff at admonition, who relinquish the fundamentals of faith and hold to hollow superstitions, who, embracing foreign teachings, would dissolve the covenant and dissipate the wealth of the Torah. These men preach homilies full of blasphemy, and even compose books in science and in philosophy, drawn from Averroes and based upon Aristotle."[136]

Ibn Adret pleaded humility, as if he did not consider himself authorized to intervene in the matters of other cities, even if he was at the head of attempts at reform and change. This is evident in his letter to Don Crescas Vidal, a native of Barcelona but residing in Perpignan. With a language that is astonishing for such a man of discretion, Ibn Adret asks his friend to rise up against all the heretical and slanderous works being produced in Languedoc and spread throughout the territories of Aragon and Castile. As we shall see, Ibn Adret's leadership initiative would extend to the entire south of Sepharad.

It is undoubtedly surprising that such a prudent and tactful man would turn to exhortations that were more ideological than reflexive: "Sound the trumpets and the bugles in alarm!"[137] Another letter was addressed to Bonafós Vidal, the brother of Crescas, and a wealthy businessman in Barcelona, with the same combative tone.

What touched off the scandal, in Baer's well-documented opinion, were the teachings of R. Levi b. Abraham b. Hayyim, the author of *Liwyat Hen* (A Garland of Grace). This author lived in the house of a wealthy and prominent Jew in Narbonne, Samuel de Scaleta, a rabbi who, although he was known as a philosophical rationalist, was a pious man, and even an admirer of Ibn Adret.[138]

The result of all this fuss was the attempt to emit a *herem* proposed by Crescas Vidal, whom Baer thinks was not the real author: "No young man under thirty years of age shall study any 'Greek or Chaldean books' (i.e., works of philosophy or science) other than medical works; and teachers of the same shall likewise fall under this ban and excommunication."[139]

It is curious that the proposal to investigate and change the customs would begin with an inquiry in Montpellier into the heresies that were studied there. Ibn Adret reacted angrily to those who let themselves be carried along by "Gentile vanities." It is strange that he seems to have thought about his project of reform with the mentality of a statesman *avant la lettre*, since he mentions as a single block the kingdoms of Castile and Aragon as if in his future projection he had in mind an entire Sepharad incorporated into the new ways of the time: "May they [the sinners] vanish and a thousand like them, but not a tittle of the Torah . . . Now this plague which threatened to destroy our home and ravage our heritage, we have expelled it from our land, empty, scorned, and despised. It left the halls of Castile and Aragon, where formerly they had sought to ensconce it. It has now been driven out completely; not one is left of the hellish throng of them."[140]

Rashba, who was so tedious and detailed in his *responsa* on legal questions, raises the tone violently when he alludes to political questions of a patriotic nature. His reference to cleansing evil, his mental scenario, geographic and visual, with gigantic dimensions, and his appeal to sinister terms that stirred up the idea of a perpetual war against diabolic evil have all the taste of Gothic political literature.

In this sense, when Ibn Adret judges Rabbi Levi b. Abraham of Narbonne, he falls into a characteristic error of the Gothic world, that of confusing the role of a peaceable and fair judge with that of an accusatory prosecutor, converted here into an efficient government official. His classification of the rabbi from Narbonne is a good example of that distortion that will become a distinctive part of the political world from now on: "He is worse than the Gentiles who differ with us in their interpretation of a few verses. His colleagues do not spare even a letter of the Torah. The Gentiles do leave most parts of the Torah intact, but he and his colleagues distort everything."[141]

Ibn Adret seems to imply that he feels closer to the Christians than to those crazy heretics, which is a very threatening opinion. His hostility must have been very intense to dare to take such a dangerous step for the

Jewish community. If he did so, it was because he understood that strategic Jewish interests were at risk in the long run, probably within a political design on a larger scale.

The Attack on Rationalism

Rashba's attack on the rationalists was ultimately an attack on Maimonides, the greatest exponent of rationalism. This led him to say that they are people "who are opposed to all religions,"[142] people who deserve the worst. With his phobia, Ibn Adret comes to insinuate that when the Gentiles find out about this, "all their gold and silver [will] not save them."[143] As Baer surmises, Ibn Adret is referring to the Inquisition as the investigative arm and justice maker with an almost exemplary efficiency. Some of Ibn Adret's investigative texts are very disturbing.

The reformist and antiheresy campaigns, which included enemies shared with the Christian inquisitions, began again in Montpellier where a letter from Ibn Adret arrived suggesting a program of practical action. In it he recommends that they learn from the example of the Christians, who, when they find Judaizers, "wrap them up in twigs and burn them in cinder." He seems to advocate harsh measures and acting with executive speed and efficiency. It is obvious that he is in tune with the administrative methods and the quasimilitary ability of the Gentiles (Christians) to find a solution to these problems of the corruption of national unity. We should note that here it is not a simple heresy that the medieval authorities were accustomed to containing, but rather certain heresies concerning the public vision of things. Here we are dealing with heresies—almost perversions—that obstructed progress toward social unity. What was at risk here was a community with a geographical domain in which a common territory was established and procedures were on course to engender a new national citizenry. The deterioration of the collective faith in the Torah, the irksome obstacles of Sephardic judicial guarantees, Maimonides' insistence on the lack of confidence in the new public entities, and the inconvenience of attaching so much importance to day to day contingency were hindering the advance of a society that was more efficient, agile, and devoted to the prestigious leadership of the Crown. This institution was sustained by an indiscriminate—homogeneous—people that arose as a collective of undifferentiated elements. It was composed of individuals who expressed themselves by choosing their elected officials, by exercising their rights, and now as the components of those massive new entities like the city, the nation, and its leaders.

Daniel Gutenmacher is correct when he states that both Ibn Adret (Rashba) and his teacher, Nahmanides (Ramban), supported "a communal idea of the Jewish community."[144]

Ibn Adret despised the contents of Christianity, but he admired their executive abilities and their administrative advances. This is why he did not hesitate to advise his followers to copy their methods. He himself had already set an example by allowing the use of Christian notaries,[145] but now he called on the authorities of Montpellier to show that they had the ability to adopt harsh measures comparable to what the Christians did: "Observe how the Gentiles punish their heretics, even for a single one of such heresies as these men expressed in their books."[146]

The proposal of Ibn Adret and his followers was none other than "to ban and excommunicate anyone who would study Greek philosophy before he has reached the age of thirty."[147] The initiative with which Ibn Adret wished to incite the Jewish authorities of Montpellier was by no means an easy task He encouraged it in Montpellier, a territory belonging to Aragon and the rearguard of Provence. The ploy was very astute in that it proposed to dismantle the rationalistic tradition that he knew was firmly rooted in that region. Provence had always shown itself to be a defender of rationalism and sensitive to the Ashkenazic advance toward Sepharad. From the first attempted coup against Maimonides it was the scholars of Provence who were the most active defenders of the great Cordoban teacher. But now the offensive begun by Ibn Adret and his band was directed against them by way of the neighboring domain of Montpellier. They did this so that they could evaluate the possibility of the change that they wished to accomplish later on throughout Languedoc and, in particular, in Provence.

The reaction in Montpellier was not long in coming, and Jacob ben Makhir was the first to respond. Rabbi Jacob was a member of the Ibn Tibbon family,[148] the emblematic caretakers of the values of Maimonides' work. Samuel ben Judah, a patriarch of the family of the so-called Tibbonides, had been a great translator of Rambam and since then, his family members were considered the guarantors of the study and respect for his work.

There are those who try to play down the harsh norms and language of Solomon ibn Adret in instigating these persecutions as the product of a particular moment in medieval history. But we should also hear another voice from the same period, that of the cultivated and scholarly R. Jacob ben Makhir, in order to understand that the language of the time had a very complete capacity for expression. Ben Makhir alleges that the nonreligious sciences are necessary and should be studied. His line of argument is crystal clear to our present-day ears: "We would do well to learn from the example of the most civilized nations who translate learned works from other languages into their own, and who revere learning and the learned without inquiring into their religion, even when they write critically of their own faith. Has any nation changed its religion because of this, or did their faith falter? How much less likely is that to happen to us who possess a rational Torah which we follow?"[149]

The resistance and the arguments of the Tibbonides must have been stronger than what the aging Ibn Adret had foreseen. In view of this, his friends in Montpellier suggested that it would be better if the Barcelona *aljama* took over the initiative. Since he had to be cautious in his own house, he was probably not enthusiastic about the idea. He did not see that it was a problem for his own city: "There is no heresy in our streets . . . the walls of the faith have not fallen within our borders."[150]

The radicals in favor of cleansing the customs in Montpellier continued to encourage and provoke unrest with their sermons and actions that would also implicate Provence in their plans. Ibn Adret's friends in Montpellier insisted on the publishing of a *herem* against the rationalists. In other words, they wanted to put the Provençal faction in its place. Nevertheless, their great political obstacle was the fact that they needed the authorization of the king.

Ultimately the Gothic reformers played their anti-Maimonides card by recruiting the two great leaders of the band, R. Asher ben Yehiel and R. Solomon ibn Adret. Ben Yehiel left Cologne in 1180, and after a brief sojourn in Provence, he went to Montpellier and finally ended up in Barcelona. Asher had had enough time to appraise the intellectual refinement and superior education of the Jewish inhabitants of the south, but he was extremely critical of their theological deviations and their tepid piety. As he shouted to the leaders of Montpellier, "The Lord will call the elders and princes of his people to account."[151]

R. Asher wrote to R. Abba Mari from Barcelona encouraging him not to become disheartened in the battle with the rationalists in Montpellier. He sincerely believed that "sin and heresy" are rampant, "and it is difficult for them to rid themselves of it."[152] Ben Yehiel is convinced of the pride of the secularized Jews of Languedoc. He believes that they are even more atheist and rationalist, more stubborn in private than they appear: "Those who now carry on their activities secretly will soon dare come out into the open and will brazenly declare, 'We have the upper hand; who dares to come and lord it over the disciples of Aristotle in their own homes?' Israel will split into sects."[153]

Ben Yehiel sees in all this the decomposition of Israel. In other words, he raises the question of the future unity of the nation in an unequivocally political tone. Thus his project is a patriotic one, if it is seen in the light of Gothic Christian politics.

For that very reason the Ashkenazic rabbi proposed a general conference of "all the leaders of the people" in one of the cities of the realm. His reference to the territory of the kingdom is not by accident, and his convocation in one of the cities of the territory indicates to us how contaminated his public view is of Gothic politics. Ben Yehiel unwittingly draws back the curtain on the mystery about who is the real political leader in this entire national movement that has such a wide scope when he says: "Rabbi Solomon will also delegate to it some of the notables of this land."[154] Ibn Adret seems to be the key person in this entire reformist design. He was a Jewish leader who had never been to Jerusalem and ended his days in Barcelona. Incidentally, Barcelona is the only city in the West that has a *barri gotic* (a Gothic quarter), a detail that may have some significance. Ibn Adret was a skillful jurist who was probably at the heart of all the operations designed to facilitate the incursion of the Gothic world into Sepharad. It was a new version of the public sphere that arrived in the Iberian Peninsula and, with the absolute hegemony of Christianity, would become converted into something like the normalization of Sephardism.

Baer believes that Rabbi Asher's suggestion was inspired by the real executors of this great patriotic project. Moreover, the idea of convoking the territorial leaders of the land reveals a geographic vision of the nation that was very alien to the tradition of Sepharad, and even innovative to a certain extent for Jewish tradition in general. In any case, this type of convocation was customarily associated with the king and called for fiscal purposes.[155] Baer considers, therefore, "that this recommendation too was formulated by the same people who were the leading spokesmen in the controversy right along."[156]

Just who were these leaders of the entire reform movement and correction of the southern deviation? Even though Solomon ibn Adret did not act in his city as he proposed they act in Provence and Montpellier, he still continued his harsh criticisms against the rationalists' sins and scandals. He was convinced that they would become more daring if they were not punished and begged the communities to act once and for all: "Let them begin to punish and to correct as they see fit, and I will marshal a goodly number of communities ready to countersign their action."[157]

In the meantime, Ibn Adret had entrusted one of his students, R. Samson ben Meir, a native of Toledo, with the task of winning over supporters to his cause.[158] The fact that Ibn Adret had dispatched his student to Toledo, as he had previously done in other parts of Castile, Navarra, and other communities, speaks to us of his vision as a statesman in the Gothic manner, with a territorial understanding of the nation that is new and announces the rise of the modern State, an eminently Gothic product. Ben Meir's journey underscored the influence of the Ashkenazic rabbi Asher ben Yehiel in Toledo.

There are so many coincidences that are so tightly linked to each other that Baer has come to the conclusion that all this "was a part of a plan carefully worked out in Barcelona."[159] The Barcelona Jews wanted to secure the signatures of all the communities of Spain and southern France, which numbered over fifty communities.[160]

The result of this thorough search for territorial consensus was the decisive step taken by the man from Montepellier, R. Abba Mari. This was the rabbi who sent Solomon ibn Adret the text of the *herem* signed by him and by the Nasi of Narbonne[161] so that it could be published in Barcelona. The movement was supposed to gather the signatures of notables in every city until it arrived "in the famed community of Toledo, the seat of R. Asher ben Yehiel."[162]

The *herem* was finally published in Barcelona in the summer of 1305. There were actually two bans: the first set a period of fifty years for the prohibition of reading the books of Maimonides, the "Greek" books, works of natural science and metaphysics, either in Arabic or in translation. Ibn Adret, however, qualifies this by saying, "We have expressly exempted from the scope of the enactment the science of astronomy and all the works of Maimonides, the *Guide* and all his other books which are more precious than gold, both those written in Hebrew and those written in Arabic."[163] Baer points out that in the text of the *herem* that he was able to consult, it says nothing about Maimonides, and an exemption was made for the study of medical books.

The second *herem* was addressed to those who interpreted the *aggadah* allegorically and not symbolically. This was a fundamental point in the confrontation. The pro-Maimonides rationalists thought that it was possible to explain many of the passages of the words of the Torah meaningfully and rationally as allegories. The pro-Gothic faction, on the contrary, held that this would trivialize them and, instead, gave them a symbolic meaning beyond rational comprehension. The works of the rationalists, according to this second ban, should be burned. As Baer reiterates, "the reformists, then, followed the way of the [Christian] Church."[164]

The protectors of tradition were very aware of the esteem for Maimonides throughout Sepharad, and perhaps for that reason they mentioned his words in the *herem*. They quoted him as an authority in trying to show that Maimonides himself would have been on their side.

A circular was added to the two bans explaining the reasons for this initiative and requesting the signatures of the *aljamas*. For Baer, the administrative language, characteristic of official documents, reveals the hand of Ibn Adret. The *herem* was signed by the notables of the Barcelona *aljama*, a community governed by a very tightly knit elite. Baer notes that no physicians or translators appear among the signatories.[165]

The results of the ban were not all as decisive as the Gothic band had hoped for. In Languedoc the reaction against this initiative was again very vehement, and great figures like Menahem Meiri, a teacher "whose outlook on learning differed from that of R. Solomon ibn Adret,"[166] opposed it categorically.

Gothic rhetoric was obliged to retreat. It is known that it was accepted in isolated cases such as that of the elders of Toledo, but few significant traces of its effect could be found anywhere. Even so, in the summer of 1306 King Philip IV decreed the expulsion of the Jews from France, which profoundly altered the state of the internal controversies and the grand designs of Ibn Adret and his followers. The death of Ibn Adret himself in 1310 was a decisive blow to the implementation of the great reform of Judaism in Sepharad.

In spite of his wise and conciliatory tone in narrating the historical facts, Baer still concludes that the program of those whom he sometimes calls "reformers" and others "zealots" "kept within the recommendations made by Nahmanides in the early stages of the conflict."[167] What was at stake in the long run was the struggle between the mythical vision of Jewish tradition[168] and its clearly mystical understanding. In sum, it is the confrontation between the deep religiosity of Maimonides, open to rational meditation, but also to rhetorical *inventio*, prophecy, and peaceful and humane dialogue as opposed to the mystical, astrological, and vigilant conception of the government of the individual.

What is at risk is the deterioration of democratic lethargy as an essential ingredient in political life in contrast to a dialectical vision of that same life, in which rhetoric becomes discredited and reduced to an *ars fallendi* or art of deception. This affects dreams, the creative imagination of human measure, prophecy as an opening of the intelligence to the significance of the divine, the *orare* of dialogue as opposed to the *sermo*, the *enthymeme* that can be used in addition to the syllogism, and good judgment as preparation for the contingency of human government.

All of the above will slowly lose their place in the world that is coming into being, with its new entities such as territory, the material seat of sovereignty and identity. The concept of a nation as territory will take precedence over all other considerations; the *national homeland* will stand out as a supreme idea against other realities. For this to happen, it is necessary to begin to shape a vigilant society, strongly rooted in wakefulness, in which will, memory, and thought will make up the foundations of the new identity of the citizen. Hannah Arendt has written many perceptive pages in this regard.[169]

As a preliminary step, night will invade the world, activated by a vigilance that will inundate the shadows and the dreams, reverie and rhetorical *inventio*. In the fourteenth century the westernmost part of Europe—England, France, and Spain—will see the birth of the perpetually vigilant society of a Christianity that will enter a new world, *modus hodiernus*, with reinforced executive powers that will reach their peak with the Calvinists.

The Gothic influence that remained at its height until the Baroque expelled the theater from the university (Petrus Ramus in the sixteenth century) and did away later on with the *viola da gamba* that was looked upon as obsolete. Moreover, it would firmly establish the principle of identity of Aristotelian *Metaphysics*, which, in turn, would open the way for the materialism of the church hierarchy and the dark and demented visions of the romantic world.

The Gothic cathedrals that were leaving their traces along the way to the southern frontier are examples of those gigantic artificial architectonic nights, those nights built on tall columns that soar toward their highest point like false nocturnal heavens. They give rise to a night—at times flamboyant—trapped within and recreated with wondrously colored subtle lights, the symbol of an enormous world of executive forces unleashed and without limits. It is a projective and persecutory world of *insomnia*, in which the individual lives as if he had a knife at his throat twenty-four hours a day.[170] Perpetual vigilance is sublimated as a tireless capacity for work, discipline, order, design, control, and programming. Rest exists only to recharge civil capacity. The infantile can only be understood as a deficiency, as preparation for only one world: that of responsible and autonomous male adults.

It is not surprising that Baer ends his meticulous historical investigation of fourteenth-century Judaism with the conclusion that it is very similar to the Christian world:

> Jewish history did not parallel the history of the Christian Church in every respect, but the historians' evaluation of thirteenth century Christianity can be applied with equal truth to contemporary Judaism. Reformist tendencies were very much in evidence. Efforts in that direction were made, but were not carried

> through. The Jewish leadership of that day was also charged with a great responsibility. They could not achieve the political salvation of their people, but they were capable of revitalizing its social and religious life by realizing in everyday activity the ideals of the sages of the Mishnah. The political structure of the Jewish communal autonomy made that possible, and the current religious awakening, stimulated by the new mysticism, created the necessary atmosphere for it.[171]

This is how this profound change is seen from a historical point of view. For political theory, however, it was a major change in public life and the conception of European governments. Baer sees it as a wasted opportunity. The potential was lost for "a social and religious reform more genuine and more pervasive than that effected in the sixteenth century by the Protestant Reformation."[172] From the standpoint of political theory these mutations also brought with them the deterioration of the tradition of *good judgment*. But they would leave as the crowning achievement of their historical task the *State*, that great new protagonist, the most successful European franchise of all time.

The Enemy Within

The problem of the internal informers or *malsínes* in the Jewish *aljamas* was always a serious threat to Jewish life. The *malsín* was a dangerous person for the life of the Jewish community because he used slander and misunderstanding in a perverse way to benefit from his denunciations. Of course the breeding ground for all this was the mutual hatred, or at least the lack of trust, between Christians and Jews.

The *malsín* was a real public menace for his *aljama* because he poisoned the atmosphere of living together between the Jewish quarter and its Christian host. The problem was that the *aljama* did not have the legal capacity to punish this public crime. With the historical loss of its sovereignty, the Jewish people also lost the capacity to have their own penal administration.[173] This made it difficult for the Jewish quarters embedded in Christian territory to provide a legal response to that very serious and almost generic problem. According to Jewish tradition, the accused always had the privilege of being present at the declaration of the witnesses, and he was always informed before he received his punishment. In the case of the *malsín*, these guarantees were reduced. As Kaufmann points out, it must be taken into account that "[t]he Jewry of the Middle Ages resembled a beleaguered city, which had to treat every attempt at betrayal with the utmost rigor."[174]

The *malsín* was a delinquent in that he put the life of the community in grave danger. In accordance with *halakhah*, which says that the active is the same as the passive, he who surrenders must be surrendered.[175] In the life of the *aljamas* of Sepharad there were frequent cases of death sentences handed down by the rabbinical authorities, but in order for them to be carried out, it was always necessary that they be sanctioned and backed up by Christian law and the permission of the king. In this regard, Américo Castro saw in this practice a precedent of the Spanish Inquisition, the new modern Inquisition that was established at the beginning of the sixteenth century. The investigation was carried out by the local Jewish Bet Din, whose secret *modus operandi* and methods of detection were similar to those used by the Inquisition. Its procedures and *pathos* are reminiscent of the Inquisitors' methods. For political theory, it is simply a matter of a common phenomenon in Gothic society, both Christian and Jewish, that would be regularized with modern procedures.

All this calls attention to the case of an important *malsín* in the city of Barcelona who came up against Solomon ibn Adret. The search for the internal enemy—*intra muros*—was the equivalent of combating the external enemy on the battlefield. The happening took place at the end of the reign of James I. The person in question had lost all his possessions as a young man and began to resort to slander and spreading false information for profit. It seems he was warned against such practices, but he repeatedly ignored them.

In the meantime, James I died in Valencia on July 27, 1278, after reigning for sixty-three years and was succeeded by his son, Peter III. As soon as Peter was crowned king, several Jewish communities complained about the activities of this informer who, it seems, enjoyed the favor and connivance of the royal court.[176]

Things changed, however, when the brothers Joseph and Moses Abravalia (Ravaya) intervened in the matter. These prominent Jews were highly regarded by the Christian authorities. Moses had become the king's minister of finance. Both brothers embarked on a campaign to put a stop to the acts of this informer who was so harmful for the stability of the *aljamas* and succeeded in convincing the king of the gravity of his crimes. The king finally ordered him to be apprehended. At the same time he ordered a Christian judge to hear the allegations of the Jewish communities against the informer that had been held back for so long.

As a result of a royal order, Rabbi Jonah Gerondi (the younger), the son of a brother of the Jonah Gerondi who had earlier had such an active role in the Maimonides controversy, was put in charge of the investigation.

Solomon ibn Adret was also dispatched by special order of the king[177] to help Rabbi Jonah. The two men had the task of taking the statements of the people of the *aljamas* involved in order to draw up a sentence against the accused.

The curious part of all this is that Gerondi and Ibn Adret, who were undoubtedly on the same ideological plane, delayed the case for an entire year while they looked in vain for a way to come to an agreement. They probably tried to avoid arriving at a verdict concerning a crime that, according to the legislation of the Crown of Aragon, was subject to the death penalty. One account of the case emphasizes the fact that the family of the accused put pressure on them to bring the case to a speedy conclusion. The result was that, under the pressure of royal threats, Gerondi and Ibn Adret handed down a report—information about the informer—to the king saying that they believed the criminal deserved the death penalty. A Christian judge was assigned to the case, and the accused was executed in public, probably in 1280.[178] He was put to death in front of the Jewish cemetery, where he bled to death, having had the veins of both arms cut.[179]

This case had kept Aragonese Jewry in suspense for several years, and after the death in 1283 of Joseph Abravalia (Ravaya), the real instigator of the trial, the family of the dead man legally contested the sentence before the Jewish authorities. They alleged that the sentence went against Jewish law and its procedures. The Jews, they said, had renounced the death penalty from time immemorial; moreover, it had been imposed without the verdict of a court of twenty-three respected men. They insisted, above all, that the evidence against the accused should have been presented in the presence of the prisoner, but it was not done in that way.

Ibn Adret found himself at the center of these counteraccusations that showed up his participation in the case. It was a case that was clearly carried out in the Gothic manner, with efficiency, discretion, and without taking into account the judicial guarantees of Jewish tradition. Because he was worried about the repercussions of these allegations and the effect that they might have not only on his name but also on the instigators of the case, the brothers Joseph and Moses Abravalia, Ibn Adret decided to submit the entire report to the Talmud scholars of northern France. The entrance on the scene of Rabbi Meir of Rothenburg,[180] one of the most prestigious rabbis in Germany, with his unconditional support of his friend Ibn Adret, would give him the backing he needed.

Shortly afterward, in June 1285, the French troops of King Philip invaded northern Catalonia forcing a part of the Jewish community to move to Gerona and Barcelona.

Ibn Adret limited his intervention in the case to a kind of technical advisory to the Christian judges, having handed over the task of judging and the responsibility for carrying it out to the government authorities. As a good legal expert and efficient administrator, he must have felt inclined to do so. It is significant that Ibn Adret resorted to an Ashkenazic rabbi to back up his stance in this case, especially if we take into account that, as Kaufmann points out, "in Germany, where the government did not come to the help of the Jews in combating this evil among them, matters were much worse than in Spain."[181] In sum, this entire incident is indicative of a significant turn in the road on the way to the entrance of Gothic Europe into a Sepharad in a profound crisis. This turn was particularly evident in the problem of the accusations of the informers that was so crucial to the everyday life of the *aljamas*.

7

Conclusions

> A city without action, without cattle, or property, *an* afflicted *people*, poor and impoverished, needy, wandering beggars.[1]
>
> —Nahmanides

The twenty-first century has shown that it is openly in favor of a society that we might term "vigilant." Perhaps it would be better to say that first it was necessary to prepare a vigilant society to establish the future State in the West. This society is characterized by several main points that function as axioms: (1) *life is a perpetual war*, a continual struggle; to live is to prepare for that struggle; (2) *knowledge is power*, thus, pedagogy and its institutions inevitably fall into the realm of politics and its confrontations; (3) *the time of wakefulness is the essential part of life*; lethargy is associated with the loss of life and directly considered to be a time of weakness, minimally necessary, but to all intents and purposes, unproductive; (4) *historical time and human action are subject to the Aristotelian principle of identity*; life always flows forward and sooner or later goes inexorably downhill.

In this book we have seen how this type of society began to crystallize in a Gothic world on top of the still-warm embers of a broad expanse of the Roman Empire. It is sufficient to observe the traces of the Cistercians and the Gothic cathedrals in Europe to comprehend the enormous ambition and scope of the enterprise. It was a formidable political project that, originating in Burgundy and the territories between the Rhine and the Elbe, spread to England, northern Italy (Milan), and as far south as the Iberian Peninsula (Granada). It was a world that, on the contrary, did not extend toward Scandinavia.

The transformation produced in Western Europe was the result of profound changes in the vision of the public. One of the main factors in this turn would be the erosion of good judgment as an essential component of the city. It was a change that brought with it, inexorably and in the medium term, the transmutation of the good judge into public prosecutor.

The Gothic affirmation implied, at the same time, the exaltation of the projective: in other words, the frenetic search for truth in the observation of the world and inquiry into the inner world as a projection. The reality of the internal world is perceived only when it is projected through our eyes onto screens. Thus, the need for the Gothic citizen—think of our own time—to relate to screens.

As a result of this fundamental attitude, the view of political science as the art of governing and the study of who commands and who obeys becomes severely curtailed. This knowledge is accepted only when it does not infringe on the inner life of the individual. The external world becomes *popularized*, almost militarized, while the internal world becomes sacred and gives itself over to the militancy of the clergy. The appearance of the military, mendicant, and preaching orders was a Gothic legacy that had long-term effects on European life. Thanks to their specialization in the internal world, the clergy would hold the key to understanding even the externally secularized world. Luther's motto, *cujus regio, eius religio*, sums up this incorporation of the religious factor into the structure of the State. From now on, religion is going to be a matter of who rules a territory, in other words, a matter of State.

In this type of society when a person suffered a misgovernment in his or her life, he or she would be referred to the clergy. From the thirteenth century on, the Christian religion would become an essential element within the government of the realm, and it was almost a foregone conclusion that it would become secularized sooner or later, as it finally happened in the sixteenth century. From then on the tasks of the control of the individual—and the correction of his lack of control—would be put in the hands of secular educators. This function would continue to gather momentum socially until it fell into the hands of teachers, social workers, ideologues, psychologists, psychiatrists, and psychoanalysts.

Western thought has always been fearful that the misgovernments of its citizens should fall into the hands of tyrants. It is odd that, precisely with the Gothic prohibition for political theory to study the government of the individual, we would end up in the long run with the homicidal experiments of Western totalitarianism. It is not by accident that Hannah Arendt studied this phenomenon in depth before taking on her masterpiece, *The Life of the Mind*, the theoretical-political study of the *foro interno*, the inner life of its citizens. Sheldon S. Wolin's recent reflection about the need for democratization of the self of the citizen runs in the same direction.[2]

But they are exceptions. Today it is not difficult to find contemporary writers who express the axiomatic convictions of the vigilant society so emphatically: "Republican civility . . . is intimately linked to the virtue of vigilance: to the virtue of keeping alert, particularly in dealing with the authorities invested with power . . . The price of freedom is, for the republican tradition, perpetual vigilance."[3]

A Book about Real Life

A Vigilant Society: Jewish Thought and the State in Medieval Spain is the result of a long look and a lengthy writing process, the reflection of years of team research, and many hours of teaching students with a vocation and a superior academic level. Moreover, its central theme is something that directly affects contemporary society.

The question might arise as to why we have resorted to such far-off periods in Europe in order to reflect on present-day political life. It is easy to justify the fact that this book concentrates on Europe. Its subject matter deals with the study of a vigilant society in exactly the same way that it was being articulated in the modern State. Both phenomena—a vigilant society and the State—are the products of Western life. It is imperative, therefore, to inquire into how it was created and to delve deeply into the background for those ideological and social conditions. Its genealogy is pertinent to the argument.

We return to the past because the origin of vigilant democracy can be found in the period between the thirteenth and fifteenth centuries. It is a time known as the Late Middle Ages or Early Renaissance, but we have characterized it as the formative period of the world and style of Gothic life.

It is possible that some readers will be uncomfortable with the term "Gothic" as it is used in this book. But this should not be the case. We should take into account that the historical description—in general, historicist—to which we are accustomed, and in which we have been educated as Western Europeans, presents itself quite rigidly in successive stages in such a way that each period displaces its dying predecessor in order to occupy its space, absorb it, and go beyond it. No matter how much we concede, particularly in Catholic countries, it was always a doubtful transition. This idea of transition helps us to recognize that, in passing from one phase to another, there were doubts and hesitations and that there was a time when one category was on its death bed as it passed the baton to the next generation. Now we know that things do not always function that way in the internal world of human beings; phenomena and their memories do not die out, nor are they manipulated in our conscience as orderly processions in time.

Some readers might question why this work concentrates so much on the Jewish communities of Europe. Others might have doubts as to whether this book is too specialized, particularly in the history of Jewish political theory.

The truth is that it does not pretend to be so. Our text merely attempts to reflect on the origins of contemporary vigilant society, and for it, we have decided to go back to the very foundations of the building, following the example of Sigmund Freud in *The Interpretation of Dreams*, where he stated his *acheronta movebo.*[4] The fact that there is interest in the genealogy of a subject does not mean that there is a lack of interest in the present or in the future possibilities of the topic, but quite the opposite.

European Jewry is the result of the Diaspora of a people who, having been defeated militarily by the Roman Empire and expelled from their land, were forced to survive dispersed and without sovereignty. It was a people without a public administration, territory, arms, formally established legal institutions, or an ideology. It did, however, preserve its identity.

But it was by no means lacking in a rich tradition of thought and practical politics. During the time when the State was being created, the Jewish communities were firmly established in two broadly defined territories: (1) the one that occupied the land that lay between the shores of the Rhine and the Elbe and surrounding areas (Ashkenaz); and (2) the other that passed through the southern lands of Alexandria, the Barbary Coast, Sicily, and finally the Iberian Peninsula (Sepharad).

Although these communities were lacking in sovereignty, they could always rely on their own organization of life: their traditional laws, religious practices, scientific culture, and a thriving literary life that, on occasion, reached a very high level. These *aljamas*, *calls*, or neighborhoods preserved strong ties of communication between them, since both the European and North African Jews always felt themselves to be a part of Knesset Israel in its entirety. The feeling of belonging to a Hebrew community, together with the fear of losing one's own identity, beat within the heart of every Jew. The teacher Solomon ibn Adret expressed it with a certain bitterness and a little indignation: "God forbid that the holy people should walk in the path of the Gentiles and follow their norms . . . Do you want to teach your children the laws of the Gentiles and build altars with the filth of their idolatry? Far from it! It will never be this way in Israel! God forbid it! Will the Torah be covered with sack cloth?"[5]

The inhabitants of the Jewish quarters also preserved a common language, although not without numerous deficiencies in this matter on the part of many Jews who hardly knew how to speak or write it.

However, these Jewish communities were forced to live in a world organized and ruled by others. In this situation they were inhabitants of territories that were under the jurisdiction of other peoples to whose authority they had to submit, or at least were obliged to live as subjects. Naturally they had to pay tribute to those rulers whose hospitality they enjoyed. They had to pay taxes and respect the laws. They lived in exile and in the power of others. This situation of living together, especially for so many centuries, implies the need to express oneself in the vernacular, to be familiar with local laws and practices and, in many cases, to develop feelings of belonging to those territories in which they were born, raised, and buried their loved ones for generations. This was why the European Jews could not be mere exiles, for many of them lived in the only land they, their parents, and their grandparents had known for centuries. It was, therefore, their land, and they expressed it as such. Nevertheless, at the same time, they also had another, very profound allegiance: their bond with the chosen people of Israel.

Our book uses these Jewish communities as sources because of their exceptional circumstances. While each *aljama* lived its daily life under Jewish law, at the same time, it was an active member of the city or kingdom in which it had settled. Like bees that carry the pollen of the flowers among which they live and are nourished, these people would also pass along the customs and ways of living from one society to another. In addition, this community, which was educated, industrious, and well traveled, also had contacts with coreligionists living in other political cultures. When they came together for family gatherings, business, study, or political exile, they could speak to each other in Hebrew—particularly the rabbis—in a mutual exchange of influences proper to the lands in which they resided.

This cross-pollination brought with it an exchange of public wisdom and knowledge that occasionally provoked harsh reactions among the different Jewish communities. Because they shared a common identity in the most profound aspects of life, this usually served to smooth over the differences between them. These internal conflicts anticipate what would take place a century later in Christian society. Moreover, some of these confrontations, such as the one that caused the rejection of Maimonides' work, also furnish a wealth of information. We should bear in mind that these controversies take place with more sincerity between these adversaries, given that their strong mutual identification as coreligionists aids them in understanding each other and because they can count on the cohesion of their community as a minority always under siege.

A Genealogy of the State

There are two main problems in the public life of the twenty-first century. The first problem is the reform of the State. The State is a European franchise, perhaps the most successful one in history and the most widely spread institution on earth. Today its engineering design reveals certain flaws and severe dysfunctions. The second problem has to do with democratic ideology. From the Renaissance on, the application of this ideology has been considered essential for the construction of the modern State. The entrance onto the scene of the masses by way of their participation in elections and their appearance in the street and in the marketplace has supposed the confirmation of the idea that power should be in the hands of the *demos*: a protagonist that, in this ideology, began by being called "the nation," "the people," or in sociological terms, "the population."

We are aware of the fact that those two examples of political ingenuity—the State and democracy—are products of Western Europe. This allows us, in times of change like our own, to return to their origins in order to better understand how they arose and with all their advantages and handicaps *ab initio*. State and democracy arose as mutations of Mediterranean components, albeit altered by Gothic elaboration.

The Neapolitan philosopher Giambattista Vico, one of the great thinkers of Mediterranean Europe, proposed an understanding of history according to the Roman tradition centered around law, jurisprudence, and rhetoric. For Vico, imagination is an active and essential part of intelligence, an aspect of human labor that transcends the memory and will of individuals while, at the same time, nurturing and fortifying them. It is easy to understand why he always showed an attitude of respect and admiration for the Jews and their spiritual tradition. Vico sustains an idea that began with Maimonides and has endured for almost six centuries: imagination has an associative function that unites disparate or incompatible things and ideas.[6]

A study of the late Middle Ages through the Jewish political thinking allows us to analyze Western European phenomena far in advance, given the fact that the above-mentioned cross-pollination that activated both theoretical thought and political engineering of Western European communities was already taking place very intensely in the *aljamas* and *calls*.

The fact that these communities were lacking in arms, burocratic structures, land, and above all, independence, forced them to live in the midst of a world that constantly wished to convert them. We have to bear in mind that the forced conversion of the Jews to Christianity meant their disappearance as a people (*Knesset Israel*) and, to a large extent, their personal destruction. Thus, by studying the years 1100 to 1400, we are not avoiding the present, but rather we are affirming a nonhistoricist dedication to the moment when those ideas and institutional changes that articulated Western life began.

A Vigilant Democracy?

The existence of the city is prior to any other evaluation. A *polis*, or a city embedded in the framework of the republic, or *commonwealth*, in the words of Thomas Hobbes (1588–1679), contains within it such a great number and wide variety of elements that it is difficult to encompass all of them. The lives of its citizens are unfathomable, and their relationships are intricate. But cities also have dense and coherent antecedents. The world of the city can hardly be captured by artists, civil engineers, or wise men. The most they can do is arrive at a mental and affective depiction of its entity.

The society that we have called "vigilant," based on the *watchfulness* that Walzer points out in the case of the Puritan clergy,[7] includes tensions that, at a given moment, can impose their domination. At that precise moment the government of the people would come under different authorities. There is no single static definition of society. In spite of the fact that the State is an engineering design, it also responds to life that flows and is occupied by people who act on it and maintain and modify it day by day. Thus, we can expect to find surprises in the evolution and contingency of its social institutions.

Both society and the State can act according to the principles that characterize vigilance. This includes cultural traditions, core convictions, and a certain type of life. While it is true that the Gothic world responds to a reality, that reality is never absolute, in spite of the omnipotent fantasies of Western man.

Who is more watchful, society or the State? This question does not have a satisfactory answer. Society occasionally responds to internal elements that take control of its government and react against an infuriated State. Likewise, the mechanisms of a reasonably organized modern State can allow for the stabilization of a demented society. The entrance of American forces into Berlin is a good example of action by a State to stop in its tracks the advance of a Gothic society harmful to mankind. The 1978 transition to democracy in Spain, with its explosion of freedom and its ability to reach a consensus among the various factions, signified an effort on the part of a generous and peaceful society to take control over the actions of a vigilant and disproportionately authoritarian State.

The phenomenon of vigilance is, therefore, a historical option that has yielded results and has left us an admirable curriculum. But behind its façade lie patches of dead zones that can constitute a danger to its citizens.

Notes

Preface

1. See Javier Roiz, *La recuperación del buen juicio* (Madrid: Foro Interno, 2003), *passim*.

2. "Thus we find small, scattered settlements of Jews in the north of Spain even before the Reconquest," Yitzhak Baer, *A History of the Jews in Christian Spain*, trans. Louis Schoffman, 2nd ed., vol. 1 (Philadelphia, PA: Jewish Publication Society, 1992), 45.

3. Sheldon S. Wolin, *Democracy Incorporated: Managed Democracy and the Specter of Totalitarianism* (Princeton, NJ: Princeton University Press, 2008), 289.

4. The term *sefardí* is explicitly defined as a *judío oriundo de España* (a Jew, native of or originally from Spain), Real Academia Española, *Diccionario de la lengua española*, 21st. ed. (Madrid, 1992), 1318.

5. H. J. Zimmels, *Ashkenazim and Sephardim: Their Relations, Differences, and Problems as Reflected in the Rabbinical Responsa* (1976) (Hoboken, NJ: Ktav Publishing House and Sephardic House New York, 1995), xi.

6. Fritz Kahn speaks of two major directions in the Jewish migration from Palestine, the two arms of the Diaspora that, throughout history, have evolved into two large groups: "two types, the 'German' or Ashkenazic and the 'Spanish' or Sephardic," Fritz Kahn, *Jüdische Lexicon* (Berlin 1930), iv, 1245. Quoted in Zimmels, 2. This culture, with such a high standard of living, spread to large sections of North Africa and the eastern Mediterranean after the Jews were expelled from the Peninsula in 1492 and 1498.

7. Baer, vol. 1, 2.

8. Ibid., 186–87. The Spanish translation reads: "we can say perfectly well that the Jews of Spain made up a national community" (*se puede decir perfectamente que los judíos de España formaban una comunidad nacional*), Baer, vol. 1, 151.

9. Jonathan Ray, *The Sephardic Frontier* (Ithaca, NY: Cornell University Press, 2006), 9.

Chapter 1

1. José Gaos, "Filosofía de Maimonides," lecture given in 1935 on the occasion of the eight-hundredth anniversary of the birth of Maimonides, Mexico: La Casa de España en Mexico, 1940. Available on line http://www.librosgratisweb.com/pdf/gaos-josé/filosofia-de-maimonides.pdf (15.12.2007), quote on last page.

2. See José Luis Lacave, "La comunidad donde nació Abraham ibn Ezra," in *Abraham ibn Ezra y su tiempo*, ed. Fernando Díaz Esteban (Actas del Simposio Internacional, Madrid, Tudela, Toledo, 1–8 Feb. 1989) (Madrid: Asociación de Orientalistas, 1990), 174.

3. The etymology of the term "*aljama*" comes from the Arabic. It refers to an aggregation of people living around a temple. Normally these people tended to live in the medieval Christian section of the city and on nearby land or in nearby towns. Just as in the case of Christian repopulations and their parishes, these groups or neighborhoods, which constituted actual communities, often lived around a temple where they often gathered for their ceremonies and other communal activities. In Christian territories the term was used for both Moorish and Jewish communities. Sometimes the name simply referred to a major temple, whether it was a principal mosque or synagogue. In other words, this leads to the idea of a temple around which people of the same religion live and congregate. In the case of the Jewish population in Christian territory, in the thirteenth century, *aljama* referred to the Jewish communities that collected their own taxes and enjoyed a certain degree of self-government. This was in accordance with special permission by the king. They were considered to be his property and linked to him by a direct bond.

4. Simon ben Zemah Duran was born in Majorca and studied with Ephraim Vidal. He was a rabbi in Saragossa or Monzón and, after the expulsion in 1391, he fled to Algeria where he practiced medicine. In 1394 he became an important leader in the Jewish community of Algeria where he worked for fifty-three years. In the opinion of Epstein, he was "one of the most remarkable figures in Israel's gallery of great Rabbis throughout the ages." Isidore Epstein, *The Responsa of Rabbi Simon B. Zemah Duran* (New York: Ktav, 1930), 105.

5. Epstein, 37.

6. Rabbenu Moshe ben Maimon, "Rambam." The acrostic or Hebrew abbreviation of his name, "RaMBaM," means, according to some interpretations, *Rosh medabrim behol makom* (the first to speak everywhere). Meir Orian, *Maimonides, Vida, pensamiento y obra*, trans. Zeev Zvi Rosenfeld (Barcelona: Riopiedras, Instituto ha-Rav Kook, n.d.), 15. In the Middle Ages teachers were often referred to by their acrostic.

7. Even when he had to flee the Iberian Peninsula because of the Almohad persecutions and live most of his life in Egypt, he continued to refer to himself as Ha Sepharadi (the Sephardic one). Zion Zohar, "A Global Perspective on Sephardic and Mizrahi Jewry: An Introductory Essay," in *Sephardic and Mizrahi Jewry*, ed. Zion Zohar (New York: New York University, 2005), 9.

8. The term "*halakhah*" is used in a number of different meanings. In its most general and usual sense, *halakhah* refers to the normative portion of the Oral Law (Torah she-be-al-peh). In this sense, *halakhah* is used in contrast with *aggadah* (or *haggadah)*, which denotes, inter alia, things, wise and ethical sayings, philosophical meditations, and admonitions. The *halakhah* includes all the precepts in Judaism—those laws involving commandments concerning the relationships between people and God ("*bein adam lamekom*") as well as those laws that are applicable to relationships in human society ("*bein adam le-havero*"). See Menachem Elon, *Jewish Law, History, Sources, Principles*, 4 vols., trans. B. Auerbach and M. Sykes (Philadelphia: Jewish Publication Society, 1994), vol. 1, 93. Obviously the Jewish legal system is based on and linked to everything that is established in the Torah, that is, the Written Law. For the literary, historical, and legal sources of Jewish law, see Elon, vol. 1, 232–39. See also n. 20 below for further explanations.

9. Haim Beinart, "España y el occidente en los días de Abraham ibn Ezra," in Díaz Esteban, 29.

10. Orian, 44, 45, 48.

11. It also took hold in other Hellenistic cities such as Antioch, Pergamum, Smyrna, Corinth, and Rhodes. The library at Pergamum (present-day Bergama, Turkey) was particularly important for its use of dried animal skin (parchment) as a substitute for Egyptian papyrus.

12. See Etienne Gilson, *La filosofía en la Edad Media*, 2nd ed. (Madrid: Gredos, 1965), 381.

13. Rabbi Moshe ben Nahman Gerondi, also known by his Greek or Latin name, Nahmanides (Gerona, 1194–Palestine, c. 1270) and by his acronym, Rabbi Moshe ben NahmaN (RaMBan). Not to be confused with Maimonides' acrostic (Rambam). He was the official principal rabbi of Catalonia and Aragon, but he was also a leader respected by all the Jewish communities. He was the Jewish leader chosen by James I the Conqueror to take part in the famous 1263 Barcelona Disputation.

14. Donald M. Nicol, *Venecia e Bisanzio* (1988) (Milan: RCS, 2001), 70.

15. Flavius Petrus Sabbatius Iustinianus, Justinian I the Great, born in Tauresium and died in Constantinople, whom the Orthodox Church venerates as a saint. Justinian, the emperor of Byzantium from 527–65, produced an exceptional compilation of Roman law, the *Corpus Iuris Civilis*, thanks to which Roman law has been preserved for posterity. He ordered this compilation to be updated with the *Novellae Leges*, some of which are written in both Latin and Greek. The work of compilation and synthesis promoted by Justinian became an essential pillar in the juridical conscience of Europe.

16. The Byzantine Empire lasted from 491 to 1453. Its first emperor was Anastasius I (491–518) and its last was Constantine XI Palaeologus (1449–1453).

17. See Nicholas de Lange, "Abraham ibn Ezra and Byzantium," in Díaz Esteban, 181, 189.

18. Angeles Navarro Peiro, "Literatura hispanohebrea," in *Memoria de Sefarad* (Toledo: Centro Cultural San Marcos, Sociedad Estatal para la Acción Cultural Exterior, 2002–2003), 300.

19. Z. Zohar, 9.

20. *Halakhah* is the jurisdictional tradition of Israel, in other words, Jewish law and its evolution throughout the centuries, including the tradition of discourse and controversy over that which is public that nurtures it. This translation, however, may be inaccurate. It is preferable to use "the word *halakhah* rather than say Jewish law, because to call *halakhah* 'law' is to prejudice our understanding of the nature of *halakhah*." Tikva Frymer-Kensky, "The Feminist Challenge to *Halakhah*," The Harvard Law School Program in Jewish Studies, *The Gruss Lectures*, 26 Oct.–30 Nov. 1994, 1, 23 Dec. 2005 http://www.law.harvard.edu/Programs/Gruss/frymer.html. For Michael Walzer, it is the tradition of moral and legal discourse of the Jewish people essentially and like Judaism, "a product of exile and exclusion." Michael Walzer, "Preface," in *Law, Politics, and Morality in Judaism*, ed. Michael Walzer (Princeton, NJ: Princeton University Press), vii. Also see Moshe Halbertal, "The History of *Halakhah*, Views from Within: Three Medieval Approaches to Tradition and Controversy," The Harvard Law School Program in Jewish Studies, *The Gruss Lectures*, 26 Oct.–30 Nov. 1994, 23 Dec. 2007 http://www.law.harvard.edu/Programs/Gruss/halbert.html.

21. See below note 72.

22. Josef Stern, *Problems and Parables of Law: Maimonides and Nahmanides on Reasons for the Commandments* (Albany: State University of New York Press, 1996), 69.

23. During this time it was considered to be impious to mix logic with faith. Averroes (1126–1198) was declared a Christianizing heretic, and his works were burned in public in 1195. Orian, 138.

24. Born in Gerona (1200?–1267?), he studied with the Tosafists in France and with Rabbi Solomon ben Abraham in Montpellier. After returning to Gerona he lived for a time in Barcelona and died in Toledo.

25. Eleazar ben Samuel of Verona (1220–1295) was an Italian physician, philosopher, and Talmud scholar who studied in Barcelona with Jonah Geronidi.

26. Nahmanides, *Torah Hashem Teminah: Kitvei Rabbeinu Moshe Ben Nahman* (C.D. Shewall, 1963), 154. Qtd. by Avietzer Ravitzky, "Maimonides: Esotericism and Educational Philosophy," in *The Cambridge Companion to Maimonides*, ed. Kenneth Seeskin (New York: Cambridge University Press, 2005), 314.

27. Daniel J. Silver, "The Resurrection Debate," in *Moses Maimonides' Treatise on Resurrection*, trans. and notes Fred Rosner (Lanham, MD: Rowman and Littlefield, 2004), 72.

28. Ahmed Chahlane, "Averroes, Maimónides y la crisis en la comunidad judía medieval," trans. Jusep Puig Montada: *Anales del Seminario de Historia de la Filosofía*. 22 (2005): 112ff.

29. "The first controversy began during the life of Maimonides and reached its climax in the thirteenth century, profoundly dividing the communities of Spain

and Provence." Ravitsky, 301. Rather than Spain, it would be more accurate in this period to speak of the kingdom of Aragon. Moreover, the king of Aragon was Seigneur de Montpellier until 1349. James I (1208–1276), of the Barcelona Disputations involving Nahmanides, was born in Montpellier. He was the son of Peter II of Aragon and Mary of Montpellier. See also Chahlane, 111–23.

30. Abraham Gross, "Gerona: A Sephardic Cradle of Jewish Learning and Religiosity," *Materia Giudaica* 6, no. 2 (2001): 161–66.

31. See Orian, 137.

32. Chahlane, 111–23.

33. Of the three versions of the Expulsion decree probably written by Torquemada, the Grand Inquisitor, the harshest is the Aragonese, which states that the Jews "for their own guilt, are condemned to perpetual servitude [to be] slaves and captives." Qtd. by Joseph Pérez, "La expulsión de los judíos," in *Memoria de Sefarad*, 385.

34. Mark R. Cohen, "The Origins of Sephardic Jewry in the Medieval Arab World," in Zohar, 27.

35. Maimonides, "Epistle to Yemen," in *A Maimonides Reader*, ed. Isadore Twersky (Springfield, NJ: Behrman House, 1972), 441.

36. Qtd. in Hanne Trautner-Kromann, *Shield and Sword* (Tübingen: Mohr, 1993), 141. Bahya ben Asher was a pupil of Solomon ibn Adret, whom he refers to as "my teacher" and a follower of Ramban in his kabbalistic studies. The quote here comes from his *Kad ha-Kemah*, (*The Jar of Flour*), a book written after 1391 that includes a collection of sermons aimed at counteracting Christian preaching, 138.

37. Epstein, 10–17.

38. Ibid., 10.

39. Ibid.

40. Zohar, 8.

41. Eliyahu Ashtor, *The Jews of Moslem Spain* (Philadelphia: Jewish Publication Society, 1992), vol. 1, 11.

42. St. Isidore of Seville called him *pace praeclarus* in contrast to his father, the Arian king Leovigild, whom he called *bello promptissimus*, Margarita Vallejo Girvés, "Los exilios de católicos y arrianos bajo Leovigildo y Recaredo," *Hispania Sacra* 55, no. 111 (2003): 35.

43. John Bowker, *The Oxford Book of World Religions* (New York: Oxford University Press, 1997), 76.

44. Zohar, 9.

45. The *Refutation of the Christian Dogmas* was written in the vernacular, possibly Catalan, by Hasdai Crescas (1340–c. 1410) and preserved thanks to the Hebrew translation with commentaries included, done in Alcalá de Henares by Joseph ben Sem Tob. There is an English translation by Daniel J. Lasquer, *The Refutation of the Christian Principles* (Albany: State University of New York Press, 1992).

46. The rabbi of the *aljama* of Carrión de los Condes (Palencia) and author of the *Proverbios Morales* written in the middle of the fourteenth century. A century later he was remembered by the influential writer and nobleman Iñigo López de

Mendoza, Marqués de Santillana, as "a Jew called Rabbi San To, who wrote very good things." See Amparo Alba Cecilia, "El poema penitencial de Sem Tob de Carrión," *Revista de Ciencias de las Religiones* 4 (1999): 8.

47. Jonathan P. Decter, "Literatures of Medieval Sepharad," in Zohar, 92.

48. Jonathan Ray, *The Sephardic Frontier* (Ithaca, NY: Cornell University Press, 2006), 15.

49. Ibid., 16.

50. A reference to this animal is also found in Maimonides: "mentioning giving free reign to his instincts and passions like the beasts and the ostriches," Maimonides, "Epistle to Yemen," 455.

51. Ray, 15.

52. Ibid., 14.

53. Ibid.

54. Daniel J. Lasquer, "Foreword to the English Translation," *The Refutation of the Christian Principles*, 11.

55. See above, note 45.

56. Aristóteles, *Retórica*, bilingual ed. and trans. Antonio Tovar (Madrid: Instituto de Estudios Políticos, 1971), book 1, 4.

57. Ursula Kirkendale, "The Source for Bach's *Musical Offering*: The *Institutio Oratoria* of Quintilian," *American Musicological Society* 31, no. 1 (Spring, 1980): 95–137.

58. See Menachem Lorberbaum, *Politics and the Limits of Law: Secularizing the Political in Medieval Jewish Thought* (Stanford: Stanford University Press, 2001), 51. Likewise, the vision of power and law in Maimonides cannot be assimilated to the Hobbesian conception of the seventeenth century that plays dangerously with the terms "word" and "sword," nor with his Calvinistic interest in "the skill of making and maintaining commonwealths," a public philosophy that reveals a Christian omnipotence exactly opposite to the vision of the Sephardic thinker.

59. Isadore Twersky, *Introduction to the Code of Maimonides* (New Haven, CT: Yale University Press, 1980), 23.

60. Maimonides, *Mishneh Torah*, book 1, "Knowledge," ch. 2, 10; *A Maimonides Reader*, ed. Isadore Twersky (Springfield, NJ: Behrman House, 1972), 46. Further references to this work are designated with the abbreviation *MT.*

61. *MT*, ch. 5, 13, 68–69.

62. Maimonides, *The Guide of the Perplexed*, a work in 3 parts, trans. and ed. Shlomo Pines, with an introductory essay by Leo Strauss, 2 vols. (Chicago: University of Chicago Press, 1963), part 2, ch. 41, vol. 2, 386. Further references to this work are designated with the abbreviation *GP*.

63. In the face of the drastic decree of King Nebuchadnessar to kill all the wise men of Babylon because they could not explain the meaning of his dream, Daniel saves his life thanks to God, who sends him "a night vision" with the interpretation of the king's dream (Dan. 2:13, 2:18).

64. *GP*, part 2, ch. 41, vol. 2, 385 (Dan. 10:8, 10:10).

65. *GP*, part 2, ch. 41, vol. 2, 385.

66. Dan. 2:30.

67. *GP,* part 1, ch. 3, vol. 1, 27.

68. See Javier Roiz, "Maimonides y la teoría política dialéctica," *Foro Interno,* no. 6, 2006, 36–37.

69. For the distinction between involuntary green memory and predatory red memory, see Javier Roiz, *El experimento moderno* (Madrid: Trotta, 1992), ch. 2, 41–89.

70. Leo Strauss speaks of the "enchanting character of the *Guide*" in his introduction, "How to Begin to Study *The Guide of the Perplexed,*" in *GP*, xiv.

71. On the internal structure of the *aljamas*, both socioeconomic and political, see Baer, *History of the Jews in Christian Spain*, vol. 1, 138–85.

72. "On the other hand, Jewish communities in Spain developed during this period a broad and comprehensive autonomy that resulted in the creation of an extremely elaborate body of logical legislation in all areas of Jewish law . . . This communal legislation often had an influence far beyond the boundaries of the enacting community; and enactments were often accepted by nearby and even by distant communities." Elon, vol. 2, 796.

73. Moisés Orfali, "Los responsa rabínicos y la vida interna en las aljamas aragonesas," in *Aragon Sefarad*, Saragossa, 2004, 164; 22 Dec, 2007 http://www.dpz.es/turismo/monograficos/aragon-sefarad/VolumenI/VolI-04.pdf.

74. Robert I. Burns, S.J., *Jews in the Notarial Culture: Latinate Wills in Mediterranean Spain, 1250–1350* (Berkeley: University of California Press, 1996), 14.

75. Burns, 14.

76. Ibid.

77. Orfali, 166.

78. Eric Amilévitch and Luc Ferrier, "Introduction," in Nahmanides, *La Dispute de Barcelone*, trans. E. Amilévitch and Luc Ferrier, 4th ed. revised and corrected (Lagrasse: Verdier, 1984), 20.

79. Nahmanides, *La Dispute de Barcelone*, 13.

80. Ibid., 88.

81. Maimonides, *Obras filosóficas y morales* (Barcelona: Ediciones Obelisco, 2006), 127.

82. Nahmanides, *La Dispute de Barcelone*, 87.

83. Vico called it "the second barbarism of reflection." See Javier Roiz, *La recuperación del buen juicio* (Madrid: Foro Interno, 2003), 25.

84. Maimonides admired Aristotle even though he recognized his severe limitations: "All that Aristotle states about that which is beneath the sphere of the moon is in accordance with reasoning . . . However, regarding all that is in the heavens, man grasps nothing but a small measure . . . shall accordingly say in the manner of poetic preciousness: '*The heavens are the heavens of the Lord, but the earth hath He given to the sons of man.*'" Ps. 115–16; *GP*, vol. 2, ch. 24, 326.

85. Haim Kreisel, "Maimonides' Political Philosophy," in Seeskin, *The Cambridge Companion to Maimonides*, 217.

86. *GP*, part 1, ch. 34, vol. 1, 73.

87. *MT*, book 1, "Knowledge," chs. 2, 4, 5, 55.

88. Isocrates, Cicero, Quintilian.

89. Steven Harvey, "Maimonides in the Sultan's Palace," in *Perspectives on Maimonides. Philosophical and Historical Studies*, ed. Joel L. Kraemer (London: Littman Library of Jewish Studies, 1996), 70.

90. Henry Purcell (1659–1695), "O Solitude," Z.406.

91. *GP*, part 1, ch. 53, vol. 1, 120.

92. See Orian, 301–03.

93. We accept Hannah Arendt's identification of the executive power of a person with his memory and will, although Arendt does not introduce the concept of lethargy in the inner part of memory. If we do so, it is possible to differentiate between green, or involuntary memory, and red, or predatory memory. For this distinction, see Roiz, *El experimento moderno*, ch. 2, 41–89.

94. Roiz, 65–71.

95. See above, note 68.

96. Peter Gay, *Freud. Una vida de nuestro tiempo* (Barcelona: Paidós, 1980), 37.

97. Exod. 33:11. See in this respect Crescas, *The Refutation of the Christian Principles*, 32.

98. Bahya ben Asher, *Mezuzah*, qtd. in Trautner-Kromann, 142.

99. Cecil Roth, "The Disputation of Barcelona (1263)," *Harvard Theological Review* 43, no. 2 (April 1950): 139. For Nahmanides, the place of faith is memory. See David Novak, *The Theology of Nahmanides Systematically Presented* (Atlanta, GA: Scholars Press, 1992).

100. The study of the Torah or Talmud was a problem for these Jewish communities, especially if the rabbis lost the confidence of their congregation due to their lack of preparation. As a consequence, sometimes improvised leaders appeared on the scene. Since the *aljamas* or Jewish neighborhoods had very few administrative structures and lacked their own political power, the rabbis were obliged to earn their prestige and gain the confidence of the people with their wisdom and hard work. The spontaneous leaders, however, were often uneducated and opportunistic, without any feeling for the community and scornful of good judgment. See Epstein, *The Responsa of Rabbi Simon ben Zemah Duran*, 12.

101. Maimonides, *Treatise on Resurrection* (1191), 12. The intervention of a rabbi or a prestigious person with knowledge of Jewish law in any trial is a guarantee. With it, there can be no possibility of abusing naïve or ignorant persons by would-be judges or arbitrators. For an example of this in a matrimonial dispute, see Epstein, 81.

102. Israel Efros, trans. and ed., *Maimonides' Treatise on Logic* (New York: American Academy for Jewish Research, 1938), 63. Efros's edition includes the original Arabic version, three Hebrew translations, and an English translation.

103. Efros, 63.

104. Ibid., 64.

105. In spite of his respect for the Arabic and Greek teachers, Maimonides demonstrates, from the very beginning of his intellectual development, his marked originality by not avoiding controversy "and occasionally carving his own path." Efros, "Introduction," 32.

106. Efros, 64.

107. This was without forgetting the obvious influence of Arabic authors such as Abu Nasr al-Farabi, whom he greatly admired.

108. Kenneth Hart Green, "Editor's Introduction: Leo Strauss as a Modern Jewish Thinker," in *Leo Strauss, Jewish Philosophy and the Crisis of Modernity: Essays and Lectures in Modern Jewish Thought*, ed. Kenneth Hart Green (Albany: State University of New York Press, 1997), 46.

109. The Svëelot u-Tësubot ("Questions and Answers") or *responsa* are rulings of eminent rabbis who acted as *dayyanim* (judges) or presided over the *yeshivot* (rabbinical academies). They were written down and answered the inquiries of other rabbis or community leaders. Today they are regarded as a source of information about the life in medieval Jewish communities. See Orfali, "Los responsa rabínicos y la vida interna en las aljamas aragonesas," 161.

110. *GP*, part III, ch. 27, vol. 2, 510–11.

111. *GP*, part III, ch. 28, vol. 2, 512.

112. *MT*, book 1, "Knowledge," ch. 1, 4, 52. See also Maimonides, "Eight Chapters," in Twersky, *A Maimonides Reader*, 368.

113. *GP*, part 3, ch. 32, vol. 2, 526.

114. *GP*, part 3, ch. 34, vol. 2, 534.

115. *GP*, 534.

116. *GP*, 534.

117. *GP*, part 3, ch. 11, vol. 2, 441. Maimonides refers to these evils later on as "these tyrannies," 441.

118. *MT*, book 1, "Knowledge," ch. 9, 2, 83.

119. In commenting on this point Lorberbaum uses the word "compliance," a term with a Hobbesian resonance. See Lorberbaum, *Politics and the Limits of the Law*, 50.

120. Oran, 289.

121. Ibid., 293.

122. Ibid., 292.

123. Lorberbaum, 39.

124. *GP*, part 2, ch. 29, vol. 2, 346.

125. *GP*, part 3, ch. 27, vol. 2, 511.

126. *GP*, part 3, ch. 45, vol. 2, 576.

127. *GP*, part 1, ch. 46, vol. 1, 97.

128. *GP*, part 1, ch. 46, vol. 1, 98.

129. After the deluge, humans become reformed; they have a second opportunity. Adam and Eve were vegetarians by order of Yahveh, because "He did not permit Adam and his wife to kill any creature and eat its meat, but all alike were

to eat herbs. But when the era of 'the sons of Noah' came, He permitted them to eat meat." Nahmanides based his arguments on Rashi (Rabbi Shlomo Yitzhaqi, 1040–1105), but he was merely expressing a very profound and lasting line of thought. See Ramban (Nahmanides), *Commentary on the Torah, Genesis*, ed. and trans. Charles B. Chavel (New York: Shilo, 1971), 56. Even so, this permission to eat the flesh of animals does not extend to eating the excised limbs of a live animal, nor its blood, since that is considered a part of its soul. Nahmanides interprets this prohibition as due to the fact that blood "is the basis of the soul." Both the limb of an animal that is still alive together with its blood contain a kind of animal soul: "Thus He has permitted the eating of the body of dumb animals after death, but not the soul itself." Nahmanides, *Genesis*, 57–58. It is curious that much later on, a descendent of Nahmanides' family, Miguel Servet (Zaporta, 1511–1553), would study in depth the mechanism of the circulation of the blood as a part of his theological interest and research. Thus he discovered the small circulation of the blood that he explained in passing in a book on theology. Nahamanides says that, in contrast to the human soul, "An animal's soul returns to its element, which is the air, and the components [of its body] are like all corporeal matters which revert to their elements and earth, whether refined or coarse." Qtd. in "The Gate of Reward," in *Ramban (Nachmanides) Writings and Discourses*, 2 vols., ed. and trans. Charles B. Chavel (New York: Shilo, 1985), vol. 2, 486.

130. *The Jewish Political Tradition*, 2 vols., ed. Michael Walzer, Menachem Lorberbaum, and Noam J. Zohar, coed. Ari Ackerman (New Haven, CN: Yale University Press, 2003), vol. 2, 445.

131. *MT*, book 1, "Knowledge," ch. 5, 11, 70.

132. *MT*, 70.

133. *MT*, 64.

134. *MT*, 66.

135. *MT*, 69–70.

136. *MT*, 65.

137. *MT*, 65.

138. Maimonides, "Eight Chapters," ch. 8, 380.

139. Ibid., 382.

140. Ibid., 383.

141. Ibid., 382–83.

142. Ibid., 384.

143. Twersky, *Introduction to the Code of Maimonides*, 359.

144. See Miguel de Cervantes, *Don Quxote*, part 2, ch. 9.

145. "Introduction to the First Part," *GP*, vol. 1, 12.

146. Human lethargy is depicted in Maimonides by the angel and dream, and knowledge is revealed by way of prophetic vision or prophetic dream. *GP*, part 2, ch. 41, vol. 2, 385–88.

147. *GP*, vol. 1, 14.

148. *GP*, vol. 1, 14.

149. *GP*, vol. 1, 68.
150. *GP*, vol. 1, 72.
151. *GP*, vol. 1, 14.
152. *MT*, book 1, "Knowledge," ch. 2, 10, 46.
153. *GP*, vol. 1, 72.
154. *GP*, vol. 1, 72–79.
155. See Joel L. Kraemer, "Maimonides' Use of (Aristotelian) Dialect," in *Maimonides and the Sciences*, ed. Robert S. Cohen and Hillel Levine (Dordrecht: Kluwer, 2001), 115.
156. Strauss even sees a kind of "deliberate self-contradiction," *GP*, xciv.
157. Yom Tov ben Avraham Asevilli (1250–1330), born in Seville (*Ishbili* in Hebrew), a noted medieval Talmud scholar. The acronym "Ritba" is sometimes spelled "Ritva."
158. Ravitzky, "Maimonides: Esotericism and Educational Philosophy," 309.
159. Yom Tov ben Abraham Ishbili, *Sefer Zikharon* (Jerusalem: Mossad ha-Rav Kook, 1988), quoted in Ravitzky, 309.
160. Pierre Abelard, *Petrus Abelardus*, the great French theologian born in Le Pallet, near Nantes.
161. Gilson, 387.
162. Berman believes that Philipp Melanchthon (1497–1560) and before him Rudolph Agricola (1443–1485), whose *De Inventione Dialectica* (1479) "strongly influenced him," were more decisive in this turn. See Harold J. Berman, *Law and Revolution II, The Impact of the Protestant Reformation on the Western Legal Tradition* (Cambridge, MA: Harvard University Press, 2003), 112.
163. Menachem Lorberbaum sees in Maimonides "a proto-Hobbesian flavor." Menachem Lorberbaum, "Medieval Jewish Political Thought," in *The Cambridge Companion to Medieval Jewish Philosophy*, ed. Daniel H. Frank and Oliver Leaman (Cambridge: Cambridge University Press, 2003), 189.

Chapter 2

1. Maimonides, "Instruction with Respect to This Treatise," in *GP*, vol. 1, 15.
2. Joel L. Kraemer, "Maimonides on the Philosophical Sciences in His Treatise on the Art of Logic," in *Perspectives on Maimonides*, 90.
3. *Domenicus Gundissalvinus*, archdeacon of Cuéllar, Segovia, presented a classification of the sciences in which "he added to the *Quadrivium* physics, psychology, metaphysics, politics, and economics, whose existence had just been revealed by the writings of Aristotle." Gilson, 373. As a translator and philosopher, he collaborated with Avendauth (Ibn Daud) and Johannes Hispanus. According to Gilson, his work "is a valuable document on the first reactions of the Christians in contact with the Arabic and Jewish philosophers prior to Averroes." Gilson, 373. Curiously, his work *De unitate* was at one time attributed to Boethius.

4. This school included Abu Bakr ibn Bajja (Avempace, b. Saragossa, d. Fez, 1139), Ibn Tufayl (Abubacer, b. Guadix, c.1105, d. 1185), Ibn Rushd (Averroes, b. Córdoba 1126, d. Marakesh 1198), and al-Bitruji (b. Córdoba, d. 1204). Kraemer, "Introduction," *Perspectives on Maimonides*, 6.

5. Al-Farabi, *El camino de la felicidad* (The Road to Happiness), trans. Rafael Ramón Guerrero (Madrid: Trotta, 2002), 68.

6. Al-Farabi, 68–69.

7. "Indeed, Strauss's own Jewish thought may be characterized as a 'return to Maimonides.'" Kenneth Hart Green, *Leo Strauss, Jewish Philosophy*, 6.

8. Leo Strauss, *Spinoza's Critique of Religion* (New York: Schocken Books, 1982), 187.

9. Harry Eckstein, "Theoretical Approaches to Explaining Collective Violence," in *Handbook of Political Violence*, ed. Ted R. Gurr (New York: Free Press, 1980), 137ff.

10. Friedrich Nietzsche, "El drama musical griego," in *El pensamiento trágico de los griegos. Escritos póstumos 1870–71*, ed. Vicente Serrano (Madrid: Biblioteca Nueva, 2004), 149.

11. The great bel canto opera was, for Nietzsche, "the caricature of musical drama . . . [something] that arose directly from the apelike imitation of antiquity." *El pensamiento trágico*, 78.

12. The *mutakallimun* were the practitioners of the *kalam* or dialectical theology. Maimonides points out that the first *mutakallimun* emerged among the Greek converts to Christianity and later among those Muslim theologians "who did not conform in their premises to the appearance of that which exists, but considered how being ought to be in order that it should furnish a proof for the correctness of a particular opinion, or at least should not refute it." *GP*, part 1, ch. 71, vol. 1, 178.

Some Maimonides scholars have posed the question of whether or not Rambam himself may have been a dialectical theologian of Judaism. See W. Z. Harvey, "Why Maimonides Was Not a *Mutakallim*," in Kraemer, *Perspectives on Maimonides*, 105. See also J. L. Kraemer, "Introduction," in *Perspectives on Maimonides*, 4. The Mu'tazilite school was one of the most important schools of Muslim theology or *kalam*. Rambam, *Readings in the Philosophy of Moses Maimonides*, Lenn Evan Goodman ed. and trans. (New York: Viking, 1976), 29.

13. Themistius Euphades Paphlago (317–387), nicknamed *sii-paili* (eloquent). Born in Paphlagonia, he lived most of his life in Constantinople, where he was a rhetorician, philosopher, and prominent public figure. Although he was a pagan, he became the adviser to several emperors during the fourth century and a senator and Praefectus Urbis under Constantine II in 355. He was the author of influential paraphrases of Aristoteles' texts, which he knew very well, such as *De Anima*, which has come down to us in the translation by William of Moerbeke. His paraphrases of the first book of *Metaphysics* are preserved in a Hebrew version later translated into Latin in Venice in 1558. He was greatly admired by the Roman philosopher and statesman Boethius.

14. "In many places they [the *mutakallimun*] follow the imagination and call it intellect . . . Thus also do those belonging to our community who imitate them and follow their ways." *GP*, part 1, ch. 71, vol. 1, 179.

15. *GP*, 179.

16. See note 12 above.

17. Strauss, "How to Begin to Study *The Guide of the Perplexed*," in *GP*, vol. 1, xiv.

18. Ibid., xiv.

19. Ibid., xiv.

20. Maimonides, "Los ocho capítulos," del *Comentario a la Mishná* (introduction to Pirkei Avot), trans. León Duvoyne, *Raíces, Revista Judía de Cultura* 60 (Fall 2004): 55.

21. This point is sometimes prejudicial to understanding Maimonides because "the rhetorical tradition has been lost in the modern age." Kraemer, in *Maimonides in the Sciences*, 115.

22. Some have attributed this idea to Philo of Alexandria (c. 20 BCE–50 CE), the Hellenized Jewish Neoplatonic philosopher who had a great influence on the Christian world in later centuries.

23. The teaching and study of religious tradition and the regulations of rabbinal tradition.

24. *GP*, part 3, ch. 12, vol. 2, 443.

25. *GP*, part 3, ch. 9, vol. 2, 436.

26. *GP*, vol. 1, 12.

27. *GP*, vol. 1, 12.

28. Pierre de la Ramée, French teacher of rhetoric, humanist, and mathematician. He taught at the Collège de Presles, Paris, where he became a professor in 1544 at the age of twenty-nine. He was a teacher and director of that institution until his death in 1572. See Peter Sharrat, "Nicolas Nacelius: Petri Rami Vita," ed. and English trans. in *Humanistica Lovainiense*, vol. 24, 1975, 183, 185. Michel Magnien, "D'une mort l'autre (1536–1572): la rhétorique reconsiderée," in Marc Fumaroli, ed., *Histoire de la rhétorique dans l'Europe moderne, 1450–1950* (Paris: Presses Universitaires de France, 1999), 380. I wish to thank Laura Adrián for this information.

Hamlet represents the opposite option to this pedagogical measure. Shakespeare uses the theater precisely as an important art for his investigations when he writes, "The play's the thing wherein I'll catch the conscience of the King" (*Hamlet* II. ii).

29. See above ch. 1, note 162.

30. Precisely the title of the "Third Part" of Hobbes's *Leviathan*.

31. Michael Walzer, *The Revolution of Saints* (New York, NY: Atheneum, 1963), 141–47.

32. Quintilian of Calahorra (Marcus Fabius Quintilianus, 30–96 ACE): *Sobre la formación del orador* ("On the education of the orator") *Institutionis Oratoriae*,

bilingual ed. and trans. Alfonso Carmona (Salamanca: Universidad Pontificia, 1997), book 2, ch. 8, 5, vol. 1, 225.

33. Quintilian echoes these doubts and misunderstandings: "And is it not so that Rhetoric does not always try to tell the truth, but always the believable?" Quintilian, *Sobre la formación del orador*, book 2, ch. 17, 39, vol. 1, 291. He answers this on several occasions with cogent arguments that could be summed up as follows: "Where there is an unjust cause, rhetoric is not present," ch. 17, 31, vol. 1, 291.

34. "Eloquence cannot grow . . . if there is no agreement between the one who transmits and the one who receives." Ch. 9, 3, vol. 1, 231.

35. "*De somno et vigilia*" in the words of Themistius.

36. For an excellent résumé of this misgovernment, see Michael Mann, *The Dark Side of Democracy: Explaining Ethnic Cleansing* (Cambridge: Cambridge University Press, 2005).

37. In-fantile not only refers to childhood. The term comes from the Latin verb *for*, *faris*, *fatus sum* which, in its past participle, *fans-fantis*, means "to say." Obviously this applies to those who do not have the ability to speak for themselves. But it also can be said of a child, an infantry soldier, a sector of the population, or aspects of the internal world of a citizen.

38. *The Consolation of Philosophy* was an important book for medieval political theory. Its author, Boethius (480?–525?), a Roman patrician by adoption, was a learned man who knew Greek very well and had probably studied in Athens or Alexandria (see note 13 above). As a Neoplatonic philosopher, he represented the resistance of solid Greek and Latin culture to the irruption of the barbarian culture of the Ostrogoths. In 510 he was appointed consul and, strangely enough, became a victim of the breakup and treachery of the two parts of the empire, Greek and Latin, Byzantium and Rome. Byzantium favored the fall of Rome into the hands of the Ostrogoths, which meant that the emperor Theodoric could not tolerate Boethius, a supporter of Byzantium. Thus he was condemned to death and executed c. 525. His famous work was written in prison while he was awaiting execution.

39. Niccolò Machiavelli, "Letter to Francesco Vettori (August 26, 1515)," in *Machiavelli: The Chief Works and Others*, trans. Allan Gilbert (Durham, NC: Duke University Press, 1965), vol. 2, 929.

40. *GP*, part 3, ch. 33, vol. 2, 532. Also qtd. by Ravitzky in Kraemer, *Perspectives*, 225.

41. Samuel ibn Tibbon, a younger contemporary of Maimonides and translator of the *Guide* from Arabic to Hebrew, translates the idea with the biblical word *medinah* meaning locality or province, although in some cases it implies the idea of a political entity. For Maimonides, the political is its own well-defined entity given that it is a distinct domain of thought and action. See Lorberbaum, *Politics and the Law*, 28.

42. Nahmanides and his pupil, Asher ben Yehiel (1250–1328), a pupil of Meir of Rothenburg, were among those largely responsible for introducing the Ashkenazic Franco-Germanic tradition into Spain. See Lorberbaum, 106.

43. Lorberbaum, 33, 93–94.

44. Isaac Pollegar was a Castilian Jew who lived in the first half of the fourteenth century. He was an exegete and was familiar with the works of Averroes, the secular sciences, and Arabic literature. He was a friend of Abner of Burgos (c. 1270–1340) until the latter converted to Christianity under the name of Alfonso of Valladolid around 1320, causing a rift between the two. The text here belongs to his *Ezer ha-Dat* (The Support of the Faith), qtd. in Trautner-Kromann, 147.

45. Aristotle, "Metaphysics," in *The Complete Works of Aristotle*, Revised Oxford Translation, ed. Jonathan Barnes, 2 vols. (Princeton, NJ: Princeton University Press, 1995), vol. 2, book 4, 4, 1007b, 18, 1591. "And it will not be possible for the same thing to be and not to be, except in virtue of an ambiguity." Vol. 2, book 4, 4, 1006b, 19–20, 1589. "But we have now posited that it is impossible for anything at the same time to be and not to be, and by this means have shown that this is the most indisputable of all principles." Vol. 2, book 4, 4, 1006a, 3–5, 1588. "[S]o that not everything will be so and not so." Vol. 2, book 4, 4, 1006a, 30, 1589.

46. Lorberbaum, 30.

47. "With what verses/ shall I sing of the kingdom of Fortune/. . . And how insulting and inopportune/ . . . everyone gathers around her throne?/ And although above, on top of all she dominates/ Commands and rules impetuously,/ This by many is called omnipotent,/ Because whoever comes into this life,/ Either sooner or later feels her power." "Di Fortuna," in *Machiavelli. Tute le opere*, ed. Mario Martelli (Milan: Sansoni, 1993), 976. Trans. Clément Godbarge.

48. It is also found in French in expressions such as *il estimait en son for intérieur*.

49. *GP*, part 3, ch. 27, vol. 2, 511.

50. *GP*, part 3, ch. 28, vol. 2, 513.

51. *GP*, part 3, ch. 27, vol. 2, 511.

52. *GP*, part 3, ch. 17, vol. 2, 471.

53. Qtd. in Goodman, *Rambam*, 16.

54. Rhetoric "*est bene dicendi scientia.*" Quintilian, *Sobre la formación del orador*, book 2, ch. 16, vol. 1, 275; rhetoric "*est bene dicendi scientia*" and the art of the orator, "*summa bene dicere*," book 2, ch. 14, 5, vol. 1, 256. He sums up: "Rhetoric would exist even if the orator remains silent." Book 2, ch. 18, 3, vol. 1, 293.

55. Lorberbaum, 20.

56. I use this word in its meaning in Spanish (extract the honey from beehives), not in its Freudian meaning.

57. Sigmund Freud, "Civilization and Its Discontents," in *The Standard Edition of the Complete Psychological Works of Sigmund Freud*, trans. and ed. James Strachey, in collaboration with Anna Freud, (London: Hogarth and Institute of Psycho-analysis, 1986), vol. 21, 77. About Freud's direct or indirect contact with Maimonides' legacy, see also David Bakan, Dan Merkur, and David S. Weiss, *Maimonides' Cure of Souls* (Albany: State University of New York Press, 2009), 137ff.

58. *GP*, part 3, ch. 12, vol. 2, 444, 443.

59. A notable French humanist and theologican, a pupil and successor of Calvin in Geneva.

60. At the end of his life Foucault turned from *dire la verité* to *dire vrai*, which signified a certain approximation to rhetoric. See Michel Foucault, "El cuidado de la verdad" (interview, May 1984), in *Estética, ética y hermeneutica. Obras esenciales*, ed. and trans. Angel Gabilondo (Barcelona: Paidós, 1999), vol. 3, 380. I wish to thank Juan Dorado Romero for this reference.

61. *GP*, part 1, ch. 53, vol. 1, 120; Goodman, 85.

Chapter 3

1. "From fair Provence's soil and sea, / who hath won thy heart away." Giorgio Germont to his son Alfredo, in Giuseppe Verdi, *La Traviata* (1853), libretto by Francesco Maria Piave, act II.

2. Israel Efros, *Maimonides' Treatise on Logic* (New York: American Academy of Jewish Research, 1938), 63. Efros's edition includes the original Arabic version, three Hebrew translations, and an English translation.

3. Eliyahu Ashtor, *The Jews of Moslem Spain*, 3 vols. (Philadelphia: Jewish Publication Society of America, 1973), vol. 1, 383.

4. Joel L. Kraemer, "The Islamic Context of Medieval Jewish Philosophy," in *The Cambridge Companion to Medieval Jewish Philosophy*, ed. Daniel H. Frank and Oliver Leaman (Cambridge, U.K.: Cambridge University Press, 2003), 38.

5. There is evidence that Lucena was a town where the majority of the inhabitants were Jews and that it was one of the major spiritual centers in Andalusia. Ashtor, *The Jews of Moslem Spain*, vol. 1, 308. Students from Morocco and northern France came to study in its schools. Ashtor, vol. 1, 384. In addition to being an important scholarly center, Lucena also was the second most important commercial center of al-Andalus in the eleventh century after Granada. It maintained commercial relations with other cities in Europe and even the Middle East. See Ashtor, *The Jews of Moslem Spain*, vol. 2, 143.

6. Joel L. Kraemer, "Moses Maimonides: An Intellectual Portrait," in *The Cambridge Companion to Maimonides*, ed. Kenneth Seeskin (New York: Cambridge University Press, 2005), 12–13.

7. The most famous Aristotelians of the Andalusian school were Abu Bakr ibn Bajja (Avempace, Saragossa, d. 1139), Ibn Tufayl (Abentofail, b. Guadix *c.* 1110–1185), and Ibn Rushd (Averroes, Córdoba, 1126–1198). See Ashtor, 14.

8. This interest in the government of the life of each individual seems to be in agreement with the fact that Spain was the first place in Western Europe where the first psychiatric establishments were set up: in Valencia (1409), Saragossa (1425), Seville, and Valladolid (1436), Palma de Majorca (1456), Toledo (1480) at the Hospital de los Inocentes over whose portal could be read "Mentis Integrae Sanitatis Procurandae." Peter Bassoe, "Spain as the Cradle of Psychiatry," *The American Journal of Psychiatry*, 101 (1945): 731–32. Franz Alexander, psychoanalyst and

pupil of Freud, took note of the fact that "[i]n Spain the treatment of psychotics began earlier than in other European countries." Franz Alexander, M.D., "Discussion of Dr. Bassoe's article 'Spain as the Cradle of Psychiatry,'" *The American Journal of Psychiatry* 102 (1945): 408.

9. Peter Gay, *Freud. Una vida de nuestro tiempo* (Barcelona: Paidós, 1989), 52.

10. Ibid., 53.

11. Ramban, "The Words of Koheleth," in *Ramban (Nahmanides), Writings and Discourses*, trans. and ed. Charles B. Chavel, 2 vols. (New York: Shilo, 1978), vol. 1, 194.

12. Leo Strauss, *Natural Right and History* (Chicago: The University of Chicago Press, 1953), *passim.*

13. Until the tenth century the Jewish population was concentrated primarily in the southern part of the peninsula and in the Ebro valley. One of the most important cities was Mérida, founded by the Romans in 23 BCE for retired (*emeriti*) soldiers. Ashtor, *The Jews of Moslem Spain*, vol. 1, 350.

14. Isidore Epstein, *The Responsa of Rabbi Simon B. Zemah Duran* (New York: Ktav, 1930), 10.

15. Suzanne Last Stone, "The Emergence of Jewish Law in Postmodernist Legal Theory," The Harvard Law School Program in Jewish Studies, *The Gruss Lectures*, October 23–November 30, 1994, 2.

16. Noam J. Zohar, "Civil Society and Government: Seeking Judaic Insights," in *Civil Society and Government*, ed. Nancy S. Rosenblum and Robert C. Post (Princeton: Princeton University Press, 2002), 276–77.

17. Yacov Guggenheim, "Jewish Community and Territorial Organization," in *The Jews of Europe in the Middle Ages (Tenth to Fifteenth Centuries), Proceedings of the International Symposium held at Speyer, 20–25 October 2002*, ed. Cristoph Cluse (Turnhout, Belgium: Brepols, 2004), 91.

18. Menachem Lorberbaum, *Politics and the Limits of Law* (Stanford, CA: Stanford University Press, 2001), 96.

19. Ibid.

20. Harold J. Berman, *Law and Revolution* (Cambridge, MA: Harvard University Press, 1983), 113–19.

21. Shalom Albeck, "Foundations of the *kehilah* in Spain up to the Ramah" (Hebrew), *The Medieval Jewish Community*, 65, as quoted by Lorberbaum in *Politics*, 97.

22. Ibid., 100.

23. Moses Maimonides, *The Guide of the Perplexed*, ed. and trans. Shlomo Pines, 2 vols. (Chicago: University of Chicago Press, 1963), vol. 1, ch. 33, 72.

24. On the five causes that, according to Maimonides, hinder the instruction of the multitude, see *GP*, vol. 1, ch. 34, 72–79.

25. Although he studied and admired their wisdom, Maimonides flatly rejected "all the first Mutakallimun from among the Greeks who had adopted Christianity and from among the Moslems who did not conform in their premises to the

appearance of that which exists, but considered how being ought to be in order that it should furnish a proof for the correctness of a particular opinion." Maimonides, *The Guide of the Perplexed*, part l, vol. 1, ch. 71, 178. Later on, in referring to this method of thought, he would be more categorical: "[M]y soul felt a very strong aversion to it." Ibid., 180. See also Warren Zev Harvey, "Why Maimonides was not a *Mutakallim*," in Kraemer, ed., *Perspectives on Maimonides*, 105–11.

Leo Strauss points out Maimonides' subtle attitude of deliberate ambiguity with respect to the philosophy of "Aristotle and the Peripatetics" as well that of the *kalam* and the *mutakallimun*, two opposing systems of thought, although he makes use of both of them. See Leo Strauss, "How to Begin to Study *The Guide of the Perplexed*," in Maimonides, *GP*, vol. 1, cxxiv.

26. Lorberbaum, *Politics and the Limits of Law*, 100.

27. Maimonides' family was forced to leave Córdoba upon the arrival of the Almohads and the capture of Seville in 1147. The Almohads imposed a veritable military dictatorship with the purpose of uniting the Muslim *taifa* kingdoms. Maimonides led an errant life, wandering with his family from one place to another; some scholars believe that they lived in the important port of Almería until 1160, when they decided to move to Fez. It is thought that they probably passed for Muslims until they were obliged to convert to Islam. For this reason, and according to the precepts of Judaism, they left Morocco for Jerusalem. Ángeles Navarro Peiro, "Literatura hispano-hebrea," in *Memoria de Sefarad* (Toledo: Centro Cultural San Marcos, Sociedad Estatal para la Acción Cultural Exterior, 2002–03), 300.

28. Lorberbaum, 103.

29. Ibid.

30. Ibid.

31. From *hagios*: sacred and *graphos*: writing, referring to the third and last part of the Jewish scriptures.

32. Lorberbaum, *Politics and the Limits of Law*, 103.

33. Ibid., 104.

34. Maimonides, *Mishneh Torah*, Book 12, Acquisitions: ch. 18, 1, in *A Maimonides Reader*, ed. Isadore Twersky (NJ: Behrman House, 1972), 46. Further references to this work are designated with the abbreviation *MT.*

35. Ibid.

36. Ibid., 171–72.

37. Juan Luis Vives devoted an important book to this subject: *De subventione pauperum. Sive de humanis necessitatibus*, published in Bruges in 1525. Juan Luis Vives, *De subventione pauperum. De comunione rerum*, trans. and notes by Francisco Calero (Valencia: Ajuntament de Valencia, 2004).

38. Maimonides, *MT*, Book 12: Acquisitions; Sales, ch. 22, 16, and 17, 173.

39. Maimonides, *MT*, Book 12: Acquisitions; Sales, ch. 22, 17, 173.

40. Maimonides, *MT*, Book 12: Acquisitions; Sales, ch. 14, 16, 172.

41. Maimonides, *MT*, Book 12: Acquisitions; Sales, ch. 14, 16, 172.

42. See ch. 1, note 13.

43. See ch. 1, note 20.

44. Asher ben Yehiel (Rosh) was born in Germany in 1250. He studied at Worms with Meir ben Baruch of Rothenburg, and after his teacher was imprisoned, he became the leader of the German Jewish community. A survivor of the slaughter of Rindfleisch in 1298, he left Germany in 1303 for Barcelona, where he was welcomed by Solomon ibn Abraham Adret. He followed closely the controversies concerning Maimonides' work. In 1305 he became the chief rabbi of Toledo. Asher was a bridge between the German commentators of the Talmud and the scholars of the Spanish Jewish communities. He died in Toledo in 1328, having written over one thousand *responsa.*

45. The Crusades were military campaigns nominally against Islam from the eleventh to the thirteenth centuries. Organized under papal initiative, they began with the preaching of sermons. In general, they were disastrous for the Jewish communities of Central Europe. The First Crusade was initiated in November 1095 by Pope Urban II at the Council of Clermont, Auvergne.

46. At the other end of Christianity, the conditions of the Jews of Byzantium were also very harsh under the Emperor Romanos I Lekapenos, who reigned from 919 to 944, which confirms the Jewish saying, "Whoever causes trouble to the Jews becomes a leader." Ashtor, *The Jews of Moslem Spain*, vol. 1, 185.

47. Robert Chazan, *Barcelona and Beyond: The Disputation of 1263 and Its Aftermath* (Berkeley: University of California Press, 1992), 199–203.

48. Ramban (Nahmanides), "Discourse on a Wedding," in *Writings and Discourses,* 2 vols. ed. and notes by Rabbi Dr. Charles B. Chavel (New York: Shilo, 1985), vol. 1, 32–33.

49. Job 28:21, *The New Jerusalem Bible* (NY: Doubleday, 1990), 788.

50. Ramban (Nahmanides), "Discourse on the Law of the Eternal Is Perfect," *Writings and Discourses*, vol. 1, 32–33.

51. The famous poet and scholar Judah Halevi (Tudela, 1075–Egypt, c. 1141) had even announced the coming of the Messiah in 1130. Navarro Peiro, "Literatura hispano-hebrea," 299.

52. Ramban, "Discourse on the Law of the Eternal Is Perfect," 40.

53. Rabbi Abraham ibn Ezra (Abenezra), born in Tudela in 1089, a city that belonged to the emirate of Saragossa, later to the Taifa kingdom of Saragossa, and finally to the kingdom of Aragon. Ibn Ezra died in Calahorra, the birthplace of Quintilian in 1164. He traveled extensively and was learned in poetry, philosophy, medicine, mathematics, and astronomy. Nahmanides took his opinions into account on many occasions. See, for example, Ramban, "Discourse on the Law of the Eternal Is Perfect," 36, 50, 102, 103, 105, 117, and 132; also see Ramban (Nahmanides), *Commentary on the Tora:. Exodus*, trans. and notes by Charles B. Chavel (New York: Shilo, 1973), 347, 419, 454, 480, 525, and 559. Sometimes the quotations are so frequent that Ibn Ezra becomes omnipresent: Ramban (Nahmanides), *Commentary on the Torah: Numbers,* trans. and notes by Charles B. Chavel (New York: Shilo, 1973). See 35, 42, 60, 71, 76, 77, 95, 109, 115, 125, 136, 141, 145, 148, 160, 174,

181, 183, 184, 187. He should not be confused with Rabbi Ezra, an important kabbalist in the circle of Gerona and the author of a "Commentary on the Song of Songs," whom Nahmanides considered as an equal in rank and close to his intimate circle, and to whom he refers as *chavaireinu* (our colleague). Ramban (Nahmanides), *Commentary on the Torah: Leviticus*, trans. and notes by Charles B. Chavel (New York: Shilo, 1974), 296.

54. Ramban, "Discourse on the Law of the Eternal Is Perfect," 36.

55. Ibid., 48–49.

56. Ramban, "The Book of Redemption," in Ramban (Nahmanides), *Writings and Discourses*, 618.

57. Ibid., 616–17. Like Ibn Ezra, when he interprets the vision of Daniel and other rabbis, Nahmanides seems to see both Greece and Rome as a single entity.

58. Ramban, "Discourse on the Law of the Eternal Is Perfect," 56.

59. Ibid.

60. Ibid.

61. Together with incest and the shedding of blood.

62. Ramban, "Discourse on the Law of the Eternal Is Perfect," 58. His discussion of enchantment and the practice of sorcery is curious.

63. Ramban, "Discourse on the Law of the Eternal Is Perfect," 54–55.

64. Ibid., 38.

65. Ibid., 66.

66. Ibid., 125.

67. Lorberbaum believes that "the two ideal opposing types of philosophies in Judaism developed by (Judah) Halevi and later by Maimonides in the first and following decades of the twelfth century respectively, mark the maturing of Jewish philosophical discourse. See Menachem Lorberbaum, "Medieval Jewish Political Thought," in *The Cambridge Companion to Medieval Jewish Philosophy*, ed. Daniel H. Frank and Oliver Leaman (Cambridge, UK: Cambridge University Press, 2003), 179. The "basic controversy" would revolve around "collective identity," 179. "A community in exile is characterized," says Lorberbaum, "by the fact that it is not the territory but the *identity* that marks the limits of its jurisdiction," 179–80. Halevi (Tudela, 1075–Egypt, 1141) studied in Lucena and was a well-known poet and physician in Córdoba.) He leans toward the charismatic identity in his *Sefer ha-Kuzari*, while Maimonides does so through a political and legal definition of identity, in which its institutionalization is essential (Lorberbaum, 179–80). The *Sefer ha-Kuzari* was originally written in Arabic and translated later into Hebrew by Judah ibn Tibbon. Subtitled "The Book of the Refutation and the Proof in Favor of the Hated Religion," it expounds a dialogue between the pagan king of the Khazars and representatives of Christianity and Islam, ending with a learned Jew who was invited to instruct them in the principles of the Jewish religion. Another translation by Judah ben Isaac Cardinal appeared at the beginning of the thirteenth century.

68. Ramban, "Discourse on the Law of the Eternal Is Perfect," 69.

69. The idea that hidden miracles exist that are not perceived by man is typical of Nahmanides. There are those who think that this is "the doctrine of Nahmanides *par excellence*." See David Berger, "Miracles and the Natural Order in Nahmanides," http://zooTorah.com/books/MiraclesNahmanides.pdf, 5.

70. Ramban (Nahmanides), *Commentary on the Torah: Leviticus*, trans. and notes by Charles B. Chavel, 460.

71. Ramban, "Discourse on the Law of the Eternal Is Perfect," 69.

72. Ibid., 70.

73. Ramban (Nahmanides), *Commentary on the Torah. Exodus*, 65.

74. Ramban, "Discourse on the Law of the Eternal Is Perfect," 71.

75. Nahmanides does accept the existence of regularities, laws, and periods implanted by God in Creation and those by which the growth of species is adjusted "so that they may not be inconstant in their functioning." Thus, on the Sabbath God can rest confidently in the knowledge that those laws that would do their work are "workers of the truth whose work is true." Ramban, "The Words of Koheleth," in Ramban (Nahmanides), *Writings and Discourses*, vol. 1, 168.

76. Maimonides, *Guide of the Perplexed*, II. 29, vol. 2, 346.

77. Ibid.

78. Ibid. Maimonides and Nahmanides obviously coincide in this essential point for the Jewish tradition, which acknowledges the Creator of the universe and diverges openly from the Greeks. As Gunnar Olsson points out, "this belief in creation ex nihilo (was) to the Greek culture the most forbidden of everything forbidden." Gunnar Olsson, *Abismal: A Critique of Cartographic Reason* (Chicago: University of Chicago Press, 2007), 43.

79. Juan Calvino (John Calvin), *Institución de la religión cristiana* (1559), trans. Cipriano de Valera (1597) (Fundación Editorial de Literatura Reformada; Netherlands, 1968), book 1, ch. xvii, 10, 145.

80. See Hugues Jean de Dianoux, "Les Saporta, marranes aragonais, professeurs de Médecine à Montpellier et leur descendants Marquis en Provence," en Carol Iancu, *Les Juifs a Montpellier et dans le Languedoc* (Montpellier: Université Paul Valery, 1988), 196–99, 210–22.

81. Francisco Javier González Echevarría and Teresa Ancín Chandía, "Miguel Servet pertenecía a la familia de judeoconversos de los Zaporta," *Pliegos de Bibliofilia* Madrid 7 (tercer trimestre, 1999): 34.

82. Jeremy Cohen, *The Friars and the Jews* (Ithaca, NY: Cornell University Press, 1982), 115.

83. In the words of Pope Clement IV, in a Papal Bull (Viterbo 1268), "our dear son, brother Paulo, known by the knickname of Christiani, of the order of preaching friars . . . who knows the language (Jewish) as he was of Jewish origin and for having been taught the Hebrew scriptures . . . but also because he possesses the zeal of the Catholic faith because he has been reborn in the sacred font," Nahmanide, 'Bulle de Clément IV, in Nahmanide, *La Dispute de Barcelona*, 4th ed. corrected and enlarged (Verdier, 1984), 87.

84. Ibid., 60.

85. After the death of Servet, John Calvin published his *Defensio orthodoxae fidei de sacra Trinitate contra prodigiosos errores Michaelis Seruet Hispani*, printed in Latin in Geneva in 1554 and in French by J. Crespin. González Echeverría and Ancín Chandía, "Miguel Servet pertenecía a la familia judeoconversa de los Zaporta," 39.

86. See note 104 in this chapter.

87. Ramban, "Discourse on the Law of the Eternal Is Perfect," 103.

88. Ibid., 120.

89. Ibid., 122.

90. Ibid., 114.

91. Maimonides, *The Guide of the Perplexed*, vol. 1, ch. 46, 96.

92. Ramban, "The Words of the Koheleth," 198 and 175.

93. Ibid., 171.

94. In one of his intrepretations Nahmanides attributes this text to Yahveh. Vigilance here is a visual observation uninterrupted on the part of the vigilant, but it functions only if the other part is vigilant, wakeful, and *disenchanted*. From this, we can deduce explicitly that God is vigilant, always awake, but not lethargic. Ramban (Nahmanides), *Commentary on the Torah: Exodus*, 290.

95. Ramban, *Commentary on the Torah: Exodus*, 315.

96. Ibid.

97. Ibid.

98. Religion is the business of him who rules.

99. Berman, *Law and Revolution*, chap. 2, 85–119.

100. See note 79 in this chapter.

101. González Echeverría and Ancín Chandía, "Miguel Servet pertenecía a la familia judeoconversa de los Zaporta," 34–42.

102. Ramban (Nahmanides), *Commentary on the Torah: Exodus*, 25, 31, 33ff.

103. Ramban, "The Words of Koheleth," 174.

104. Ibid., 166.

105. Ibid., 224–31.

106. Charles B. Chavel, "Translator's Introduction to 'Letter to the French Rabbis,'" in Ramban (Nahmanides), *Writings and Discourses*, vol. 2, 357.

107. Chavel, 358–59.

108. An allusion to Psalms 106:35.

109. Ramban, "Letter to the French Rabbis," in Ramban (Nahmanides), *Writings and Discourses*, vol. 2, 375.

110. Ibid., 375.

111. Ibid.

112. Zechariah 1:14, the words of the angel of Yahveh alluding to Jerusalem.

113. An allusion to the words of King Ahashuerus to his court in Esther 1:4: "Thus he displays the riches and splendor of his empire and the pomp and glory of his majesty." *The New Jerusalem Bible* (New York: Doubleday, 1990), 660; Quoted in Nahmanides, "Letter to the French Rabbis," in *Writings and Discourses,* vol. 2, 388.

114. Ramban, "Letter to the French Rabbis," 388.

115. Ibid., 389.

116. *The New Jerusalem Bible*, 837.

117. An allusion to Isaiah 30:15: "your strength (lay) in serenity and trust."

118. Ibid., 389.

119. Ibid., 395–96.

120. Ibid., 397.

121. *The New Jerusalem Bible*, 1147.

122. Ramban, (Nahmanides), "Rosh Hashanah," in *Writings and Discourses*, vol. 1, 351.

123. Ramban arrived in the land of Israel in 1267 at the port of Akko where he stayed a few months before continuing on to Jerusalem. In 1972 a valuable copper ring was found on a hill in Akko with his name and an inscription in Hebrew. Translator's note. *Exodus*, 627.

124. The Tosefta was a complementary supplement to the Mishnah dating from the second century, written in Hebrew and Aramaic, with a structure similar to the Mishnah.

125. Ramban (Nahmanides), *Commentary on the Torah: Leviticus*, 97.

126. Ramban, "Rosh Hashanah," 284.

127. Ibid., 264.

128. Ibid., 271.

129. Ramban, "The Words of the Koheleth," 177.

130. Ibid., 198.

131. "Amo la patria mia più dell' anima," "Niccolò Machiavelli a Francesco Tettori, Forlì, April 16, 1527." *Machiavelli. Tutte le opere*, ed. Mario Martelli (Milan: Sandone, 1993), 1250; Niccolò Machiavelli, "Letter to Francesco Vettori, April 16, 1527," in Allan Gilbert, trans., *Machiavelli: The Chief Works and Others*, 2 vols. (Durham: Duke University Press, 1989), vol. 2, 1010; Maurizio Viroli, *For Love of Country* (Oxford: Clarendon, 1995), 37.

132. Ramban, "Rosh Hashanah," 295.

133. Lorberbaum, *Politics and the Limits of Law*, 106.

134. Harold J. Berman, *Law and Revolution*, 362.

135. Ibid., 361–62.

136. Isidore Epstein, *The "Responsa" of Rabbi Solomon Ben Adret of Barcelona (1235–1310)* (New York: Ktav, 1968), 96.

137. Michael Waltzer, "Preface," in *Law, Politics, and Morality in Judaism*, ed. Michael Walter (Princeton, NJ: Princeton University Press, 2006), vii.

138. Berman, *Law and Revolution*, 362.

139. See note 120.

140. Lorberbaum, *Politics and the Limits of Law*, 108.

141. Ibid., 108.

142. "[T]his vast and dreadful desert, a land of fiery snakes, scorpions, thirst . . ." Deuteronomy 8:16.

143. Exodus 16:35.

144. Michael Waltzer, "Preface," in *Law, Politics, and Morality in Judaism*, vii.

145. As Rabbi Moses ben Samuel Sofer (1762–1839), an ultraorthodox leader of the romantic period, indicates strictly: "All novelty is prohibited by the Torah," in *Law, Politics, and Morality in Judaism*, ix.

146. Robert M. Cover, "Obligation: A Jewish Jurisprudence of the Social Order," in *Law, Politics, and Morality in Judaism*, 5.

147. Suzanne Last Stone, "Judaism and Civil Society," 30.

148. Ibid., 12, 21.

149. A good example of these differences can be found in Leo Strauss, *Natural Right and History*, a work that is frequently misinterpreted because of this.

150. Lorberbaum, 108.

151. Ibid.

152. Ibid.

153 Ibid., 107.

154. Rabbi Meir of Rothenburg (Worms c. 1215–1293) was a noted scholar, respected leader of his community, and witness to numerous anti-Semitic persecutions.

155. The Cortes of Toledo had already forced the Jews to live in separate quarters of the city. Torquemada's decree of March 20, 1492, recalls that the Jews "for their own fault are forced to endure perpetual servitude . . . to be servants and captives . . . we [therefore] command all Jews, of both sexes and all ages, who live, dwell, and are in any way present in our kingdoms and lands to be gone and never return or even pass through these realms." See Joseph Pérez, "La expulsion de los Judíos, "in *Memoria de Sefarad* (Toledo: Centro Cultural San Marcos, 2002–03), 385.

156. Many Jews in the kingdom of Aragon emigrated because of this to Tudela, in the neighboring kingdom of Navarra. The tribunal of the Holy Office was not established in Navarra until 1513, when its seat was transferred precisely to Tudela in 1515. See González Echevarría and Ancín Chandía, "Miguel Servet pertenecía a la familia de judeoconversos de los Zaporta," 41. The first accusations of blood libel against Jews date from 1144, in Norwich, England. See below n. 167. In this degrading line, there is the very famous case of a child of Toledo in 1490, in which Jewish inhabitants were accused of the ritual killing of a Christian boy. See Isidro G. Bango Torviso, "Inquisition," in *Memoria de Sefarad* (Toledo, Sociedad Estatal, 2002–03), 420.

157. Arabic *aljamiado*, that is, Arabic written in Hebrew characters.

158. Nahmanides seems to see Greece subsumed into a greater Rome, and, as such, he believes that, for the tradition of the rabbis, both are seen as a single reality. Nahmanides, "The Book of Redemption," 616–27.

159. An example of this critical position toward the significance of Maimonides can be found in the Catalan poet in the Hebrew language, Meshulam ben Solomon de Piera, the leader of his *aljama*, a pupil of the kabbalistic circle of Gerona and, as he himself recognized, an admirer of Nahmanides: "[T]o our eyes we a second son for Ben Nahman, but destiny is also our second son." Josep

Ribera-Florit, "El poeta judío catalán Mesulam ben Selomó de Piera y sus poemas laudatorios," 7. I do not have the complete bibliographic data of the Spanish version, but for the Catalan version of this article, see J. Ribera, "El poeta jueu català Meshul.lam ben Shelomo de Piera I els seus poems laudatoris," in *Homenatge a Antoni Comas* (Barcelona, 1985), 371–84. In Spanish it can be found in PDF in http://www.aeehj.org/. See also J. Ribera, "Meshulam ben Shelomo de Piera y la controversia maimonista en Cataluña," *El Olivo*, 9 (1985): 211–34.

160. Ahmed Chalane, "Averroes, Maimónides y la crisis en la comunidad judía medieval," trans. Joseph Puig Montada, *Anales del Seminario de Historia de la Filosofía* 22 (2005): 112ff.

161. Suzanne Last Stone, "Judaism and Civil Society," 14. Ritva, or Rabbi Yom Tov ibn Asevilli, was a prominent leader of the Jews of Seville. He was born in the second half of the thirteenth century and probably lived into the first half of the fourteenth century. He was a pupil of the great Rashba, the rabbi and judge of Toledo Jewry. See also Rabbi Jonah ben Abraham of Gerona, *The Gates of Repentance* (Shaarei Tesuvah), trans. Shraga Silverstein (Jerusalem-New York: Feldheim, 1976), 191.

162. Ahmed Chalane, "Averroes, Maimónides y la crisis en la comunidad judía medieval," *Anales del Seminario de Historia de la Filosofía*, 22 (2005): 112.

163. Cohen, *The Friars and the Jews*, 103–28.

164. Many people witnessed this famous disputation of July 20, 1263, to which Nahmanides was summoned by order of the king and with the consent of Fray Raimundo de Penyafort: "the King [seated] in his usual throne against the wall. The bishop was also there and many nobles, Guillem de Cervelló, Pere de Berga, and numerous knights and people of the lower classes from every part of the city." Quoted in *Disputa de Barcelona de 1263 entre Mestre Mossé de Girona i Fra Pau Cristià*, translation into Catalan of the Hebrew and Latin texts by Eduard Feliu, with an introduction by Jaume Riera i Sans (Barcelona: La Columna, 1985), 5, 47, 81. Nahmanides, who was also accompanied by other Jews who seemed to be and were held to be the wisest among them" (*Disputa*, 65) had a dispute, it seems, with Fray Paulo Christiani and his advisers, among whom was Fray Peter of Genoa (*Disputa*, 13). It seems that Fray Raimundo de Penyafort also intervened occasionally (*Disputa*, 58). The event took place in the royal palace in Barcelona before James I, king of Aragon, Majorca, and Valencia, count of Barcelona and Urgel, and seigneur of Montpellier (*Disputa*, 69). The pro-Christian Latin text (*Disputa*, 65–60), which refers to these happenings, is from the same period and bears the seal of the chancery. The first Hebrew version of the same event is also included here (*Disputa*, 3–61) and dates from the end of the fifteenth or beginning of the sixteenth century. It is unclear whether its origin comes directly from Nahmanides.

165. Étienne Gilson, *La filosofía en la Edad Media*, 2nd ed. (Madrid: Gredos, 1965), 392.

166. Andrei Oisteanu, "Jews, Christians, and Muslims: Some Theological Disputations in Medieval Europe," *Studia Hebraica* 6 (2006): 95.

167. Quoted in Robert Chazan, *Barcelona and Beyond: The Disputation of 1263 and Its Aftermath* (Berkeley: University of California Press, 1962), 10.

168. Beginning with the fourth Lateran Council (1215), European Jews were obliged to wear distinctive badges on their clothing. The Hispanic kingdoms were very reluctant to accept this disposition of Pope Innocent III. Bango Torviso, "Inquisition," 105.

169. Robert J. Burns, S.J., *Latinate Wills in Mediterranean Spain, 1250–1350* (Berkeley: University of California Press, 1996), 15.

170. Ibid.

171. The first case of blood libel appeared in Norwich, England, in 1144 and has appeared at certain times in European culture until the present. The Jews were accused of having abducted a Christian boy in order to torture him just as they had done earlier with Jesus on Passover. As a consequence, massacres took place in several towns, the most serious occurring in York.

172. Mossé ben Nahman, "Comentari sobre la perícopa 'el meu servidor serà intel.ligent,'" a text included in *Disputa de Barcelona de 1263 entre Mestre Mossé de Girona i Fra Pau Cristià*, trans. into Catalan of the Hebrew and Latin text by Eduard Feliu, 81.

Chapter 4

1. Ramban (Nahmanides), *Commentary on the Torah, Numbers*, trans. and notes Charles B. Chavel (New York: Shilo, 1973), 73.

2. In the sense of received tradition, from the Hebrew term *qabbalah*, the nominal form of the verb *qibbel* (to receive); the kabbalist is the *mequbbal*, the receiver of the teachings.

3. Gershom Scholem, *Major Trends in Jewish Mysticism*, with a new Foreward by Robert Alter (New York: Schocken Books, 1995), 1.

4. Ibid., 2.

5. Ibid.

6. Ibid., 3.

7. See Eric Voegelin, "Anxiety and Reason" (1963), in "What Is History? And Other Late Unpublished Writings," *The Collected Works of Eric Voegelin*, vol. 28, ed. Thomas A. Hollbeck and Paul Caringella (Baton Rouge: Louisiana State University Press, 1990); Eric Voegelin, "Order and History, vol. 1, Israel and Revelation," *The Collected Works of Eric Voegelin*, vol. 14, ed. Maurice P. Hogan (Columbia: University of Missouri Press, 2001).

8. Ari Ackerman, "Jewish Philosophy and the Jewish-Christian Philosophical Dialogue in Fifteenth-century Spain," in *The Cambridge Companion to Medieval Jewish Philosophy*, 372.

9. The First Crusade was preached by the pope in 1095 at the Council of Clermont and reached Constantinople in 1097.

10. For Elfenbein, "The political machinery of the Spanish communities of this period is almost as varied as is nature itself. There is no single and uniform system of government in the *aljama*. We can discover from the point of view of suffrage a variety of governmental features ranging from democracy to tyranny." Rabbi Israel Elfenbein, "Jewish Communal Government in Spain," *Student's Annual, Journal of Theological Studies* 2 (1915): 102–03.

11. Epstein, *Responsa*, 60–61.

12. Ibid., 75.

13. Ibid., 57.

14. Ibid., 58.

15. Ibid., 61.

16. Ibid., 62–71.

17. This was the case of Maimonides' family, who emigrated to Fez. Moisés Orfali, *Biblioteca de autores lógicos hispano-judios (siglos XI–XIV)* (Granada: Editorial Universidad de Granada, 1997), 70–71. Others like Judah Halevi emigrated to Castile before going to Egypt, and still others such as Judah ibn Tibbon and Joseph Qimhi ended up in Languedoc. Orfali, 60, 89, 104.

18. Arthur Green, "Introduction," in the *Zohar*, Pritzker Edition, trans. of original manuscripts and commentaries by Daniel C. Matt (Stanford, CA: Stanford University Press, 2004), vol. 1, xxxi.

19. The author says that he happened to find a notebook "written in characters I knew to be Arabic" in the Alcaná (old clothes market) of Toledo. The book was supposedly written by "Cide Hamete Benengeli, an Arabic historian." Miguel de Cervantes, *Don Quijote de la Mancha*, edición del iv centenario (Madrid: Real Academia Española, Asociación de Academias de la Lengua Española, 2004), part 1, ch. 9, 85–86. Later on he refers to him as an "Arabic and Manchegan author." Part 1, ch. 22, 199.

20. Idel, "Jewish Philosophy and Kabbalah in Spain," *in Sephardic and Mizrahi Jewry*, 120.

21. The author of important works in Hebrew such as the *Explanation of the Ten Sefirot*. Nevertheless, Azriel is strongly in favor of teaching this knowledge orally.

22. Among his pupils were "R. Solomon ibn Adret, R. Yom Tov Ashvili, R, Isaac ben Todros, and R. David ha-Kohen." Moshe Idel, "We Have No Kabbalistic Tradition on This," in *Rabbi Moses Nahmanides (Ramban): Explorations in His Religious Virtuosity* (Cambridge, MA: Harvard University Press, 1983), 65.

23. There is speculation that he may have been the author of *Sefer el-Bahir*, a pioneering book on kabbalah.

24. Born in Saragossa in the middle of the thirteenth century, he studied with the teachers of kabbalah in Barcelona. He was an admirer of Maimonides, whom he believed was compatible with and similar to the kabbalah. He traveled widely, spreading kabbalistic teachings based on the *Sefer Yetsirah* (The Book of Creation) throughout Italy and Greece. He is one of the first teachers to give music a central role in the understanding of knowledge.

25. Idel, "Jewish Philosophy and Kabbala in Spain," 130.

26. Born into a wealthy Sevillian family around the time of the Expulsion Decree, he was the assistant of Abraham Senior, the chief tax collector and chief rabbi of the kingdom of Castile. Isaac was also the father of the famous humanist, León Hebreo (Judah Abravanel).

27. Cedric Cohen Skalli, "Discovering Isaac Abravanel's Humanistic Rhetoric," *The Jewish Quarterly Review* 97, no. 1 (Winter 2007): 86.

28. Skalli, 78ff. See also Eric Lawee's monography, *Abrabanel's Stance toward Tradition: Defense, Dissent, and Dialogue* (Albany: State University of New York Press, 2001); Leo Strauss, "On Abravanel's Philosophical Tendency and Political Teaching," in *Isaac Abravanel, Six Lectures*, ed. J. B. Trend and H. Loewe (Cambridge, UK: Cambridge University Press, 1937), 95–129.

29. Skalli, 80.

30. Ibid., 78.

31. Scholem, *Major Trends*, 7.

32. Ibid., 10–11.

33. Ibid., 11 and ff.

34. Ibid., 12.

35. Ibid., 13.

36. Ibid.

37. R. Jonah of Gerona (Rabbeinu. Yonah b. Abraham Gerondi, *The Gates of Repentance* (Shaarei Teshuvah), bilingual version in Hebrew and English, trans. Shraga Silverstein, (Jerusalem, New York: Feldheim, 1976), 11, 143.

38. Ibid., 131.

39. Ibid.

40. Ibid., 117.

41. Ibid., 119.

42. Ibid.

43. This idea also appears in Abraham ibn Ezra (1080–1167) in his work *Yesod Mora* (Treatise on Reverence), for whom the imprisonment of the soul in the body "has no other goal that that of giving it an individualized and autonomous existence." Orfali, *Biblioteca de autores lógicos*, 53.

44. Jonah of Gerona, 111.

45. In some passages by this author there seems to be a certain confusion between the concept of judgment and sentence. Jonah of Gerona, 127.

46. Jonah of Gerona, 99.

47. Ibid., 129.

48. Ramban, *Commentary on the Torah: Numbers*, 25.

49. The *Zohar*, vol. 2, 3, 1:77a.

50. Ibid., 14.

51. Ibid.

52. Ibid.

53. Nahmanides, *Exodus*, 333.

54. Scholem, 14.

55. Ibid., 15.

56. Ibid.

57. The medieval Arabic translators had translated most of Aristotle's works, including, of course, his *Rhetoric*. See Kraemer, "The Islamic Content of Medieval Jewish Philosophy," in *The Cambridge Companion*, 51.

58. Scholem, 135.

59. Ibid., 15.

60. Ibid.

61. Ibid., 37.

62. The *Zohar*, vol. 2, 218 (1:126b), 245 (1:123b). The texts I have extracted here are very far apart in the work, but they make up a single thought that runs throughout the book. On the impurity of woman and her inclination toward witchcraft, see 219 (1:127a), 220 (1:127b), 230 (1:130b), and 235 (1:131b).

63. Exod. 33:11. See in this respect, H. Crescas, *The Refutation of the Christian Principles*, 32.

64. Scholem, 16.

65. Ibid., 17.

66. See note 24 in this chapter.

67. Scholem, 17.

68. Nahmanides uses this expression on several occasions in his monumental *Commentary on the Torah,* which has been discussed in other parts of this book.

69. Epstein, *The Responsa of Rabbi Simon B. Zemah Duran*, 7.

70. Stern, *Problems and Parables of Law*, 98.

71. The *Zohar*, vol. 2, 182 (1:117b).

72. Scholem, 21.

73. Moses Nahmanides is highly esteemed as "a great kabbalist, legal scholar, and biblical commentator." David Shatz, "The Biblical and Rabbinic Background to Medieval Jewish Philosophy," in *The Cambridge Companion to Medieval Jewish Philosophy*, 28. Solomon ibn Adret is recognized as "the halakhic leader of Aragonese Jewry." H. Tirosh-Samuelson, "Philosophy and Kabbalah: 1200–1600," in *The Cambridge Companion*, 232.

74. Scholem, 24.

75. Ibid.

76. These are the words of the assembly of representatives of the communities of Aragon and Valencia who met in Barcelona in 1354 in an attempt to withstand the persecution that arose as a consequence of the Black Death of 1348. See Elon, *Jewish Law*, vol. 2, 798.

77. Nahmanides, *Exodus*, 3.

78. Kraemer, "The Islamic Context of Medieval Jewish Philosophy," 49.

79. Scholem, 28.

80. Ibid., 31.

81. Kraemer, 55.

82. Ibid.

83. *Don Quxote*, first part, ch. 19, regarding the conversation between Sancho and Don Quixote and the adventure with a dead body.

84. The *Zohar*, vol. 2, 70 (1:90b).

85. Juan Calvino (John Calvin), *Institución de la religión cristiana* (1559), trans. Cipriano de Valera (1597) (Rijswijk, Netherlands: Fundación Editorial de Literatura Reformada, 1968), book 1, ch. 17, 10, 145.

86. Shatz, 34.

87. Kraemer, 46.

88. Y. Tzvi Langermann, "Maimonides' Repudiation of Astrology," in *Maimonids and the Sciences*, ed. Robert S. Cohen and Hillel Levine (Dordrecht: Kluwer, 2001), 131.

89. Idel, "Jewish Philosophy and Kabbala in Spain," 127.

90. The medieval Arabic philosophers also distinguished between *zahir* and *bahir* "the external and internal (deep structure) sense of texts and the inner truth and outer aspect of the religious law. This *zahir-batin* dichotomy was prominent in the milieu of Shi' ism and Sufism." Kraemer, 60–61.

91. Tirosh-Samuelson, 237.

92. Ibid.

93. Nahmanides, *Leviticus*, 297.

94. Ibid., 296–97.

95. Ibid., 101.

96. Tirosh-Samuelson, 237.

97. R. Jonah of Gerona, 173. "Our Sages have said that such a man is called a thief, for he steals men's minds" (Shevuoth 39a).

98. See Tirosh-Samuelson, 237.

99. Ibid., 240–41.

100. Ibid., 231.

101. Scholem, 33.

102. This same idea is found in the Quietism of Miguel de Molinos in the sixteenth century in Valencia.

103. Scholem, 37.

104. An example of this can be found in two great German operas: the beginning of Mozart's *Magic Flute* (1791) ("*Zu Hilfe, zu Hilfe, sonst bin ich verloren*") ("Help, help, or I am lost!"); and Wagner's *Siegfried* (1876) (*Hoiho! Hoiho!/ Hau'ein! Hau'ein! /Friss ihn! Friss ihn!/den Fratzenschmied!/ Ha ha ha ha)* (Hoiho! Hoiho!/ Attack! Attack!/ Bite him! Bite him! Bite that sloppy forger! Ha, ha, ha).

105. Scholem, 105.

106. See Tirosh-Samuelson, 228–29.

107. Nahmanides, *Leviticus*, 454.

108. Nahmanides' confidence in the Tosefta regarding those subjects is obvious, as it shows in his commentary on Leviticus, the third book of the Pentateuch, which he considers to be "the law of the priests and the Levites," *Leviticus*, 3. There

are numerous mentions of the Tosefta; see for example 97, 179, 335, 429, 430, 448, 454, 460, 483.

109. Scholem, 118.

110. Norman Roth, "Las reacciones rabínicas ante Maimonides," in *Maimonides y su época*, ed. Carlos del Valle, Santiago García-Jalón, and Juan Pedro Monferrer (Madrid: Sociedad Estatal de Conmemoraciones Culturales, 2007), 74.

111. Zion Zohar, in *Sephardic and Mizrahi Jewry*, 9.

112. The economy of Muslim Spain always had a highly developed financial system. See Ashtor, vol. 1, 275.

113. Toledo was linked to Córdoba and Seville by a constant flow of trade among the three cities. See Ashtor, vol. 1, 275.

114. The situation must have been uncomfortable for many Sephardim, taking into account the advances in the field of medicine that they were aware of and enjoyed in Sepharad. As Gilson admitted, even in the latter years of the thirteenth century "the teaching of medicine was still in its infancy at the University of Paris," Gilson, 387.

115. Nahmanides, *Exodus*, 265.

116. Ibid.

117. Ibid.

118. Ibid.

119. Moses' father-in-law for whom he worked as a shepherd.

120. Nahmanides, *Exodus*, 266.

121. Scholem, 145.

122. These schools were active from the fifth century BCE until 529 CE, when the emperor of Byzantium, Justinian I, ordered the closing of the School of Athens.

123. Chayim J. Henoch, *Ramban, Philosopher and Cabalist* (Northvale, NJ: Aronson, 1998), 5.

124. Henoch, 6. Nevertheless, this author understands that the kabbalist way starts from a "duality of profound dialectical implication between two aspects of God," 6. This interpretation of the subject seems to lose a part of the Mediterranean rhetorical wisdom of the kabbalah.

125. It is not by accident that, in referring to the great opponents of the school of Maimonides such as the Catalan Hasdai Crescas, some scholars attribute to them a "dialectical agility and astuteness." Orfali, *Biblioteca de autores lógicos hispano-judíos (siglos XI–XIV)*, 152. Hasdai ben Abraham (or ben Judah) Crescas (Barcelona, 1340–Saragossa, c. 1411) was a member of a wealthy and distinguished family of Catalan scholars and a pupil of Rabbi Nissim ben Reuben Gerondi (Barcelona, 1320–1380). His works on philosophy and theology include *The Light of the Lord* (1410) and *The Refutation of the Christian Principles*.

126. Henoch, 6.

127. Ibid.

128 Ibid., 7.

129. Ibid., 116. Ibn Ezra also emphasizes the importance of this divine commandment to "banish the foreign gods" from the land of Israel. Henoch, 126.

130. Henoch, 126.
131. Ibid., 137.
132. Ibid., 237.
133. Ibid., 235.
134. Rabbi Shlomo Yitzchaki (1040–1105), "Rashi," born in Troyes, France, and educated in the Jewish schools of Mainz and Worms before he returned to his native city to found his own *yeshiva*. He was a Talmud scholar and exegete, held in esteem by his contemporaries and later generations.
135. Solomon Gaon, *The Influence of Catholic Theologian Alfonso Tostado on the Pentateuch Commentary of Isaac Abravanel* (Hoboken, NJ: Ktav, 1993), 42.
136. Henoch, 241.
137. Nachmanides, *Deuteronomy*, 365.
138. Henoch, 201.
139. Ibid.
140. Quoted in ibid.
141. From the Greek *dia-ballein*, to throw somewhere else; contrary to *syn-ballein*.
142. (Medinaceli 1248–Peñafiel c. 1305). A pupil in his youth of Abraham Abulafia and probably a friend of Moses de Leon, the author of the *Zohar*.
143. Henoch, 203.
144. Ibid., 204.

Chapter 5

1. The *Zohar*, Pritzker Edition, translation of original manuscripts and commentaries by Daniel C. Matt (Stanford, CA: Stanford University Press, 2004), vol. 2, 185 (1:118b).
2. "The Book of the *Zohar* . . . constitutes one of the richest spiritual legacies of Judaism." Haim Beinart, *Los Judíos en España* (Madrid: Mapfre, 1992), 111.
3. Scholem, *Major Trends*, Fifth Lecture, 156.
4. "Pseudooepigraphy is far removed from forgery." Scholem, 204.
5. Scholem, 194.
6. Nevertheless, "He is careful to avoid expressions which appear to have too much of a modernistic sound, such as *Kabbalah* and *Sefiroth*. In their place he employs paraphrases." Scholem, 165.
7. Arabic influence appears only in a few words, but the influence of Spanish can be seen in the vocabulary, expressions, and use of certain prepositions. See Scholem, 165.
8. Idel, "Jewish Philosophy and Kabbalah in Spain," 126.
9. Scholem, 157.
10. Ibid., 158.
11. Carles Giol, "Introducción," in *El Zohar. El libro del esplendor*, trans. Carles Giol, 2nd ed. (Barcelona: Ediciones. Obelisco, 2002), 21.

12. Scholem, 168.

13. Ibid., 163.

14. "Aramaic was the spoken language of Jews, both in the land of Israel and in Babylonia, from late biblical times (fourth–third century BCE) until after the Islamic conquest and its replacement by Arabic . . . By the time the *Zohar* was written, Aramaic was a purely literary language for all but a tiny group of Jews in the mountains of Kurdistan." Arthur Green, "Introduction," in *Zohar*, vol. 1, lxxiv.

15. See Scholem, "Fifth and Sixth Lectures," 157–243.

16. Scholem, 166–67.

17. *Zohar*, vol. 1, 108 (1:15a).

18. Ibid., 109 (1:15a).

19. Ibid., 257 (1:47b).

20. Ibid., 127 (1:17a).

21. Scholem, 167.

22. Ibid.

23. Ibid., 169. Arthur Green also finds certain concomitances between the narrative technique of the *Zohar*, which he sees as "a sort of novel in formation," and Cervantes' work. Green, "Introduction," *Zohar*, vol. 1, lxvii.

24. *Zohar*, vol. 2, 183 (1:118a).

25. Ibid.

26. A reference to the curtain that covers the heavens from the sight of men. See *Zohar*, vol. 1, 262 (1:48a).

27. *Zohar*, vol. 2, 183 (1:118a). The cloud is an allusion to war.

28. *Zohar*, vol. 2, 183 (1:118a).

29. Ibid., 183–64 (1:118a–118b).

30. *Don Quixote*, part 1, chs. 32–35.

31. Ibid., ch. 32.

32. *Zohar*, vol. 2, 184 (1:118b).

33. Nahmanides also understands enchantment as a matter for the enchanter or the specialist in prophecy. Ramban, *Commentary on the Torah: Numbers*, 270–71.

34. The same expression also appears in Jonah Gerondi, *The Gates of Repentance*, 173.

35. *Don Quixote*, part 1, ch. 7.

36. Ramban, *Numbers*, 270; see also 271, 273.

37. *GP*, vol. 1, xiv. See also, ch. 1, note 70. Although there are some who have raised the question of whether "there could have been in all the history of Jewish thought, two works that are more different than the *Zohar* and *The Guide of the Perplexed*." Moshe Halbertal, *Concealment and Revelation*, trans. Jackie Feldman (Princeton, NJ: Princeton University Press, 2007), 40.

38. Scholem, 173.

39. This attitude is just the opposite of Solomon ibn Adret (Rashba), "who stands in the tradition of his teacher Ramban, as opposed to that of Rambam." R. David Horwitz, "Rashba's Attitude toward Science and Its Limits," *The Torah u-Madda Journal*, 3 (1991–1992): 68.

40. There are, however, vestiges of this line of transformation of rhetoric in Isidore of Seville (560–636).

41. Scholem, 174.

42. Aaron Kirschenbaum, *Equity in Jewish Law: Beyond Equity* (Hoboken, NJ: Ktav, 1991), 1.

43. Idel, "Jewish Philosophy and Kabbalah in Spain," 127. This Talmudist was also the teacher of Mordecai ben Hillel, who took refuge in Spain at the end of the thirteenth century. Although he was respected for his Talmudic scholarship, Dan Ashkenazi, who received his nickname in Spain from his northern origin, ran into difficulties with Solomon ibn Adret for having given a letter of guarantee—that some think was a forgery—to an alleged prophet, Abraham of Avila, and for his favorable comments on animal sacrifice by Christians. Yitzhac Baer describes this person as a "German Pietist living in Saragossa who, in his rabbinical arguments, had sometimes reached conclusions that Rabbi Solomon ben Adret considered to be close to heresy." Yitzhac Baer, *Historia de los judíos en la España cristiana*, 2 vols., trans. José Luis Lacave (Madrid: Altalena, 1981), vol. 1, 222. This paragraph is omitted in the English translation.

44. *Zohar*, vol. 3, 415ff.

45. The Mishnah is the *repetition*, always preserved in memory, of the legal tradition of Israel. It includes the exegesis and application of the precepts received and preserved orally from the time of Moses. Together with the written law, the Torah, it makes up *halakhah*. The written compilation of the Mishnah was carried out around 200 CE by Rabbi Juda Ha-Nasi in the face of the serious difficulties of the Jewish community in Palestine, a Roman province, and the fear that it might be lost in the Diaspora. In contrast to the Torah, the Mishnah is presented as a systematized and organized *corpus juris*. The commentaries done by rabbinical tradition in the three centuries after the appearance of the Mishnah make up the Gemara. The Talmud is composed of both the Mishnah and the Gemara. Talmud means "study," and it is the abbreviation of the phrase "Talmud Torah" (study of the law); Moisés Orfali, *Talmud y Cristianismo* (Barcelona: Riopiedras, 1998), 11.

46. "De fide catholica ex Veteri et Novo Testamento, contra Iudaeos."

47. Yvonne Friedman, "Introduction," in Petri Venerabilis, *Adversus Iudeorum Inveterataam Duritiem* (Against the Inveterate Obstinacy of the Jews) a book written before 1144, *editio princeps*, 1522), ed. Yvonne Friedman (Turnhout, Belgium: Brepols, 1985), viii. "Remoue igitur, Iudee, stultitiae scandalum de corde tuo, separa bestialem intellectum a mente tua . . ." (Set aside from your heart, Jew, the temptation of stupidity, separate from your mind the bestial discernment . . ."), II, 598–99, 33. "O Iudei, hic bouinus intellectus cordibus uestris insederit, nec scriptura Dei uidere, nec Christum agnoscere . . ." (Oh, Jews, this bovine discernment will take possession of your souls, and you will not be able to see God's scriptures, nor recognize Christ . . ."), III, 47–48, 43. "Vere Sathanas de uobis ut hominess de simiis ludit, uere ut iumentum uilissimus chamo stultitiae quo uult trahit, uere ut pater mendacii multa uobis promittit ut cuncta substrahat, somnia dat, ut res

aufera . . ." ("The truth is that Satan mocks you as if you were monkeys, the truth is that he mocks you as if he would drag a miserable beast of burden with a yoke of stupidity, the truth is that he mocks you like an untruthful father who promises you many things and takes away others, who grants you dreams and deprives you of others . . .") III, 528–30, 57. "Videor michi Iudee . . . Cur enim non dicaris animal brutum, cur non bestia, cur non iumentum? Adhibe tecum bouem, vel si mauis asinum quo nichil in pecoribus stolidius est, et simul cum eo quaecumque possunt ausculta . . . Produco igitur portentuosam bestiam de cubili suo, et eam in theatro totius mundi, ins conspectus omnium populorum ridendam propono.Profero tibi coram uniuersis, Iudee, bestia . . ." ("It seems to me, Jews . . . Why do you not consecrate the stupid animal, why do you not consecrate the beast, why do you not consecrate the beast of burden? Bring with you the ox, and if you so prefer, the donkey, who among the beasts is not stupid, and at the same time listen with him to everything you can . . . I then lead ahead the monstrous beast far from his lair, and I show him off in the theater of the world for everyone to see. I present you publicly to everyone, Jew, beast . . .") V, 15–18, 125 and V, 33–34, 125–26. Peter the Venerable traveled to Spain in 1142.

48. Friedman, "Introduction," vii. She also cites J. Kritzeck, *Peter the Venerable and Islam* (Princeton, NJ: Princeton University Press, 1964), 216.

49. Friedman, "Introduction," lxviii.

50. Ibid., lxix: "quis continet manus nostrorum a sanguine uestro, nisi praecaeptum illius qui uos abiecit et nos elegit, Dei dicentis per prophetam uestrum: Ne occidas eos?" P. Venerabilis, V, 603–05, 141.

51. Chazan, 189.

52. In the thirteenth century the persecution of the Talmud began in earnest with very aggressive movements against Judaism. These initiatives were frequently headed by conversos like Nicolas Donin, the author of a petition (*memorial*) to Gregory IX in 1236 that led to the Paris *Disputatio* of 1240. Orfali, 13.

53. Chazan, 193.

54. Ibid., 189.

55. See note 5 in this chapter.

56. Cluse, "Section II: Around the Mediterranean. Editor's Notes," 94.

57. Sheldon S. Wolin, "Fugitive Democracy," in *Democracy and Difference*, ed. Seyla Benhabib (Princeton, NY: Princeton University Press), especially, 31–33.

58. It is curious that this confrontation with omnipotence appeared in political theory at a time when we began to reflect on the possibility of thermonuclear war. For examples of this type of literature, see Herman Kahn, *Thinking about the Unthinkable* (New York: Horizon Press, 1962); H. Kahn, *Thinking about the Unthinkable in the 1980s* (New York: Simon and Schuster, 1984); H. Kahn, *On Thermonuclear War* (Princeton, NJ: Princeton University Press, 1961). See also Joel Kovel, *Against the State of Nuclear Terror* (London: Pan Books, 1983); Robert W. Tucker, "Morality and Deterrence," *Ethics* 95 (April 1985); Joseph S. Nye Jr. *Nuclear Ethics* (New York: Macmillan, 1986).

59. *Zohar*, vol. 3, 215 (1:198b).

60. In the original meaning of the term, which is derived from the Latin verb *for, fari, fatus sum*, to speak or be able to say. *Fans-fantis* is the present participle. See also ch. 2, n. 37, in this text.

61. Scholem, 217.

62. Ibid., 237.

63. *Zohar*, vol. 1, 223 (1.35b). Quoted from the Torah "A river watering the garden flowed from Eden" (Genesis, 2:10).

64. *Zohar*, vol. 1, 224 (1:35b).

65. Ibid., vol. 3, 179 (1:193a).

66. In October 1299 "James II (1291–1327) authorizes M. Raimundo Lull to preach in the synagogues on Saturdays and Sundays throughout his realm, and in order to expound to the Jews the truth of the Catholic faith . . . he orders all the Jews in his lands to go on feast days to hear the preaching of R. Lull." Régné, 505.

67. Giambattista Vico, *Ciencia Nueva* (1744), trans. Rocío de la Villa (Madrid: Tecnos, 1995), 526.

68. David ben Saul, also a kabbalist and student of Solomon of Montpellier, was involved along with Jonah Gerondi. The polemic spread to entire communities in France, Italy, and Germany causing mutual excommunications and dividing Judaism for many years. See Dov Schwartz, *Central Problems of Medieval Judaism* (Leiden: Brill, 2005), 229.

69. Trautner-Kromann, 132. Also, see below, ch. 6.

70. Baer, vol. 1, 260. Also see Jeremy Cohen, "The Christian Adversary of Solomon ibn Adret," *The Jewish Quarterly Review*, new series 71, no. 1 (July 1980): 48.

71. Baer, vol. 1, 281.

72. Lorberbaum, 117–19. See ch. 6, "The Enemy Within."

73. Scholem, 239.

74. Ibid.

75. Some scholars think that this is an unjustified exaggeration, given that "Spain was never the first in any field of creativity, even in those that reached to high levels of development" and suggests the possibility that "in many respects Spanish-al-Andalus Jewry was, until the twelfth century, quite similar to other Jewish communities under Islam." Menahem Ben-Sasson, "The So-Called 'Golden Age' of Spanish Jewry," in Cluse, 123. According to Ben-Sasson, it was only in poetry that the Spanish school reached excellent heights, even though "Spain was not a stable place and was not regarded as the most affluent country, nor even the most affluent Jewish community." Cluse, 132.

76. A reference to the demoniacal realm, *Zohar*, vol. 3, 268 (1:207a).

77. *Zohar*, vol. 2, 4 (1:77b).

78. An allusion to the Psalms (119:62): "At midnight I rise to give you thanks for your righteous laws."

79. *Zohar*, vol. 2, 26 (1:82b). See also vol. 3, 271 (1:207b).

80. Ibid., vol. 3, 26 (1:169b).

81. Ibid., vol. 2, 30 (1:83a). See also vol. 3, 116 (1:183a).

82. Ibid., 31 (1:83b). See also 229 (1:130b) where he insists on the same idea.

83. Ibid., 79 (1:92a).

84. Ibid., 173 (1:115a).

85. Baer, vol. 1, 279.

86. *Zohar*, vol. 3, 115 (1:183a) and 117 (1:183b).

87. Ibid., 117–18 (1:183b).

88. Sigmund Freud, *New Introductory Lectures on Psycho-analysis and Other Works*, in *The Standard Edition* 22 (1933–1936), 171.

89. Bernat Metge, *Lo somni* ed. Ferran Gadea and Jordi Tiñena (Barcelona: ECSA, 2004), 250. "Treball, per lo qual los hòmens són nats, llunyen així d'ells como si era verí, e si usaven de raó, abraçarien aquell, car és dissipador de les humors supèrflues que són en lo cos. En dormir, qui és cosí de la mort, despenen lo terç de llur vida, e lo restant en servei dellur cos, del qual són servidors e catius."

90. *Zohar*, vol. 2, 228 (1:130a).

91. Ibid.

92. Ibid., 19 (1:181b); see also 8 (1:78a).

93. Ibid., 52 (1:86b); see also, 257 (1:134b).

94. Ibid., vol. 3, 268 (1:207a) and 270 (1:207b). The concept of *dormita*, or deep sleep, akin to death, is curious in this respect.

95. Ibid., vol. 2, 80 (1:92a).

96. Ibid., 188 (1:119a).

97. Ibid., 85 (1:93a).

98. A particularly worrisome description of this Gothic vision of the night is found in *Zohar*, vol. 3, 400–01 (1:231a, and 1:231b). On this point, the *Zohar* definitively moves away from what we called the Sephardic world, a world in which there is room for *The Guide of the Perplexed*, *The Celestina*, and *Don Quixote*.

99. *Zohar*, vol. 2, 84 (1:92b).

100. Ibid., 80 (1:92a).

101. Ibid., 173 (1:115a).

102. Ibid., vol. 3, 133 (1:186a).

103. In the Christian culture of the thirteenth century, lethargy, connected with the mythical Greek river Lethe, is clearly associated with forgetfulness, which is understood as an executive function of the mind, almost like a mental muscle dependent on will: "In a cave there is a river called Lethe, and the souls that enter there drink from necessity, and once they have done so, forget everything," B. Metge, 160.

104. *Zohar*, vol. 2, 204 (1:121b).

105. Ibid.

106. Ibid., 194 (1:119b).

107. Ibid., 204 (1:121b) and 205 (1:22a).

Chapter 6

1. Baruch Spinoza, "Ethics," in *The Collected Works of Spinoza*, ed. and trans. Edwin Curley (Princeton, NJ: Princeton University Press, 1985), 589.

2. Norman A. Stillman, *Sephardi Religious Responses to Modernity* (London: Routledge, 1995), 2.

3. Ibid., 5.

4. Ibid., 70.

5. See charts in Gerard Nahon, "Zarfat: Medieval Jewry in Northern France," 214; Alfred Haverkamp, "Jews and Urban Life," 63; Rainer Barzen, "Jewish Regional Organization in the Rhineland," 240–41; and Jörge R. Müller, *Eretz gezerah*—'Land of Persecution'; Pogroms against the Jews in the *regnum Teutonicum* from c. 1280 to 1350," 253, in Cluse, *The Jews of Europe.*

6. Hirsch Jakob Zimmels, *Ashkenazim and Sephardim: Their Relations, Differences, and Problems as Reflected in the Rabbinical Responsa* (New York: Ktav, 1996), 9–10.

7. Ibid., 1.

8. Z. Zohar, 8.

9. The expulsions from Judea in the first century CE brought a large number of Jews to Babylonia. Its emigration or Diaspora is known as the *golah* and was present for centuries. In the first century it was the most numerous population in exile, and in some cities the Jews made up a substantial part of the population. Elon, vol 3, 1087. "Rav" and Samuel, pupils of Rabbí Judah ha-Nasi, took their teacher's Mishnah with them to Babylonia. Elon, vol. 3, 1088.

Rabbi ha-Nasi's Mishnah was compiled in the second century CE and was commentated and studied in the yeshivas of Babylonia by the *amoraim*, giving rise to the Babylonia Talmud. See Elon, vol. 3, 1091–95. The Babylonian Talmud, however, only covers thirty-three of the sixty-three tracts in the Mishnah; Elon, vol. 3, 1094. In Jerusalem, commentaries and interpretations of the Tannaitic (oral tradition) were also compiled, edited and followed by commentaries and interpretations of the *amoraim* of the land of Israel that would give rise to the Israel Talmud; Elon, vol. 3, 1905–96. On the differences between the two, see Elon, vol. 3, 1085–1100.

10. Zimmels, 4.

11. Qtd. in ibid., 2–3.

12. Zimmels, 4.

13. Qtd. in ibid., 5–6.

14. Zimmels, 6.

15. Ibid.

16. "The communal ordinance, the *takkanah* regulated all the aspects of Jewish life." Epstein, *Responsa of Ben Adret,* 89. It was backed up by the *herem*, the public ban that was issued by the community as a "moral weapon intended to enforce discipline by invoking the wrath and punishment of the Almighty." Epstein, 77–78.

"The Anathema, or Herem . . . was the most powerful and terrible weapon in the hands of the communal chiefs to maintain discipline, to check insubordination, to enforce their regulations, and to impose their authority . . . the chief weapon in the hands of the *aljamas* to enforce obedience and adherence to the ordinances." Epstein, 77, 44. For the punishments imposed by the *herem* see Epstein, *Responsa of Zemah Duran*, 69–70.

17. Rabbi Gershom ben Judah, Meor Hagolah, "The Light of the Exile," was born in Metz in Lorraine and lived in Mainz, Germany. He was an eminent exegete and commentator of the Talmud. He was widely consulted and wrote many *responsa* on *halakhic* questions.

18. Epstein, b. *Zemah Duran,* 88.

19. Epstein, *Responsa of Ben Adret*, 87. According to Baer, "There is reason to believe that monogamy was the rule of most Jewish families in Spain, but in those circles which were still under the influence of the social concepts of Moslem culture, there were to be found Jews who had two wives or kept concubines." Baer, vol. 1, 236.

20. Epstein, 87.

21. Ibid., 88.

22. Feliu, 86.

23. Ibid., 86, 87.

24. Ibid., 87.

25. Ibid.

26. Zimmels, 11.

27. Ibid., 24. See also Chazan, 36–37.

28. Isaac b. Shesheth, "Responsa num. 376," qted in Zimmels, 25.

29. Rabbi Shlomo Yitzchaki. See above ch. 4, n. 135.

30. Zimmels, 25. Rabbi Jacob ben Meir (1100–1171) "Rabbeinu Tam," born in Ramerupt, northern France, was the grandson of Rashi and became a well-known *halakhist* and Tosafist as well as a leader of the Troyes community.

31. Zimmels, 25.

32. Ibid.

33. José Gaos, "Filosofía de Maimonides," (1935), published in Mexico, 1945. Also available in http.//www.librosgratisweb.com/pdf/gaos-josé/filosofia-de-maimonides.pdf (15.12.2007), 5.

34. Nahmanides also tends toward the visual and its impact: "because ugly things give rise to ugliness in the soul and they confound the intent of the pure heart, but when it is hidden from the seeing eye there is no harm." Ramban, *Deuteronomy*, 287.

35. Isaac b. Shesheth, "Responsa num. 394," qted in Zimmels, 25.

36. Spinoza, 589.

37. Ibid., 604.

38. Ibid., 584.

39. Ibid.

40. Ibid., 616.

41. Ibid., 495.

42. Hannah Arendt studied the three political powers of the citizen in depth *in foro interno*. She devoted the second part of her masterpiece *The Life of the Mind*—which was unfortunately unfinished at the time of her death—to the executive power. See Hannah Arendt, *The Life of the Mind* (London: Harcourt Brace Jovanovich, 1978), vol. 2, "Willing," 11–39.

43. Spinoza, 497.

44. On the influence of the kabbalah in his work and the influence of the kabbalist, Joseph Gikatila, with his identification of the idea of nature with *Elohim*, or the creative power of God, see Moshe Idel, "Deus sive Natura," in *Maimonides and the Sciences*, 106–07. On Joseph Gikatila, see, ch. 4, n. 143.

45. An example to the contrary would be the frustrated attempt to understand the importance of forgetting that we see in some Ashkenazic works, including some of the most sensible and interested in this respect. See Yosef Hayim Yerushalmi, *Zajor. La historia judía y la memoria judia*, trans. from the 3rd ed, by Ana Castaño and Paticia Villaseñor (Madrid: Anthropos, 2002), 125–139.

46. Here Spinoza reaches a height that is unattainable for much later Sephardic philosophers such as Jacques Derrida, for whom this point is already lost.

47. Spinoza, 497.

48. See above ch. 2, n. 37.

49. Spinoza, 496.

50. Ibid., 575.

51. Freud, *New Introductory Lectures on Psycho-analysis and Other Works*, in *The Standard Edition of the Complete Psychological Works* 22 (1933–1936): 171.

52. Michel Foucault, *Surveiller et punir: naisance de la prison* (1975), coll. Bibliothéque des histoires (Paris: Gallimard, 1989); *Discipline and Punish: the Birth of the Prison*, trans. Alan Sheridan (NY: Random House, 1975).

53. Member of a large and very pious family, he was a Talmud scholar, and like other members of his family, devoted to the systematic study of legal tradition and the codification of Jewish law. He made a meager living as a money lender, thanks to which he could dedicate his time to his studies. See above ch. 3, note 44.

54. Adret was "one of the greatest, if not the greatest," rabbis of his time. Epstein, 96. "The Jews had great confidence in Adret, and the authority and influence of his *responsa* were immense," Trautner-Kromann, 96. Baer calls him "[t]he great rabbinic authority of the day." Baer, vol. 1, 260. For Feliu, "He was the most outstanding Jewish personality in the rabbinical culture of Catalonia in the second half of the thirteenth century." Feliu, "Salomó ben Adret, mestre de la llei jueva," 37. Also see ch. 5 in this work and notes 69, 70, 71, and Peter J. Haas, "Political Liberty: The Rhetoric of the Responsa," in *On Liberty, Jewish Philosophical Perspectives*, ed. Daniel H. Frank (Richmond, UK: Curzon, 1999), 207.

55. The decisive battle of Las Navas de Tolosa, near La Carolina, Jaen, took place in July 1212. It had been preached by Pope Innocent III as a crusade against

the Almohads. Soldiers from the entire Iberian Peninsula and many from the other side of the Pyrenees from the French bishoprics of Narbonne, Bordeaux, and Nantes participated, although the French retreated without fighting, with the exception of a small contingent from Languedoc. Construction on the Cathedral of Toledo began at this time over the Friday mosque in 1226, probably in response to the extraordinary advance of the Christian Reconquest. The definitive reconquest of Seville took place in 1248.

56. Baer mentions the conditions imposed by international relations. See vol. 2, 8. "At the close of the fourteenth century, the kingdom [of Castile] was drawn into the general currents of European politics." Baer, vol. 1, 307.

57. Moisés Orfali characterizes him as a "rabbi and prominent leader of the *aljama* of the Jews of Barcelona . . . for almost fifty years." M. Orfali, "La cuestión de la venida del Mesías en un *responsum* de Rabí Shelomó ibn Adret al Cahal de Lérida," *Helmántica*, 43, nos. 130–31 (1992): 203.

58. R. David Horwitz, "Rashba's Attitude towards Science and Its Limit," *The Torah ut-Madda Journal* 3 (1991–1992): 68.

59. Zimmels, 22.

60. Chazan, 188.

61. Zimmels, 22.

62. According to Baer, R. Jonah Gerondi, "whose last years—he died in 1263—were spent in Toledo," vol. 1, 250

63. Lorberbaum, 106.

64. Zimmels, 24.

65. Something similar was happening in the fifteenth century in Christian Spain. In the field of law it was customary to emit *consilia* and *responsa* with which eminent jurists would issue opinions on legal matters of municipal types, canon, feudal, and criminal law, wills, contracts, and other matters. The great jurists, Andreas Alciatus (Andrea Alciato, 1492–1550) and Uldaricus Zasius (Ulrich Zäsi, 1461–1535) issued hundreds of legal rulings in this respect. See Berman, *Law and Revolution II*, 107.

66. Zimmels, 28.

67. Ibid., 30.

68. *Tefillin* (pl. *tefillah*, phylacteries), the set of small black leather boxes containing writing on parchment which are bound by black leather straps to the left hand and head during weekday services. See *Zohar*, vol. 1, note 719, 96.

69. Zimmels, 31.

70. *Zohar*, vol. 1, 96 (1:13b).

71. Zimmels, 32.

72. Ibid.

73. Nahmanides would have understood it: "because in time of religious persecutions, we are obligated to suffer death for any of the commandments." Ramban, *Exodus*, 302. Maimonides also considered that "he who gives up his life [so as not to convert] . . . acts with righteousness and honesty and will greatly be rewarded

before the Lord . . . Now then, if someone asks us [what to do], die or confess? We would answer him: 'Confess and do not die, but do not remain in the dominions of that king.'" Orfali, *Los converses españoles en la literature rabínica*, 19.

74. Zimmels, 33. The author does not clarify where this incident took place, although the date seems to coincide with the anti-Jewish attacks in Catalonia.

75. Haas, "Political Liberty," 203.

76. Ibid., 203–04.

77. Ibid., 204.

78. Zimmels, 33.

79. Ibid., 33.

80. See Sarah Stroumsa, "Maimonides and the Mediterranean Cultures," in Cluse, 103.

81. Ramban, "Letter to the French Rabbis," in *Writings and Discourses*, vol. 2, 388.

82. Z. Zohar, "A Global Perspective," 9; and Moshe Idel, "Jewish Philosophy," 132, in Zohar, *Sephardic and Mizrahi Jewry*.

83. Lorberbaum, 109.

84. Ramban, *Exodus*, 210.

85. Bava Kamma 80b–81a, the first in the series of three Talmudic tractates of the order Nezikin or "Damages" that deal with civil law. Ramban, *Exodus*, 210.

86. Ramban, *Exodus*, 210.

87. Rabbi Simon b. Zemah Duran mentions that the Majorcan Jews who came from the peninsula after the 1391 persecutions turned to the non-Jewish courts rather than their own, a practice that, as a follower of Maimonides, displeased him. Apparently the Jewish tribunals were not permitted in Majorca by the Christian rulers. Epstein, 65.

88. "Nahmanides' attitude is very different [from that of Maimonides] . . . It is possible that this change is connected to the growing Ashkenazic influence on *halakhists* in Spain." Lorberbaum, 106.

89. The eminent French Tosafist, Rabbi Samuel ben Meir (Rashbam), was the grandson of Rashi and brother of R. Tam. See n. 30 in this chapter. A Talmud exegete, he came from a family with a long rabbinical tradition in northern France (Ramerupt, near Troyes) and was a renowned scholar of Jewish theology. In addition he was a sheep herder and owner of vineyards.

90. Novak, 127; *The Jewish Social Contract*. See also ch. 4, n. 135.

91. Novak, 127. "Nahmanides was the first great Spanish figure belonging totally to the cultural environment of Christian Europe." Bernard Septimus, "'Open Rebuke and Concealed Love': Nahmanides and the Andalusian Tradition," in *Rabbi Moses Nahmanides*, ed. Twersky, 11.

92. In August 1260 James I appointed a Christian to the office of notary public of the Jews of Jaca. See Regné, 25.

93. The Lérida *cahal* did not accept this change, in spite of the fact that the Christian authorities already accepted the documents written up by the Jewish scribe

of the *cahal*, but without the need for the two witnesses required by the Jewish authorities. Obviously, in many business transactions between Jews and Christians the two parties chose to obtain the document and do away with the inconvenience of having to appear with two witnesses, a practice that slowed and probably made the procedures more expensive." See Burns, *Latinate* Wills, 31.

94. Burns, 21.

95. Ibid., 20.

96. Ibid., 30.

97. Lorberbaum, 111.

98. Ramban, *Exodus*, 337.

99. Lorberbaum, 111.

100. *Responsum* 48, qtd. in Lorberbaum, 112.

101. Feliu, 35.

102. "Nahmanides draws a parallel between communal and national leadership in terms of the legislative powers they have in common but never explicitly uses the term 'political leadership' to describe the community activities." Lorberbaum, 112.

103. Bernard Septimus, "'Open Rebuke and Concealed Love': Nahmanides and the Andalusian Tradition," in *Rabbi Moses Maimonides*, ed. Twersky, 26.

104. Septimus, 27.

105. Ibid., 28.

106. His youngest son "was an official of the Castilian court," Baer, vol. 1, 257.

107. Septimus, 29.

108. Ramban, together with R. Meshullam Dapiera, produced a profound turn in Hispano-Hebrew poetry. According to Fleischer, these transformations are authentic and came from their own tradition: "I cannot see any European influence explaining the formidable changes Ramban and R. Meshullam effected in the very substance of Spanish Hebrew poetry." Ezra Fleischer, "The Gerona School of Hebrew Poetry," in Twersky, 47.

109. Qtd. in Septimus, 31.

110. Ibid., 30.

111. Ibid., 32.

112. Septimus, 34. Nahmanides had many connections with the south. Beinart points out that one of his sons, R. Joseph, collaborated with the famous School of Translators of Toledo, in addition to other Jewish translators such as R. Yishaq ibn Cid, Don Judah Mosca (R. Yehuda ben Mose ha-Cohen) and the German kabbalist R. Abraham of Cologne. Haim Beinart, *Los judíos en España* (Madrid: Mapfre, 1992), 100. See n. 106 in this chapter.

113. Joseph Agassi, "Maimonides in Context," in *Maimonides and the Sciences*, 14.

114. Anicius Manlius Severinus Boethius was a Roman patrician born in Rome. He was a mathematician, geomcter, theologian, musician, and translator of Aristotle and Porphyry (232–304), a student of Plotinus. He enjoyed a great deal

of popular prestige and occupied a high place at the court of Theodoric. Accused by his enemies of conspiring in favor of the Byzantine Empire, he was put in prison without being able to defend himself and executed by the king of the Ostrogoths. He wrote *De consolatione philosophiae* in prison. See ch. 2, nn. 13, 38.

115. Judah Halevi, "Songs of Zion," qtd. in David R. Carr, "Judaism in Christendom," *The Blackwell Reader in Judaism*, ed. Jacob Neusner and Alan J. Avery-Peck (Malden, MA: Blackwell, 2001), 115. Judah Halevi was born in Tudela, c. 1075 and died in Egypt in 1141. He was a refined poet, scholar, and physician. For Beinart, "[h]e is one of the outstanding figures of Spanish Jewry." Haim Beinart, 62. An inveterate traveler, he lived in Granada, Córdoba, Toledo, and Seville, "the city of poets," according to his friend, Moses ibn Ezra. Beinart, 65. He is the author of *The Kuzari*, a work written in Arabic in defense of Judaism in contrast to Christianity and Islam. In Arabic he was called Abu Alhasan ibn Allavi. See also ch. 4, and n. 17.

116. *Las Siete Partidas, Volume Five, Underworlds: The Dead, the Criminal, and the Marginalized*, trans. and notes by Samuel Parsons Scott, ed. Robert I. Burns, S.J. (Philadelphia: University of Pennsylvania Press, 2001), 1433.

"Et la raçon porque la Eglesia et los Emperadores et los Reyes et los otros principes sufrieron a los judios vivir entre cristianos, es esta: porque ellos viviesen en cativerio para siempre, et fuesse remembranza á los omes quellos vienen del linaje de aquellos que crucificaron á Nuestro Señor Jesucristo." Alfonso X The Wise, Ley 1ª, título xxiv, Partida VIIª of *Las Siete partidas*, José Amador de los Ríos, *Historia de los judíos de España y Portugal* (1875), 3 vols. (Madrid: Turner, 1984), vol. 1, 466–67.

This king of Castile (1221–1284) drew up a Code of Law in 1256, although it did not go into effect until the middle of the fourteenth century, in which he devoted an entire chapter to the Jewish people. Even though it places certain restrictions on the Jews and reinforces prejudices based on canon law, it does include "a certain measure of humane treatment to the Jews." Baer, vol. 1, 116.

117. De los Ríos, vol. 2, 72–78.

118. I think that José Faur's idea is correct in the sense that the types of Hebrew and Greek perception correspond to two different levels of reality. "The Greek truth is visual. Therefore it is related to the spatial World-Out-There. For the Hebrews the highest form of truth is perceived at the auditory level." Jose Faur, *Golden Doves with Silver Dots* (Bloomington: Indiana University Press, 1980), 29.

119. Extract taken from the "Report" of the scholar Bonastruc Demaistre to the holy Jewish religious congregation of Gerona concerning "all that occurred" in the Tortosa *Disputatio*. Qtd. in Hyam Maccoby (ed. and trans.), *Judaism on Trial* (1982) (Oxford: Littman Library, 2003), 170. "Gerónimo" refers to the *converso* Joshua Alorki, a convert to Christianity known as Jerónimo de Santa Fe.

120. Baer, vol. 1, 287.

121. This same lack of originality is mentioned in regard to another of Ibn Adret's public texts, an important *responsum* addressed to the Lérida *cahal*. Orfali, "La cuestión de la venida del Mesias," 213.

122. Regné, 68.

123. Lorberbaum, 128.

124. In this sense *dina de-malkuta dina* (the law of the kingdom is the law) is the Talmudic phrase that Ibn Adret repeats frequently in his legal opinions in order to back up the pragmatism of his advice. Feliu, 39, 63.

125. Baer, 288.

126. Ibid.

127. As we have said elsewhere, Solomon of Montpellier was a subject of the Aragonese king, given that the domain of Montpellier was a part of the Crown, as was the domain of Urgell.

128. These were tied together and hung around one's neck. Feliu, 44.

129. It was thought that the topaz cooled down the body and passion. Feliu, 44.

130. Feliu, 45.

131. Ibid., 47.

132. Nissim ben Reuben Gerondi, "Ninth Sermon," quoted in Lorberbaum, 141.

133. Ramban, *Deuteronomy*, 365.

134. See above, ch. 4, n. 24.

135. Baer, vol. 1, 291.

136. Ibid.

137. Ibid., 230, in the Spanish edition. "*¡A tu boca la trompeta y los cornetines de alarma!*" This phrase is omitted from the English version.

138. Baer, vol. 1, 292.

139. Ibid., 293.

140. Ibid., 293–94.

141. Ibid., 294.

142. Ibid.

143. Ibid.

144. Daniel Gutenmacher, "The Legal Concept of Political Obligation in Medieval Spanish Jewish Law," *Dine Israel* 15 (1989–1990): 65.

145. He probably didn't have any choice in the face of royal initiatives. See n. 92 in this chapter.

146. Baer, vol. 1, 295.

147. Ibid.

148. Judah Saul ibn Tibbon (1120–1190), born in Granada, was the first Tibbon to emigrate to Lunel. Samuel ben Judah ibn Tibbon (Lunel 1150-Marseille 1230) was a translator of Maimonides' work. Other members of the family participated actively in the controversies between partisans and adversaries of Maimonides and were in favor of philosophical and scientific activities that they believed did not harm the Jewish faith.

149. Baer, vol. 1, 296.

150. Ibid., 233 of the Spanish edition. This passage is omitted from the English edition.

151. Baer, vol. 1, 298.

152. Ibid.

153. Ibid.

154. Ibid.

155. In this regard, Peter III called on all the Jewish *aljamas* to each send two of their procurators to Egea. Regné, 202.

156. Baer, vol. 1, 299.

157. Ibid.

158. Ibid., 300.

159. Ibid.

160. Ibid.

161. The presence of Jews in Spain and France apparently dates from before the taking of Jerusalem by the emperor Titus (66–70 ACE). The Jewish communities were governed by a leader and a council of elders. The leader acted as the head of the community in matters of paying taxes or tribute to the kings and emperors. He acted as a "prince," with the right to appoint religious representatives, judges, and other officials in the community. As Narbonne was the most important city, it was established that its leader would be the *nasi* (prince), with authority over all the Jewish communities of Sepharad. The cities such as Jaca, Gerona, Barcelona, and Tarragona, which belonged to the Marca Hispana, were under the authority of the *nasi* of Narbonne, who governed like any other ruler in collaboration with the Carolingian kings (717–814). Andrés J. Bonet, "The Bonet-Kalonymos-Shem Tovs: Direct Descendants of King David and the Prince of Septimania," *Sharsheret Hadorot* 17, no. 2 (June 2003): 1.

162. Baer, vol. 1, 301.

163. Ibid., 301–02.

164. Ibid., 236 of the Spanish edition. "*Los reformistas seguían, pues, el camino de la Iglesia.*" This passage does not appear in the English edition.

165. Baer, vol. 1, 304.

166. Ibid.

167. Ibid., 305.

168. What Sheldon S. Wolin called, in the twentieth century, "the mythical-historical man." Sheldon S. Wolin, *The Presence of the Past* (Baltimore, MD: Johns Hopkins University Press, 1989), 1–2. On this point, see Javier Roiz, *La recuperación del buen juicio* (Madrid: Foro Interno, 2003), 208.

169. See n. 42 in this chapter.

170. John Calvin, *Institución de la religión cristiana* (1559), trans. Cipriano de Valera (1597) (Rijswijk: Fundación Editorial de Literatura Reformada, 1968), book 1, ch. xvii, 10, 145.

171. Baer, vol. 1, 305. The Spanish text differs slightly from the English translation: "*[F]ueron capaces de renovar los ideales de los sabios de la Misnhá, y de edificar su vida social sobre los cimientos de la tradición mítico-popular, antigua y viva, gracias a la organización político democratica de entonces*" ("[T]hey were capable of renewing the ideals of the sages of the Mishnah and building their social life on the foun-

dations of the mythical-popular tradition, both ancient and modern, thanks to the political-democratic organization of the time"), Baer, vol. 1, 238.

172. Baer, vol. 1, 305.

173. D. Kaufmann, "Jewish Informers in the Middle Ages," *The Jewish Quarterly Review,* new series 8, no. 2 (1896): 217.

174. Ibid. For this case, see also Baer, vol. 1, 168–70.

175. Kaufmann, 217.

176. Ibid., 222.

177. Ibid., 223.

178. Ibid., 225.

179. Ibid., 224.

180. Considered the greatest authority in the Ashkenazic world of his time, he was born in Worms and educated in the Ashkenazic Talmudic schools of Würzburg, Mainz, and Paris. He was a notable rabbi and poet in the line of the Tosafists. He taught in several communities in Germany, and among his pupils were R. Mordechai ben Hillel Ashkenazi and R. Asher ben Yehiel, who became chief rabbi of Toledo. He was imprisoned during the pogroms of 1286 instigated by Rudolph of Habsburg (1218–1291), king of Germany, king of Romanos, and count of Habsburg. He died in prison in Alsace after several years of incarceration.

181. Kaufmann, 226.

Chapter 7

1. Nahmanides, "Prayer at the Ruins of Jerusalem," in *Writings and Discourses*, vol. 2, 713.

2. Sheldon S. Wolin, *Democracy Incorporated: Managed Democracy and the Specter of Totalitarianism* (Princeton, NJ: Princeton University Press, 2008), 289.

3. Philip Pettit, *Republicanismo. Una teoría sobre la libertad y el gobierno* (Barcelona: Paidos, 1999), 340. I am grateful to Victor Alonso for this reference.

4. *Flectere si nequo superos, acheronta movebo* ("If I cannot bend the Higher Powers, I will move the infernal regions."). A line from Virgil (*Aeneid*, VII, 312), qtd. by Sigmund Freud in "The Interpretation of Dreams." *The Standard Edition of the Complete Psychological Works of Sigmund Freud*, ed. James Strachey, vol. 5 (1900–1901) (London: Hogarth, 2001), 608. For the theoretical political meaning of this quotation, see Javier Roiz, *El experimento moderno* (Madrid: Trotta, 1992), 11.

5. Rabbi Abraham A. Neuman, "Some Phases of the Condition of the Jews in Spain in the Thirteenth and Fourteenth Centuries," *Publications of the American Jewish Historical Society* 22 (1914): 67.

6. José Faur, "Imagination and Religious Pluralism: Maimonides, Ibn Verga, and Vico," *New Vico Studies* 10 (1992): 40.

7. Michael Walzer, *The Revolution of the Saints* (New York: Atheneum, 1965), 134.

References

Ackerman, Ari. "Jewish Philosophy and the Jewish-Christian Philosophical Dialogue in Fifteenth-century Spain." In *The Cambridge Companion to Medieval Jewish Philosophy*, ed. Daniel H. Frank and Oliver Leaman. Cambridge University Press, Cambridge, U. K., 2003.

Agassi, Joseph. "Maimonides in Context." In *Maimonides and the Sciences*, ed. Robert S. Cohen and Hillel Levine. Dordrecht, Kluwer. 2001.

Alba Cecilia, Amparo. "El poema penitencial de Sem Tob de Carrión." *Revista de Ciencias de las Religiones* 4 (1999).

Alexander, Franz. "Discussion of Dr. Bassoe's article 'Spain as the Cradle of Psychiatry.'" *The American Journal of Psychiatry* 102 (1945).

Al-Farabi. *El camino de la felicidad*, trans. Rafael Ramón Guerrero. Madrid 2002.

Alfonso X (the Wise). *Las Siete Partidas, vol. 5, Underworld: The Dead, the Criminal, and the Marginalized*, trans. and notes Samuel Parsons Scott, ed. Robert I. Burns, S.J. Philadelphia, University of Pennsylvania Press, 2001.

Amilévitch, Eric, and Luc Ferrier. "Introduction." In Nahmanide, *La Dispute de Barcelone*, trans. Eric Amilévitch and Luc Ferrier, 4th ed. revised and corrected. Éditions Verdier, Lagrasse, 1984.

Arendt, Hannah. *La vida del espíritu. El pensar, la voluntad y el juicio en la filosofía y en la política* (1971), trans. Ricardo Montoro and Fernando Vallespín. Centro de Estudios Constitucionales, 1984.

———. "Willing." In *The Life of the Mind*, vol. 2. Harcourt Brace Jovanovich, 1972.

Aristotle. "Metaphysics." In *The Complete Works of Aristotle*, the revised Oxford translation, ed. Jonathan Barnes, 2 vols. Princeton University Press, Princeton, NJ, 1995.

Aristóteles. *Retórica*, bilingual ed. and trans. Antonio Tovar. Instituto de Estudios Políticos, Madrid, 1971.

Ashtor, Eliyahu. *The Jews of Moslem Spain*, 3 vols. Jewish Publication Society, Philadelphia, 1973.

Baer, Yitzhak. *Historia de los judíos en la España cristiana* (1959), trans. from the Hebrew by José Luis Lacave, 2 vols. Altalena, Madrid, 1981.

———. *A History of the Jews in Christian Spain* (1961), trans. from the Hebrew by Louis Schoffman, introduction by Benjamin R. Gampel, 2 vols. Jewish Publication Society, Philadelphia-Jerusalem, 1992.

Bakan, David, David Merkur, and David S. Weiss. *Maimonides' Cure of Souls: Medieval Precursor of Psychoanalysis*. Albany, State University of New York Press, 2009.

Bango Torviso, Isidro G. "Inquisición." In *Memoria de Sefarad*. Centro Cultural San Marcos. Sociedad Estatal para la Acción Cultural Exterior, Toledo, 2002–2003.

Barzin, Rainer. "Jewish Regional Organization in the Rhineland." In *The Jews of Europe in the Middle Ages (Tenth to Fifteenth Centuries)*, ed. Cristoph Cluse. Proceedings of the International Symposium held at Speyer, 20–25 October 2002, Brepols, Turnhout, Belgium, 2004.

Bassoe, Peter. "Spain as the Cradle of Psychiatry." *The American Journal of Psychiatry* 101 (1945).

Beinart, Haim. "España y el occidente en los días de Abraham Ibn Ezra." In *Abraham Ibn Ezra y su tiempo* (Actas del Simposio Internacional, ed. Fernando Díaz Esteban. Madrid, Tudela, Toledo, 1–8 febrero 1989), Asociación Española de Orientalistas, Madrid, 1990.

———. *Los judíos en España*. Mapfre, Madrid, 1992.

Benhabib, Seyla (ed.). *Democracy and Difference*. Princeton University Press, Princeton, NJ, 1996.

Ben-Sasson, Menahem. "The So-Called 'Golden Age' of Spanish Jewry." In *The Jews of Europe in the Middle Ages (Tenth to Fifteenth Centuries)*, ed. Cristoph Cluse. Proceedings of the International Symposium held at Speyer, 20–25 October 2002, Brepols, Turnhout, Belgium, 2004.

Berger, David. "Miracles and the Natural Order in Nahmanides." In *Rabbi Moses Nahmanides (Ramban): Explorations in His Religious Virtuosity*, ed. Isadore Twersky. Harvard University Press, Cambridge, MA., 1983.

Berman, Harold J. *Law and Revolution, The Formation of Western Legal Tradition*. Harvard University Press, Cambridge, MA, 1983.

———. *Law and Revolution II, The Impact of the Protestant Reformations on the Western Legal Tradition*. Harvard University Press, Cambridge, MA, 2003.

Bonet, Andrés J. "The Bonet-Kalonymos-Shem Tovs. Direct Descendants of King David and the Prince of Septimania." *Sharsheret Hadorot* 17, no. 2 (June 2003).

Burns, Robert I., S. J. *Jews in the Notarial Culture: Latinate Wills in Mediterranean Spain, 1250–1350*. University of California Press, Berkeley, 1996.

Calvino, Juan, (John Calvin). *Institución de la religión cristiana* (1559), trans. Cipriano de Valera (1597). Fundación Editorial de Literatura Reformada, Rijswijk, Netherlands, 1968.

Carr, David R. "Judaism in Christendom." In *The Blackwell Reader in Judaism*, ed. Jacob Neusner and Alan J. Avery-Peck. Blackwell, Maldin, MA, 2001.

Cervantes, Miguel de. *Don Quijote de la Mancha,* edición del 4º centenario, Real Academia Española, Asociación de Academias de la Lengua Española. Madrid, Santillana, 2004.

Chahlane, Ahmed. "Averroes, Maimónides y la crisis en la comunidad judía medieval," trans. Josep Puig Montada. *Anales del Seminario de Historia de la Filosofía* 22 (2005).

Chavel, Charles B. "Translator's Introduction" to Ramban, "Letter to the French Rabbis." In Ramban (Nachmanides), *Writings and Discourses*, trans. and ed. Charles B. Chavel, 2 vols. Shilo Publishing House, New York, 1985, vol. 2.

Chazan, Robert. *Barcelona and Beyond: The Disputation of 1263 and Its Aftermath.* University of California Press, Berkeley, CA, 1992.

Cluse, Cristoph. "Section II: Around the Mediterranean. Editor's Notes." In *The Jews of Europe in the Middle Ages (Tenth to Fifteeenth Centuries),* ed. Cristoph Cluse. Proceedings of the International Symposium held at Speyer, 20–25 October 2002, Brepols, Turnhout, Belgium, 2004.

———, ed. *The Jews of Europe in the Middle Ages (Tenth to Fifteenth Centuries),* Proceedings of the International Symposium held at Speyer, 20–25 October 2002, Brepols, Turnhout, Belgium, 2004.

Cohen, Jeremy. "The Christian Adversary of Solomon Ibn Adret." *The Jewish Quarterly Review*, New Series 71, no. 1 (July 1980).

———. *The Friars and the Jews.* Cornell University Press, Ithaca, NY, 1982.

Cohen, Mark R. "The Origins of Sephardic Jewry in the Medieval Arab World." In *Sephardic & Mizrahi Jewry*, ed. Zion Zohar. New York University Press, New York, 2005.

Cohen, Robert S. and Hillel Levine, eds. *Maimonides and the Sciences.* Kluwer Academic Publishers, Dordrecht, 2001.

Cover, Robert M. "Obligation: A Jewish Jurisprudence of the Social Order." In *Law, Politics, and Morality in Judaism*, ed. Michael Walzer. Princeton University Press, Princeton, NJ, 2006.

Crescas, Hasdai. *The Refutation of the Christian Principles*, trans. and notes, Daniel J. Lasker. State University of New York Press, Albany, NY, 1992.

Decter, Jonathan P. "Literatures of Medieval Sepharad." In *Sephardic & Mizrahi Jewry*, ed. Zion Zohar. New York University, New York, 2005.

De Los Ríos, José Amador. *Historia de los judíos de España y Portugal* (1875), 3 vols. Turner, Madrid, 1984.

Del Valle, Carlos, Santiago García-Jalón, and Juan Pedro Monferrer, eds. *Maimónides y su época.* Sociedad Estatal de Conmemoraciones Culturales, Madrid, 2007.

Dianoux, Hugues Jean de. "Les Saporta, marranes aragonais, professeurs de Médecine à Montpellier et leur descendants Marquis en Province." In Carol Iancu, *Les Juifs à Montpellier et dans le Languedoc.* Université Paul Valery, Montpellier, 1988.

Díaz Esteban, Fernando, ed. *Abraham Ibn Ezra y su tiempo* (Actas del Simposio Internacional, Madrid, Tudela, Toledo, 1–8 Feb. 1989), Asociación Española de Orientalistas, Madrid, 1990.

Disputa de Barcelona de 1263 entre Mestre Mossé de Girona i Fra Pau Cristià, translation into Catalan of the Hebrew and Latin texts by Eduard Feliu, with a "Estudi introductori" by Jaume Riera i Sans. La Columna, Barcelona, 1985.

Eckstein, Harry. "Theoretical Approaches to Explaining Collective Violence." In *Handbook of Political Conflict*, ed. Ted R. Gurr. Free Press, New York, 1980.

Efros, Israel. "Introduction" in Maimonides' *Treatise of Logic*, trans. and ed., Israel Efros. American Academy for Jewish Research, New York, 1938.

Elfenbein, Rabbí Israel. "Jewish Communal Government in Spain." *Student's Annual, Journal of Theological Studies* 2 (1915).

Elon, Menachem. *Jewish Law: History, Sources, Principles*, trans. from the Hebrew by Bernard Auerbach y Melvin J. Sykes, 4 vols. Jewish Publication Society, Philadelphia, 1994.

Epstein, Isidore. *The Responsa of Rabbi Simon B. Zemah Duran*. Ktav, New York, 1930.

———. *The 'Responsa' of Rabbi Solomon Ben Adret of Barcelona (1235–1310)*. Ktav. New York, 1968.

Faur, José. *Golden Doves with Silver Dots*. Indiana University Press, Bloomington, 1986.

Faur, José. "Imagination and Religious Pluralism: Maimonides, Ibn Verga, and Vico." *New Vico Studies* 10 (1992).

Feliu, Eduard. "Salomó ben Adret, mestre de la llei jueva." *Tamid* (Barcelona) 4 (2002–2003).

Fleischer, Ezra. "The 'Gerona School' of Hebrew Poetry." In *Rabbi Moses Nahmanides (Ramban): Explorations in His Religious Virtuosity*, ed. Isadore Twersky. Harvard University Press, Cambridge, Massachusetts, 1983.

Foucault, Michel. *Surveiller et punir: naissance de la prison* (1975). Bibliothèque des histoires, Gallimard, Paris, 1989. English translation, *Discipline and Punish: The Birth of the Prison*, trans. Alan Sheridan. Random House, NY, 1975.

———. "El cuidado de la verdad" (interview May 1984). In *Estética, ética y hermenéutica. Obras esenciales. vol. 3*, ed. and trans. Ángel Gabilondo. Paidós, Barcelona, 1999.

Frank, Daniel H. *On Liberty, Jewish Philosophical Perspectives*. Curzon, Richmond, U.K., 1999.

Frank, Daniel H., and Oliver Leaman eds. *The Cambridge Companion to Medieval Jewish Philosophy*. Cambridge University Press, Cambridge, 2003.

Freud, Sigmund. *La interpretación de los sueños*. In *Obras completas*, trans. Luis López Ballesteros. Biblioteca Nueva, Madrid, 1972, vol. 2.

———. "El Malestar en la Cultura." In *Obras Completas*, trans. Luis López Ballesteros. Biblioteca Nueva, Madrid, 1972, vol. 8.

———. "Nuevas lecciones introductorias al psicoanálisis" (1932). In *Obras Completas*, trans. Luis López-Ballesteros. Biblioteca Nueva, Madrid, 1972, vol. 8.

———. "Civilization and Its Discontents." In *The Standard Edition of the Complete Psychological Works of Sigmund Freud*, vol. 21 (1927–1931), translated under the General Editorship of James Strachey, in collaboration with Anna Freud. Hogarth Press and the Institute of Psycho-Analysis. Vintage, London, 1986.

———. "Civilization and Its Discontents." In *The Standard Edition of the Complete Psychological Works of Sigmund Freud,* vol. 21 (1927–1931), translated under the General Editorship of James Strachey, in collaboration with Anna Freud. Hogarth Press and the Institute of Psycho-Analysis. Vintage, London, 1986.

———. *New Introductory Lectures on Psycho-Analysis and Other Works*. In *The Standard Edition of the Complete Psychological Works of Sigmund Freud, vol. 22 (1933–1936),* translated from the German under the General Editorship of James Strachey, in collaboration with Anna Freud, assisted by Alix Strachey and Alan Tyson. Hogarth Press and The Institute of Psycho-Analysis. Vintage, London, 2001.

———. *The Interpretation of Dreams*. In *The Standard Edition of the Complete Psychological Works of Sigmund Freud,* vol. 5 (1900–1901), translated under the General Editorship of James Strachey, in collaboration with Anna Freud. Hogarth Press and the Institute of Psycho-Analysis. Vintage, London, 2001.

Friedman, Yvonne. "Introduction." In Petri Vinerabilis, *Adversus Iudeorum Inveteratam Duritiem (Against the Inveterate Obstination of the Jews)* (a work written before 1144, *editio princeps* 1522), ed. by Yvonne Friedman. Brepols, Turnhout, Belgium, 1985.

Frymer-Kinsky, Tikva. "The Feminist Challenge to Halakhah." The Harvard Law School Program in Jewish Studies, *The Gruss Lectures*, Oct. 26–Nov. 30, 1994. http://www.law.harvard.edu/programs/Gruss/frymer.html (23.12.2007).

Fumaroli, Marc, ed. *Histoire de la rhétorique dans l'Europe moderne, 1450–1950.* Presses Universitaires de France, Paris 1999.

Gaon, Solomon. *The Influence of Catholic Theologian Alfonso Tostado on the Pentateuch Commentary of Isaac Abravanel.* Ktav Publishing House, Hoboken, NJ, 1993.

Gaos, José. "Filosofía de Maimónides," conferencia pronunciada en1935 con motivo del VIII Centenario del nacimiento de Maimónides. Published by the Casa de España en México, México, 1940. http://www.librosgratisweb.com/pdf/gaos-jose/filosofia-demaimonides.pdf (15.12.2007).

Gay, Peter. *Freud. Una vida de nuestro tiempo*. Paidós, Barcelona, 1989.

Gerondi, Jonah (Rabbeinu Yonah of Gerona). *The Gates of Repentance (Shaarei Teshuvah),* bilingual version in Hebrew and English, trans. Shraga Silverstein. Feldheim Publishers, Jerusalem, New York, 1976.

Gilson, Étienne. *La filosofía en la Edad Media.* Gredos, Madrid, 2nd. ed., 1965.

Giol, Carles. "Introducción." In *El Zohar. El libro del esplendor*, trans. Carles Giol. Ediciones Obelisco, Barcelona, 2nd. ed., 2002.

González Echevarría, Francisco Javier, and Teresa Ancín Chandía. "Miguel Servet pertenecía a la familia de judeoconversos de los Zaporta." *Pliegos de Bibliofilia*, Madrid 7 (tercer trimestre de 1999).

Goodman, Lenn Evan, ed. and trans. *Rambam, Readings in the Philosophy of Moses Maimonides.* Viking Press, New York, 1976.

Green, Arthur. "Introduction." In *The Zohar*, Pritzker Edition, trans. of original manuscripts and commentaries by Daniel C. Matt. Stanford University Press, Stanford, CA, 2004.

Gross, Abraham. "Gerona: A Sephardic Cradle of Jewish Learning and Religiosity." *Materia Giudaica* 6, no. 2 (2001).

Guggenheim, Yacov. "Jewish Community and Territorial Organization." In *The Jews of Europe in the Middle Ages (Tenth to Fifteenth Centuries)*, ed. Cristoph Cluse. Proceedings of the International Symposium held at Speyer, 20–25 October 2002, Brepols, Turnhout, Belgium, 2004.

Gutenmacher, Daniel. "The Legal Concept of Political Obligation in Medieval Spanish Jewish Law." *Diné Israel*, 15 (1989–1990).

Haas, Peter J. "Political Liberty: The Rhetoric of the Responsa." In *On Liberty, Jewish Philosophical Perspectives*, ed. Daniel H. Frank. Curzon, Richmond, U.K., 1999.

Halbertal, Moshe. "The History of Halakhah, Views from Within: Three Medieval Approaches to Tradition and Controversy." The Harvard Law School Program in Jewish Studies, *The Gruss Lectures*, October 26–November 30, 1994. Available on http://www.law.harvard.edu/Programs/Gruss/halbert.html (23.12.2007).

Halbertal, Moshe, *Concealment and Revelation*, trans. Jackie Feldman. Princeton University Press, Princeton, 2007.

Harvey, Steven. "Maimonides in the Sultan's Palace." In *Perspectives on Maimonides: Philosophical and Historical Studies*, ed. Joel L. Kraemer. Littman Library of Jewish Civilization, London, 1996.

Harvey, Warren Zev. "Why Maimonides Was Not a *Mutakallim*." In *Perspectives on Maimonides: Philosophical and Historical Studies*, ed. Joel L. Kraemer. Littman Library of Jewish Civilization, London, 1996.

Hart Green, Kenneth. "Editor's Introduction: Leo Strauss as a Modern Jewish Thinker." In *Jewish Philosophy and the Crisis of Modernity: Essays and Lectures in Modern Jewish Thought*, ed. Leo Strauss. State University of New York Press, Albany, 1997.

Haverkamp, Alfred. "Jews and Urban Life." In *The Jews of Europe in the Middle Ages (Tenth to Fifteenth Centuries)*, ed. Cristoph Cluse. Proceedings of the International Symposium held at Speyer, 20–25 October 2002. Brepols, Turnhout, Belgium, 2004.

Henoch, Chayim J. *Ramban: Philosopher and Cabalist*, Jason Aronson, Northvale, NJ, 1998.

Horwitz, R. David. "Rashba's Attitude towards Science and Its Limits." *The Torah u-Madda Journal* 3 (1991–1992).

Iancu, Carol. *Les Juifs à Montpellier et dans le Languedoc.* Université Paul Valery, Montpellier, 1988.

Idel, Moshe. "We Have No Kabbalistic Tradition on This." In *Rabbi Moses Nahmanides (Ramban): Explorations in His Religious Virtuosity*, ed. Isadore Twersky. Harvard University Press, Cambridge, Massachusetts, 1983.

———. "Deus sive Natura." In *Maimonides and the Sciences*, ed. Robert S. Cohen and Hillel Levine. Kluwer Academic Publishers, Dordrecht, 2001.

———. "Jewish Philosophy and Kabbalah in Spain." In *Sephardic & Mizrahi Jewry*, ed. Zion Zohar. New York University Press, New York, 2005.

Ishbili, Yom Tov ben Abraham. *Sefer Zikharon*. Mossad ha-Rav Kook, Jerusalem, 1983.

Kahn, Herman. *On Thermonuclear War*. Princeton University Press, Princeton, NJ, 1961.

———. *Thinking about the Unthinkable*. Horizon Press, New York, 1962.

———. *Thinking about the Unthinkable in the 1980s*. Simon and Schuster, New York, 1984.

Kaufmann, D. "Jewish Informers in the Middle Ages." *The Jewish Quarterly Review new series* 8, no. 2 (1896).

Kirkendale, Ursula. "The Source for Bach's *Musical Offering:* The *Institutio Oratoria* of Quintilian." *American Musicological Society, Journal* 31, no. 1 (1980, Spring): 95–137.

Kirschenbaum, Aaron. *Equity in Jewish Law: Beyond Equity*. Ktav, Hoboken, NJ, 1991.

Kovel, Joel. *Against the State of Nuclear Terror*. Pan Books, London, 1983.

Kraemer, Joel L. "Maimonides on the Philosophic Sciences in His Treatise on the Art of Logic." In *Perspectives on Maimonides: Philosophical and Historical Studies*, ed. Joel L. Kraemer. The Littman Library of Jewish Civilization, London, 1996.

———. "Maimonides' Use of (Aristotelian) Dialectic." In *Maimonides and the Sciences*, ed. Robert S. Cohen and Hillel Levine. Kluwer Academic Publishers, Dordrecht, 2001.

———. "The Islamic Context of Medieval Jewish Philosophy." In *The Cambridge Companion to Medieval Jewish Philosophy*, ed. Daniel H. Frank and Oliver Leaman. Cambridge University Press, Cambridge, U. K., 2003.

———. "Moses Maimonides: An Intellectual Portrait." In *The Cambridge Companion to Maimonides*, ed. Kenneth Seeskin. Cambridge University Press, New York, 2005.

———, ed. *Perspectives on Maimonides: Philosophical and Historical Studies*. Littman Library of Jewish Civilization, London, 1996.

Kreisel, Haim. "Maimonides' Political Philosophy." In *The Cambridge Companion to Maimonides*, ed. Kenneth Seeskin. Cambridge University Press, New York, 2005.

Lacave, José Luis. "La comunidad donde nació Abraham Ibn Ezra." In *Abraham Ibn Ezra y su tiempo* (Actas del Simposio Internacional, Madrid, Tudela, Toledo, 1–8 febrero 1989), ed. Fernando Díaz Esteban. Asociación Española de Orientalistas, Madrid, 1990.

Lange, Nicholas de. "Abraham Ibn Ezra and Byzantium." In *Abraham Ibn Ezra y su tiempo* (Actas del Simposio Internacional, Madrid, Tudela, Toledo, 1–8 febrero 1989), ed. Fernando Díaz Esteban. Asociación Española de Orientalistas, Madrid, 1990.

Langermann, Tzvi. "Maimonides' Repudiation of Astrology." In *Maimonides and the Sciences*, ed. Robert S. Cohen and Hillel Levine. Kluwer Academic Publishers, Dordrecht, 2001.

Last Stone, Suzanne. "Judaism and Civil Society." In *Law, Politics, and Morality in Judaism*, ed. Michael Walzer. Princeton University Press, Princeton, NJ, 2006.

———. "The Emergence of Jewish Law in Postmodernist Legal Theory." The Harvard Law School Program in Jewish Studies, *The Gruss Lectures*, October 26–November 30, 1994. Available on http://www.law.harvard.edu/programs/Gruss/stone.html (23–12–2007).

Lawee, Eric. *Abrabanel's Stance toward Tradition: Defense, Dissent, and Dialogue*. State University of New York Press, Albany, NY, 2001.

Lorberbaum, Menachem. *Politics and the Limits of Law*. Stanford University Press, Stanford, CA, 2001.

———. "Medieval Jewish political thought." In *The Cambridge Companion to Medieval Jewish Philosophy*, ed. Daniel H. Frank and Oliver Leaman. Cambridge University Press, Cambridge, 2003.

Maccoby, Hyam (ed. and trad.). *Judaism on Trial* (1982). The Littman Library of Jewish Civilization, London, 2003.

Machiavelli, Niccolò. "Letter to Francesco Vettori (26 August 1515)." In *Machiavelli: The Chief Works and Others*, trans. Allan Gilbert, 2 vols., Duke University Press, Durham, NC, 1965.

———. "Di Fortuna." In *Machiavelli. Tutte le opere*, ed. Mario Martelli. Sansoni, Milan, 1993.

———. "Letter to Francesco Vettori (16 April 1527)." In *Machiavelli: The Chief Works and Others*, trans. Allan Gilbert, 2 vols. Duke University Press, Durham, NC, 1965; and in *Machiavelli: Tutte le opere*, ed. Mario Martelli. Sansoni, Milan, 1993.

Magnien, Michel. "D'une mort l'autre (1536–1572): la rhétorique reconsiderée." In *Histoire de la rhétorique dans l'Europe moderne, 1450–1950*, ed. Marc Fumaroli. Presses Universitaires de France, Paris, 1999.

Maimonides (Moses ben Maimon). *Treatise of Logic*, trans and ed. Israel Efros. American Academy for Jewish Research, New York, 1938.

———. *The Guide of the Perplexed*, a work in three parts, trans. and ed. Shlomo Pines, with an introductory essay by Leo Strauss, 2 vols. University of Chicago Press, Chicago, 1963.

———. "Eight Chapters." In *A Maimonides Reader*, ed. Isadore Twersky. Behrman House, Springfield, NJ, 1972.

———. "Epistle To Yemen." In *A Maimonides Reader*, ed. Isadore Twersky. Behrman House, Springfield, NJ, 1972.

———. "Mishneh Torah." In *A Maimonides Reader*, ed. Isadore Twersky. Behrman House, Springfield, NJ, 1972.

———. *Treatise on Resurrection* (1191), trans. and ed. Fred Rosner. Rowman & Littlefield, Lanham, MD, 2004.

Maimonides (Moses ben Maimon). "Los ocho capítulos." Del *Comentario a la Mishná* (escritos como introducción al Comentario a la Mishná de Abot), trans. León Duvojne. *Raíces, Revista Judía de Cultura* 60 (otoño 2004).

———. *Obras filosóficas y morales*. Ediciones Obelisco, Barcelona, 2006.

Mann, Michael. *The Dark Side of Democracy: Explaining Ethnic Cleansing*. Cambridge University Press, Cambridge, 2005.

Metge, Bernat. *Lo somni*, ed. Ferran Gadea and Jordi Tiñena. ECSA, Barcelona, 2004.

Müller, Jörg R. "*Erez gezerah* 'Land of Persecution': Progroms against the Jews in *regnum Teutonicum* from c. 1280 to 1350." In *The Jews of Europe in the Middle Ages (Tenth to Fifteenth Centuries)*, ed. Cristoph Cluse. Proceedings of the International Symposium held at Speyer, 20–25 October 2002, Brepols, Turnhout, Belgium, 2004.

Nahon, Gerard. "Zarfat: Medieval Jewry in Northern France." In *The Jews of Europe in the Middle Ages (Tenth to Fifteenth Centuries)*, ed. Cristoph Cluse, Proceedings of the International Symposium held at Speyer, 20–25 October 2002. Brepols, Turnhout, Belgium, 2004.

Nahmanides (Ramban, Nachmanides). *Torah Hashem Temimah: Kitvei Rabbeinu Moshe Ben Nahman*. C. D. Shewall, 1963.

———. *Commentary on the Torah: Genesis*, trans. and ed. Charles B. Chavel. Shilo Publishing House, New York, 1971.

———. *Commentary on the Torah: Exodus*, trans. and ed. Charles B. Chavel. Shilo Publishing House, New York, 1973.

———. *Commentary on the Torah: Numbers*, trans. and ed. Charles B. Chavel. Shilo Publishing House, New York, 1973.

———. *Commentary on the Torah: Leviticus*, trans. and ed. Charles B. Chavel. Shilo Publishing House, New York, 1974.

———. *Commentary on the Torah: Deuteronomy*, trans. and ed. Charles B. Chavel. Shilo Publishing House, New York, 1976.

———. *La Dispute de Barcelone*, trans. Eric Amilévitch and Luc Ferrier, 4th ed. revised and corrected. Éditions Verdier, Lagrasse, 1984.

———. "Bulle de Clément IV." In *La Dispute De Barcelone*, trans. Eric Amilévitch and Luc Ferrier, 4th ed. revised and corrected. Éditions Verdier, Lagrasse, 1984.

———. "Comintari sobre la perícopa 'el meu servidor serà intelligent.'" In *Disputa de Barcelona de 1263 entre Mestre Mossé de Girona i Fra Pau Cristià*, trans. into Catalan from the Hebrew and Latin texts by Eduard Feliu, with a "Estudi introductori" by Jaume Riera i Sans. La Columna, Barcelona, 1985.

———. "Discourse on a Wedding." In Ramban (Nachmanides), *Writings and Discourses*, trans. and ed. Charles B. Chavel, 2 vols. Shilo Publishing House, New York, 1985, vol. 1.

———. "Discourse on the Law of the Eternal Is Perfect." In Ramban (Nachmanides), *Writings and Discourses*, trans. and ed. Charles B. Chavel, 2 vols. Shilo Publishing House, New York, 1985, vol. 1.

———. "Letter to the French Rabbis." In Ramban (Nachmanides), *Writings and Discourses*, trans. and ed. Charles B. Chavel, 2 vols. Shilo Publishing House, New York, 1985, vol. 2.

———. "Prayer at the Ruins of Jerusalem." In Ramban (Nachmanides), *Writings and Discourses,* trans. and ed. Charles B. Chavel, 2 vols. Shilo Publishing House. New York, 1985, vol. 2.

———. "Rosh Hashanah." In Ramban (Nachmanides), *Writings and Discourses,* trans. and ed. Charles B. Chavel, 2 vols. Shilo Publishing House, New York, 1985, vol. 1.

———. "The Book of Redemption." In Ramban (Nachmanides), *Writings and Discourses*, trans. and ed. Charles B. Chavel, 2 vols. Shilo Publishing House, New York, 1985, vol. 2.

———. "The Gate of Reward." In Ramban (Nachmanides), *Writings and Discourses*, trans. and ed. Charles B. Chavel, 2 vols. Shilo Publishing House, New York, 1985.

———. "The Words of Koheleth." In Ramban (Nachmanides), *Writings and Discourses*, trans. and ed. Charles B. Chavel, 2 vols. Shilo Publishing House, New York, 1985, vol. 1.

———. *Writings and Discourses*, trans. and ed. Charles B. Chavel, 2 vols, Shilo Publishing House, New York, 1985.

Navarro Peiro, Ángeles. "Literatura hispanohebrea." In *Memoria de Sefarad.* Centro Cultural San Marcos. Sociedad Estatal para la Acción Cultural Exterior, Toledo, 2002–03.

Neuman, R. Abraham A. "Some Phases of the Condition of the Jews in Spain in the Thirteenth and Fourteenth Centuries." *Publications of the American Jewish Historical Society* 22 (1914).

Neusner, Jacob, and Alan J. Avery-Peck, eds. *The Blackwell Reader in Judaism.* Blackwell, Maldin, MA, 2001.

Nietzsche, Friedrich. "El drama musical griego." In *El pensamiento trágico de los griegos. Escritos póstumos 1870–71*, ed. Vicente Serrano. Biblioteca Nueva, Madrid, 2004.

Nicol, Donald M. *Venezia e Bisanzio* (1988). RCS Libri, Milan, 2001.

Novak, David. *The Theology of Nahmanides Systematically Presented.* Scholars Press, Atlanta, GA, 1992.

———. *The Jewish Social Contract.* Princeton University Press, Princeton, NJ, 2005.

Nye, Joseph S. Jr. *Nuclear Ethics.* Macmillan, New York, 1986.

Oisteanu, Andrei. "Jews, Christians and Muslims: Some Theological Disputations in Medieval Europe." *Studia Hebraica* 6 (2006).

Olsson, Gunnar. *Abismal: A Critique of Cartographic Reason.* University of Chicago Press, Chicago, 2007, 43.

Orian, Meir. *Maimónides. Vida, Pensamiento y obra,* trans. Zev Zvi Rosenfeld. Riopiedras, Instituto ha-Rav Kook, Barcelona, nd.

Orfali, Moisés. *Los conversos españoles en la literatura rabínica: problemas jurídicos y opiniones legales durante los siglos XII–XVI*. Universidad Pontificia de Salamanca, Salamanca, 1982.

———. "La cuestión de la venida del Mesías en un *responsum* de Rabbí Shelomó ibn Adret al Cahal de Lérida." *Helmántica* 43, nos. 130–31 (1992).

———. *Biblioteca de autores lógicos hispano-judíos (siglos XI–XIV)*. Editorial Universidad de Granada, Granada, 1997.

———. *Talmud y cristianismo*. Riopiedras, Barcelona, 1998.

———. "Los responsa rabínicos y la vida interna en las aljamas aragonesas." In *Aragón Sefarad*, Saragossa, 2004. Available on http://www.dpz.es/turismo/monograficos/aragon-sefarad/VolumenI/VolI-04.pdf (22.12.2007).

Pérez, Joseph. "La expulsión de los judíos." In *Memoria de Sefarad*. Centro Cultural San Marcos. Sociedad Estatal para la Acción Cultural Exterior, Toledo, 2002–2003.

Pettit, Philip. *Republicanismo. Una teoría sobre la libertad y el gobierno*. Paidós, Barcelona, 1999.

Quintiliano De Calahorra (Marcus Fabius Quintilianus). *Sobre la formación del orador (Institutionis Oratoriae)*, 12 books in 4 vols., bilingual ed. and trans. Alfonso Carmona. Universidad Pontificia de Salamanca, Salamanca, 1997.

Ravitzky, Aviezer. "The Days of the Messiah." In *Perspectives on Maimonides: Philosophical and Historical Studies*, ed. Joel L. Kraemer. Littman Library of Jewish Civilization, London, 1996.

———. "Maimonides: Esotericism and Educational Philosophy." In *The Cambridge Companion to Maimonides*, ed. Kenneth Seeskin. Cambridge University Press, New York, 2005.

Ray, Jonathan. *The Sephardic Frontier*. Cornell University Press, Ithaca, NY, 2006.

Régné, Jean. *History of the Jews in Aragon*, edition and notes by Yom Tov Assis and Adam Gruzman. Hebrew University, Magnes Press, Jerusalem, 1978.

Ribera-Florit, Josep. "Meshulam ben Shelomo de Piera y la controversia maimonista en Cataluña." *El Olivo* 9 (1985).

———. "El poeta judío catalán Mesulam ben Selomó de Piera y sus poemas laudatorios." In *Hominatge a Antoni Comas*, Barcelona, 1985.

Roiz, Javier. *El experimento moderno*. Trotta, Madrid, 1992.

———. *La recuperación del buen juicio*. Foro Interno, Madrid, 2003.

———. "Maimónides y la teoría política dialéctica." *Foro Interno* 6 (2006).

Rosenblum, Nancy S., and Robert C. Post, eds. *Civil Society and Government*. Princeton University Press, Princeton, 2002.

Roth, Cecil. "The Disputation of Barcelona (1263)." *Harvard Theological Review* 43 (April 1950).

Roth, Norman. "Las reacciones rabínicas ante Maimónides." In *Maimónides y su época*, ed. Carlos del Valle, Santiago García-Jalón, and Juan Pedro Monferrer. Sociedad Estatal de Conmemoraciones Culturales, Madrid, 2007.

Scholem, Gershom. *Grandes temas y personalidades de la Cábala* (1988). Riopiedras, Barcelona, 1994.

———. *Major Trends in Jewish Mysticism*, with a new foreward by Robert Alter, reprinted from the third revised edition. Schocken Books, New York, 1995.

———. *Las grandes tendencias de la mística judía*, trans. Beatriz Oberländer. Ediciones Siruela. Madrid, 2nd. ed., 2000.

Schwartz, Dov. *Central Problems of Medieval Judaism*. Brill, Leiden, 2005.

Seeskin, Kenneth, ed. *The Cambridge Companion to Maimonides*. Cambridge University Press, New York, 2005.

Septimus, Bernard. "'Open Rebuke and Concealed Love': Nahmanides and the Andalusian Tradition." In *Rabbi Moses Nahmanides (Ramban): Explorations in His Religious Virtuosity*, ed. Isadore Twersky. Harvard University Press, Cambridge, MA, 1983.

Shakespeare, William. "Hamlet, Prince of Denmark." In *The Complete Works*, ed. Peter Alexander. Collins, London, 1951.

Sharrat, Peter. "Nicolas Nacelius: Petri Rami Vita," edited with English trans. in *Humanistica Lovaniinsa* 24 (1975).

Shatz, David. "The Biblical and Rabbinic Background to Medieval Jewish Philosophy." In *The Cambridge Companion to Medieval Jewish Philosophy*, ed. Daniel H. Frank and Oliver Leaman. Cambridge University Press, Cambridge, 2003.

Silver, Daniel J. "The Resurrection Debate." In *Moses Maimonides' Treatise on Resurrection,* trans. and notes, Fred Rosner. Rowman & Littlefield, Lanham, MD, 2004.

Skalli, Cedric Cohen. "Discovering Isaac Abravanel's Humanistic Rhetoric." *The Jewish Quarterly Review* 97, no. 1 (Winter 2007).

Spinoza, Baruch. "Ethics." In *The Collected Works of Spinoza*, ed. and trans. Edwin Curley. Princeton University Press, Princeton, NJ, 1985.

Stern, Josef. *Problems and Parables of Law*. State University of New York Press, Albany, 1998.

Stillman, Norman A. *Sephardi Religious Responses to Modernity*. Routledge, London, 1995.

Strauss, Leo. "On Abravanel's Philosophical Tendency and Political Teaching." In *Isaac Abravanel, Six Lectures*, ed. J. B. Trend and H. Loewe. Cambridge University Press, Cambridge, 1937.

———. *Natural Right and History*. University of Chicago Press, Chicago, 1953.

———. "How to Begin to Study *The Guide of the Perplexed*." In Moses Maimonides, *The Guide of the Perplexed*, a work in three parts, trans. and ed. Shlomo Pines. University of Chicago Press, Chicago, 1963.

———. *Spinoza's Critique of Religion*. Schocken Books, New York, 1982.

———. *Jewish Philosophy and the Crisis of Modernity*: *Essays and Lectures in Modern Jewish Thought*. State University of New York Press, Albany, 1997.

Stroumsa, Sarah. "Maimonides and the Mediterranean Cultures." In *The Jews of Europe in the Middle Ages (Tenth to Fifteenth Cinturies)*, ed. Cristoph Cluse.

Proceedings of the International Symposium held at Speyer, 20–25 October 2002, Brepols, Turnhout, Belgium, 2004.

Tirosh-Samuelson, Hava. "Philosophy and Kabbalah: 1200–1600." In *The Cambridge Companion to Medieval Jewish Philosophy*, ed. Daniel H. Frank and Oliver Leaman. Cambridge University Press, Cambridge, 2003.

Trautner-Kromann, Hanne. *Shield and Sword.* J. C. B. Mohr (Pauls Siebeck). Tubingen, 1993.

Tucker, Robert W. "Morality and Deterrence." *Ethics* 95 (April 1985).

Twersky, Isadore, ed. *A Maimonides Reader*. Behrman House, Springfield, NJ, 1972.

———. *Introduction to the Code of Maimonides.* Yale University Press, New Haven, 1980.

———, ed. *Rabbi Moses Nahmanides (Ramban): Explorations in His Religious Virtuosity*. Harvard University Press, Cambridge, MA, 1983.

Vallejo Girvés, Margarita. "Los exilios de católicos y arrianos bajo Leovigildo y Recaredo." *Hispania Sacra* 55, no. 111 (2003).

Venerabilis, Petri. *Adversus Iudeorum Inveteratam Duritiem* (Against the Inveterate Obstinacy of the Jews) (a work written before 1144, edition princeps 1522), ed. Yvonne Friedman. Brepols, Turnhout, Belgium, 1985.

Vico, Giambattista. *Ciencia Nueva* (1744), trans. Rocío de la Villa. Tecnos, Madrid, 1995.

Viroli, Maurizio. *For Love of Country*. Clarendon Press, Oxford, 1995.

Vives, Juan Luis. *De subventione pauperum, De comunione rerum*, trans. and notes by Francisco Calero. Ajuntament de Valencia, Valencia, 2004.

Voegelin, Eric. "Anxiety and Reason" (1963). In "What Is History? and Other Late Unpublished Writings," ed. Thomas A. Hollbeck and Paul Caringella, *The Collected Works of Eric Voegelin*, vol. 28. Louisiana State University Press, Baton Rouge, 1990.

———. "Order and History, vol. 1, Israel and Revelation," ed. Maurice P. Hogan, *The Collected Works of Eric Voegelin,* vol. 14. University of Missouri Press, Columbia, 2001.

Walzer, Michael, Menachem Lorberbaum, and Noam J. Zohar, eds. Ari Ackerman, coed. *The Jewish Political Tradition*, 2 vols. Yale University Press, New Haven, 2003.

Walzer, Michael. *The Revolution of the Saints*. Atheneum, New York, 1965.

———. "Preface." In *Law Politics, and Morality in Judaism,* ed. Michael Walzer. Princeton University Press, Princeton, NJ, 2006.

———, ed. *Law, Politics, and Morality in Judaism*. Princeton University Press, Princeton, NJ, 2006.

Williams, A. Lukyn, *Adversos Judaeos*. Cambridge University Press, London, 1935.

Wolin, Sheldon S. *The Presence of the Past.* Johns Hopkins University Press, Baltimore and London, 1989.

———. "Fugitive Democracy." In *Democracy and Difference*, ed. Seyla Benhabib. Princeton University Press, Princeton, NJ, 1996.

Yerushalmi, Yosef Hayim. *Zajor. La historia judía y la memoria judía*, trans. from the 3rd. ed. (1966) Ana Castaño and Patricia Villaseñor. Anthropos, Madrid, 2002.

Zimmels, Hirsch Jakob. *Ashkenazim and Sephardim: Their Relations, Differences and Problems as Reflected in the Rabbinical Responsa* (1976). Ktav Publishing House and Sephardic House New York, Hoboken, NJ, 1996.

Zoha. El. El libro del esplendor, trans. Carles Giol. Ediciones Obelisco, Barcelona, 2nd. ed., 2002.

Zohar, The. Pritzker Edition, 3 vols., trans. of original manuscripts and commentaries by Daniel C. Matt. Stanford University Press, Stanford, CA, 2004.

Zohar, Noam J. "Civil Society and Government: Seeking Judaic Insights." In *Civil Society and Government*, ed. Nancy S. Rosenblum y Robert C. Post. Princeton University Press, Princeton, 2002.

Zohar, Zion. *Sephardic & Mizrahi Jewry*. New York University Press, New York, 2005.

———. ed. "A Global Perspective on Sephardic and Mizrahi Jewry: An Introductory Essay." In *Sephardic & Mizrahi Jewry*, ed. Zion Zohar. New York University Press, New York, 2005.

Index